speakout 2ND EDITION

Pre-intermediate
Teacher's Book

with Resource and Assessment Disc

Jenny Parsons and Matthew Duffy
with Nick Witherick

contents

TEACHER'S BOOK

Introduction

Students' Book contents	4–7
Welcome to *Speakout Second Edition*	9
Overview of the components	10–11
A unit of the Students' Book	12–15
Additional components	16–18
Workbook	16
MyEnglishLab	17
ActiveTeach	17
Website	18
Speakout Extra	18
Teaching approaches	19–22
The Global Scale of English	23

Teacher's notes

Index and Lead-in	24
Units 1–12	25–144

Resource bank

Photocopiable activities index	145–146
Photocopiable activities	147–194
Teacher's notes for photocopiable activities	195–204

TEACHER'S RESOURCE AND ASSESSMENT DISC

Extra resources

- Class audio scripts
- Class video scripts
- BBC interviews
- Worksheets for BBC interviews

Tests

- Unit tests
- Achievement tests
- Mid-course test
- End of course test
- Test audio
- Test audio scripts
- Test answer key

STUDENTS' BOOK CONTENTS

LESSON	GRAMMAR/FUNCTION	VOCABULARY	PRONUNCIATION	READING
UNIT 1 LIFE page 7 ◑)) BBC interviews | What do you look for in a friend?				
1.1 Feeling good? page 8	question forms	free time	stressed words	understand an article about the secrets of happiness
1.2 True love page 10	past simple	relationships	past simple verbs: -ed endings	
1.3 Nice day, isn't it? page 12	making conversation	conversation topics	linking	
1.4 Someone Special page14				
UNIT 2 WORK page 17 ◑)) BBC interviews | What do you do?				
2.1 The company 4U? page 18	present simple and continuous	work	word stress	
2.2 A risky business page 20	adverbs of frequency	jobs	stressed syllables	read a newspaper article about dangerous jobs
2.3 I like working outside page 22	expressing likes/dislikes	types of work	intonation: sound interested	
2.4 Dream Commuters page 24				read the results of a survey about work/life balance
UNIT 3 TIME OUT page 27 ◑)) BBC interviews | What do you like doing in your their free time?				
3.1 Free in NYC page 28	present continuous/ be going to for future	time out	fast speech: going to	
3.2 Relax! page 30	questions without auxiliaries	places to visit	stress in compound nouns	read about how people spend their free time around the wor
3.3 Can I take a message? page 32	making a phone call	collocations	linking: can	
3.4 Rio de Janeiro page 34				
UNIT 4 GREAT MINDS page 37 ◑)) BBC interviews | Are you learning anything at the moment?				
4.1 Hidden talent page 38	present perfect + ever/never	make and do	weak forms: have	
4.2 Schools of thought page 40	can, have to, must	education	weak forms: have to	read an article about different schools
4.3 What should I do? page 42	giving advice	language learning	silent letters	read replies to a website message
4.4 Inventions page 44				
UNIT 5 TRAVEL page 47 ◑)) BBC interviews | Do you enjoy travelling to different countries?				
5.1 Fantastic film trips page 48	past simple and past continuous	transport	weak forms: was/were	read about amazing journeys in film
5.2 Travel tips page 50	verb patterns	travel items	stressed syllables	
5.3 You can't miss it page 52	asking for/giving directions	tourism	intonation: questions	read a text about a man who works in three countries every d
5.4 Full Circle page 54				
UNIT 6 FITNESS page 57 ◑)) BBC interviews | What do you do to keep fit?				
6.1 Keeping fit page 58	present perfect + for/since	health	sentence stress	identify specific information in an article about types of exerc
6.2 The future of food page 60	may, might, will	food	intonation: certainty/ uncertainty	
6.3 How are you feeling? page 62	seeing the doctor	illness	difficult words: spelling v. pronunciation	
6.4 Monitor Me page 64				

DVD-ROM: ■■■ DVD CLIPS AND SCRIPTS   ◑) BBC INTERVIEWS AND SCRIPTS   ▷ CLASS AUDIO AND SCRIPTS

LISTENING/DVD	SPEAKING	WRITING
	ask and answer questions about holidays and weekends	
listen to stories about offers of marriage	ask and answer personal questions	write about an important year in your life; improve your use of linking words
understand routine exchanges	making conversation	
Miranda: watch an extract from a sitcom about a woman called Miranda	talk about important people in your life	write about your best friend
listen to interviews about jobs	talk about what motivates you at work	write an email about work experience
	talk about dangerous jobs	
listen to a man talking about his job	talk about your perfect job	
The Money Programme: Dream Commuters: watch an extract from a BBC documentary about commuting	describe your work/life balance	write a web comment about work/life balance
listen to a radio programme about going out in New York	talk about your future plans	write an email invitation
	discuss how you spend your free time	
understand some problem phone calls	make and receive phone calls	
Going Local: Rio: watch an extract from a BBC travel programme about visiting Rio de Janeiro	plan a perfect day out	write an invitation for a day out
listen to someone describing how he used his hidden talent	talk about hidden talents	check your work and correct mistakes
	talk about rules in schools	
	give advice and make suggestions for language learners	
Supersized Earth: The Way We Move: watch an extract from a BBC documentary about developments that have changed the world	talk about inventions	write a forum post about inventions
	tell a anecdote	
understand travel advice	discuss travel	write an email describing a trip or weekend away
	ask for and give directions	
Full Circle: watch an extract from a BBC travel programme	present ideas for an award	write an application for an award
	talk about your lifestyle	
listen to a radio interview with a food expert	discuss food preferences	write about food
listen to conversations between a doctor and her patients	explain health problems	
Horizon: Monitor Me: watch an extract from a BBC documentary about health	talk about healthy habits	write a blog post about health advice

STUDENTS' BOOK CONTENTS

LESSON	GRAMMAR/FUNCTION	VOCABULARY	PRONUNCIATION	READING
UNIT 7 CHANGES page 67 ◁» BBC interviews | How has your life changed in the last ten years?				
7.1 Living the dream page 68	used to	verbs + prepositions	weak forms: used to	read about living the dream
7.2 The great impostor page 70	purpose, cause and result	collocations	rhythm in complex sentences	read and predict information in a story
7.3 Can you tell me? page 72	finding out information	facilities	intonation: checking information	read about studying abroad
7.4 A Greek Adventure page 74				
UNIT 8 MONEY page 77 ◁» BBC interviews | How do you feel about shopping?				
8.1 Treasure hunt page 78	relative clauses	money	pronouncing the letter 's'	read the story of a treasure hunt
8.2 Pay me more! page 80	too much/many, enough, very	multi-word verbs	multi-word verb stress	
8.3 I'm just looking page 82	buying things	shopping	weak forms: do you/can I	read a questionnaire about shopping
8.4 soleRebels page 84				
UNIT 9 NATURE page 87 ◁» BBC interviews | How do you feel about being in the countryside?				
9.1 Green living page 88	comparatives/superlatives	nature	stressed syllables	read about great green ideas
9.2 Into the wild page 90	articles	the outdoors	word stress, weak forms: a and the	understand an article about an experience in the wild
9.3 It could be because ... page 92	making guesses	silent letters	animals	
9.4 The Northern Lights page 94				
UNIT 10 SOCIETY page 97 ◁» BBC interviews | How do you feel about city life?				
10.1 Top cities page 98	uses of like	describing a city	sentence stress	read about the best cities for young people
10.2 Crime and punishment page 100	present/past passive	crime and punishment	weak forms: was/were	read an article about crime and punishment
10.3 There's a problem page 102	complaining	problems	sentence stress	
10.4 Mary's Meals page 104				
UNIT 11 TECHNOLOGY page 107 ◁» BBC interviews | How do you feel about technology?				
11.1 Keeping in touch page 108	present perfect	communication	sentence stress	
11.2 Make a difference page 110	real conditionals + when	feelings	weak forms: will	read an article about social media
11.3 I totally disagree page 112	giving opinions	internet terms	polite intonation	read about wasting time
11.4 Is TV Bad For Kids? page 114				
UNIT 12 FAME page 117 ◁» BBC interviews | Would you like to be famous?				
12.1 Caught on film page 118	reported speech	film	contrastive stress	read a magazine article about writing a blockbuster
12.2 A lucky break page 120	hypothetical conditionals present/future	suffixes	word stress	read a magazine article about internet fame
12.3 What can I do for you? page 122	requests and offers	collocations	polite intonation: requests	read a text about concierges
12.4 Billion Dollar Man page 124				

IRREGULAR VERBS page 127   LANGUAGE BANK page 128   PHOTO BANK page 152

LISTENING/DVD	SPEAKING	WRITING
listen to a radio programme about a woman who changed her life	talk about how your life has changed	use paragraphs to write about a decision that changed your life
	talk about why people tell lies	
understand short, predictable conversations	learn to check and confirm information	
BBC **My Family And Other Animals**: watch an extract from the beginning of a BBC film about a family that moves to Greece	talk about new experiences	write a blog/diary

	talk about a project that people should invest in	
listen to a discussion about salaries	talk about why you should earn more	write an opinion piece
listen to conversations in shops	describe items; go shopping	
BBC **BBC News: soleRebels**: watch an extract from the BBC news about an Ethiopian business	present a money-making idea	write a competition entry for a business investment

listen to a radio programme about green ideas	talk about green issues	write about your views on the environment
	give your views on life in the city or the country	
listen to people discussing quiz questions	talk about different animals	
BBC **Joanna Lumney in the Land of the Northern Lights**: watch an extract from a BBC documentary about the Northern Lights	talk about amazing places	write a travel blog

listen to conversations about different cities	discuss qualities of different places	use formal expressions to write an email
	discuss alternative punishments to fit the crimes	
listen to people complaining	talk about problems in a school	
BBC **Mary's Meals**: watch an extract from a BBC documentary about an internet sensation	talk about an important issue	write about an issue

listen to people talking about how they keep in touch	talk about things you've done/would like to do	improve your use of pronouns
	talk about future consequences	
listen to a discussion about the internet	give your opinion	
BBC **Panorama: Is TV Bad For Kids?**: watch an extract from a BBC documentary about giving up television	talk about technology you couldn't live without	write a web comment about technology

	talk about your favourite film	
listen to people talking about fame	talk about being famous	write about a famous person
listen to people making requests	make requests and offers	
BBC **Lewis Hamilton: Billion Dollar Man**: watch an extract from a BBC documentary about Lewis Hamilton	talk about your ambitions	write about your childhood ambitions

COMMUNICATION BANK page 160   AUDIO SCRIPTS page 168

Our first priority in writing *Speakout Second Edition* was to find out what people liked about the first edition and what could be improved. To that end, we asked teachers and learners around the world for feedback on every level of the course. What did they like? What worked well in class? What changes would they like to see?

We then took a fresh look at every single exercise in the series and improved or updated it based on the feedback we'd received. We revised the grammar, vocabulary and skills syllabuses in line with the *Global Scale of English*, we ensured that there was more recycling and practice of key language, and we included a wealth of up-to-date new material:

- **New BBC video clips** – The BBC video clips which accompany each unit are one of the most original features of the course. We've retained the most popular clips and included some wonderful new material from the BBC archive to engage and motivate learners.

- **New reading/listening texts** – Teachers really appreciated the range of authentic texts in the first edition. We've broadened the range of genres in the second edition to reflect the types of texts learners read outside the classroom. Listening texts are also more authentic and we've included a wider variety of international accents.

- **New pronunciation sections** – We've developed a stronger pronunciation syllabus. Teachers wanted more support in this area, so we now have a wider range of pronunciation features in the three input lessons in each unit. Further pronunciation practice can also be found in *Speakout Extra*.

- **New images and clearer design** – The overall design is lighter, less cluttered and easier to navigate. We've refreshed the photos and illustrations completely, and selected dramatic images to introduce each new unit. Great images motivate learners, and provide excellent prompts for language activities.

- **New supplementary material** – One thing teachers always ask for is 'more'. More grammar, more vocabulary, more pronunciation. There's only so much we can fit into the Students' Books but, for those who want more practice in specific areas, *Speakout Extra* provides a bank of additional exercises that can be accessed via the *Speakout* website. *Speakout Extra* includes grammar, vocabulary, pronunciation and skills practice as well as ideas and activities for exploiting the BBC clips and interviews. *Speakout Extra* will be updated regularly so don't forget to check it out.

We really appreciate the feedback you've given us and hope you find *Speakout Second Edition* even more stimulating and user-friendly than the first edition.

From left to right: Steve Oakes, Antonia Clare, JJ Wilson and Frances Eales

OVERVIEW OF THE COMPONENTS

- Twelve units with 90 to 120 hours of teaching material
- Comprehensive *Language bank* with detailed explanations and extra practice
- *Photo bank* to expand vocabulary
- Audio material for use in class
- DVD content (BBC clips and interviews)
- Audio and video scripts

CLASS AUDIO CDs

- Audio material for use in class

WORKBOOK

- Additional grammar, vocabulary and pronunciation exercises to complement material in the Students' Book
- Additional functional language practice exercises
- Additional reading, listening and writing practice
- Regular review sections
- With- and without-key versions

WORKBOOK AUDIO

- Audio material to practice listening, pronunciation and functional language
- Visit www.english.com/speakout to download the audio

MYENGLISHLAB

Learning Management System that provides:

- Interactive Workbook with instant feedback
- Extra practice in grammar, vocabulary and skills
- Unit and achievement tests
- Mid- and end of course tests
- BBC interviews and interactive exercises

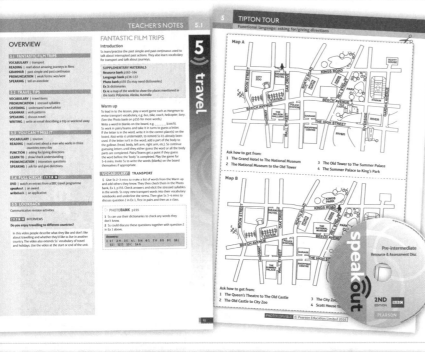

TEACHER'S BOOK WITH RESOURCE AND ASSESSMENT DISC

- Teacher's notes for every unit with warmers, fillers, alternative suggestions, culture notes and answer keys
- Generic teaching tips on useful areas such as grammar, lexis, pronunciation, using video, etc.
- Photocopiable grammar, vocabulary, and functional language worksheets for every unit
- Class audio and video scripts
- BBC interviews, worksheets and scripts
- Unit and achievement tests
- Mid- and end of course tests
- Test audio, audio scripts and answer keys

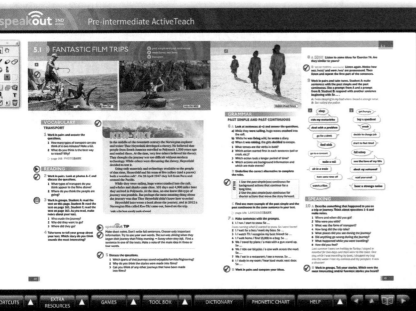

ACTIVETEACH

Software for classroom use to help teachers get the most out of the course:

- Integrated audio and video content
- Answer-reveal feature
- Large extra resources section
- Grammar and vocabulary review games
- BBC interviews and worksheets
- Assessment package containing all the course tests
- A host of useful classroom tools

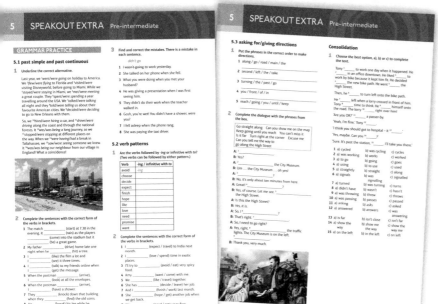

WEBSITE AND SPEAKOUT EXTRA

- Information about the course
- Sample materials
- Placement test
- Teaching tips and ideas
- Free downloadable worksheets provide additional grammar, vocabulary, pronunciation and skills practice (*Speakout Extra*)
- Extra video-exploitation activities to help learners get the most out of the course (*Speakout Extra*)

Speakout Extra and other teacher's resources available at:

www.pearsonelt.com/speakout

A UNIT OF THE STUDENTS' BOOK

Speakout Second Edition Students' Book is clearly designed and easy to use. Each unit follows the same pattern with an introductory page, two main input lessons covering grammar, vocabulary, pronunciation and skills work, a functional lesson and a skills-consolidation lesson based on a clip from a BBC programme. The unit culminates with a page of *Lookback* exercises and there is a detailed *Language bank, Photo bank* and *Communication bank* at the back of the book.

1. Striking images provoke interest in the topic
2. Language focus and outcomes clearly stated at the start of each lesson
3. BBC interviews provide 'models' of authentic language
4. Grammar presented in context with clear explanations and plenty of practice
5. Learners referred to Language bank at the back of the book for further practice
6. Key lexis introduced in context and expanded in Photo bank at the back of the book
7. Special pronunciation sections in each lesson
8. Focus on reading and/or listening in every spread
9. Writing sections focus on different genres and sub-skills
10. Focus on useful functional language
11. *Learn to* sections develop listening/speaking skills
12. Useful learning tips in each unit

5 travel

FANTASTIC FILM TRIPS p48   TRAVEL TIPS p50   YOU CAN'T MISS IT p52   FULL CIRCLE p54

SPEAKING 5.1 Tell a travel anecdote 5.2 Discuss travel 5.3 Ask for and give directions
5.4 Present ideas for an award

LISTENING 5.2 Understand travel advice 5.3 Understand and follow directions in a city
5.4 Watch an extract from a BBC travel programme

READING 5.1 Read about amazing journeys in films
5.3 Read a text about a man who works in three countries every day

WRITING 5.2 Write an email describing a trip or weekend away
5.4 Write an application for an award

BBC INTERVIEWS Do you enjoy travelling to different countries?

5.1 FANTASTIC FILM TRIPS

G past simple and past continuous
P weak forms: was/were
V transport

Kon-Tiki

Into the Wild

Rabbit-Proof Fence

VOCABULARY
TRANSPORT

1 Work in pairs and answer the questions.
1 How many types of transport can you think of in two minutes? Make a list.
2 What do you think is the best way to travel? Why?
▷ page 155 PHOTOBANK

READING

2 Work in pairs. Look at photos A–C and discuss the questions.
1 What types of transport do you think appear in the films above?
2 Where do you think the people are going?

3 Work in groups. Student A: read the text on this page. Student B: read the text on page 161. Student C: read the text on page 163. As you read, make notes about your text.
1 Who made the journey?
2 Why did they want to go?
3 Where did they go?

4 Take turns to tell your group about your text. Which story do you think sounds the most interesting?

KON-TIKI

In the middle of the twentieth century the Norwegian explorer and writer Thor Heyerdahl developed a theory. He believed that people from South America travelled to Polynesia 1,500 years ago and settled there. At the time, very few others believed his theory. They thought the journey was too difficult without modern technology. While others were discussing the theory, Heyerdahl decided to test it.

Using only materials and technology available to the people of that time, Heyerdahl and his team of five sailors (and a parrot) built a wooden raft*. On 28 April 1947 they left from Peru and crossed the Pacific.

While they were sailing, huge waves crashed into the raft, and whales and sharks came close. 101 days and 4,300 miles later they arrived in Polynesia. At the time, no one knew this type of journey was possible. But perhaps the most amazing thing about the journey was that Thor Heyerdahl didn't know how to swim!

Heyerdahl later wrote a book about the journey, and in 2012 a Norwegian film called *Kon-Tiki* came out, based on the trip.

*raft: a flat boat usually made of wood

speakout TIP

Make short notes. Don't write full sentences. Choose only important information. Try to use your own words. *The sun was shining when they began their journey that Friday morning.* → *Sunny when they left.* Find a sentence in one of the texts. Make a note of the main idea in three or four words.

5 Discuss the questions.
1 Which (parts of the) journeys sound enjoyable/terrible/frightening?
2 Why do you think the stories were made into films?
3 Can you think of any other journeys that have been made into films?

GRAMMAR
PAST SIMPLE AND PAST CONTINUOUS

6 A Look at sentences a)–c) and answer the questions.
a) While they **were sailing**, huge waves **crashed** into the raft.
b) While he **was living** wild, he **wrote** a diary.
c) When it **was raining**, the girls **decided** to escape.
1 What tenses are the verbs in bold?
2 Which action started first in each sentence (*sail* or *crash*, etc.)?
3 Which action took a longer period of time?
4 Which actions are background information and which are main events?

B Underline the correct alternative to complete the rules.

RULES
1 Use the *past simple/past continuous* for background actions that continue for a long time.
2 Use the *past simple/past continuous* for shorter actions that move the story forward.

C Find one more example of the past simple and the past continuous in the same sentence in your text.

▷ page 136 LANGUAGEBANK

7 A Make sentences with the prompts.
1 I / run / start to snow. So ...
I was running when it started to snow. So I went home!
2 I / wait for a bus / meet my boss. So ...
3 I / watch TV / recognise my best friend! So ...
4 I / walk home / find $5,000 in a bag. So ...
5 We / travel by plane / a man with a gun stand up. So ...
6 We / ride our bicycles / a cow walk across the road. So ...
7 We / eat in a restaurant / see a mouse. So ...
8 I / study in my room / hear loud music next door. So ...

B Work in pairs and compare your ideas.

---

8 A ▶ 5.1 Listen to some ideas for Exercise 7A. Are they similar to yours?

B WEAK FORMS: *was/were* Listen again. Notice how *was* /wəz/ and *were* /wə/ are pronounced. Then listen and repeat the first part of the sentences.

9 Work in pairs and take turns. Student A: make sentences with the past simple and the past continuous. Use a prompt from A and a prompt from B. Student B: respond with another sentence beginning with *So ...*.
A: *I was sleeping in my bed when I heard a strange noise.*
B: *So I called the police.*

A
sleep
ride my motorbike
deal with a problem
go for a drink
feel sick
go to a concert
make a call
sit in a train
have some time off
watch a film

B
get hungry
buy a speedboat
crash
decide to change job
start to feel tired
fall asleep
see the love of my life
check my voicemail
read your email
hear a strange noise

SPEAKING

10 A Describe something that happened to you on a trip or journey. Think about questions 1–8 and make notes.
1 Where and when did you go?
2 Who were you with?
3 What was the form of transport?
4 How long did the trip take?
5 What places did you see during the journey?
6 Did anything go wrong during the journey?
7 What happened while you were travelling?
8 How did you feel?
Last summer I went on holiday to Turkey. I stayed in Istanbul for two days and then went to the coast. One day, while I was travelling by boat, I dropped my bag into the water. I lost my camera and my passport. It was a disaster.

B Work in groups. Tell your stories. Which were the most interesting and/or funniest stories you heard?

48   49

5.2 ▶ TRAVEL TIPS

G verb patterns
S stressed syllables
V travel items

6 VOCABULARY

TRAVEL ITEMS

1 Work in pairs. Discuss the questions.
1 Do you travel light?
2 What do you usually pack when you go away for a short trip/long holiday?

2 A Work in pairs. Look at the words in the box and choose two things for travellers 1–3 below.

suitcase notebook digital camera souvenirs
waterproof clothes dictionary walking boots sun hat
backpack money belt binoculars map umbrella

1 a grandmother visiting her grandchildren in Australia
2 a student travelling around the world
3 a tourist visiting the sights in New York

7 B ▶ 5.2 STRESSED SYLLABLES Listen and repeat the words. Underline the stressed syllables.

C Work in pairs. Discuss. Which of the things in Exercise 2A do you take on holiday with you?

▷ page 155 PHOTOBANK

8 LISTENING

3 A ▶ 5.3 Listen to people describing what they take on holiday. Which of the items in Exercise 2A do the travellers mention?

B Work in pairs and complete the notes.
1 I try to learn _____.
2 I love _____.
3 I take a lot of _____.
4 I usually spend my holidays in _____.
5 I sometimes travel in _____ places.
6 I don't carry too much _____.
7 I write things down because I like to _____ them.

C Listen again to check.

4 GRAMMAR

VERB PATTERNS

4 A Look at sentences 1–9 below and underline the verb + verb combinations.
1 We always expect to hear English.
2 I always want to talk to local people.
3 I love walking when I go on holiday.
4 I always seem to take hundreds and hundreds of photos.
5 I usually choose to go to a warm place.
6 I enjoy travelling in wild places.
7 If you decide to go walking, a backpack is easier to carry.
8 It's best to avoid carrying too much money.
9 I need to write things down.

B Complete the table below with the verbs in the box.

expect want seem choose enjoy
decide avoid need

verb + -ing	verb + infinitive with to
	expect

C Work in pairs. Add the verbs in the box below to the table above. Which two verbs can go in both columns?

hope finish imagine hate
would like love

5 ▷ page 136 LANGUAGEBANK

5 Cross out the verb combination that is not possible in each sentence.
1 I hope/enjoy/expect to get a free plane ticket.
2 I want/would like/imagine to visit Australia.
3 She loves/avoids/needs travelling.
4 Where did you like/decide/choose to go on your next holiday?
5 They hate/want/love working with tourists.
6 He doesn't seem/need/enjoy to know this area well.
7 Do you like/expect/love going to different countries?
8 Why did you avoid/decide/hope to become a travel writer?

6 A Complete the sentences and make them true for you. The next word must be either the infinitive with to or the -ing form of a verb.
1 When I travel:
   I always avoid …
   I hate …
   I love …
2 On my last holiday:
   I chose …
   I decided …
   I enjoyed …
3 For my next holiday:
   I want …
   I hope …
   I would like …

B Work in pairs and compare your ideas.

SPEAKING

7 Work in pairs. Discuss the questions.
1 What type of holidays can you see in the photos? Which do you prefer? Why?
2 Is there anything that you really love doing when you are on holiday?
3 When you travel, do you try to learn about the place, its customs and its language? Why/Why not?
4 Do you enjoy visiting tourist areas, old cities, new cities, or none of these?
A: I really like sightseeing holidays. I love spending time looking at beautiful old buildings.
B: I love taking photos. I put them on my Facebook page when I get back.
A: Me, too.

9 WRITING

USING SEQUENCERS

8 A Work in pairs. Read an email describing a trip and discuss. What were the good/bad things about the trip?

Hi Paolo,
I hope you're well. I've just got back from my trip to Poland. It was wonderful. First we flew to Warsaw. We were only there for two days, but we managed to see lots of interesting sights like the Royal Castle and the National Museum. Then we had a day in Kraków, which was beautiful, especially the huge square in the Old Town. Unfortunately, after a while, it started raining so we spent the afternoon chatting with locals in a bar. After that, we took a train to Łódź. I loved it. We visited various museums and walked along the famous Piotrkowska Street. Finally, we caught the plane back home. It was a great trip and we met lots of really friendly Poles, who promised to visit us in Spain!
Love,
Irina

B Underline five words/phrases that help us to understand the order of events. The first one has been done for you.

C Write an email to a friend about a trip or a weekend away. Use the words you underlined.

5.3 ▶ YOU CAN'T MISS IT

F asking for/giving directions
I intonation: questions
V tourism

VOCABULARY

TOURISM

1 Work in pairs. Look at the words in the box. Which things can you see in the photos?

tour guide boat trip coach tour tourists
sightseeing natural wonder tax-free shopping

2 A Look at the title of the text below. Discuss. What do you think the man does? Why do you think he works in three countries every day?

B Read the text to find out.

C Discuss. Would you like Juan's job? Why/Why not?

 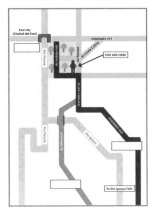

THE MAN WHO WORKS IN THREE COUNTRIES EVERY DAY

JUAN OLIVEIRA was born in Argentina, grew up in Paraguay and now lives in Brazil. He says he loves the three countries equally, and he works in all three of them every day.

Juan is a tour guide in Foz do Iguaçu, a Brazilian town which is close to the borders of both Argentina and Paraguay. He takes tourists around the Iguaçu Falls, one of the great natural wonders of the world.

First, he shows tourists the waterfall from the Brazilian side. Then they cross the border to see the water from the Argentinian side. After that, they go on a boat trip which takes them under the waterfall. Finally, he takes them on the short journey to Ciudad del Este in Paraguay to do some tax-free shopping.

He says the Falls are amazing, especially in the rainy season. He sees them every day and he never gets tired of them.

10 FUNCTION

ASKING FOR/GIVING DIRECTIONS

3 A ▶ 5.4 Look at the map. Where is the tourist? Now listen and follow the routes on the map. For each route, write the destination (the country) on the map.

B Listen again and read audio script 5.4 on page 171. Underline useful phrases for giving directions.

East city
(Ciudad del Este)
HIGHWAY 277
YOU ARE HERE
Río Paraná
Río Iguazu
HIGHWAY AZ4
To the Iguazu Falls

4 Label pictures A–J with the phrases in the box.

go along the main road go straight on
in front of you go past the turning go left
take the first right at the corner cross a bridge
keep going until you reach (the border)
go through the (centre of the town)

A go left
B
C
D
E
F
G
H
I
J

5 A ▶ 5.5 Listen to three conversations. Are the statements true (T) or false (F)?
1 Speaker 1 takes the bus.
2 Speaker 2 has a map.
3 Speaker 3 will see a restaurant before arriving at The Grand Motel.

B Complete the notes. Listen again to check.

Conversation 1 Carnival
It takes _____ minutes. Go straight on. You'll hear the _____!

Conversation 2 Plaza Hotel
Go past the cinema. Take the first _____. Keep going for _____ minutes. You'll see the _____.

Conversation 3 The Grand Motel
Go to the end of this street. Go _____ and go past the _____. It's on the _____.

▷ page 136 LANGUAGEBANK

11 LEARN TO

SHOW/CHECK UNDERSTANDING

6 A ▶ 5.6 Read and listen to the extracts from the audio script. Are the phrases in bold asking for information (A), explaining directions (E) or showing understanding (U)?

Extract 1
A: **Can we walk?** A
B: Yes, **it takes about ten minutes** from here. E

Extract 2
C: **Excuse me, can you help me?** I'm looking for the Plaza Hotel. **Is this the right way?**
D: Um … Plaza Hotel, Plaza Hotel. Yes, **keep going**, past the cinema and take the first left.
C: **OK.**
D: Then keep going for about fifteen minutes until you reach the end of the road. And **you'll see** the sign for the hotel. **You can't miss it.**
C: OK. **Can you show me on the map?**
D: Sure.

Extract 3
E: Excuse me, we want to get to The Grand Motel. **Is it far?**
F: Umm … sorry, I've no idea. Jim, do you know?
G: What?
F: The Grand Motel?
G: The Grand Motel? Yeah, it's just over there. Just go to the end of this street. **Go left** and go past the … um … there's a restaurant. Go past the restaurant and it's on the left.
E: On the left. **So I need to** go to the end of the street, turn left, go past the restaurant and it's on the left.

B Which phrases mean:
1 Am I going in the right direction?
2 Continue.
3 It's easy to see it.

C ▶ 5.7 INTONATION: questions Listen to five questions. Which words are said louder and with a higher voice: words at the beginning (is, can) or near the end of the question? Listen again to check.

7 Work in pairs. Look at audio script 5.5 on page 171 and practise the first two conversations.

SPEAKING

8 Work in pairs. Student A: look at the map on page 161. Student B: look at the map on page 163. Ask for and give directions.
A: How do I get to the station?
B: Go straight on until you reach the Greek restaurant, then turn right.

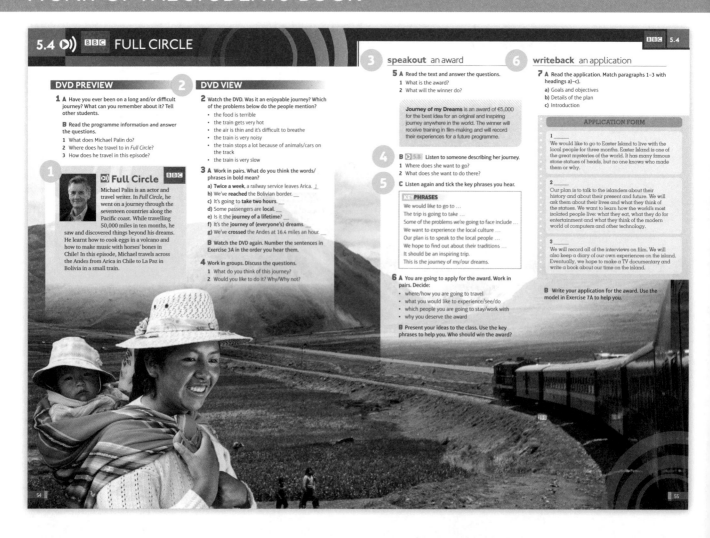

5.4 ◁)) **BBC** FULL CIRCLE

DVD PREVIEW

1 A Have you ever been on a long and/or difficult journey? What can you remember about it? Tell other students.

B Read the programme information and answer the questions.
1 What does Michael Palin do?
2 Where does he travel to in *Full Circle*?
3 How does he travel in this episode?

◁)) **Full Circle** **BBC**

Michael Palin is an actor and travel writer. In *Full Circle*, he went on a journey through the seventeen countries along the Pacific coast. While travelling 50,000 miles in ten months, he saw and discovered things beyond his dreams. He learnt how to cook eggs in a volcano and how to make music with horses' bones in Chile! In this episode, Michael travels across the Andes from Arica in Chile to La Paz in Bolivia in a small train.

2 DVD VIEW

2 Watch the DVD. Was it an enjoyable journey? Which of the problems below do the people mention?
• the food is terrible
• the train gets very hot
• the air is thin and it's difficult to breathe
• the train is very noisy
• the train stops a lot because of animals/cars on the track
• the train is very slow

3 A Work in pairs. What do you think the words/phrases in bold mean?
a) **Twice a week**, a railway service leaves Arica. ⊥
b) We've **reached** the Bolivian border. __
c) It's going to **take two hours**. __
d) Some passengers are **local**. __
e) Is it the **journey of a lifetime**? __
f) It's the **journey of (everyone's) dreams**. __
g) We've **crossed** the Andes at 16.4 miles an hour. __

B Watch the DVD again. Number the sentences in Exercise 3A in the order you hear them.

4 Work in groups. Discuss the questions.
1 What do you think of this journey?
2 Would you like to do it? Why/Why not?

3 speakout an award

5 A Read the text and answer the questions.
1 What is the award?
2 What will the winner do?

Journey of my Dreams is an award of €5,000 for the best idea for an original and inspiring journey anywhere in the world. The winner will receive training in film-making and will record their experiences for a future programme.

4 B ▷ 5.5 Listen to someone describing her journey.
1 Where does she want to go?
2 What does she want to do there?

5 C Listen again and tick the key phrases you hear.

KEY PHRASES

We would like to go to ...
The trip is going to take ...
Some of the problems we're going to face include ...
We want to experience the local culture ...
Our plan is to speak to the local people ...
We hope to find out about their traditions ...
It should be an inspiring trip.
This is the journey of my/our dreams.

6 A You are going to apply for the award. Work in pairs. Decide:
• where/how you are going to travel
• what you would like to experience/see/do
• which people you are going to stay/work with
• why you deserve the award

B Present your ideas to the class. Use the key phrases to help you. Who should win the award?

6 writeback an application

7 A Read the application. Match paragraphs 1–3 with headings a)–c).
a) Goals and objectives
b) Details of the plan
c) Introduction

APPLICATION FORM

1 _____
We would like to go to Easter Island to live with the local people for three months. Easter Island is one of the great mysteries of the world. It has many famous stone statues of heads, but no one knows who made them or why.

2 _____
Our plan is to talk to the islanders about their history and about their present and future. We will ask them about their lives and what they think of the statues. We want to learn how the world's most isolated people live: what they eat, what they do for entertainment and what they think of the modern world of computers and other technology.

3 _____
We will record all of the interviews on film. We will also keep a diary of our own experiences on the island. Eventually, we hope to make a TV documentary and write a book about our time on the island.

B Write your application for the award. Use the model in Exercise 7A to help you.

Speakout Second Edition Students' Book has a motivating DVD spread at the end of every unit. Based on authentic clips from the BBC's rich archive, these lessons are designed to consolidate language and act as a springboard for further speaking and writing tasks.

The *Lookback* page provides a review of key language covered in the unit with exercises that can be done altogether at the end of the unit or individually as and when appropriate. *Speakout Second Edition* also has a detailed *Language bank*, a *Photo bank* and *Communication bank*.

① Learners read about the DVD clip in preparation for viewing

② Different viewing tasks help learners understand and appreciate the DVD clip

③ *Speakout* tasks consolidate language and build learners' confidence

④ 'Models' are provided to help learners perform the task

⑤ Key phrases give learners the language they need to perform the task

⑥ *Writeback* tasks provide further communicative practice

⑦ *Lookback* exercises are an enjoyable 'test' of language covered in unit

⑧ *Language bank* provides detailed explanations and further practice

⑨ *Photo bank* extends key lexical sets

⑩ *Communication bank* provides further opportunities to practise key language

---

5.5 ◁ LOOKBACK

7

○ TRANSPORT

1 A Choose four types of transport from the box below. Write a sentence about each type. Don't mention the name.

train tram minibus taxi
motorbike ferry speedboat
coach lorry helicopter

It travels through water and is very fast.

B Work in pairs and take turns. Student A: read your sentences. Student B: guess which type of transport it is.
A: It's a fast type of transport. It goes on the road. It has two wheels.
B: A motorbike.

○ PAST SIMPLE AND PAST CONTINUOUS

2 A Put the verbs in brackets into the past simple or past continuous.
1 While they (walk), they (see) a fence.
While they were walking, they saw a fence.
2 While they (cross) the sea, a terrible storm nearly (destroy) the raft.
3 They (run) away one night while it (rain).
4 While he (wander) in the wilderness, he (meet) some people who helped him.
5 When the men (sail) on the ocean, they (see) many sea creatures.
6 While he (live) in an abandoned bus, he (realise) he might die.

B Work in pairs. Discuss. Which films from Lesson 5.1 do the sentences go with?

3 Work in pairs and take turns. Ask and answer the question.
Where were you and what were you doing at these times yesterday?

| 5:00 | 10:00 | 13:00 |
| 16:00 | 19:00 | 22:00 |

○ TRAVEL ITEMS

4 A Add the vowels.
1 stcs *suitcase* 6 svnrs
2 bckpck 7 bnclrs
3 wtrprf clths 8 ntbk
4 wlkng bts 9 dgtl cmr
5 sn ht 10 mny blt

B Work in pairs. Decide which of the items above are important for the holidays below.

beach walking
sightseeing adventure

A sun hat is important for a beach holiday.

○ VERB PATTERNS

5 A Complete the sentences with the correct form of the verbs in brackets.
1 I sometimes choose _____ (go) somewhere on holiday because a friend recommends it.
2 I hope _____ (visit) more cities in my own country this year.
3 I seem _____ (have) good luck with the weather when I go on holiday. It never rains!
4 I want _____ (travel) to places where tourists never go.
5 I always avoid _____ (travel) by boat because I get sick.
6 I don't enjoy _____ (fly) very much.
7 I can't imagine _____ (go) on a camping holiday – I prefer hotels!
8 I wouldn't like _____ (have) a holiday with a big group of people.

B Work in pairs. Discuss. Are sentences 1–8 true for you? Why/Why not?

○ ASKING FOR/GIVING DIRECTIONS

6 A Find and correct the mistakes. There are two mistakes in each conversation.

Conversation 1
A: Excuse me. I'm looking for the Natural History Museum. Is this right way?
B: Keep going until you reach the crossroads. It's in the right.

Conversation 2
A: Hello. We want to go to the Italian Embassy. Is far?
B: No. Just turn left and you'll see the sign for it. You can't miss.

Conversation 3
A: Excuse me, do you know where the university is?
B: Keep going along the main road. Then you'll see a sign and it's in front to you.

B Work in pairs and practise the conversations.

C Work in pairs and take turns.

Student A: ask for directions:
• from a well-known place in the town to Student B's house
• from Student B's house to the school

Student B: ask for directions:
• from the school to a nearby restaurant
• from a nearby restaurant to a well-known place in the town
A: OK. How do I get from the station to your house?
B: Well, you take the first right ...

8 GRAMMAR

5.1 past simple and past continuous

	past simple	past continuous
+	I watched a film yesterday.	I was watching a film yesterday.
–	He didn't play here.	He wasn't playing here.
?	Did you talk to John?	Were you talking to John?

Use the past simple to talk about completed actions.
I ate a salad last night.
Use the past continuous to talk about actions in progress at a particular time.
At 8a.m. yesterday I was travelling to work.

I was sleeping → → → → → → → →

11p.m.   the thief entered (3a.m.)
past ────■────────────■──── present

It is common to use the past simple and the past continuous together to tell stories. The past continuous describes an action that starts first, but is interrupted by a second action. Use the past simple for the second (usually short) action.
What were you doing when the bus crashed?
I was sleeping when the thief entered the house.
It is common to use *when* or *while* to link the two actions. Use *while* before the continuous action.
While he was sleeping, it started to rain.
Use *when* before the continuous action or the short action.
When we were talking, the bus appeared.
We were talking when the bus appeared.
Do NOT use *while* before the short action.
I was sleeping ~~while~~ it started to rain.

5.2 verb patterns

Sometimes we use two verbs together.
I love playing football.
After some verbs, put the second verb in the infinitive with *to*.
She decided to go to Mexico.
We need to make a phone call.
After some verbs, use the *-ing* form.
I enjoy running.
They avoided travelling by bus.

some common verb patterns	
verb + -ing	verb + infinitive with to
enjoy	choose
finish	hope
avoid	expect
imagine	would like
stop	decide
like	seem
don't mind	want
spend (time)	need
	help
	promise

Many verbs that show preference (things that we like or don't like) are followed by *-ing*, e.g. *like, enjoy, don't mind.*
After some verbs it is possible to use the *-ing* form OR the infinitive with *to*, e.g. *love, hate.*
I love dancing. I love to dance.
I hate getting up early. I hate to get up early.
There is little change in meaning.

5.3 asking for/giving directions

go left | go past the turning | go along the main road | take the first right

keep going until you reach … | at the corner | go through the centre | cross a bridge

go straight on | in front of you

useful questions	directions	saying you understand
Can we walk? Excuse me, can you help me? Is this the right way? Can you show me on the map? Is it far?	It takes about twenty minutes. Keep going … You'll see … You can't miss it.	OK, so I need to … Right.

PRACTICE

5.1 **A** Complete the story with the correct form of the verbs in brackets. Use the past simple or past continuous.

Alvin Straight, a 73-year-old, [1]_____ (live) quietly on his farm in Iowa, USA, when he heard the news that his brother, Lyle, was seriously ill. After ten years with no contact between the brothers, Alvin [2]_____ (decide) to visit Lyle. Alvin couldn't drive so he [3]_____ (buy) a lawnmower, which moved at five miles per hour, and [4]_____ (begin) the 250-mile-journey.
While he [5]_____ (travel), he met many people, including a priest and a teenage girl who was running away from her family. He helped them all simply by talking about life. Some of them also [6]_____ (help) him. For example, one day when he [7]_____ (drive) the lawnmower, it broke down. While two mechanics [8]_____ (fix) it, he met a friendly couple and [9]_____ (stay) with them.
The journey took him six weeks. And [10]_____ the story _____ (end) happily? See the 1999 film, *The Straight Story*, to find out!

B Make sentences with the prompts and the correct form of the verbs in the box. Use the past simple or past continuous.

pass know like play dance swim travel have

1 He / tennis when he hurt his leg.
2 Sarah / the job because it was boring.
3 While they / they met lots of other tourists.
4 How / you / my name?
5 Who / you / with in that nightclub when I saw you?
6 I / in the sea when I saw the shark.
7 I / my exam?
8 The thief broke in while Jack / breakfast.

5.2 **A** Complete the sentences with the correct form of the verbs in the box.

live read drink swim visit have play finish

1 They want _____ the monuments tomorrow morning.
2 I can't imagine _____ in that flat – it's so small!
3 I don't like _____ water from a bottle.
4 They decided _____ football this morning.
5 Would you like _____ dinner in this restaurant?
6 Do you enjoy _____ in the sea?
7 I hope _____ my degree next year.
8 I love _____ books about adventures.

B Find and correct the mistakes. There are eight mistakes in the advertisement.

✱ Are modern holidays too boring for you?
✱ Would you like doing something more exciting?

Mad Dog Tours is perfect for people who hate spend time asleep on a beach. If you enjoy to travel to strange places, if you don't mind to stay in cheap hotels and want knowing how the local people really live, we promise helping you. Cheap holidays are our speciality. If you choose booking your holiday with *Mad Dog Tours*, you can expect living your dreams!

5.3 **A** Match 1–10 with a)–j) to make sentences or questions.

1 Excuse me, can | a) about an hour.
2 Is this the | b) need to go left here.
3 Is | c) restaurant on your right.
4 Can you show | d) it far?
5 It takes | e) right way?
6 You can't | f) going.
7 Can we | g) me on the map?
8 So I | h) you help me?
9 You'll see the | i) walk?
10 Keep | j) miss it.

B Underline the correct alternative to complete the conversations.

Conversation 1
A: Excuse me, how do I get to the swimming pool?
B: You need to go [1]along/at/with the main road. Keep going until you [2]go/have/reach the town hall. Then [3]go/make/be left and it's [4]the/in/to front of you.

Conversation 2
A: Excuse me, is this the right way to the Bach Concert Hall?
B: No, you need to turn around, then [5]do/cross/go the bridge. After that, you [6]have/are/take the first right and go [7]at/with/through the centre of town. The concert hall is the [8]first/corner/cross of Ducane Road and Bright Street.

---

9 Lesson 5.1 TRANSPORT

1 Match photos A–N to the types of transport.

1 aeroplane
2 coach
3 ferry
4 helicopter
5 hot air balloon
6 lorry
7 minibus
8 moped
9 motorbike
10 ship
11 speedboat
12 taxi
13 tram
14 underground

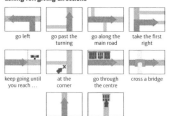

2 Work in pairs. Discuss. Which types of transport do you use regularly? Which do you think are the most enjoyable ways to travel?

Lesson 5.2 TRAVEL ITEMS

1 Match photos A–R to the travel items.

1 alarm clock
2 aspirin
3 binoculars
4 dictionary
5 digital camera
6 first aid kit
7 map
8 money belt
9 notebook
10 backpack
11 soap
12 souvenirs
13 suitcase
14 sun hat
15 travel guide
16 umbrella
17 walking boots
18 waterproof clothes

2 Work in pairs and take turns.
Student A: describe an item.
Student B: guess the item.
A: *You wear these when it is raining.*
B: *Waterproof clothes.*

---

10 COMMUNICATION BANK

Lesson 1.3

4 **A** Student A: make questions or comments with the prompts for Student B. Listen to Student B's responses.
1 would / like / drink?
2 watch / match / last night?
3 nice / day?
4 work / here?

B Listen to Student B's questions and comments. Choose the correct response.
1 Hi, Pete. Pleased to meet you./ Dear Mr Pete. How do you do?
2 Yes, thanks. I didn't do much./ Yes, thank you. I am enjoying it.
3 I'm coming from Toledo, near Madrid./ I'm from Toledo, near Madrid.
4 It's nice to meet you./ Yes, see you soon.

Lesson 3.5

4 **C** Answers to quiz
2 Reagan
3 *A Night at the Opera*
4 Raphael
5 Elton
6 One Love
7 Venice
8 Céline
9 Nelly Furtado

Lesson 4.3

9 **A** Student A: explain your problem. Then listen and respond to the advice.
Your son is eighteen years old and lives at home. He needs to study for his exams, but in the evening he goes out with friends until late. He often misses lessons or falls asleep when he is studying. At home you do all the cooking and cleaning and give your son money every week.

B Listen to another student's problem. Give the student some advice.

Lesson 2.2

4 **B** Student B

Danger Rating 8/10

Motorbike courier, Brazil

In Brazil, they are called motoboys, and on average, one of them dies in traffic every day. Foreign correspondent Peter Lane met the motoboys of São Paulo. He learnt that accidents are not the only problem – there are also robberies. It happened to Roberto Coelho.

'It was terrible, a really bad time for me. I lost everything. We don't have insurance and the company doesn't help us.' The motoboys usually earn just $450 a month.

Lane asks, 'When you know the streets are dangerous, why do you still drive so fast?' Coelho says it's because they often work under time pressure. 'We know it's dangerous, but we have no choice.'

Lane also spoke to some car drivers. One said, 'These motorcycle couriers are so dangerous. They drive too fast and they don't care about the rules of the road.' Another said, 'Most of them are just kids. It's no surprise they have accidents.'

Once in a while, they try to change the traffic laws – they want the motoboys to drive like everyone else. But the changes all failed, so the motoboys continue to risk their lives in one of the most dangerous jobs in the world.

Lesson 3.3

8 Student A: think about what you are going to say when you receive and make phone calls in these situations. Role-play the situations with Student B.

Answer the phone
1 You work for Nova Restaurant. Take a message.
2 You work for Amber Cinema. Answer the phone and tell a customer the times of the film *The Magic Hat*: 2.30p.m., 5.00p.m., 7.30p.m. and 10.00p.m., with a special extra showing at 12.00p.m. at the weekend.
3 Answer the phone normally. Listen and respond to the invitation.

Make a call
4 You are calling Ripping Yarns, a theatre company. You would like six tickets for *Hamlet* for Friday.
5 You are calling Brandon's Restaurant. You want to change your reservation from 7.30p.m. on Tuesday to 8.00p.m. next Wednesday. There will now be ten people, not five, so you need a bigger table.
6 Ask your partner if he/she wants to go for a snack after class.

5.1

5 TRAVEL

1 VOCABULARY
TRANSPORT

1 A Find fourteen types of transport in the word snake.

(taxi) ship motorbike tram moped aeroplane lorry speedboat helicopter coach ferry airballoon underground minibus

B Complete the word web with the types of transport in Exercise 1A.

WATER

FOUR WHEELS OR MORE — taxi

TWO WHEELS

TRANSPORT

AIR

PUBLIC TRANSPORT (CITY)

C What types of transport are the people talking about?

1 'I always call one to get home at night.'
taxi
2 'I use it every morning to get to work. The roads are full of cars, so it's the quickest way to travel.'
3 'It's my dream to travel in one of these, to feel the wind in my face and look down at the world below.'
4 'We enjoy touring foreign cities in them. They are perfect for groups of thirty or forty people.'
5 'I drive it for twelve hours a day. It's my job. I transport products for food companies across the country.'
6 'I can take you to your house. It's big enough for two people and I have two helmets.'
7 'It's the fastest way to travel on water. I use mine for waterskiing.'
8 'In the past, everyone used these to visit other continents. It took three weeks to get to the USA! Now this type of travel is only for rich people.'

1 GRAMMAR
PAST SIMPLE AND PAST CONTINUOUS

2 Match the sentence halves.
1 The last time they spoke to Marina ___
2 The teacher explained the exercise to us, but ___
3 Were there any calls for me ___
4 It started to rain ___
5 My mobile phone rang while ___
6 I fell asleep while I ___
7 Were you doing something important ___
8 I didn't go out last night ___

a) while we were playing football.
b) when I phoned you?
c) while I was shopping?
d) I was cooking.
e) because I was studying.
f) we weren't listening.
g) she was working in a bar.
h) was watching TV.

3 Complete the conversations with the past simple or past continuous form of the verbs in brackets.

Conversation 1
A: I came to see you yesterday, but you weren't at home. What 1_____ were you doing _____ (you/do)?
B: I was here, but I 2_____ (play) with my son in the garden, so I 3_____ (not hear) the doorbell.

Conversation 2
A: I heard you broke your leg. How 4_____ (it/happen)?
B: It happened when I 5_____ (climb) a mountain two weeks ago. I fell and I 6_____ (land) badly.

Conversation 3
A: Wendy told me you 7_____ (see) Jim last week.
B: Yes. I 8_____ (study) in the library and he 9_____ (say) 'hello'.

Conversation 4
A: I hear you crashed the car again.
10_____ (you/drive) too fast?
B: No! It wasn't my fault! I 11_____ (go) at thirty miles an hour when this other car suddenly 12_____ (come) out of a side street.

Conversation 5
A: I 13_____ (see) you on your bicycle yesterday. Where 14_____ (you/go)?
B: I 15_____ (go) to the shops, but I 16_____ (drop) my wallet on the way!

4 A Match the phrases in the box with the pictures.

drop his ticket | try to sleep
decide to use his mobile phone | go for a walk
go through security | pay the taxi driver

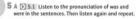

B Complete the story with the past simple or past continuous form of the phrases in Exercise 4A.

This is the story of Tim Bobo's first trip in an aeroplane. He was very excited, but as he was going out of the house, he 1_____ dropped his ticket _____ on the floor. He took a taxi to the airport, but while he 2_____, someone took his bag. Luckily, there was nothing important in the bag. He checked in, but while he 3_____, he found some keys in his pocket. Soon he was on the aeroplane. When it was taking off, he 4_____ around the plane! The flight attendant told him to sit down immediately. Then soon after this he noticed that everyone seemed unhappy, so he started singing. Unfortunately, the other passengers 5_____ and they told him to be quiet. A few hours later, he made one more mistake: while the plane was landing, he 6_____ his mobile phone!

2

5 A ▶ 5.1 Listen to the pronunciation of was and were in the sentences. Then listen again and repeat.

B Read audio script 5.1 on page 79. Listen again, read and repeat.

3 LISTENING

6 A ▶ 5.2 Listen to a story about a German tourist. Choose the map which shows his journey.

A

B

B Listen again. Are the sentences true (T) or false (F)?
1 A German man wanted to visit his girlfriend in Sydney, Australia. ___
2 When he was booking his ticket, he made a mistake. ___
3 His flight took him to the wrong town in Australia. ___
4 He was wearing summer clothes because the weather in Montana was hot. ___
5 His parents and friends sent him warm clothes. ___
6 After a few days, he bought a ticket to Australia. ___

7 A Read the sentences from the recording. Can you remember the rest of the second sentence?
1 A twenty-one-year-old German tourist called Tobi Gutt wanted to visit his girlfriend in Sydney, Australia. Unfortunately, _____
2 When he looked at the plane to Sidney, he became confused. Strangely, _____
3 A few friendly people helped him with food and drink until eventually, _____

B ▶ 5.3 Listen, check and complete the sentences.

28 / 29

WORKBOOK

Speakout Second Edition Workbook contains a wide variety of review and practice exercises and covers all of the language areas in the corresponding Students' Book unit. It also contains regular review sections to help learners consolidate what they have learned.

1. Extensive practice of vocabulary and grammar covered in the Students' Book
2. Additional practice of pronunciation points covered in the Students' Book
3. Reading and listening texts develop learners' skills
4. Writing exercises focus on useful sub-skills

Speakout Second Edition Workbook Audio is available online. Visit www.english.com/speakout to download audio material to accompany the pronunciation, listening and functional practice exercises.

5.2

3 READING

4 A Read the article and match topics a)–d) with paragraphs 1–4.
a) dealing with problems ___
b) having the best experience ___
c) doing something different ___
d) preparing for your trip ___

My top travel tips

Sandy Graves is an experienced travel writer who regularly travels all over the world. Here she shares some of her top tips.

1 When you start packing, leave your suitcase open somewhere. As you think of something you need to take, pack it. Don't leave it until later or you might forget. Make photocopies of all your important documents and put them in your suitcase, too. If you lose your passport, having a copy will make it easier to get a new one. Pack earplugs. They're great for long flights and noisy hostels, when you really need to sleep.

2 While you're travelling, be patient. Everybody wants to leave on time, but it doesn't always happen. Buses can be late, you can have problems with your documents or your card might not work in the ATM. Don't worry, there's always a way to get there. Smile and enjoy it — you won't have another chance to!

3 If you want more than just a holiday, try volunteering, spending some time learning new skills and meeting new people. You can travel anywhere in the world to do all kinds of different jobs, from building in Tanzania to looking after elephants in Thailand. Just think what you could do.

4 Do your best to try everything around you. Try the local food, buy the terrible, cheap souvenirs (they won't feel terrible when you're back home) and take lots of photos. And talk to local people — you can get so much more out of your trip if you do. Keep an open mind, and don't criticise the local culture. You might see or experience things which seem strange to you, but are normal there.

B Read the article again. Are the statements true (T) or false (F)?
1 Try to pack things at the same time as you think of them. ___
2 It's a good idea to take earplugs for when you want to go swimming. ___
3 It's best not to worry when you have problems. ___
4 There aren't many opportunities to do anything different when you travel. ___
5 Don't buy souvenirs if they're not good. ___
6 Try to accept things which seem strange to you. ___

C Find words in the article that match these meanings.
1 things you put in your ears to keep out noise (paragraph 1): _____
2 places where you can eat and sleep cheaply for a short time (paragraph 1): _____
3 able to wait calmly (paragraph 2): _____
4 a machine where you can get money from your bank (paragraph 2): _____
5 abilities; things you can do (paragraph 3): _____
6 from the place where you are (paragraph 4): _____

4 WRITING
USING SEQUENCERS

5 A Look at the pictures of two stories. Put sentences a)–i) in the correct order to tell the stories.
a) We had a great night out.
b) First, we met in a bar in town.
c) Finally, when we arrived, the hotel didn't have our reservation.
d) After the meal, we went dancing.
e) Then, our taxi broke down on the way to the hotel.
f) First, the flight was cancelled.
g) The holiday was a disaster.
h) Then we went out for a pizza.
i) We waited, and after a while we had to fly to a different airport.

Story 1
a ___ , ___ , ___ , ___

Story 2
g ___ , ___ , ___ , ___

B Write about a time when you went on holiday or had a good night out. Write 50–100 words. Use the sequencers in the box.

first | then | after that/after a while | finally

31

MYENGLISHLAB

MyEnglishLab provides a fully blended and personalised learning environment that benefits both teachers and learners. It offers:

- An interactive Workbook with instant feedback and automatic grade book
- A common error report that highlights mistakes learners are making
- Tips and feedback that direct learners to reference materials and encourage them to work out answers themselves
- Unit and achievement tests
- Mid- and end of course tests
- BBC interviews and interactive exercises

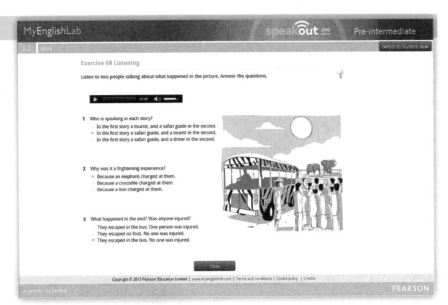

ACTIVETEACH

Speakout Second Edition ActiveTeach contains everything you need to make the course come alive. It includes integrated whiteboard software that allows you to add notes, embed files, save your work and reduce preparation time.

- Answers to exercises are revealed at the touch of a button
- Audio and video content fully integrated with time-coded scripting
- Shortcuts to the relevant pages of the *Language bank* and *Photo bank* make navigation easy

- Extra resources section includes editable scripts, photocopiable worksheets, tests and BBC interviews for every unit with accompanying worksheets
- Grammar and vocabulary review games
- Assessment package containing all the course tests
- Useful tools include a regular keyboard, a phonetic keyboard, a stopwatch and scoreboard.

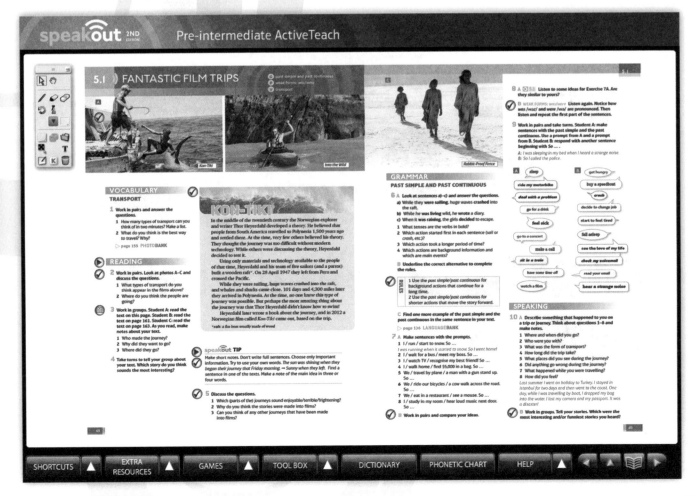

ADDITIONAL COMPONENTS

WEBSITE

Speakout Second Edition's website provides a wealth of information to support the course including:

- Information about the course, components and authors
- Introductory videos by the authors of the course
- Sample materials and free downloadable worksheets
- Teaching tips
- Placement test
- Editable audio and video scripts
- Global Scale of English mapping documents

Visit www.pearsonelt.com/speakout to check out the range of material available.

SPEAKOUT EXTRA

Speakout Extra provides a bank of additional downloadable exercises that can be accessed via the companion website:

- Downloadable grammar, vocabulary, pronunciation and skills worksheets
- BBC interviews and accompanying worksheets
- Additional worksheets to accompany DVD clips in the Students' Books
- Updated regularly with new material

Visit www.pearsonelt.com/speakout to check out the range of material available.

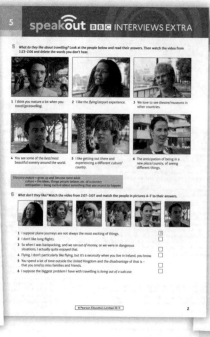

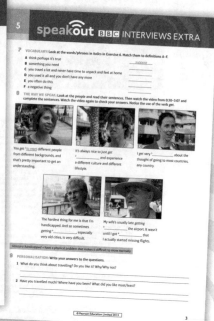

The thinking behind
Speakout Second Edition

Speakout Second Edition has been significantly updated and refreshed following feedback from students and teachers from around the world. It offers engaging topics with authentic BBC material to really bring them to life. At the same time it offers a robust and comprehensive focus on grammar, vocabulary, functions and pronunciation. As the name of the course might suggest, speaking activities are prominent, but that is not at the expense of the other core skills of reading, writing and listening, which are developed systematically throughout.

With this balanced approach to topics, language development and skills work, our aim has been to create a course book full of 'lessons that really work' in practice. Below we will briefly explain our approach in each of these areas.

TOPICS AND CONTENT

In *Speakout Second Edition* we have chosen topics that are relevant to students' lives and are global in nature. Where a topic area is covered in other ELT courses we have endeavoured to find a fresh angle on it. It is clear to us that authenticity is important to learners, and many texts come from the BBC's rich resources (audio, visual and print) as well as other real-world sources. At lower levels, we have sometimes adapted materials by adjusting the language to make it more manageable for students while trying to keep the tone as authentic as possible. We have also attempted to match the authentic feel of a text with an authentic interaction. Every unit contains a variety of rich and authentic input material including BBC interviews (filmed on location in London, England) and DVD material, featuring some of the best drama, documentary and light entertainment programmes that the BBC has to offer.

GRAMMAR

Knowing how to recognise and use grammatical structures is central to our ability to communicate with each other. Although at first students can often get by with words and phrases, they increasingly need grammar to make themselves understood. Students also need to understand sentence formation when reading and listening, and to be able to produce accurate grammar in professional and exam situations. We share students' belief that learning grammar is a core feature of learning a language and believe that a guided discovery approach, where students are challenged to notice new forms, works best. At the same time, learning is scaffolded so that students are supported at all times in a systematic way. Clear grammar presentations are followed by written and oral practice.

In *Speakout Second Edition* you will find:

- **Grammar in context** – We want to be sure that the grammar focus is clear and memorable for students. Grammar is almost always taken from the listening or reading texts, so that learners can see the language in action, and understand how and when it is used.

- **Focus on noticing** – We involve students in the discovery of language patterns by asking them to identify aspects of meaning and form, and complete rules or tables.

- **Cross-references to *Language bank*** – As well as a summary of rules within the unit, there are also cross-references to the *Language bank* at the back of the book which provides further explanation of the grammar point in focus as well as additional practice.

- **Plentiful and varied practice** – We ensure that there is plenty of practice, both form- and meaning-based, in the *Language bank* to give students confidence in manipulating the new language. Additional form-based grammar practice is also provided in the Workbook and in *Speakout Extra*. On the main input page we include personalised practice, which is designed to be genuinely communicative, and to offer students the opportunity to say something about themselves or the topic. There is also regular recycling of new language in the *Lookback* pages. Again, the focus here is on moving learners towards communicative use of the language.

VOCABULARY

Developing a wide range of vocabulary is key to increasing communicative effectiveness; developing a knowledge of high-frequency collocations and fixed and semi-fixed phrases is key to increasing spoken fluency. An extensive understanding of words and phrases helps learners become more confident when reading and listening, and developing a range of vocabulary is important for effective writing. Equally vital is learner-training, equipping students with the skills to record, memorise and recall vocabulary for use.

There is a prominent focus on vocabulary in *Speakout Second Edition*. We include vocabulary in almost all lessons, whether in a lexical set linked to a particular topic, as preparation for a speaking activity, or to aid comprehension of a DVD clip or a listening or reading text. Where we want students to use the language actively, we encourage them to use the vocabulary to talk about their own lives or opinions. At lower levels, the *Photo bank* also extends the vocabulary taught in the lessons, using memorable photographs and graphics to support students' understanding. Vocabulary items have been selected according to their usefulness with a strong focus on the following:

- **Vocabulary 'chunks'** – As well as lexical sets, we also regularly focus on how words fit together with other words, often getting students to notice how words are used in a text and to focus on high-frequency 'chunks' such as verb-noun collocations or whole phrases.

- **Vocabulary systems** – We give regular attention to word-building skills, a valuable tool in expanding vocabulary. At higher levels, the *Vocabulary plus* sections deal with systems such as affixation, multi-word verbs and compound words in greater depth.

- **Recycling** – Practice exercises ensure that vocabulary is encountered on a number of occasions: within the lessons, on the *Lookback* page, in subsequent lessons and in the *Photo bank/Vocabulary bank* at the back of the book. Additional vocabulary practice is also provided in the Workbook and in *Speakout Extra*.

- **Learner training** – One of the main focuses of the *Speakout* tips – which look at all areas of language learning – is to highlight vocabulary-learning strategies, aiming to build good study skills that will enable students to gain and retain new language.

FUNCTIONAL LANGUAGE

One thing that both teachers and learners appreciate is the need to manage communication in a wide variety of encounters, and to know what's appropriate to say in given situations. These can be transactional exchanges, where the main focus is on getting something done (buying something in a shop or phoning to make an enquiry), or interactional exchanges, where the main focus is on socialising with others (talking about the weekend, or responding appropriately to good news). As one learner commented to us, 'Grammar rules aren't enough – I need to know what to say.' Although it is possible to categorise 'functions' under 'lexical phrases', we believe it is useful for learners to focus on functional phrases separately from vocabulary or grammar.

The third lesson in every unit of *Speakout Second Edition* looks at one such situation, and focuses on the functional language needed. Learners hear or see the language used in context and then practise it in mini-situations, in both a written and a spoken context. Each of these lessons also includes a *Learn to* section, which highlights and practises a useful strategy for dealing with both transactional and interactional exchanges, for example, asking for clarification, showing interest, etc. Learners will find themselves not just more confident users of the language, but also more active listeners.

SPEAKING

The dynamism of most lessons depends on the success of the speaking tasks, whether the task is a short oral practice of new language, a discussion comparing information or opinions, a personal response to a reading text, or a presentation where a student might speak uninterrupted for a minute or more. Students develop fluency when they are motivated to speak. For this to happen, engaging topics and tasks are essential, as is the sequencing of stages and task design. For longer tasks, students often need to prepare their ideas and language in a structured way. This all-important rehearsal time leads to more motivation and confidence as well as greater accuracy, fluency and complexity. Also, where appropriate, students need to hear a model before they speak, in order to have a realistic goal.

In *Speakout Second Edition* there is a strong focus on:

- **Communicative practice** – After introducing any new language (vocabulary, grammar or function) there are many opportunities for students to use it in a variety of activities which focus on communication as well as accuracy. These include personalised exchanges, dialogues, flow-charts and role-plays.

- **Fluency development** – Opportunities are included in every unit for students to respond spontaneously. They might be asked to respond to a series of questions, to comment on a BBC DVD clip, interview or text, or to take part in conversations, discussions and role-plays. These activities involve a variety of interaction patterns such as pairs and groups.

- **Speaking strategies and sub-skills** – In the third lesson of each unit, students are encouraged to notice in a systematic way features which will help them improve their speaking. These include, for example, ways to manage a phone conversation, the use of mirror questions to ask for clarification, sentence starters to introduce an opinion and intonation to correct mistakes.

- **Extended speaking tasks** – In the *Speakout Second Edition* BBC DVD lesson, as well as in other speaking tasks throughout the course, students are encouraged to attempt more adventurous and extended use of language in tasks such as problem solving, developing a project or telling a story. These tasks go beyond discussion; they include rehearsal time, useful language and a concrete outcome.

LISTENING

For most users of English, listening is the most frequently used skill. A learner who can speak well but not understand at least as well is unlikely to be a competent communicator or user of the language. We feel that listening can be developed effectively through well-structured materials. As with speaking, the choice of interesting topics and texts works hand in hand with carefully considered sequencing and task design. At the same time, listening texts can act as a springboard to stimulate discussion in class.

The listening strands in *Speakout Second Edition* focus on:

- **Authentic material** – In *Speakout Second Edition*, we believe that it is motivating for all levels of learner to try to access and cope with authentic material. Each unit includes a DVD extract from a BBC documentary, drama or light entertainment programme as well as a BBC Interview filmed on location with real people giving their opinions. At the higher levels you will also find unscripted audio texts and BBC radio extracts. All are invaluable in the way they expose learners to real language in use as well as different varieties of English. Where recordings, particularly at lower levels, are scripted, they aim to reflect the patterns of natural speech.

- **Sub-skills and strategies** – Tasks across the recordings in each unit are designed with a number of sub-skills and strategies in mind. These include: listening for global meaning and more detail; scanning for specific information; becoming sensitised to possible misunderstandings; and noticing nuances of intonation and expression. We also help learners to listen actively by using strategies such as asking for repetition and paraphrasing.

- **Texts as a context for new language** – We see listening as a key mode of input and *Speakout Second Edition* includes many listening texts which contain target grammar, vocabulary or functions in their natural contexts. Learners are encouraged to notice this new language and how and where it occurs, often by using the audio scripts as a resource.

- **Texts as a model for speaking** – In the third and fourth lessons of each unit the recordings serve as models for speaking tasks. These models reveal the ways in which speakers use specific language to structure their discourse, for example, with regard to turn-taking, hesitating and checking for understanding. These recordings also serve as a goal for the learners' speaking.

READING

Reading is a priority for many students, whether it's for study, work or pleasure, and can be practised alone, anywhere and at any time. Learners who read regularly tend to have a richer, more varied vocabulary, and are often better writers, which in turn supports their oral communication skills. Nowadays, the internet has given students access to an extraordinary range of English language reading material, and the availability of English language newspapers, books and magazines is greater than ever before. The language learner who develops skill and confidence in reading in the classroom will be more motivated to read outside the classroom. Within the classroom, reading texts can also introduce stimulating topics and act as springboards for class discussion.

The reading strands in *Speakout Second Edition* focus on:

- **Authentic texts** – As with *Speakout Second Edition* listening materials, there is an emphasis on authenticity, and this is reflected in a number of ways. Many of the reading texts in *Speakout Second Edition* are sourced from the BBC. Where texts have been adapted or graded, there is an attempt to maintain authenticity by remaining faithful to the text type in terms of content and style. We have chosen up-to-date, relevant texts to stimulate interest and motivate learners to read. The texts represent a variety of genres that correspond to the text types that learners will probably encounter in their everyday lives.

- **Sub-skills and strategies** – In *Speakout Second Edition* we strive to maintain authenticity in the way the readers interact with a text. We always give students a reason to read, and provide tasks which bring about or simulate authentic reading, including real-life tasks such as summarising, extracting specific information, reacting to an opinion or following an anecdote. We also focus on strategies for decoding texts, such as guessing the meaning of unknown vocabulary, understanding pronoun referencing and following discourse markers.

- **Noticing new language** – Noticing language in use is a key step towards the development of a rich vocabulary and greater all-round proficiency in a language, and this is most easily achieved through reading. In *Speakout Second Edition*, reading texts often serve as valuable contexts for introducing grammar and vocabulary as well as discourse features.

- **Texts as a model for writing** – In the writing sections, as well as the *Writeback* sections of the DVD spreads, the readings serve as models for students to refer to when they are writing, in terms of overall organisation as well as style and language content.

WRITING

In recent years the growth of email and the internet has led to a shift in the nature of the writing our students need to do. Email has also led to an increased informality in written English. However, many students need to develop their formal writing for professional and exam-taking purposes. It is therefore important to focus on a range of genres, from formal text types such as essays, letters and reports to informal genres such as blog entries and personal messages.

There are four strands to writing in *Speakout Second Edition* which focus on:

- **Genres** – In every unit at the four higher levels there is a section that focuses on a genre of writing, emails, for example. We provide a model to show the conventions of the genre and, where appropriate, we highlight fixed phrases associated with it. We usually then ask the students to produce their own piece of writing. While there is always a written product, we also focus on the process of writing, including the relevant stages such as brainstorming, planning, and checking. At Starter and Elementary,

we focus on more basic writing skills, including basic written sentence patterns, linking, punctuation and text organisation, in some cases linking this focus to a specific genre.

- **Sub-skills and strategies** – While dealing with the genres, we include a section which focuses on a sub-skill or strategy that is generally applicable to all writing. Sub-skills include paragraphing, organising content and using linking words and pronouns, while strategies include activities like writing a first draft quickly, keeping your reader in mind and self-editing. We present the sub-skill by asking the students to notice the feature. We then provide an opportunity for the students to practise it.

- **Development of fluency** – At the end of every unit, following the DVD and final speaking task, we include a *Writeback* task. The idea behind these tasks is to develop fluency in their writing. While we always provide a model, the task is not tied to any particular grammatical structure. Instead the emphasis is on using writing to generate ideas and personal responses.

- **Writing as a classroom activity** – We believe that writing can be very usefully employed as an aid to speaking and as a reflective technique for responding to texts – akin to the practice of writing notes in the margins of books. It also provides a change of pace and focus in lessons. Activities such as short dictations, note-taking, brainstorming on paper and group story writing are all included in *Speakout Second Edition* and additional writing practice is provided in *Speakout Extra*.

PRONUNCIATION

In recent years, attitudes towards pronunciation in many English language classrooms have moved towards a focus on intelligibility: if students' spoken language is understandable, then the pronunciation is good enough. We are aware, however, that many learners and teachers place great importance on developing pronunciation that is more than 'good enough', and that systematic attention to pronunciation in a lesson, however brief, can have a significant impact on developing learners' speech.

In *Speakout Second Edition*, we have taken a practical, integrated approach to developing students' pronunciation, highlighting features that often cause problems in conjunction with a given area of grammar, particular vocabulary items and functional language. Where relevant to the level, a grammatical or functional language focus is followed by a focus on a feature of pronunciation, for example, the weak forms of auxiliary verbs or connected speech in certain functional exponents. Students are given the opportunity to listen to models of the pronunciation, notice the key feature and then practise it.

Each input lesson looks at a specific feature of pronunciation and the following strands are covered:

- **Sentence stress** – We help learners to identify which words are stressed in a sentence. This is particularly important for helping learners to understand rapid spoken English where the important information is highlighted by the speaker.

- **Word stress** – When dealing with new vocabulary, we emphasise the importance of using the correct word stress patterns. This helps listeners to identify the word being used and helps the speaker to use the correct vowel sounds.

- **Intonation** – We look at how intonation and the way we deliver a sentence can influence its meaning, or how the sentence is received.

- **Connected speech** – We help learners to understand rapid spoken English by looking at how the sounds change in fast speech. To encourage fluency we also help learners to produce rapid speech.

- **Individual sounds** – Sometimes specific individual sounds can cause problems for learners. We help learners to identify and produce specific sounds where they are important.

Additional pronunciation practice is provided in the Workbook and in *Speakout Extra*.

TEACHING PRE-INTERMEDIATE LEARNERS

Pre-intermediate students have usually not yet reached a plateau. This makes them potentially very rewarding to teach. While they have enough English to have a basic conversation, they will be able to see progress during the course in terms of the range, fluency and accuracy of output.

Pre-intermediate students still probably see the English language in terms of small, discrete pieces – verb tenses learned sequentially and basic lexical sets such as colours, jobs, hobbies, animals, etc. – which they have not yet 'put together'. One of the keys to teaching at this level is to provide students with deeper encounters with the language: setting more challenging tasks than at elementary, and sometimes asking students to deal with the complexities of authentic material – text and film – in order to develop strategies for coping with incomplete understanding. Strategy development, both metacognitive (learning habits such as keeping a vocabulary notebook, watching films, etc.) and cognitive (ways to deal with tasks at hand, e.g. using phrases to ask for help, predicting content by reading a title, etc.), as at other levels, are essential for students' progress.

Typically, pre-intermediate students are able to make themselves understood in a wider variety of situations than they could at elementary. They are also able to deal with short basic texts. However, they may have problems with extended discourse. This applies to all four skills: their spoken utterances will probably be short and their written compositions brief; they probably do little extensive reading, and they may have difficulty in sustaining concentration while listening to recordings or conversations that are longer than two minutes. One of the teacher's roles at this level is to gradually expose students to longer pieces of discourse while providing both linguistic and motivational support. Teachers should do thorough, personalised pre-reading/pre-listening tasks, break long pieces into shorter sections, and use whole-class activities in order to foster students' confidence.

As regards the syllabus, it is very important for learners at this stage to encounter the same language again and again. Pre-intermediate students need a lot of review and recycling of grammar and vocabulary that they may have encountered but not yet mastered. Pre-intermediate is a key stage at which they begin to change passive knowledge (language they know) into active knowledge (language they can use).

Here are our Top Tips for teaching at this level:

- Recycle grammar and vocabulary. Although they will have covered many key points such as the past simple, they will not have mastered them.

- Introduce learning strategies – e.g. for recording vocabulary – by modelling them. By now the students are beyond 'survival English' and should be able to start 'collecting' vocabulary from the texts they encounter.

- Look at how words work together. At elementary students probably need to learn mainly one-word items in order to name things, but at pre-intermediate they are more able to work with phrases and chunks of language.

- Get students into the habit of reviewing language frequently. You could begin each class with a short review of grammar and vocabulary learnt in the previous lesson, perhaps by using a game or photocopiable activity.

- Do a lot of work on pronunciation through short drills. At this level, the students need to continue familiarising themselves with the sounds of English, particularly the ways in which the sounds of words change in the context of connected speech.

- Get students to self-correct. At pre-intermediate level, many students start to develop awareness of correct and incorrect English. You could try having small signals on the board, for example, -s for third person 's', -ed for past tense endings. When the students make a mistake, you can just point to the board to remind them.

- Where possible, begin to use short authentic texts such as menus, brochures and newspaper articles.

- Use role-plays and structured speaking tasks to encourage students to extend speaking skills.

- Encourage fluency by having conversations at the beginning or the end of the class. Use topics that students should all be able to talk about, like what they did at the weekend, or what their plans are for after the class.

Antonia Clare, Frances Eales, Steve Oakes and JJ Wilson

The Global Scale of English

The Global Scale of English (GSE) is a standardised, granular scale that measures English language proficiency. The scale is part of a wider GSE ecosystem that includes Learning Objectives or 'can do' statements that describe exactly what a learner can do at each point on the scale, teaching and learning materials in a variety of media, and low- and high-stakes tests – all aligned to the Global Scale of English. Using the Global Scale of English students and teachers can now answer three questions accurately: Exactly how good is my English? What progress have I made towards my learning goal? What do I need to do next if I want to improve?

Unlike some other frameworks that measure English proficiency in broad bands, the Global Scale of English identifies what a learner can do at each point on a scale from 10–90, across each of the four skills: listening, reading, speaking and writing. This allows learners and teachers to understand a learner's exact level of proficiency, what progress they've made and what they need to learn next.

The Global Scale of English is designed to motivate learners by making it easier to demonstrate granular progress in their language ability. Teachers can use their knowledge of their students' Global Scale of English levels to choose course materials that are precisely matched to ability and learning goals. The Global Scale of English serves as a standard against which English language courses and assessments worldwide can be benchmarked, offering a truly global and shared understanding of language proficiency levels.

Visit English.com/gse for more information about the Global Scale of English.

SPEAKOUT SECOND EDITION AND THE GSE

The authors and editorial team were informed by the GSE Learning Objectives for Adult Learners during the writing and development of *Speakout Second Edition*. Revisions to the grammar, vocabulary and skills syllabuses were influenced by these GSE Learning Objectives, and they helped to ensure that the outcomes of each lesson are clear, meaningful and relevant to learners. The spread below shows how the GSE Learning Obectives for Adult Learners are reflected in the skills content of a typical lesson in *Speakout Intermediate Second Edition*:

1. Can find specific information in simple letters, brochures and short articles. (Reading GSE 38)
2. Can follow the main points of short talks on familiar topics if delivered in clear, standard speech. (Listening GSE 45)
3. Can ask and answer questions about basic plans and intentions. (Speaking GSE 37)
4. Can write a basic letter of application with supporting details. (Writing GSE 47)

Visit www.pearsonelt.com/speakout for the full list of GSE Learning Objectives for Adult Learners covered in each level of *Speakout Second Edition*.

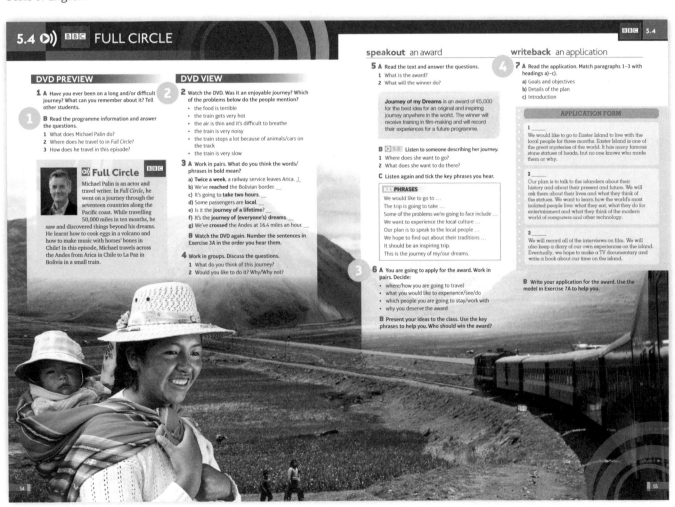

INDEX

UNIT 1	25
UNIT 2	35
UNIT 3	45
UNIT 4	55
UNIT 5	65
UNIT 6	75
UNIT 7	85
UNIT 8	95
UNIT 9	105
UNIT 10	115
UNIT 11	125
UNIT 12	135

LEAD-IN

Introduction

The activities on the Lead-in page are designed to provide revision and communicative practice in language that pre-intermediate Ss should be familiar with. Use the Lead-in page to assess your Ss existing knowledge and revise/teach the target language in each activity.

CLASSROOM LANGUAGE

Answers:
1A 1 does 2 do 3 are 4 to 5 you 6 say
1B 1 b) 2 f) 3 c) 4 e) 5 a) 6 d)

SPELLING

Answers: 2A 1 would 2 which 3 friend 4 know 5 people

Lead in Recording 1

1 would – as in 'Would you like a drink?'   would – w-o-u-l-d
2 which – as in 'Which film did you see?'   which – w-h-i-c-h
3 friend – as in 'What is the name of your best friend?'   friend – f-r-i-e-n-d
4 know – as in 'Do you know the answer?'   know – k-n-o-w
5 people – as in 'How many people are in your class?'   people – p-e-o-p-l-e

PARTS OF SPEECH

Answers: 3 2 article 3 noun 4 preposition of place 5 auxiliary 6 adjective 7 adverb

TENSES AND STRUCTURES

Answers:
4 1 **present simple:** My name is …
   2 **present continuous:** I'm living …
   3 **present perfect:** I've been here for …
   4 **past simple:** I was born in …
   5 *going to* **for future plans:** I'm going to visit my uncle …

QUESTION WORDS

Answers: 5 1 What 2 Who 3 Where 4 When 5 How 6 Why

AUXILIARY VERBS

Answers: 6 1 do 2 does 3 did 4 don't 5 doesn't 6 didn't 7 Are 8 isn't

VOCABULARY

Answers:
7 **family:** uncle, grandmother, cousin
   food: tomato, sugar, pasta
   jobs: shop assistant, lawyer, doctor
   shops: bookshop, bakery, supermarket
   transport: car, bike, train

OVERVIEW

1.1 FEELING GOOD?

VOCABULARY | free time
READING | understand an article about the secrets of happiness
GRAMMAR | question forms
PRONUNCIATION | stressed words
SPEAKING | ask and answer questions about holidays and weekends

1.2 TRUE LOVE

VOCABULARY | relationships
LISTENING | listen to stories about offers of marriage
GRAMMAR | past simple
PRONUNCIATION | past simple verbs: -ed endings
SPEAKING | ask and answer personal questions
WRITING | write about an important year in your life; improve your use of linking words

1.3 NICE DAY, ISN'T IT?

VOCABULARY | conversation topics
LISTENING | understand routine exchanges
FUNCTION | making conversation
LEARN TO | sound natural
PRONUNCIATION | linking

1.4 SOMEONE SPECIAL BBC⏺ DVD

DVD | watch an extract from a sitcom about a woman called Miranda
speakout | a special person
writeback | a competition entry

1.5 LOOKBACK

Communicative revision activities

BBC⏺ INTERVIEWS

What do you look for in a friend?

This video extends discussion of the unit topic to friendship. It will also extend Ss' language on friendship, relationships and keeping in touch. Use the video at the start or end of the unit.

FEELING GOOD?

Introduction

Ss revise/practise asking and answering questions with *be* and the auxiliary verb *do* in the context of happiness.

> **SUPPLEMENTARY MATERIALS**
> **Resource bank** p148
> **Language bank** p128–129

Warm up

It's very important to build rapport with a new class. The activity here is designed to give Ss the opportunity to get to know each other and help you to assess their language and speaking skills, in particular the use of question forms (reviewed later in the lesson). First, tell Ss the aims of the activity and elicit the information they need to get to know each other, e.g. *name, age, home town, nationality/country, job/occupation, hobbies/interests, reasons for learning English*. Write the prompts on the board and elicit a suitable question for each one, e.g. *What's your name? How old are you? Where are you from?* Write the questions on the board if necessary. Ss then work in groups of 4–6 and take turns to ask and answer the questions. They should note down at least five facts about each person in their group for feedback. In feedback, nominate each student in each group to tell the class about one person in their group. The class listens and writes down another question to ask that person. This ensures that Ss pay attention and listen to each other. Ss then move around the class in an informal way, asking and answering the questions they wrote down.

> **Teaching tip**
>
> While Ss work through speaking activities like this, monitor and note down any particular strengths and weaknesses, including how well they use the target language. This will help you to decide how much support and input will be needed in the grammar section later.

VOCABULARY FREE TIME

1A First, elicit two or three examples from different Ss. Ss then work in pairs to discuss their ideas. In feedback, nominate Ss to tell the class about their partner's answers.

B Give Ss 2–3 mins to do the exercise alone but don't pre-teach new language at this point. Ss then complete the phrases and compare answers in pairs. Monitor while they do the exercise and check/teach phrases Ss don't know in feedback, e.g. *have time off = not go to work/have a holiday*.

> **Answers:** 2 spend   3 eat   4 have   5 play

C Give Ss 3–4 mins to do the exercise in pairs. Meanwhile, write the verbs from Ex 1B on the board. In feedback, nominate Ss to give their answers. Write the extra activities on the board under the correct verb or invite Ss to write them.

> **Suggested answers:**
> 1 go out/to the cinema/to work/running
> 2 spend £50/the morning in bed/a week in the mountains
> 3 eat a meal/a hamburger/a lot/at home/alone
> 4 have a party/friends round
> 5 play football/tennis/in a team

READING

2A First, introduce the text and check the rubric. Give Ss 2–3 mins to read the text. They then discuss their answers in pairs, small groups or as a whole class.

Teaching tip

The aim of strict time limits is to encourage Ss to skim texts quickly and check the main ideas. Tell them not to worry about unknown vocabulary at the moment.

B Give Ss 2–3 mins to rank the ideas in order of importance and discuss in their pairs. In feedback, elicit answers and ask Ss to justify their opinions. Also, check the meaning of any useful vocabulary from the text, e.g. *brain, unexpected, curious, satisfaction, network, opportunity*.

GRAMMAR   QUESTION FORMS

3A Elicit an answer for each question from the class. Then give Ss time to prepare their answers. Encourage them to make brief notes. Monitor and provide vocabulary Ss need if necessary.

B Model and drill the questions. Ss then work in small groups and take turns to ask and answer them. Monitor and make notes on their performance, particularly with the accuracy of the tenses used. Check Ss' answers in open pairs across the class, i.e. nominate two students at a time to ask and answer a question.

4A Ss look at the tables. Check the meaning of *auxiliary* and other meta-language (*subject, infinitive*, etc.) if necessary. Ss should use the questions in Ex 3A to help them complete the tables. While Ss complete the tables, write the questions on the board with gaps. Elicit the answers and complete the gaps. Ask: *Which is a 'yes/no' question? Which are information (wh-) questions?* Then ask: *What tense are the questions in? How do you know?* Elicit Ss' answers.

Answers: 1 do   2 When   3 Are   4 Where

Teaching tip

Stronger classes can work alone but *weaker Ss* might need more support. In *mixed-ability classes*, strong Ss could work with weak ones. Done sensitively, this is a useful strategy for most classes; the need to help/explain language challenges stronger Ss and increases their language awareness.

B Ss read the rules of form and discuss their answers in pairs. In feedback, elicit and underline the auxiliary verbs and *be* in the questions on the board.

Answers: 1 before   2 before

▷ **LANGUAGEBANK 1.1** p128–129

Stronger classes can study the tables and notes at home when they do the exercises. Otherwise, check the tables and notes with Ss, especially the difference between *which* and *what*. Elicit more examples using question words, e.g. *What are you doing? Why are you learning English? Which languages do you speak?* *Weaker Ss* could do Ex A–C in class. If you do Ex A and B in class, make them into a competition. The first pair to finish with all the correct answers wins. If there are words/places/names Ss don't understand, tell them to use the answers in Ex B to work them out.

Answers:
A 1 How many   2 Who   3 What/Which   4 What   5 When
   6 Where   7 Which   8 How
B 1 e)   2 b)   3 h)   4 f)   5 c)   6 d)   7 a)   8 g)
C 1 How much *does* this cost?
   2 *Do* you have/*Have you got* any brothers or sisters?
   3 What time *does* the film start?
   4 How often do you *play* football?
   5 Who *is your new teacher*?
   6 Do *you want* to come and have a pizza?
   7 Why don't you *like* grammar?
   8 Where *did* you go on holiday last year?

5A Check the rubric and do the first question as an example. Ss then work alone to write the questions and then compare answers in pairs. Monitor and prompt Ss to self-correct, but don't do feedback yet. Ss will check their answers in Ex 5B.

B Play the recording, pausing for a few seconds after each question for Ss to check/correct their answers.

Answers:
1 How many <u>people</u> **are** in your <u>family</u>?
2 How often **do** you <u>see</u> your <u>parents</u>?
3 **Do** you <u>enjoy</u> spending time with your <u>family</u>?
4 <u>When</u> **was** your <u>last</u> family <u>celebration</u>?
5 <u>Who</u> **do** you <u>live</u> with?
6 How often **do** you <u>eat</u> <u>out</u> with <u>friends</u>?
7 Where **does** your <u>best</u> <u>friend</u> <u>live</u>?

C Play the first question again and elicit the stressed words: *people, family*. Ss then do the others alone/in pairs. Play the recording again for Ss to check their answers before they repeat the questions.

Answers: See Ex 5B above.

D Pair Ss who don't know each other well, especially in *monolingual classes*; this will create a wider information gap. They take it in turns to ask and answer the questions and make brief notes on their partner's answers. In feedback, nominate Ss to report back their own and their partner's answers to the class, e.g. *There are six people in my family, but there are ten in Diego's*.

SPEAKING

6A First, ask: *Where are the people in the pictures? What are they doing?* Elicit Ss' answers, e.g. *in Paris, taking a photo; in a café, spending time/having a coffee with friends.* Do an example, then give Ss 3–4 mins to finish the exercise in pairs. In feedback, elicit the questions and prompt Ss to self-correct.

Suggested answers:
Holidays
How long do you usually go on holiday for?
Who do you usually go with?/Who do you like going with?
What do you like doing?
Where do you like going?
Where do you want to go on your next holiday?
Weekend
What do you usually do/like doing at the weekend?
Where do you (like to) go?
Do you ever/usually/often (have to) work or study?
What time do you usually get up?

B In groups, Ss take it in turns to ask and answer the questions. Monitor discreetly while Ss talk and make notes of examples of good language and problems.

C Ss report back to the class about their group's answers. In feedback, write some examples of Ss' errors and good language on the board. Ss discuss and correct them in pairs, groups or as a whole class.

Optional extra activity
Ss write a short paragraph about one of the Ss in their group but do *not* mention their names, e.g. *X often plays chess at the weekend. He also paints pictures. He started when he was sixteen. He enjoys it because he likes art.* Ss then pass their texts round for other groups to read and guess who they are about. Alternatively, put the texts on the classroom walls. Ss walk round and guess who the people are.

Homework ideas
- **Ex 6B:** Ss write two paragraphs about their answers to the questions (or they write about another person in their group).
- **Language bank** 1.1 Ex A–C, p129
- **Workbook** Ex 1–4, p5–6

TRUE LOVE

Introduction
Ss revise and practise the past simple in the context of relationships. They also practise using linking words in texts.

SUPPLEMENTARY MATERIALS
Resource bank p147 and 149
Language bank p128–129
Warm up: 12 verb prompts (see notes below)

Warm up
Review irregular past forms with a *pelmanism* activity on the board. Before class, write six irregular verbs and their past simple forms, e.g. *become – became, fall – fell, meet – met, get – got, go – went, see – saw,* on A4 sheets of paper (one on each sheet). On the other side of each sheet, write a number from 1 to 12. In class, stick the sheets on the board with the numbers face up and do an example. Elicit any two numbers from Ss, e.g. 3 and 9, and turn over the corresponding sheets for them to see the words. If there's a verb and a past simple form that match to make a pair, e.g. *go – went,* remove them from the board. If not, put them back in the same places. Ss should try to remember where they are so they can choose a matching pair of words later. Ss work in pairs/teams and take it in turns to choose two numbers. The pair/team with the most matching pairs wins.

Teaching tip
Use similar pelmanism activities with any word game involving the matching of two items.

SPEAKING

1 Read and check the questions with Ss. Teach/Check *love at first sight.* Then give them 3–4 mins to discuss the questions in pairs. In feedback, elicit their answers and have a brief class discussion.

Suggested answers:
2 at work/college, in clubs/societies, playing sports, at parties, at friends' houses

VOCABULARY   RELATIONSHIPS

2A Give Ss 3 mins to read the sentences and match the phrases with the definitions. In feedback, elicit their answers and check the meaning and pronunciation of the phrases where necessary.

Answers: 1 b) **2** f) **3** h) **4** a) **5** g) **6** e) **7** d) **8** c)

B Ss put the stages of a relationship in order and check answers in pairs before class feedback.

Suggested answers: 7, 5, 2, 8, 1, 6, 4, 3

C Ask Ss to work alone and monitor discreetly while they write their sentences. Ss then work in pairs and read their sentences to each other. Encourage them to ask follow-up questions about each of their partners' sentences. In feedback, elicit any interesting or unusual information from Ss.

speakout TIP

Read the Speakout tip with Ss and write the verbs *get* and *have* on the board. Give them 2 mins to write down phrases they remember in pairs. In feedback, elicit the phrases and write them on the board (or invite Ss to do it). They then copy the lists into their notebooks.

Teaching tip

It's important for Ss to record their vocabulary in a logical and accessible way so they can review it easily. Suggest that they either have a separate section in their English notebooks or a smaller notebook which they could carry around in their bag/ pocket to refer to at suitable times.

LISTENING

3A Here Ss practise their prediction skills. Ask them to discuss the questions in pairs and then play the recording for them to check their ideas.

Answers:
Story 1: The man put the engagement ring in the woman's salad but she didn't see it and put it in her mouth.
Story 2: They went on a dive and the man proposed to the woman underwater.
Story 3: The man made a video of him proposing to his girlfriend and put it on YouTube.

Teaching tip

It is important to build Ss' confidence with listening by asking them to compare their answers in pairs. If they don't agree about their answers, play the recording again for them to double-check: this gives them the chance to get the right answers.

B Play the recording and get Ss to check answers in pairs before class feedback.

Answers:
1 in a restaurant
2 She put the ring in her mouth and nearly swallowed it.
3 Egypt
4 She said yes.
5 He made a two-minute YouTube video of him proposing and sent her a link.
6 She made a video of herself saying yes.

C Put Ss in pairs and give them 2 mins to decide which stories the sentences are from. Check answers, then give Ss 3–4 minutes to retell the stories. Monitor and help where necessary. In feedback, nominate Ss/pairs to retell the stories in open class.

Answers: 1 Story 1 2 Story 2 3 Story 3 4 Story 2 5 Story 3 6 Story 1

D Ss could discuss the questions in pairs or small groups. Monitor and provide vocabulary they may need. In feedback, nominate Ss from each group to tell the class their opinions.

1 My boyfriend and I were at a restaurant and I don't know how he did it, but he put the engagement ring in my salad. I didn't see it and I put it in my mouth. I think he panicked and tried to stop me. Anyway, luckily, I felt something hard as I bit into my food and I didn't swallow it. I took it out, saw what it was and accepted! So that was how we got engaged. It was almost a disaster. We got married one month later.

2 We decided to go on holiday in Egypt as we both liked diving. This was me and my girlfriend at the time. So we went on a dive and I proposed to her underwater. I didn't say anything. I just gave her the ring while we were, I don't know, ten feet under. Luckily, she smiled. We got back on the boat and she said yes.

3 My husband and I are video artists. We met at art school and honestly, we fell in love immediately. And what he did was, he made a funny two-minute video, he put it on YouTube and sent a link to me. And it was him proposing. And in the video there was music and then all of our friends suddenly appeared, singing and dancing. It was amazing and such a surprise. I watched it and then I surprised him. I accepted his proposal, but I didn't tell him. Instead, I made a video of me saying yes.

GRAMMAR   PAST SIMPLE

4A Give Ss 2–3 mins to underline the past simple on their own and then compare answers in pairs. In feedback, check answers and ask Ss to tell you whether each verb is regular or irregular. (These are indicated as *(I)* or *(R)* in the answer key below.)

Answers: 1 were (I)   **2** didn't say (I), gave (I)   **3** met (I)
4 smiled (R)   **5** accepted (R), didn't tell (I)   **6** tried (I)

B Ss can refer to the audio script on p168 to help them complete the tables before comparing their answers in pairs. Write the gapped sentences from the second table on the board. In feedback, elicit the regular and irregular past forms and the spelling of -ed endings, e.g. *marry – married*. Then nominate Ss to complete the gapped sentences on the board. Check the form of the past simple. Ss then copy down the three sentences.

Answers:
regular: liked, decided, tried
irregular: went, fell, got, said
negative: didn't
question: Did
short answer: didn't

5A Ss now practise recognising the pronunciation of -ed endings. Write the phonemic symbols on the board and model/drill them. Teach Ss that /d/ is a voiced sound and /t/ is unvoiced. Illustrate this: tell Ss to touch their throat with their fingers. When they say /d/, they will feel a vibration in their throat, but with the /t/ sound, they won't. Then play the recording while Ss read the sentences.

Watch out!

The pronunciation of the -ed endings of regular verbs is a common problem for Ss. They overgeneralise from the rule for verbs like *started*, *decided* and pronounce all -ed endings in the same way (/ɪd/). It's very important to highlight, drill and correct this mistake at all times to prevent fossilisation.

B Check the examples and play the recording. Pause after each verb for Ss to write it in the correct column. Elicit/Check Ss' answers. To give practise of *producing* the sounds, Ss can listen and repeat again. Drill the verbs chorally (with the whole class) and then individually. With **stronger classes**, you could teach the rules of pronunciation for *-ed* endings: verbs end with the /d/ sound after vowels and voiced consonants except /d/, e.g. /b/ /v/ /z/ /g/ /m/ /n/ /l/. Verbs end with /t/ after unvoiced consonants except /t/, e.g. /p/ /f/ /s/ /k/. Verbs end in /ɪd/ after /d/ and /t/, e.g. *started*, *decided*.

> **Answers:**
> /d/: smiled, studied
> /t/: worked, stopped, walked, talked, helped
> /ɪd/: wanted, needed, decided

> ▷ **LANGUAGEBANK 1.2** p128–129
>
> Ss can refer to the notes on p128 when they do the exercises. **Weaker Ss** should do Ex A and B in class. Check new vocabulary before Ss do each exercise or in feedback.
>
> **Answers:**
> A 2 saw 3 got 4 knew 5 emailed 6 fell 7 decided
>   8 asked 9 arrived 10 said 11 got
> B 1 taught 2 did, grow up 3 met 4 didn't get on
>   5 left, got 6 lived, didn't see 7 Did, enjoy 8 didn't have
>   9 finished 10 studied

6A Do an example. Ss then complete the sentences alone and compare answers in pairs. In feedback, elicit answers and for each verb, ask: *Is it a regular or irregular verb?* It would also be useful to revise the time phrases in each sentence before Ss do Ex 6B and 6C. Elicit and write them on the board, e.g. *three months ago, last summer, all night*. Ss copy them down and add three more examples of each phrase, e.g. *two weeks/a year/five minutes ago.* Check answers and write them on the board for Ss to copy if necessary.

> **Answers:** 1 saw 2 went 3 stayed 4 went 5 cooked 6 spent

B Check the example and give Ss 3–4 mins to write the questions in pairs. In feedback, elicit and drill the questions with the class, and then elicit possible answers with time phrases.

> **Answers:**
> 1 When did you last see your best friend?
> 2 When did you last go to a wedding?
> 3 When did you last stay up all night?
> 4 When did you last go on holiday?
> 5 When did you last cook a meal (for (some) friends/someone)?
> 6 When did you last spend the day with your sister/brother/
>   boyfriend/etc.?

C Model/Drill the example question and elicit personalised answers using time phrases. While Ss work in pairs, monitor and prompt them to self-correct errors with the target language. Give feedback on persistent errors with the past simple.

SPEAKING

7A Give Ss 3–4 mins to write down five dates and make notes about them. Monitor closely to provide help with vocabulary, especially with **weaker Ss**. To provide a model for Ss, you could tell them about an important date for you.

B Check the example and point out that Ss can only use *yes/no* questions. Limit the number of questions to ten. In feedback, nominate Ss to tell the class about one of their partner's dates.

WRITING   **LINKING WORDS**

8A This should be revision for most Ss, so use the exercise to check. Check new words if necessary, e.g. *degree, flat-mate*.

> **Answers:** 1 c) and   2 d) because   3 b) so   4 a) but

B Ss look at the cartoon. Ask: *What's the man doing?* Elicit/Teach *internet chatroom*. Ss complete the text. In feedback, elicit answers and ask some comprehension questions, e.g. *What happened in 2011? Where do they live now?*

> **Answers:** 1 because   2 and   3 but   4 so

C Give Ss time to think and make notes on an important year, using the linking words. It would be helpful for them to talk about it in pairs/small groups for 3–4 mins while you monitor and provide language they need. Give Ss 8–10 mins to write their text. If time, Ss exchange texts with a different partner and answer questions about it. Otherwise, they can finish writing it at home.

> **Teaching tip**
>
> Encourage a collaborative approach to writing: Ss show each other their work and exchange advice/help.

> **Homework ideas**
>
> * **Ex 7:** Ss write sentences about their (or their partner's) five important dates.
> * **Ex 8C:** Ss write a final draft of their text.
> * **Language bank** 1.2 Ex A–B, p129
> * **Workbook** Ex 1–8, p7–8

NICE DAY, ISN'T IT?

Introduction

Ss learn and practise ways of making conversation when they first meet people. They also learn how to make their spoken English sound more natural.

> **SUPPLEMENTARY MATERIALS**
> **Resource bank** p150
> **Language bank** p128–129
> **Warm up:** Prepare a short descriptive narrative like the example below (or use the one provided).

Warm up

Lead in to the lesson topic with a *live listening*. In a live listening, you tell Ss a story/anecdote or give a description of an event which relates to/provides a model of a speaking activity that Ss will do in the lesson. You can ask comprehension questions about it, use target language that Ss will focus on later or just allow Ss to listen – and practise hearing authentic English. Give Ss a short description – real or invented – based on the questions in Ex 1A.

Example text:

Last weekend I went to stay with my friend James in Oxford and he took me to a local artisans' market on Sunday morning. It was fantastic. There was home-made bread and cakes, jewellery, clothes, cards and paintings – all sorts of things. It was great. James introduced me to a friend of his called Jane – she makes beautiful silver rings and necklaces and sells them in the market. I've recently started making necklaces too, so James thought we should meet. He was right. We got on really well and talked about our work for ages – I learnt lots of interesting things and got some new ideas for my necklaces. And I'm thinking of making earrings now.

When you've finished, ask comprehension questions about your description. Then move to Ex 1, where Ss will talk about their own experiences.

VOCABULARY   CONVERSATION TOPICS

1 Lead in to the topic. Ask: *Do you like going to parties/meeting new people?* Elicit Ss' answers and have a brief class discussion. Then check the questions in Ex 1. Give Ss 3–4 mins to discuss them in pairs. In feedback, elicit and discuss Ss' answers.

2A Elicit/Check the meaning of the words in the box, and also check *conversation killers* in the title of the article. Give Ss 3–4 mins to read and complete the article, then ask them to compare answers in pairs. Check answers in feedback.

> **Answers:** 1 conversation   2 tells   3 interrupt   4 saying
> 5 gossip   6 joke   7 talk

B Ss discuss the questions in pairs. Elicit answers in feedback and encourage Ss to give reasons.

> **Answer:** The article talks about the kinds of problems you can have when trying to have a conversation with someone.

C Ask Ss to cover the article and give them 2 mins to make a list of the tips they remember. They can then compare their notes in pairs. In feedback, elicit the tips if possible or give Ss 1 min to check their lists in the article by themselves.

FUNCTION   MAKING CONVERSATION

3A Tell Ss that they are going to listen to people 'making conversation'. Play the recording and then ask them to discuss the question in pairs. In feedback, elicit the answer and ask Ss to give reasons.

> **Answer:** Conversation 2 is better because it flows more easily and both speakers sound interested.

B First, elicit possible answers to question 1, then play the recording again. Ss listen, complete the responses, then compare their answers in pairs. If they have any doubts, play the recording again. Check Ss' answers and teach new words/phrases as necessary.

> **Answers:** 1 Pleased   2 love   3 from   4 lovely   5 OK   6 terrible
> 7 soon

4 Put Ss in A/B pairs and tell them to look at the relevant exercises on p160 and p162. Do question 1 as an example: elicit Student A's question (*Would you like a drink?*) and Student B's answer (*I'd love an orange juice, please.*). Tell Ss to face each other and not show their books. Monitor while Ss work and make notes of problems they have. With **mixed-ability** or **weaker classes**, provide more support for the preparation stage. Divide the class into Student As and Student Bs. In pairs/small groups, Student As work together to prepare their questions and Student Bs do the same with their questions. Pair **stronger Ss** with **weaker ones** and monitor to provide extra help with accuracy where needed. In feedback, nominate Student As and Bs to ask and answer each question across the class. Then write problems Ss had on the board and ask them to correct the mistakes in pairs.

> **Answers:**
> **Student A questions/Student B answers**
> 1 **A:** Would you like a drink?
>   **B:** I'd love an orange juice, please.
> 2 **A:** Did you watch the match last night?
>   **B:** Yes, it was brilliant.
> 3 **A:** Nice day, isn't it?
>   **B:** Yes, it's lovely.
> 4 **A:** Do you work here?
>   **B:** No, I'm a student.
> **Student B questions/Student A answers**
> 1 **B:** This is my friend, Pete.
>   **A:** Hi, Pete. Pleased to meet you.
> 2 **B:** Did you have a good weekend?
>   **A:** Yes, thanks. I didn't do much.
> 3 **B:** Where exactly are you from?
>   **A:** I'm from Toledo, near Madrid.
> 4 **B:** I'll see you later.
>   **A:** Yes, see you soon.

> ▷ **LANGUAGEBANK 1.3** p128–129
>
> Ss can refer to the information in the tables to help them with Ex A and B.
>
> **Answers:**
> **A** 2 Hi. Pleased to ~~know~~ *meet* you.
>   3 ~~Do~~ *Would* you like a drink?
>   4 Where *exactly* do you come from?
>   5 Did you have *a* good weekend?
>   6 I'*ll* see you later.
> **B** 1 Pleased to meet you.
>   2 I would love a coffee.
>   3 So, what do you do?
>   4 I'll see you later.
>   5 Where exactly do you come from?
>   6 See you soon.

LEARN TO SOUND NATURAL

5A Ss may already be aware of how words are linked in English, especially if they studied *Speakout Elementary*. Play the recording while Ss listen and read. Then ask: *How/When do we link words in sentences in English?* Give Ss time to look at the sentences again and discuss their answers. Elicit the answer: when one word ends in a consonant and the following word begins with a vowel, e.g. *would you*.

B Play the recording again for Ss to listen and repeat. Play it as many times as necessary until Ss are confident. Then do individual repetition and correction as needed. If Ss find the word linking difficult, drill the pairs of linked words in isolation and then drill the whole phrase again.

speakout TIP

Read the Speakout tip with Ss and check the examples. Ss then look at the conversations in Ex 3B and find questions where they could add *so* in a natural way. It would also be useful to point out the use of *exactly* to ask for more detail. Elicit other examples: *Where exactly do you come from? What exactly do you do?*

> **Answers:**
> **Conversation 1**
> So, would you like a drink, Rachel?
> So, where exactly do you come from?
> **Conversation 2**
> So, did you have a good weekend?
> So, did you watch the match last night?

SPEAKING

6A Check the rubric and elicit an example question for the first topic, e.g. *So, what kind of films do you enjoy?* Then give Ss 3–4 mins to prepare the questions. They should also practise *saying* the questions to each other. Monitor to check the accuracy of their questions and help with pronunciation where needed.

B First, check the rubric and examples. Ss then work in groups or stand up and walk around the class, having conversations with other Ss. **Weaker classes** could first practise the conversation in pairs before moving on to the group activity. You can then monitor and provide support as necessary. During the activity, monitor discreetly, making notes of both good language and errors. In feedback, ask Ss what they learnt about their classmates. Then write 4–6 examples of the language you noted on the board. Ss correct the errors in pairs.

> **Alternative approach**
>
> Ss choose another identity to use in the conversations – an invented one or a famous person. Give them time to prepare facts about their new identity before they start the conversations.

> **Homework ideas**
>
> • **Ex 6B:** Ss write two conversations similar to the ones they had in class.
> • **Language bank** 1.3 Ex A–B, p129
> • **Workbook** Ex 1–4, p9

SOMEONE SPECIAL

Introduction

Ss watch an extract from the BBC situation comedy *Miranda*. They then learn and practise how to talk about a special person in their lives, and write a competition entry about their best friend.

> **Culture notes**
>
> *Miranda* was a popular BBC sitcom, written by and starring comedian Miranda Hart. It was developed from Hart's earlier semi-autobiographical radio series *Miranda Hart's Joke Shop* and revolved around socially awkward Miranda, who often found herself in bizarre situations. The show aired from 2009 to 2015, lasting three series, and was filmed in front of live audiences.

Warm up

Lead in and create interest in the lesson. Tell Ss to cover the texts and look at the photo across the bottom of the pages. Ask: *Who do you think these people are? What do you think they are talking about?* Discuss briefly in open class, then elicit or explain that the photo is from the BBC sitcom *Miranda*, and tell Ss they will be watching an excerpt from it later in the lesson.

DVD PREVIEW

1A Check the questions and elicit one or two initial answers. Then give Ss 3–4 mins to discuss in their pairs. In feedback, nominate pairs to share their answers with the class. The other Ss can add extra ideas and agree/disagree.

B Give Ss 1–2 mins to read the text. Check any new words, e.g. *panic, respond, work something out*. Ss then discuss the questions in pairs, groups or as a whole class.

> **Suggested answers:**
> 1 Miranda always panics when her boyfriend says 'I love you' and doesn't know what to say.
> 2 She might be uncertain of her feelings and/or it might be something to do with her old friend, Gary.

DVD VIEW

2A Tell Ss that they will now watch the DVD and check their answers to Ex 1B. Play the recording and elicit answers in feedback. Ask: *Were your guesses correct? What else did you find out?*

> **Answers:** She can't say 'I love you' to Mike because she's in love with Gary. She needs to work out how to end her relationship with Mike.

> **Teaching tip**
>
> Tell Ss to focus on answering the question and not worry about language they don't understand. They'll watch the DVD again in Ex 3B.

B Give Ss time to read the sentences before they watch the DVD again. In feedback, check *doughnuts, freak out, it's only fair, split up, make sb's heart skip*. With **weaker classes**, play the DVD again if Ss are unsure.

> **Answers:** 2 a) 3 e) 4 b) 5 d) 6 f)

3A Ss read the sentences first. Elicit/Teach the phrases *have to dash, spring to mind*. With **stronger classes**, you could do this in feedback. Play the DVD. Ss watch, listen and complete their answers individually. Do not confirm answers yet – Ss will check them in Ex 3B.

B Play the DVD again. Ss watch, check their answers and then compare them in pairs. If necessary, pause/rewind the sentences containing the answers (in bold in the DVD script below).

Answers:
1 Mike – to Miranda
2 the man – to Miranda
3 Stevie – to Miranda
4 Miranda – to her friends (Stevie and the man)
5 Gary – to Miranda
6 Miranda – to Stevie

4 Give Ss 2 mins to discuss the questions in pairs, then discuss in open class.

DVD 1 Miranda

MR = Miranda   MK = Mike   G = Gary   C = Clive   S = Stevie

MR: So news – Mike and I are still together, all good. But when he tells me he loves me I freak out, can't say it back.
MK: I love you.
MR: Oh well, well done and you're welcome and what a boost.
MR: Gary, look at you in your own restaurant.
MK: Are you renaming it?
MR: What, Gary's?
G: What's wrong with Gary's?
MR: No, seriously, what are you calling it?
MK: It's very you.
MR: No, that's lovely, no that's perfect, classy, sort of manly, yeah.
G: Manly? Good, cos now I'm manning up to put sign up.
MK: Oh **I'm gonna have to dash, I will see you later**. I love you.
MR: Oh well, um *(hums mobile phone ringtone)* – hello …
C: Right, OK, well, uh, **what springs to mind when I say, 'What do you love?'**
MR: Good, liking this, don't worry, Stevie, I've got a new friend.
C: OK, what do you love?
MR: Doughnuts.
C: Again, what was your first love?
MR: Doughnuts.
C: More emotional, what makes your heart skip?
MR: Doughnuts.
C: I think I know what this means. You're not in love with your boyfriend, it's only fair you split up with him.
MR: What, what?! No, no, no! You can't leave me with that! Oh my lovely Mike, I'm going to beanbag myself. Stevie! Stevie!!!
S: Miranda?!
MR: He said oh!
S: Alright, calm … now step back!
MR: She's back, love'ou.
S: Love'ou.
C: Love'ou.
S and MR: No!
S: Now, as this suggests, Mike is not what makes your heart skip. I mean, you love him but you're not in love with him, that's why you can't say it. I'm right, aren't I?
MR: Yes.
S: **Now we need to work out how you'll end it.**
C: Can't you just tell him?
S: Just tell him?! This guy! Miranda can't be direct, it's a condition.
MR: **I'm going to have to write Mike a letter. It's the only way.**
S and C: It's too mean!
S: Come on, think and pace.
C: No I really should be–
MR: Think and pace!!!
G: Hi!
MR: Oh are you OK?
G: Oh I'm stressed, um, cooking, deliveries, **listen, uh, I really, really need your help. Um, do you think you could spare a few hours this afternoon?**
MR: Yeah, sure, I'll come over later.
G: Oh thank you, thank you. Oh and by the way, uh, man has put up sign. Don't laugh.
MR: I wouldn't laugh, it's one of the reasons I love you.
S: Uh, what did you just say?

MR: I just said, 'I love you,' but, I mean, just flippantly, like I say it to you.
S: Well, that's where you're mistaken, my massive friend. We say it in a silly way. But tell me you love me.
MR: Love'ou.
S: Can you see you're finally getting this? What truly makes your heart skip?
MR: Gary.
S: How do you see Mike? How do you see Gary? Who do you love?
MR: Gary, I'm in love with Gary!!!
S: Yes! Waited three years for this, she said I love you!!!
C: To who?
MR: Gary! I love Gary! **I'm in love with Gary!**

speakout a special person

4A Ss now talk about people they know. Check the rubric and questions and give Ss 3 mins to think about their answers. They should note down the names with reasons for their choices. Monitor and provide help if necessary.

B First, elicit some answers before Ss work in pairs, making sure that Ss give reasons for their choices. Then monitor to ensure they are giving reasons. In feedback, nominate each student to tell the class about one of their choices.

5 Check the questions, especially question 2. Elicit examples of people who are important to your Ss, e.g. family members, friends, teachers. Give Ss time to think and note down their answers. They will be able to expand on these in Ex 6C, after listening to the model text. Monitor and help where needed.

6A Check the rubric and questions. Ss then listen to the model and compare answers in pairs. Check these in feedback.

Answers:
1 They met at school.
2 They get on really well; they've got lots of things in common; the speaker thinks she can rely on Michelle and that Michelle is a great person; they have a real laugh together.
3 She's a bit competitive.

B First, read/check the key phrases with Ss, then play the recording again. Ss tick the ones they hear. In feedback, play the recording and pause at each phrase (in bold in the audio script below). Elicit/Drill the complete sentences and ask further comprehension questions, e.g. *How did they meet? What's one thing they have in common?*

Answers:
I've known [name] for …
We met …
We get on really well [because …] …
We've got lots of things in common …
The only problem with [name] is …
He/She's a great person.

Unit 1 Recording 7

I've known Michelle for a long time and **we met** when we were at school together. We were about eleven years old and I had to show her to her peg to hang up her coat and we've been mates ever since. Er … **we get on really well**. She's one of those people that if you haven't seen for six months, six days, it's the same. It's like time hasn't passed. **We've got lots of things in common.** We play tennis together. **The only problem with Michelle is** that she's a bit competitive and we've fallen out over tennis. Sometimes if she wins, I haven't spoken to her … erm … and she's just one of those people you can rely on. She's sort of like number one in my phone book. Erm … and yes, **she's a great person**. We have a real laugh together.

C First give Ss time to check their notes from Ex 5 and add to or revise them using the key phrases. They can also use the audio script on p168 to help. Provide support to Ss who need it or ask *stronger Ss* to help *weaker ones*. Ss then take turns to talk about their special person in pairs. Remind them to ask questions from Ex 5 as often as possible to keep the conversation going. Monitor discreetly and note down the strengths and weaknesses of the language Ss use. In feedback, Ss tell the class about their own/ their partner's special person. The class then decide which person was the most 'special' and why. Give feedback on Ss' strengths and weaknesses now or in the next lesson.

writeback a competition entry

7A Ss first read a model of a competition entry about a best friend. Check the rubric and title of the competition. Ss then read the text and answer the question. In feedback, elicit Ss' answers and teach/check expressions in the text, e.g. (*be*) *there for me*, *help me through, sense of humour*.

> **Suggested answers:**
> She is always there for me.
> She has helped me through some difficult times.
> We know everything there is to know about each other.
> I can talk to Julie about anything.
> She will be a friend forever.

B Give Ss time to think and make notes about who they'll write about. It might be the same person as in Ex 5 or a different one. They should use the key phrases and refer to the text in Ex 7A for help. Provide support where needed. Ss could add photos to their texts and/or put them on the class blog.

> **Homework ideas**
> • **Ex 6C:** Ss write a description of their special person.
> • **Ex 7B:** Ss write a final draft of their competition entry.

LOOKBACK

Introduction

The notes below provide ideas for exploiting the exercises and activities, but your approach will depend on your aim, e.g. as a diagnostic test/assessment or for fluency practice/revision. For example, if you wanted to assess/test Ss' knowledge, then it would *not* be appropriate to monitor and help them.

FREE TIME

1A Ss complete the sentences alone and then compare answers in pairs. In feedback, elicit and drill the questions to prepare Ss for Ex 1B.

> **Answers:** **1** have   **2** off   **3** spend   **4** spending   **5** eat   **6** go

B While Ss ask/answer the questions, note down problems for feedback or assessment if required. In feedback, write examples of correct/incorrect sentences on the board for Ss to correct alone/ in pairs. Alternatively, write the sentences on an A4 sheet of paper after the lesson. Photocopy it for your Ss as a warm up for the next class (or use an OHP or IWB if available).

QUESTION FORMS

2 First, give Ss time to read the application form and write the questions. Monitor and prompt them to self-correct if appropriate. Then put Ss in pairs, preferably with a partner they don't know very well so that there is a real information gap, and get them to ask and answer the questions on the form. Monitor and give feedback as needed.

> **Answers:**
> How old are you?
> Where were you born?
> Are you married?
> What is your address?
> What is your telephone number?
> Have you got a mobile phone number?
> What is your email address?
> What do you do?
> Do you have/Have you got any hobbies?

3A Give Ss 3–4 mins to write questions about their chosen topics. In a *mixed-ability class*, you could either put *strong/weak Ss* together or put *weaker Ss* together and provide support.

> **Suggested answers:**
> **love:** Have you got a girlfriend/boyfriend? When did you meet?
> **home:** Where do you live?
> **family:** How many people are there in your family? Have you got any children?
> **work:** Where do you work? Do you enjoy your job?
> **food:** Do you like cooking? Do you eat junk food?
> **holidays:** Where do you usually go on holiday?

B Ss take it in turns to ask their questions in groups and make notes of the answers. Each student could then write a short summary of the answers. Monitor discreetly, making notes of Ss' performance for feedback/remedial work later. In feedback, nominate Ss to tell the class about their group.

RELATIONSHIPS

4A Give Ss 3–4 mins to work alone and correct the mistakes in the paragraph. Monitor and help Ss if necessary. Do not confirm answers yet – Ss will check them in Ex 4B.

B First, Ss compare their answers to Ex 4A in pairs. Check the answers, then ask Ss to close their books and do the speaking activity. Note down problems for feedback or assessment if required.

> **Answers:**
> I met Layla at a market. She was selling bread. We started chatting and *got on well*. At the time I didn't *have* a girlfriend, so I asked her on a date. We went to a local bakery! We soon fell *in* love and I proposed *to* her after a month. I hid the ring in a piece of cake. Fortunately, she accepted, and she didn't eat the ring! It was a good way to get engaged. A week later we *got* married.

PAST SIMPLE

5A Give Ss 3–4 mins to write the questions. In **weaker classes**, Ss could work in pairs.

> **Answers:**
> 1 Where did you go?
> 2 Why did you go there?
> 3 Did you stay in a hotel?
> 4 What did you do during the day?
> 5 Did you go out in the evenings?
> 6 Was the weather hot?
> 7 What language did you speak?
> 8 Did you make any new friends?

B While Ss ask/answer the questions, note down problems with the past simple for feedback or assessment if required.

6A Depending on your aims, **weaker classes** could refer back to the verbs on p10–11 in their books.

B Ss could make a note of the number of incorrect answers their partners gave. The activity could also be done as a team game.

C Ss work alone to write questions for the verbs they chose in Ex 6A. Monitor and make notes of problems with the question forms for feedback.

D Give Ss 5–6 mins to ask and answer the questions and make notes. They could then work with another pair and tell them about their partners' answers.

> **Optional extra activity**
> Provide further practice of past simple forms. Draw a grid on the board with 12 squares numbered 1–12. Put Ss in teams and name them A, B, C, etc. Demonstrate the activity. Ask Team A to choose a number from the grid. Give them the verb from the grid below, e.g. 1 *meet*. Ss must make a correct sentence in the past simple, e.g. *I met my husband in my English class.* Ss take it in turns to choose a number and select a student from their team to make a sentence. They get a point for each correct sentence. The team with the most points wins.
>
> Example verb grid:
>
> | 1 meet | 5 fall | 9 go |
> |---|---|---|
> | 2 cook | 6 study | 10 get |
> | 3 start | 7 decide | 11 say |
> | 4 have | 8 stop | 12 live |

MAKING CONVERSATION

7A Ss work alone to complete the conversations, though **weaker Ss** could work together. Ss should practise saying the conversations alone. Monitor and help them with pronunciation where needed.

> **Suggested answers:**
> **Conversation 1**
> **A:** Hi, (name). Nice day, isn't it?
> **B:** Yes, it's lovely.
> **Conversation 2**
> **A:** This is my friend (name).
> **B:** Hi. Pleased to meet you.
> **Conversation 3**
> **A:** So, do you work here?
> **B:** No, I'm a student.
> **Conversation 4**
> **A:** Where exactly do you come from?
> **B:** I'm from Reading.
> **Conversation 5**
> **A:** Did you have a good weekend?
> **B:** Yes, it was OK. I didn't do much.
> **Conversation 6**
> **A:** Did you watch the match last night?
> **B:** Yes, it was terrible.
> **Conversation 7**
> **A:** We lost 3–0.
> **B:** Oh no! I'm sorry to hear that.
> **Conversation 8**
> **A:** I'll see you later.
> **B:** Yes, see you soon.

B While Ss practise the conversations, note down problems with pronunciation and do remedial work in feedback if appropriate. Ss could also choose one or two conversations and memorise/rehearse them to perform to the class.

> **BBC interviews and worksheet**
>
> **What do you look for in a friend?**
> This video extends discussion of the unit topic to friendship. It will also extend Ss' language on friendship, relationships and keeping in touch.

OVERVIEW

2.1 THE COMPANY 4 U?

VOCABULARY | work
PRONUNCIATION | word stress
SPEAKING | talk about what motivates you at work
LISTENING | listen to interviews about jobs
GRAMMAR | present simple and continuous
WRITING | write an email about work experience

2.2 A RISKY BUSINESS

VOCABULARY | jobs
PRONUNCIATION | stressed syllables
READING | read a newspaper article about dangerous jobs
GRAMMAR | adverbs of frequency
SPEAKING | talk about dangerous jobs

2.3 I LIKE WORKING OUTSIDE

VOCABULARY | types of work
LISTENING | listen to a man talking about his job
FUNCTION | expressing likes/dislikes
LEARN TO | respond and ask more questions
PRONUNCIATION | intonation: sound interested
SPEAKING | talk about your perfect job

2.4 DREAM COMMUTERS BBC))) DVD

DVD | watch an extract from a BBC documentary about commuting
READING | read the results of a survey about work/life balance
speakout | work/life balance
writeback | a web comment

2.5 LOOKBACK

Communicative revision activities

BBC))) INTERVIEWS

What do you do?

In this video people describe their jobs and the best and worst things about them. The video also consolidates and extends Ss' vocabulary of work and jobs. Use the video at the end of Lesson 2.2 or at the start or end of the unit.

THE COMPANY 4 U?

Introduction

Ss revise and practise the present simple and continuous in the context of work and learn vocabulary to talk about jobs/work. They also learn how to start and end an email.

> **SUPPLEMENTARY MATERIALS**
> **Resource bank** p152
> **Language bank** p130–131
> **Ex 2A:** dictionaries
> **Ex 9C, optional extra activity:** realia: job advertisements (similar to the one in Ex 9B)

Warm up

Tell Ss to think of a person they know well who has a job. Then ask them questions about the person, e.g. *Where is he/she now? What's he/she doing at the moment? Where does he/she work? What time does he/she usually go to work? When does he/she get home? Does he/she work alone or with other people? Does he/she work inside or outside?* You could write the questions on the board or dictate them to Ss. Ss note down their answers individually and then, in pairs, read each other's answers and guess the person's job.

VOCABULARY   WORK

1 Give Ss 1 min to look at the photo and memorise the details. They then cover the photo and answer question 1 in pairs. Check answers and teach new vocabulary, e.g. *open-plan office, work on the computer*. Give Ss another 2–3 mins to discuss the other two questions.

2A Check the example and the meaning of *provide services*. Ss do the exercise and compare answers in pairs. In feedback, check/teach, e.g. *products, desks, manage, fixed, regular* and *sum (of money)* if necessary. With **weaker classes**, you may want to check this language before Ss do the exercise. Alternatively, Ss could check it in their dictionaries.

> **Answers:** 1 <u>com</u>pany   2 <u>cus</u>tomer   3 <u>bo</u>nus   4 <u>off</u>ice
> 5 emplo<u>yee</u>   6 <u>task</u>   7 boss   8 <u>staff</u>   9 <u>sal</u>ary   10 em<u>ploy</u>er

B Ss listen and repeat the words. Elicit the main stress in each word (see answer key above). Play the recording as many times as necessary until Ss are confident. They then copy the words and underline the main stress.

SPEAKING

3A First, check new words in the prompts, e.g. *flexible, chance, develop, skills*. Then give Ss 4–5 mins to discuss and decide their answers in pairs.

B Ss now work in groups and compare their ideas. Monitor discreetly while Ss work and make notes of examples of good language and problems. To make the task more challenging, **stronger classes** could discuss and agree on the top three items in order of importance. In feedback, write examples of Ss' errors and good language on the board. They discuss and correct them in pairs, groups or as a whole class.

LISTENING

4A Check the definition of *motivate* from the *Longman WordWise Dictionary*. If Ss want advice about buying a monolingual dictionary, this is a good one to recommend for this level. Teach/Check new language in the pictures, e.g. *thank-you note*. Elicit Ss' ideas for the first picture. This is a prediction activity, so encourage them to be imaginative. Give Ss 2–3 mins to discuss their ideas in pairs. In feedback, elicit and write their ideas on the board but do not confirm answers yet.

Answers:
A Yahoo employees have a free bus ride to work.
B Yahoo employees watch films together once a month.
C Pontiflex provides a nap room for its employees.
D At one company, the boss writes thank-you notes to employees.

B Play the recording. Ss listen and check their ideas from the board, and make notes of other ideas they hear. In feedback, refer to the ideas on the board. Elicit/Check those that were the same and then discuss the other ideas that were mentioned. Ss then discuss which ideas they think are the best. (The ideas related to the pictures are in bold in the audio script below. The other ideas mentioned are underlined.)

Answers: At Yahoo there's a dentist and a hairdresser at the office. At Google lunch is free and you can get a cheap massage at the office. At another company the staff does a job swap two days a year.

Unit 2 Recording 2

A: Today we're looking at how companies motivate their staff. Sarah, can you tell us more?
B: Absolutely. Internet companies are famous for this type of thing. **At Yahoo there's a free bus ride to work for employees.** There's also a dentist and a hairdresser at the office.
A: Makes life easier for employees …
B: Exactly. And, wait for it, **one day a month the staff watch films together**.
A: Great ideas.
B: Yep. Now at Google, lunch is free, and you can also get a cheap massage at the office.
A: Wow!
B: And other companies are bringing in new ideas, too. **A company called Pontiflex in New York created a nap room, where employees could sleep for fifteen minutes.**
A: Nice idea.
B: At several companies we're hearing that the relationship between bosses and employees is changing. **At one company, the boss writes thank-you notes to employees.** At another, the staff does a job swap two days a year. So a senior manager might clean floors for the day, and the cleaner can sit in an air-conditioned office.
A: Does that motivate everybody?
B: Well, it helps employees to see what everyone else is doing in the company, which I think is … very valuable and, of course, …

5A Check the meaning of the phrases in the box. Tell Ss to focus on the task and not worry about language they don't understand yet. Ss listen, tick the activities they hear and then compare answers in pairs. In feedback, nominate Ss to answer (see answers in bold in the audio script below). Elicit information about the companies mentioned.

Answers: **1** choosing a CD **2** studying **3** checking emails

B Check *agreement* in question 1. Ss listen again and make notes. In feedback, check answers (underlined in the audio script below) and replay the relevant sections if necessary. For further exploitation of the language/content of the recording, Ss could listen again and read audio script 2.3 on p168 at the same time.

Answers:
1 The employees at the music shop get free coffee at Kinko's. The employees at Kinko's get one free CD a week from the music shop.
2 It pays for employees to do courses.
3 Because the company has flexible hours.

Unit 2 Recording 3

Conversation 1

M = Man   I = Interviewer

M: Hi. I work at Kinko's coffee shop across the street. But, er, at the moment I'm having a break here in the music shop.
I: And what are you doing on your break?
M: **I'm choosing my free CD for the week.**
I: Free CD? Can you tell us a bit more? Why are you doing this?
M: Sure. Kinko's, the coffee shop, has an agreement with the music shop. The employees at the music shop get free coffee at Kinko's. They all come in during their break. And we get one free CD a week from the music shop.
I: Great!
M: We all know each other and it works really well.

Conversation 2

W = Woman   I = Interviewer

W: So, this is the clothes shop. **And this is the study area.**
I: Right. So you have a study area?
W: Yeah. **As you can see, David, over there, is studying.** And these two are doing an online course.
I: And this is during company hours? Does the boss know about this?
W: It's the boss' idea. The company pays for employees to do courses. So during our breaks or after seven when the shop closes, we can stay on and study.
I: That's excellent. And are you studying at the moment?
W: Yeah, but I'm not studying anything connected with fashion.
I: What are you studying?
W: I'm studying history.
I: And the company pays?
W: The company pays. It pays for about six of us. I think six of us are doing online courses.
I: Brilliant.

Conversation 3

E = Employee   I = Interviewer

E: Hi there. I work for a software company.
I: And what are you doing now?
E: Well, **I'm checking my emails at the moment** because I need to see what work I have to do today.
I: At one o'clock?
E: Well, the company has flexible hours. You can arrive when you want and go home at any time.
I: That sounds good.
E: It's great. We get a salary for good work, not for the time we spend in the office. So, really, the important thing is to do your job well. That's what the boss says, anyway!

GRAMMAR PRESENT SIMPLE AND CONTINUOUS

Watch out!

Ss may make mistakes with both the meaning and form of the two tenses, e.g. *I am not work in an office. He's coming from Japan.* Check the concepts carefully and monitor/correct at all stages of the practice.

6A Check *temporary* in question 2. Ss answer the questions alone and then compare answers in pairs. In feedback, elicit other examples of sentences in audio script 2.3 that use the present simple/continuous.

Answers: 1 a) 2 b) 3 a) 4 b)

B Follow the same procedure as in Ex 6A and elicit other examples of the two concepts.

Answers: 1 a) and b) 2 c) and d)

▷ LANGUAGEBANK 2.1 p130–131

Stronger Ss can study the tables and notes at home when they do the exercises. Otherwise, check the tables and notes with Ss, especially the use of state verbs. *Weaker Ss* should do Ex A–B in class.

Answers:
A 1 isn't 2 's working 3 'm playing 4 do, know
  5 are, wearing 6 don't eat 7 'm waiting
B 1 John works in sales and he ~~is going~~ *goes* to the office every day at 8a.m.
  2 The new employee says she's eighteen, but ~~I'm not believing~~ *I don't believe* it.
  4 Don't buy a bottle of wine for her. She ~~isn't drinking~~ *doesn't drink* alcohol.
  5 I can't speak Chinese, but my friend ~~teaches~~ *'s teaching me*.
  8 Hey! What ~~do you do~~ *are you doing* with that knife?

7 Check the examples. Ss then do the exercise alone and compare answers in pairs. Monitor and prompt them to self-correct. Recheck the concept of the two tenses in feedback.

Answers:
2 I'm looking for a job at the moment. I look at my emails when I get to work.
3 I don't use English for my job. I'm not using the photocopier at the moment.
4 Do you watch the news on TV every day? Are you watching TV right now?
5 I'm not reading any good books at the moment. I don't read a newspaper every morning.
6 Are you having a good time at this party? Do you have a company car?
7 I'm selling my house. I sell IT products to companies in Asia.

8A Monitor while Ss write the questions. In *mixed-ability classes*, *stronger* and *weaker Ss* can work together. Elicit/Drill the questions in feedback to prepare Ss for Ex 8B.

Answers:
2 Do you speak any other languages?
3 Why are you learning English?
4 Are you studying for an exam now?
5 Are you working on a special project at the moment?
6 Do you have your own office?
7 Do you like your boss?

B Monitor and prompt Ss to correct errors with the target language. In feedback, elicit the similarities and differences that Ss found with their partners.

WRITING STARTING/ENDING AN EMAIL

9A Check the example and elicit one or two more. Ss then work alone and compare answers in pairs before feedback. Check any new language, e.g. *Regarding, Cheers, look forward to.*

Answers:
Formal: Dear Sir, Dear Dr Bryce, I am writing about, Regarding, Best wishes, I look forward to hearing from you, Best regards, Yours sincerely
Informal: Hi, Hello, Dear All, Hi everyone, It's about, See you soon, Bye for now, Speak soon, Take care, Cheers, Love

B Give Ss 3–4 mins to read the email and answer the question. In feedback, check new vocabulary, e.g. *apply for, position, qualities, candidate, mobile apps.*

Answer: She designs apps.

C Check the rubric and give Ss 1 min to read the advert. While Ss write their first draft, monitor and provide support. Also encourage them to show their work to a partner before they write a final draft. If you have a class blog, Ss could post their email on it or send it to you.

Model answer:
Dear Mr Balik,
My name is Patricia Gonzalez. I am from Venezuela, but I am living in London at the moment.
I am writing about your advertisement for work experience.
I am twenty years old and I am studying industrial design at the Royal College of Art in London.
Could you send me some information about your work experience programme?
I look forward to hearing from you.
Yours sincerely,
Patricia Gonzalez

Optional extra activity

If you've brought authentic job advertisements, Ss choose one and write another email in class or at home. Alternatively, Ss interview each other for the job in Ex 9C. Divide the class into pairs/groups of interviewers/applicants. Interviewers decide what qualities/qualifications they are looking for, while applicants decide what qualities/qualifications they need. Interviewers talk to at least three applicants and choose the best one.

Homework ideas

* **Ex 9C:** Ss write a final draft of their email or another one using a different job advertisement.
* **Language bank** 2.1 Ex A–B, p131
* **Workbook** Ex 1–6, p10–11

A RISKY BUSINESS

Introduction

Ss revise and practise the use of adverbs of frequency in the context of work routines and dangerous jobs.

> **SUPPLEMENTARY MATERIALS**
> **Resource bank** p151 and 153
> **Language bank** p130–131
> **Photo bank** p152 (Ss may need dictionaries.)
> **Ex 4B (and optional extra activity):** dictionaries
> **Ex 7A:** photos of a variety of dangerous jobs, e.g. racing driver, police officer, soldier, jockey, circus performer, stuntman

Warm up

Play the *Alphabet game* to revise jobs. Say *A* and brainstorm all the jobs Ss can think of beginning with *A* (e.g. *artist, actor*). Do the same for each letter of the alphabet. This is a quick revision activity, so keep the pace lively and move on if Ss can't think of jobs for certain letters – they will revise/learn job words in the Photo bank later.

VOCABULARY   JOBS

1A Check new language, e.g. *opportunities, deal with*. Elicit answers for one job and give Ss 4–5 mins to decide on the best/worst jobs in pairs. In feedback, ask Ss to vote on the best/worst job and elicit their reasons.

B Ss first cover the words and describe/guess the jobs in the photos in pairs. They then match the words with the photos. Elicit/Check Ss' answers and the abbreviations *rep* (*representative*) and *IT* (*Information Technology*).

> **Answers: A** fashion designer   **B** rescue worker
> **C** motorcycle courier   **D** sales rep   **E** IT consultant
> **F** foreign correspondent   **G**   personal trainer

C Check the example. Read the Speakout tip with Ss before they listen and repeat the jobs. With **stronger classes**, you could point out that the main stress in noun + noun compounds is usually on the first word, but in adj + noun compounds, it's in the second word.

speak**out** TIP

Encourage Ss to use the Speakout tip with Ex 1C and with other new vocabulary they come across.

> **Answers:** <u>sales</u> rep, <u>fa</u>shion de<u>sig</u>ner, IT con<u>sult</u>ant,
> <u>for</u>eign corre<u>spon</u>dent, <u>per</u>sonal <u>train</u>er, <u>res</u>cue <u>work</u>er,
> <u>mo</u>torcycle <u>cou</u>rier

> **Teaching tip**
>
> Use the finger highlighting technique to elicit stress: hold up one hand and elicit/say each syllable of a word while touching your fingers with the thumb/first finger of your other hand, e.g. *accountant* has three syllables, so you touch three fingers: a-ccount-ant. Then ask: *Where's the stress?* Elicit: *on the second syllable: -ccount*. Then elicit/drill the word again: *ac<u>count</u>ant*.

> ▷ **PHOTOBANK** p152
>
> **1** Ss can check the job words in their dictionaries if they have difficulty matching them. In feedback, elicit the main stress in each word.
> **2** Check the meaning of *dangerous* and *enjoyable*. Give Ss 5 mins to discuss the questions, giving reasons for their choices. In feedback, Ss vote on each one.
>
> > **Answers:**
> > **1** 1 P   2 I   3 E   4 G   5 J   6 B   7 H   8 O   9 M   10 D   11 K
> >   12 N   13 L   14 C   15 F   16 A

2A Check *risk* in the word box and refer Ss to the title of the lesson, *A risky business*. Ss then complete the phrases in pairs. In feedback, check the meaning of each phrase by giving/eliciting examples of jobs they could refer to, e.g. *Police officers risk their lives*. This will prepare them for Ex 2B.

> **Answers: 1** get   **2** work   **3** risk   **4** deal with

B While Ss talk about the jobs, monitor and note down problems they have with the new phrases and give feedback afterwards.

> **Optional extra activity**
>
> Ss work in pairs/groups. They choose a job and describe it, using the phrases from Ex 2A and other language they know. Their partner(s) have to guess the job.

3A Ss practise the phrases further here. Give them 2–3 mins to complete the sentences and compare answers in pairs before class feedback.

> **Answers: 1** get   **2** under   **3** holidays   **4** risk   **5** team   **6** deal

B Discuss the first sentence as a class, eliciting reasons, e.g. *I agree because a good salary motivates people to work hard.* In feedback, nominate Ss to tell the class their opinions. Give feedback on language problems afterwards.

READING

4A Check the rubric and give Ss 3–4 mins to discuss the question. They can then compare answers with another pair and change their minds about their first opinions if they wish. In feedback, nominate Ss to give one opinion and reason each.

B Set up this jigsaw reading activity carefully. Divide Ss into groups of three and name them A, B or C. Ss look at the title of their text. Teach *danger rating*. Then check the rubric and give Ss 3–4 mins to read their texts and make notes of the answers. They can use their dictionaries to check new words, but tell them to only look up essential vocabulary they need to answer the questions (see also the optional extra activity after Ex 4C).

> **Teaching tip**
>
> In a jigsaw reading activity, Ss read different texts about similar topics, but have the same questions. They work on their own texts first and then exchange information with those who read the other texts.

C Ss take it in turns to tell their group about their texts, using their notes. They mustn't look at each others' books. Monitor to check that Ss do this correctly. In feedback, nominate Ss to tell the class about their text.

Answers:
job: A mountain rescue worker   **B** motorbike courier   **C** jockey
country: A Austria   **B** Brazil   **C** France
people interviewed:
A Martin Schmidt, emergency doctor; Marius Adler, paramedic; Klaus Hartmann, helicopter pilot
B Roberto Coelho, motorbike courier; car drivers
C Vincent Dax, jockey
why the job is dangerous:
A bad weather conditions; people often panic, which makes the team's job more difficult/dangerous
B accidents and robberies
C broken bones and occasional deaths
special memories/stories:
A They once rescued a woman after a skiing accident. Her husband brought them a box of chocolates to say *thank you.*
B He was robbed and lost everything.
C He once fell off his horse and was knocked unconscious.

Optional extra activity

Ss check 3–4 new words/phrases (from the text they read in Ex 4B) in their dictionaries, e.g. Text A: *view, avalanche, conditions, panic, reward;* Text B: *on average, robbery, insurance, respect, traffic laws;* Text C: *gun, gates, glory, generation, ribs, knock unconscious.* Ss can then read the other two texts and 'teach' the new words/phrases to their partners from Ex 4C.

GRAMMAR   **ADVERBS OF FREQUENCY**

Watch out!

The position of adverbs or adverbial phrases in a sentence varies considerably, so Ss need to be made aware of this. Expose them to the language in natural contexts and provide sufficient controlled practice and feedback.

5A The sentences are from the texts in Ex 4. Ss work alone and then compare their answers in pairs. In feedback, draw the line on the board and invite Ss to write the adverbs in the correct place.

Answers: never, hardly ever, rarely, occasionally/once in a while, sometimes, often, usually, always

B Do an example from each text. Then give Ss 2–3 mins to underline the adverbs/expressions. **Fast-finishers** can also read the other texts. In feedback, nominate Ss to read out the sentence containing the language. Elicit/Check the position of each adverb/expression in each sentence, e.g. before the main verb, at the beginning/end of the sentence.

Answers:
Text A
they <u>sometimes</u> get angry with the people they rescue; Climbers <u>always</u> risk their lives; they <u>usually</u> fly in much worse weather conditions; <u>often</u>, the people they rescue are frightened; <u>occasionally</u>, they get a surprise; The people they rescue … <u>hardly ever</u> say thank you
Text B
The motoboys <u>usually</u> earn just $450; they <u>often</u> work under time pressure; <u>Once in a while</u>, they try to change the traffic laws
Text C
it is <u>sometimes</u> easy to forget; Life as a jockey is <u>rarely</u> safe and it <u>usually</u> involves a few broken bones; <u>Once in a while</u> jockeys even die; he <u>never</u> worries

▷ **LANGUAGEBANK 2.2** p130–131

Read/Check the notes with Ss. They can refer to them when they do the exercises. **Weaker Ss** should do Ex A–B in class. Check *waste money* in Ex A and *my boss is out* in Ex B.

Answers:
A 2 Once in a while, I go swimming./I go swimming once in a while.
3 I never waste my money.
4 Najim doesn't often play tennis.
5 Akiko and Toshi usually stay at home in the evening.
6 Why are you always late?
7 I rarely work late on Fridays.
8 Mary hardly ever deals with customers.
9 Occasionally, I work in a team./I occasionally work in a team./I work in a team occasionally.
B 1 Usually   **2** every day   **3** sometimes   **4** rarely   **5** always
6 Once in a while   **7** every year   **8** occasionally

6A Do an example. Ss then correct the sentences alone and compare answers in pairs. In feedback, nominate Ss to write the answers on the board.

Answers:
1 I *always work* at night.
2 Once *in* a while I study at weekends.
3 I *hardly ever* study alone.
4 I work at home *occasionally*.
5 It is *sometimes* difficult to study and work at the same time.
6 I don't *usually* miss classes because of work.

B Check the example and give Ss 2–3 mins to write their sentences. Point out that they should use adverbs/expressions of frequency. Monitor and help them with language they need.

C Monitor and prompt Ss to self-correct errors with adverbs/expressions. In feedback, invite Ss to tell the class about their partner's job.

SPEAKING

7A Check the rubric and questions. Then elicit ideas for suitable jobs. If you've brought photos of dangerous jobs, use them as prompts, especially for **weaker classes**. Give Ss 5–6 mins to discuss the questions and decide on their three jobs. They can use the texts from Ex 4 as a model for question 3. Monitor closely to provide help with ideas and vocabulary where needed.

B Give Ss time to prepare their presentation to the other group. They should take it in turns to give their answers to each question in Ex 7A. While Ss talk, make notes on their use of the language they've studied in this lesson and do any remedial work needed later. In feedback, invite each group to tell the class what they thought of the other group's programme.

Optional extra activity

Ss 'present' their TV programme on a poster, using photos and texts related to the questions in Ex 7A.

Homework ideas

- **Ex 7:** Ss write a description of their TV programme or make a poster of it. They could add photos/texts.
- **Language bank** 2.2 Ex A–B, p131
- **Workbook** Ex 1–6, p12–13

I LIKE WORKING OUTSIDE

Introduction

Ss learn and practise ways of expressing likes/dislikes about work. They also learn how to respond to what people say and ask more questions in order to sound interested.

> **SUPPLEMENTARY MATERIALS**
> **Resource bank** p154
> **Language bank** p130–131
> **Warm up and Ex 1A:** bilingual dictionaries

Warm up

Lead in to the lesson via the photos. Ss work in pairs and describe the people, say what they're doing/wearing and guess the jobs if possible. Monitor and provide useful vocabulary. Ss could also use bilingual dictionaries to look up words they need. In feedback, check Ss' answers using the following ideas. *Photo A: A man is in the sea. He's holding a net. He's a fisherman. Photo B: The woman is standing in a classroom. She's a teacher. Photo C: The man is holding a branch of a tree and showing it to the other people. He's a tour guide. Photo D: The woman is standing in a meeting room and talking to people. She's a businesswoman.*

VOCABULARY   TYPES OF WORK

1A Check the types of work that Ss are not familiar with, e.g. *retail*. Ss could use bilingual dictionaries for words they need in their answers or ask you. Tell them to write at least three answers to questions 3 and 4. In feedback, write Ss' answers to questions 3 and 4 on the board and check/teach and drill new words.

> **Suggested answers:**
> 1 the food industry
> 2 the fashion industry
> 3 actor, singer, presenter, cameraman, make-up artist, researcher
> 4 designer, sales assistant, shop manager

B Ask Ss to work in pairs and decide which industries the people in the photos work in. Check answers in feedback.

> **Suggested answers:** A the food industry   B education
> C the tourist industry   D sales and marketing

FUNCTION   EXPRESSING LIKES/DISLIKES

2A Check the rubric. Tell Ss to focus on what the job is and what the man *likes* about his job. They listen and note down their answers and then compare them in pairs. Play the recording again if necessary. In feedback, check answers and *marine biologist*.

> **Answers:** He's a marine biologist. He likes working outside, travelling, working alone and learning new things, being his own boss.

B With **weaker classes**, pause the recording after each sentence in the exercise for Ss to write. Play the recording again and elicit Ss' answers after each question (see answers in bold in the audio script below). Check the meaning of *can't stand, don't mind* and *be keen on*. Also check *get my hands dirty* (do manual work) and *be my own boss* (work for myself). Ask: *What do you notice about these verbs?* Elicit that they all end in *-ing*. Teach the rule: verbs that follow the expressions/verbs in the exercise end in *-ing*. Ss should write the new expressions in their notebooks.

> **Answers:** 1 working   2 sitting   3 travelling   4 working
> 5 getting   6 learning   7 working   8 working

> **Unit 2** Recording 5

> **I = Interviewer   M = Man**
>
> **I:** Can you tell us a little about what you do and what you like about your job?
> **M:** Yes. I'm a marine biologist. I work mainly in the sea and also in the lab. One good thing about my job is that **I like working outside.**
> **I:** I see.
> **M:** In fact, **I can't stand sitting at a desk all day**. Um, what else?
> **I:** Maybe you get to travel …
> **M:** I travel a lot and **I absolutely love travelling**, particularly in South America and Australia.
> **I:** Right. And what about your colleagues, people you work with?
> **M:** Actually, most of my time is spent alone, which kind of suits me. **I don't like working in a team. I prefer working alone.**
> **I:** Really? And what about the type of work?
> **M:** It's interesting – there's a lot of lab work, but it's a very practical job. You're working with animals and plant life the whole time. And, y'know, **I don't mind getting my hands dirty**. That's important. Also, **I'm keen on learning new things** – and you do learn all the time in this job. You're always discovering new things.
> **I:** That's great. It sounds wonderful.
> **M:** I couldn't do an office job because **I hate working under pressure**. And **I'm not very keen on working for a company**. I just **want to be my own boss.**
> **I:** So, you found the right job for you.
> **M:** I found the right job for me, yes.

C Do questions 1 and 2 as examples. Ss then work in pairs and discuss the others. In feedback, check Ss' answers. To prepare Ss for the next exercise, elicit examples of sentences that are true for them, e.g. *I like working in the garden. I can't stand junk food.*

> **Answers:** 1 +   2 – –   3 + +   4 –   5 *   6 +   7 – –   8 –

3A Ss work alone and tick sentences that are true for them. They then rewrite the sentences that they *didn't* tick to make them true for them. Monitor and support Ss who need help.

B Demonstrate the activity. Ask: *What do you love/like/hate?* Elicit an answer from Ss' sentences in Ex 3A for each question. Ss then ask and answer in pairs and make notes of their partner's answers. In feedback, nominate Ss to tell the class about their partner.

> ▷ **LANGUAGEBANK 2.3** p130–131
>
> Refer Ss to the note about *like* + infinitive and elicit more examples. Ss can refer to the information in the tables to help them with this exercise.
>
> **Answers:**
> A 1 listening   2 don't   3 on   4 doesn't   5 loves   6 stand

LEARN TO   RESPOND AND ASK MORE QUESTIONS

4A Play the recording for Ss to complete the extracts. In feedback, check answers and ask: *What does the listener do when she responds?* Elicit/Explain that she responds to what the speaker says to show interest and/or asks another question to find out more information.

> **Answers:** 2 about   3 Really   4 sounds

B Play the recording. Ss listen and repeat. Encourage them to copy the intonation and extend their voice range. For example, with the phrase *I see*, illustrate the rise of the intonation on *see* with your arms and hands, as if you were conducting an orchestra. Play the recording for Ss to repeat as many times as necessary until they are confident.

C Give Ss 3–4 mins to underline the phrases and compare their answers. In feedback, elicit and drill the phrases. Play the recording again as a model if necessary.

> **Answers:**
> **comments:** Right. That's great. It sounds wonderful.
> **questions:** Really?

5A Organise Ss into A/B pairs. Elicit an answer to question 1 as an example. Monitor while Ss complete their answers and prompt them to self-correct any errors.

B Check/Drill the example conversation. Ss should sound as interested as they can in their responses. Do feedback in open pairs across the class (nominate one student to ask another). Have a class vote on the student(s) who sounded the most interested.

SPEAKING

6A Check the rubric and prompts. Then give Ss 5–6 mins to make notes in pairs. Monitor and support *weaker Ss* if necessary.

B Check the example and give Ss 1–2 mins to prepare. Provide help and support while they do this, especially with intonation. While Ss work in their groups, monitor discreetly, making notes of both good language and errors. In feedback, ask Ss to talk about their partners' perfect jobs.

> **Homework ideas**
> * **Ex 1:** Ss write about two or three types of industries they would like to work in, giving reasons.
> * **Ex 6:** Ss write a short description of their perfect job.
> * **Language bank** 2.3 Ex A, p131
> * **Workbook** Ex 1–4, p14

DREAM COMMUTERS

Introduction

Ss watch an extract from the BBC's *The Money Programme: Dream Commuters*, which explores the life of a man who decided to move abroad with his family and commute to work in the UK. Ss then learn and practise how to talk about work/life balance and write a comment on a website.

> **SUPPLEMENTARY MATERIALS**
>
> **Ex 3B:** maps of England (showing Hampshire and Gatwick airport) and France (showing Toulouse and the River Lot)

Warm up

Lead in and create interest in the lesson. Tell Ss to cover the texts and look at the photo on p25. Ask: *What kind of place is this? Where is it, do you think? What's it like? Would you like to live there? Why/Why not?* Discuss briefly in open class.

DVD PREVIEW

1 Give Ss 2–3 mins to discuss the questions in pairs. In feedback, invite Ss to tell the class about their partner's journey to college/work. Ask: *Who has a good/bad journey to work or college?* Ask for a show of hands to see which is most common.

2A Give Ss 1–2 mins to read the programme information and answer the questions. In feedback, check Ss' answers, but don't teach new vocabulary yet – this is done in Ex 2B.

> **Answers:**
> 1 Justin was unhappy about his work/life balance.
> 2 He decided to buy a property in France and commute from there.

B Teach/Check any new language in the definitions and do the first question as an example. Tell Ss to look at the words in bold in the text and work out which one fits the definition. Ss then work alone and compare their answers in pairs. In feedback, elicit/check and drill the words. Ask further checking questions, e.g. *What makes you feel fed up? Do you own a property?* Refer Ss to the photo. Ask: *Who is the man? Where is he?* Ss can speculate, but will find out the answers in Ex 3.

> **Answers:** 1 transformed 2 flights 3 commuters 4 traffic
> 5 commute 6 property 7 fed up with

DVD VIEW

> **Culture notes**
>
> **Budget flights** are typically offered by airlines such as Easyjet and Ryanair in the UK. Flights are cheaper than normal scheduled flights: seats are not reserved, check-in baggage is restricted and free meals are not provided.
> **Gatwick** is one of London's major airports, about 40 miles south of the city.
> **Toulouse** is in southwest France.
> The **River Lot** flows into the Garonne.
> **BT** is British Telecom, a UK telecom company.

3A Tell Ss to focus on answering the question and not worry about language they don't understand. They'll watch the DVD again in Ex 3B. Play the DVD. Ss complete the task and compare their answers in pairs. Also check Ss' predictions from Ex 2. (The man in the photo is Justin Saunders. He is outside his new home in France.)

> **Answer:** Justin's life is better now because he and his family are happier.

B Check the questions and play the DVD again. Ss complete the task and compare their answers in pairs. In feedback, elicit answers. If you've brought some maps, elicit/point out where Hampshire, Gatwick Airport and Toulouse are and show Ss the River Lot, where Albas is situated.

> **Answers:** 1 T 2 T 3 F 4 F 5 T

4 Ss read the sentences. Check *available* and *terrace*. Ss watch the DVD, complete the exercise and compare their answers in pairs. Play the DVD again if necessary. Ask Ss to tell you to pause the DVD when they hear the answers (in bold in the DVD script below).

> **Answers:** 1 the traffic 2 commuters 3 much cheaper
> 4 terrace 5 lifestyle

> **Optional extra activity**
>
> Play the DVD again, pausing at suitable points. Ask questions about what Ss can see, e.g. *What's he/she doing now? Where are they? What do you think of the plane/house/view/Albas?* You can do this kind of activity with any DVD clip. It involves Ss and gives them the opportunity to learn/focus on language and ideas in an authentic context.

> **DVD 2** The Money Programme: Dream Commuters

P = Presenter   L = Libby Potter   J = Justin Saunders
R = Rebecca Saunders   W = Woman

P: Do you hate your journey to work? Do you feel like you're wasting time sitting in traffic jams or on busy trains? People in Britain spend longer in their cars and trains than anyone else in Europe. So, some people are choosing to live in Europe, but commute to work in the UK. They travel to work like this. Libby Potter, a reporter for the *Money Programme*, meets Justin Saunders, one of Britain's 'Dream Commuters'.
It's Friday evening and Justin Saunders has just finished work. He is manager of an online business based in the UK. He's going home. But his home is in France. Justin is a Euro commuter.

W: Boarding starts at six o'clock and the gate number will be on the screens in Departures.

P: Justin flies from Gatwick to his house in southwest France. **He's one of a group of commuters who take the same flight to Toulouse every week.** There's a hotel operator, an IT worker, a charity manager and a BT consultant. But this week there is an extra traveller: Libby, who is here to interview Justin. The flight takes off. There's no time for shopping with these guys.

L: So why did you decide to make this move in the first place?

J: We basically decided to move to France for the better quality of life. We thought … **we looked on the internet and we saw properties available much cheaper than in Britain. We were fed up with the commuting and the traffic.**

L: But what's the cost of the commute?

J: When I book the flights early enough, I'm paying something like thirty-eight pounds return.

P: Justin's life is in a village in southwest France, an hour's drive from Toulouse Airport and over seven hundred miles from his Hampshire office.

R: Daddy's home.

J: Where's Georgie?

R: She's asleep.

J: She's asleep.

R: So, how was the flight?

J: Oh, not too bad. Nice to be back home, though.

P: It's morning in the French village of Albas, beside the River Lot, and Justin Saunders seems pretty happy.

R: **That's the house down there. With the terrace.**

L: The one just here with the river view.

R: The river view, yeah.

J: **We've just transformed our lifestyle.**

P: Well, wouldn't you commute by plane for this?

5 Check the questions and give Ss 3–4 mins to discuss in their pairs. Then discuss briefly in open class.

speakout work/life balance

6 Ss now have the opportunity to talk about the work/life balance in their own countries. First, teach *on average* and *percent* in the text. Then check the questions and give Ss 4–5 mins to read and discuss them in pairs or groups. In **multilingual classes**, Ss might want to work with others from the same part of the world. They should note down their answers. Monitor and provide help if necessary. Discuss Ss' answers in feedback.

7 First, read and check the key phrases with Ss. They then listen and tick the answers, and compare them in pairs. In feedback, play the recording again, pausing at each key phrase (in bold in the audio script below). Elicit/Drill the complete sentences. Also elicit the answer to the question in the rubric. If time, you could ask further comprehension questions, e.g. *How long does Zeinab spend studying? How often does she have a holiday?*

> **Answers:**
> **Question:**
> Yes, she has a good work/life balance.
>
> **Key phrases:**
> How much time do you spend … (sleeping/relaxing/commuting)?
> Do you ever … (have a holiday)?
> What about your … (social life/weekends)?

Unit 2 Recording 8

A = Alistair   Z = Zeinab

A: Zeinab, can I ask you a few questions about your work/life balance?

Z: Of course.

A: OK. First question: **how much time do you spend sleeping?**

Z: Lots! Probably about eight or nine hours a night!

A: Really?!

Z: Yep.

A: OK. And what about studying?

Z: Well, I suppose usually about five or six hours a day, although it depends. I mean, if I have an exam coming up or something, it's probably more.

A: And **do you ever have a holiday?**

Z: Oh yeah. Probably twice a year I try and go abroad and just completely relax.

A: OK. **What about your weekends?** Do you ever study at the weekend?

Z: Not usually, but once in a while I open a book!

A: Right. And do you think you have a good work/life balance?

Z: I think so, yeah. I'm not too stressed or anything.

A: Easy life being a student.

Z: Oh yeah!

8A First, elicit more example questions using the key phrases. Ss should then write at least one question for each topic. **Stronger Ss** could also refer to the audio script on p169 for ideas. Provide support to Ss who need it or ask **stronger Ss** to work with **weaker ones**. Monitor closely to check the accuracy of Ss' questions.

B Ss take turns to ask and answer their questions in groups. Monitor discreetly and note down the strengths and weaknesses of the language Ss use. In feedback, Ss talk about a person from their group with a similar work/life balance to theirs. Give feedback on Ss' performance, either now or at the beginning of the next lesson.

writeback a web comment

9A Check the questions. Give Ss 3 mins to read the text and answer the questions. They can compare them in pairs or small groups. In feedback, discuss Ss' answers and teach/check useful vocabulary from the text, e.g. *in general, get stressed, balanced lifestyle, move house.*

> **Suggested answer:**
> **1** This is not a stressful job because the work/life balance is good. He/She can manage their own time to suit his/her needs.

B Give Ss time to think and make notes for their comment. They should use the key phrases and refer to the text in Ex 9A for help. Provide support where needed.

> **Homework ideas**
> - **Ex 5:** Ss write about the benefits and problems of being a 'dream commuter'.
> - **Ex 9B:** Ss write the final draft of their comment or another comment for the website/class blog.

LOOKBACK

Introduction

Lookback activities are designed to provide revision and communicative practice in a motivating way. This helps Ss and gives you the opportunity to assess their ability to use the language they've learnt in the unit. It's a good idea to monitor and assess individual Ss while they do the activities and compare their performance with their results in more formal tests.

PRESENT SIMPLE AND CONTINUOUS

1 Ss first read the sentences. Check the meaning of *keep fit*, *published*, *divorced*. Ss should decide on the verbs they can use first and discuss them in pairs. They then complete the sentences alone and compare answers in pairs. In feedback, ask Ss to justify the tense they chose: present simple for routines or things that are generally true and present continuous for things happening now or around now.

> **Answers:**
> **2** a) 'm doing   b) do
> **3** a) play   b) 's playing
> **4** a) write   b) 's writing
> **5** a) 's working   b) works
> **6** a) makes   b) 'm making
> **7** a) has   b) 's having
> **8** a) 're getting   b) get
> **9** a) reads   b) 'm reading
> **10** a) 'm visiting   b) visit

2A Elicit some examples to show Ss what to do, e.g. *I usually sing opera in the bath.* Give Ss 4–5 mins to write their sentences. Monitor and prompt them to self-correct where necessary.

B Check the example. Point out that Ss must use words from each box in Ex 2A in both their statements and responses, e.g. *rarely, work, at my desk* and *often, work, at home.* They can respond to their partner's sentences with a follow-up question or statement. Do more examples to illustrate this if necessary. Ss then work in pairs and take turns to read out their sentences and respond to each other. They should try to extend the conversation for as long as possible, e.g. *A: I never drink tea at my desk. B: Do you usually drink coffee? A: No, I always drink water. B: Oh, I occasionally drink water, but I prefer coffee.* Monitor and note down problems Ss have with tense, word order or meaning/use of the adverbs for feedback (or use the information for assessment if required). In feedback, nominate Ss to act out one of their conversations to the class. The pair with the longest string of follow-up questions and statements wins.

ADVERBS OF FREQUENCY

3A First, check new language in the exercise, e.g. *texts, wake (me) up, prefer.* Give Ss 3–4 mins for the exercise. They then compare answers in pairs and discuss the ones they don't agree on. Encourage them to justify/explain the answers they gave during this checking stage. In feedback, check answers and recheck the meaning of *once in a while/occasionally, hardly ever.* With **weaker classes**, drill the questions and answers chorally and then in open pairs across the class. Correct pronunciation mistakes as required.

> **Answers: 1** d)   **2** a)   **3** f)   **4** e)   **5** b)   **6** g)   **7** c)

B Give Ss time to rehearse the questions by saying them to themselves. Monitor and help them with their pronunciation where needed. Ss then take turns to ask/answer the questions. They should note down their partner's answers so that they can report back to the class in feedback. Monitor discreetly, making notes of individual students' performances. In feedback, Ss tell the class about their partner. Give feedback and do remedial work as required.

WORK AND JOBS

4 Check the example and elicit another one to demonstrate the activity clearly, e.g. *A personal trainer doesn't have to risk his/her life.* First, give Ss 2–3 mins to think about which words/phrases can be used together to make sensible statements. Monitor and provide help if needed. Then put Ss in pairs of similar ability. They take turns to go first. They should give each other a point for a correct answer. The one with the most points is the winner. Do feedback in open pairs across the class: one student says a word/phrase and the other must choose another and explain the connection between them. Prompt Ss to correct themselves/each other. Finally, do remedial work.

EXPRESSING LIKES/DISLIKES

5A First, ask Ss to sit with a classmate they think they know well. They then read the statements. Elicit one or two example questions that Ss think they know how their partner will answer, e.g. *A: Do you like opera, Olga? B: No, I can't stand it.* Give Ss 3–4 mins to write a question for each answer. Monitor and prompt them to self-correct any errors they make. Try to check all Ss' work so that the questions they ask in Ex 5B are grammatically correct.

B Read/Check the example conversation. Tell Ss that they can give themselves 3 points for each question their partner answers as predicted, e.g. *A: Do you like Italian food? B: I absolutely love it.* They can also get one extra point for each follow-up question they ask. Tell them you will be assessing their use of follow-up questions while they work. In feedback, find out who had the most points. Then invite pairs to act out their conversations to the class. Tell the other Ss to listen and write down any other follow-up questions to ask once each pair has finished talking. Finally, give feedback and do remedial work as needed.

> **BBC interviews and worksheet**
>
> **What do you do?**
>
> In this video people describe their jobs and the best and worst things about them. The video also consolidates and extends Ss' vocabulary of work and jobs.

OVERVIEW

3.1 FREE IN NYC

VOCABULARY | time out
LISTENING | listen to a radio programme about going out in New York
GRAMMAR | present continuous/*be going to* for future
PRONUNCIATION | fast speech: *going to*
SPEAKING | talk about your future plans
WRITING | write an email invitation

3.2 RELAX!

VOCABULARY | places to visit
PRONUNCIATION | stress in compound nouns
READING | read about how people spend their free time around the world
GRAMMAR | questions without auxiliaries
SPEAKING | discuss how you spend your free time

3.3 CAN I TAKE A MESSAGE?

VOCABULARY | collocations
LISTENING | understand some problem phone calls
FUNCTION | making a phone call
LEARN TO | manage phone problems
PRONUNCIATION | linking: *can*
SPEAKING | make and receive phone calls

3.4 RIO DE JANEIRO BBC ᴰ⁾ DVD

DVD | watch an extract from a BBC travel programme about visiting Rio de Janeiro
speakout | a day in your city
writeback | an invitation

3.5 LOOKBACK

Communicative revision activities

BBC ᴰ⁾ INTERVIEWS

What do you like doing in your free time?

This video consolidates and extends Ss' vocabulary of free time activities and exemplifies real usage of the present continuous for future. Use the video at the end of Lessons 3.1 or 3.2 or at the start or end of the unit.

FREE IN NYC

Introduction

Ss revise and practise the present continuous and *be going to* for future plans and arrangements. They learn vocabulary to talk about going out, and how to write an invitation email.

> **SUPPLEMENTARY MATERIALS**
> **Resource bank** p155–156
> **Language bank** p132–133
> **Photo bank** p153 (Ss may need dictionaries.)
> **Warm up:** photos of the famous New York sights listed; photocopies of words for the activity (See notes below.)

Warm up

Introduce some famous sights in New York. Write the names of the places below on the board or give Ss photocopies of the names if you have them. Leave gaps in the words, e.g. *St_ _ _ _ o_ L_ _ _ _ _y* (Statue of Liberty). In pairs or groups, Ss complete the names of the places. Elicit/Check the names and discuss what Ss know about them. If you've brought photos of the places, Ss can match them with the names.
Places: Statue of Liberty, Empire State Building, Central Park, Times Square, Broadway, Rockefeller Centre, Metropolitan Museum of Art, Ellis Island, Brooklyn Bridge, Fifth Avenue

VOCABULARY   TIME OUT

1A Give Ss time to look at the word webs. Check/Teach and drill unknown words. Ss write their answers alone and then check in pairs. Check answers and then get Ss to copy the word webs into their notebooks. Advise them to use a separate section in their notebooks for recording new vocabulary.

> **Answers:** **1** go to **2** see **3** get **4** go **5** have

B Tell Ss to use at least one example from each word web in their questions. Monitor while Ss do the exercise and give feedback on problems you noticed.

> ▷ **PHOTOBANK** p153
>
> **1** Ss can use their dictionaries to check any words they don't know.
> **2** *Stronger classes* may know how to use the present perfect with *ever/never*. However, to help **weaker classes**, write these prompts on the board for Ss to use in their answers: I've never *collected/been to/seen/played/surfed/walked/cycled … I'd like to …* Elicit some sentences using the prompts before Ss work in pairs.
>
> **Answers:**
> **1** 1E 2O 3L 4B 5D 6C 7N 8F 9M 10G
>   11H 12A 13K 14J 15I

LISTENING

> **Culture notes**
>
> Home to the Empire State Building, Times Square, the Statue of Liberty and other iconic sites, New York City has a population of over 8 million people and is a fast-paced, globally influential centre of art, culture, fashion and finance. The city's five boroughs sit where the Hudson River meets the Atlantic Ocean, with the island borough of Manhattan at the 'Big Apple's' core.

2A Before Ss discuss in pairs, give an example for question 1. Say: *When I'm in a city, I like to …* . Alternatively, elicit one or two examples from Ss. Then give Ss 2–3 mins to discuss in their pairs. In feedback, nominate pairs to share their ideas with the class.

B Give Ss time to read the questions first. Ss then listen and answer the questions individually, then compare in pairs. Elicit answers in feedback (in bold in the audio script below).

> **Answers:** **1** yes **2** yes **3** $20 (each) **4** They have to organise a great day out without going over their budget.

3A Ask Ss to read the information, and check new vocabulary (e.g. *bagel, finance, ferry, exhibition, atmosphere*) before Ss complete the exercise. Ss work alone; monitor and help them where necessary. Do not confirm answers yet, as Ss will check them in Ex. 3B. (The answers are underlined in the audio script below.)

> **Answers:** **1** Central Park **2** Museum **3** views **4** live
> **5** sculpture/art **6** Square **7** Italian **8** dance/hip-hop

B After Ss have listened and compared answers in pairs, play the recording again if necessary. Check answers in feedback (in italics in the audio script below).

> **Answers:** Central Park (musicians), High Line (bridge), Staten Island Ferry, Times Square

C While Ss talk, monitor and make notes for remedial work to focus on in feedback.

Unit 3 Recording 1

P = Presenter   R = Rafael   C = Carmen

P: You probably think there's nothing to do for free in New York, right? Well, **New York may be one of the most expensive cities in the world**, but if you look carefully, **there are still lots of fun things to do that will cost you next to nothing or may even be free**. We sent two journalists, Rafael and Carmen, out onto the streets of New York with just **twenty dollars to spend**. Their challenge was to **organise a great day out, but not go over their budget**. Let's listen to their plans. Rafael?

R: Yes.

P: Rafael, hi, can you tell us what you're planning to do with your twenty dollars?

R: Hi, yes, well, actually, I'm going to start the day with a delicious bagel from a great bagel shop I've discovered on Third Avenue. They are really cheap and tasty. <u>Then I'm going to spend the morning in *Central Park*</u>. The park is filled with free events and street musicians, so I'm just going to listen to music and watch people. In the afternoon, <u>I'm going to the Museum of American Finance</u>. You have to pay to go in, but I'm really interested to find out about the history of American banking. After that, <u>I'm taking the *Staten Island Ferry*</u>. It's free and it's a great way to see views of New York from the water. <u>In the evening, I'm going to see some live music</u> on Second Avenue. I'll need to buy one drink, but the music is free.

P: That sounds great, Rafael. Enjoy the day.

R: Thank you. I'm sure I will.

P: OK, so Rafael has chosen bagels, Central Park, the Finance Museum and live music in the evening. Let's hear about what Carmen is planning for her day. Carmen?

C: Hi.

P: Carmen, can you tell us what you've planned for your day in New York City?

C: Yes, of course. I'm really excited because I'm going to the *High Line* to see some sculptures and just walk around and see what's happening.

P: The High Line? What's that?

C: It's an old railway track. Now it's used as a park, and there are lots of different activities and artists there. It's a really peaceful and beautiful place, right in the middle of the city. Lots of people go jogging there. I'm not going running, though. <u>I'm going to see a free art exhibition</u>. After that, <u>I'm going to *Times Square*</u>. It's such a famous place, and there are a lot of tourists there, but <u>I really like the atmosphere</u>, and <u>there's an Italian restaurant that does the best cheesecake just nearby</u>. So, I'm going to have something to eat and then, <u>in the evening, I'm meeting with a friend and we're going to a free hip-hop class</u>. I'm going to learn to dance like a real New Yorker.

P: Wow, that sounds good. So, first you're going to eat cheesecake and then you're going dancing. Right?

C: Exactly!

P: That sounds like a great plan. So, two great plans there. Which would *you* choose?

GRAMMAR   PRESENT CONTINUOUS/ BE GOING TO FOR FUTURE

> **Watch out!**
>
> Ss are often confused when they learn that the present continuous is more commonly used for arrangements (plans which involve other people and a fixed time/place) and *be going to* is more commonly used for plans which *don't* involve other people, e.g. *I'm going to relax this weekend*. It's very important to check the differences carefully and correct/give feedback at all stages of the lesson.

4A Ss do the exercise alone and compare answers in pairs while you write sentences a)–d) on the board. In feedback, elicit/check Ss' answers using the sentences on the board. Elicit and write on the board *present continuous* and *be going to*. Check the forms and drill the sentences. With **stronger classes**, add *at the club on Saturday/with John today* to sentences b) and d) respectively. Explain that it's more common to use the present continuous for arrangements with *other people* and *at a fixed time/place*, and also that *be going to* is more common for plans that *don't involve other people*, as in sentences a) and c). However, reassure them that both the present continuous and *be going to* can usually be used for future plans/arrangements.

> **Answers:** **1** the future **2** yes **3** present continuous: b) and d); *be going to*: a) and c)

B Ss listen and repeat the sentences. Play the recording as many times as necessary until Ss are confident. Do individual repetition and correction as needed.

Unit 3 Recording 2

1 gonna – I'm gonna see a free art exhibition.
2 gonna – I'm gonna see some live music.
3 gonna – We're gonna have a pizza.
4 gonna – Are you gonna come with us?

▷ **LANGUAGEBANK 3.1** p132–133

Read and check the notes with **weaker classes**. Ss can do Ex A and B now and Ex C after Ex 5A. In Ex B, remind Ss to try to mention other people and a time/place in their sentences. In Ex C, both tenses would be acceptable in 4, 5, 6, 9 and 10.

Answers:
A 1 C 2 B 3 D 4 A
B (Suggested answers)
   A I'm having a meeting with my boss next week.
   B I'm staying at home to watch TV with my wife this evening.
   C John's playing football for his school team on Saturday.
   D I'm going to the cinema with Jane next weekend.
C 1 are, doing
   2 'm going to
   3 're going to be
   4 are, going to take/are, taking
   5 're going to bring/'re bringing
   6 're not going to bring/'re not bringing
   7 is, going to have
   8 's going to play
   9 are, going to get/are, getting
   10 're going to drive/'re driving

5A Do question 1 with Ss. Point out that when the main verb is *go*, it isn't necessary to use *going to go*. We can say *We're going to the cinema on Friday* (the same applies to question 6). After Ss have written and compared their answers in pairs, check them in feedback.

Answers:
1 We're going to the cinema on Friday.
2 Are you going to stay at home this evening?
3 She isn't working this weekend.
4 What time are we meeting tomorrow?
5 I'm going to watch a/the football match later.
6 They're going out for a pizza on Saturday.

B Elicit an example before Ss do the exercise. Monitor and check their work for accuracy.

C Ss compare their answers in pairs and find out if they have anything in common.

SPEAKING

6A Check the rubric and elicit examples of Ss' plans. Then give them 3 mins to complete the *you* column in the table.

B Drill the example question and answer chorally and in open pairs across the class. Ss then do the exercise. To follow up, they can work with a different partner/pair and exchange information about their plans. Monitor and make notes of Ss' problems for feedback.

WRITING INVITATIONS

7A Check the meaning of *invitations*. Ss then do the exercise alone. After they have compared answers in pairs, check them with the class.

Answers:
1 Hi Sonia – I'm going to be in …
2 Great to hear from you. I'm sorry, but …
3 We're going out for a meal. Do you …
4 I'd love to. Sounds great! …

B Elicit an example. Ss then underline the other answers. In feedback, elicit and drill the sentences.

Answers:
inviting: Would you like to come? Do you want to meet us for dinner?
responses: I'm sorry, but I'm busy. I'd love to.

C Do the first email with Ss. Then give them 4–5 mins to write the others alone/in pairs. Monitor closely and prompt Ss to correct any errors they make. In feedback, Ss write the emails on the board. Discuss and correct them with the class.

Answers:
Hi Matt,
What are you doing tonight? A few people are coming to watch the football at my house. Do you want to come?
Ali

Ali,
Great to hear from you. I'd love to. What time's everyone coming?
Matt

Tilly,
What are you doing at the/this weekend? Would you like to go dancing on Saturday night?
Frank

I'm sorry, but I'm busy on Saturday evening. Do you want to go to the cinema on Sunday?
T

That's a great idea. I'd love to. What do you want to see?
Frank

D Ss should work with the same partner as in Ex 6. Monitor and take notes of examples of good language and problems, and write them on the board. Ss discuss and correct them in pairs in feedback.

Homework ideas
- **Ex 6:** Ss write two paragraphs about their own or their partner's plans.
- **Ex 7D:** Ss write a final draft of their email or a different one.
- **Language bank** 3.1 Ex A–C, p133
- **Workbook** Ex 1–6, p15–16

RELAX!

Introduction

Ss revise and practise the use of questions without auxiliary verbs in the context of free time.

> **SUPPLEMENTARY MATERIALS**
> **Resource bank** p157
> **Language bank** p132–133
> **Warm up:** photos of different indoor and outdoor leisure activities
> **Ex 1B:** dictionaries

Warm up

Show Ss photos of different indoor and outdoor leisure activities and distribute them to pairs/groups of Ss if possible. Give Ss 3–4 mins to name and describe the activities and places in the photos in as much detail as possible, e.g. *This is a photo of an art gallery. People are looking at the paintings.* In feedback, elicit and discuss Ss' answers. Teach/Check only essential vocabulary, as Ss will learn more later in the lesson.

VOCABULARY   PLACES TO VISIT

1A Give Ss 2–3 mins to answer the questions and compare their answers in pairs. In feedback, check/elicit the meaning of the words in the box. Do not confirm whether each activity takes place indoors or outdoors – this will be done in Ex 1B.

> **Suggested answers:**
> 1 See Ex. 1B below.
> 2 **concert hall:** listen to live music
> **countryside:** go for walks, go birdwatching
> **sports field:** watch or play all kinds of sports
> **nightclub:** dance
> **street market:** go shopping
> **shopping mall:** go shopping
> **nature trail:** go hiking
> **waterfront:** go for walks, go to restaurants/bars, look at boats

B Give Ss 3–4 mins to complete the word webs. Monitor and provide help if necessary. Ss can also use dictionaries to check words they're not sure about. Check Ss' answers in feedback, but note that pronunciation is checked in Ex 2A and 2B.

> **Suggested answers:**
> **indoors:** concert hall, nightclub, shopping mall; other places: cinema, museum, art gallery
> **outdoors:** countryside, sports field, street market, nature trail, waterfront; other places: park, the street

2A When you check the example, hold up three fingers and ask: *Where's the main stress?* Elicit *on the first syllable of the first word.* Then drill *concert hall.* Use the same technique with problem words when you check Ss' answers in feedback.

> **Answers:** <u>count</u>ryside, <u>sports</u> field, <u>night</u>club, <u>street</u> market, <u>shopping</u> mall, <u>nature</u> trail, <u>water</u>front
> The first word is usually stressed in compound nouns.

B Ss should be able to repeat the words with more confidence. If not, use the finger highlighting technique again.

READING

3A Give Ss 2–3 mins to discuss the questions in pairs and then discuss them with the class in feedback.

B Introduce the article and give Ss 5 mins to read it and find the answers to the questions in Ex 3A. Ss then compare answers in pairs and see if any of their guesses were correct. In feedback, elicit answers and check useful vocabulary from the text, e.g. *per week, two hours' drive, inhabitants, easily, annual, a good choice.*

> **Answers:** 1 people from Canada   2 football   3 New Zealanders
> 4 Spain   5 the UK   6 Thailand   7 It's impossible to say.
> 8 people from Greece and Estonia

C Ss discuss the questions in pairs. In feedback, elicit answers, then discuss what Ss learnt about the countries/activities mentioned in the article.

GRAMMAR   QUESTIONS WITHOUT AUXILIARIES

> **Watch out!**
>
> Ss usually find auxiliary verbs in English quite difficult to get used to as many languages don't use them. For this reason, they may not find questions without auxiliaries particularly strange. However, they will probably confuse the two forms initially. Clarify the difference carefully and provide sufficient controlled practice and feedback.

4 Ss should answer the questions alone and then compare their answers in pairs. In feedback, check answers and then illustrate the language further. Write the questions and answers on the board and ask: *Is question a) asking about the subject or object?* Elicit *the subject* and draw a box around *Greeks.* Then ask the same question about question b). Elicit *the object* and draw a box around *a party.* Ss then copy the sentences into their notebooks.

> **Answers:** 1 a)   2 b)   3 object questions

> ▷ **LANGUAGE BANK 3.2** p132–133
>
> Read/Check the table and notes with Ss. In feedback for Ex B, check if Ss know the answers to the questions.
>
> **Answers:**
> A 2 Who ~~does read~~ *reads* the most in your family?
>   3 Who ~~be~~ *is/was* your favourite writer?
>   5 What ~~did be~~ *was* your favourite book when you were a child?
>   6 Who ~~did write~~ *wrote* it?
>   7 How often *do* you read on the internet?
> B 1 What colour was The Beatles' submarine? (yellow)
>   2 Who wrote *Stairway to Heaven*? (Jimmy Page from Led Zeppelin)
>   3 Whose home was Graceland? (Elvis Presley's)
>   4 Which country did Diego Rivera come from? (Mexico)
>   5 Who painted the *Mona Lisa*? (Leonardo da Vinci)
>   6 Which painter invented Cubism? (Pablo Picasso/Georges Braque)

5 Do the first question as an example. Ss then complete the questions alone and compare answers in pairs. Monitor to see what type of problems they're having. Check answers in feedback.

> **Answers:** 1 Who   2 Which   3 do   4 Who   5 is   6 won
> 7 makes   8 did

SPEAKING

6A Set up the activity in two stages carefully, to ensure greater accuracy. Check the examples and then elicit a suitable answer for question 1, e.g. *I listen to music every day.* Give Ss 4–5 mins to prepare the questions they need for the other topics, alone or in pairs. Monitor closely and provide support where needed. Check the questions with the class before they do the information-finding activity. To find out the information for questions 1–8, Ss can do it as a class mingling activity. They ask their questions and note down the answers. Alternatively, assign one of the questions to each student/pair: they ask the question and report their findings back to the class.

Suggested questions:
3 How much time do you spend on the internet?
4 How often do you go to art galleries and/or museums?
5 When was the last time you went to the cinema?
6 How often do you go to parties?
7 How much TV do you watch?
8 How often do you watch or play sports?

B Give Ss time to analyse their findings. They then report back to the class. The other Ss are free to agree/disagree with the results!

Homework ideas

- **Ex 3:** Ss write about the free time activities they like best/least and say why.
- **Language bank** 3.2 Ex A–B, p133
- **Workbook** Ex 1–4, p17–18

CAN I TAKE A MESSAGE?

Introduction

Ss learn and practise making phone calls in both informal and formal situations. They also learn how to manage problems they might experience during phone calls.

> **SUPPLEMENTARY MATERIALS**
> **Resource bank** p158
> **Language bank** p132–133
> **Ex 8:** recording facilities

Warm up

Lead in to the lesson with common collocations for using the phone. Write these verbs on the board for Ss to copy: *make, answer, call, switch on, leave, put*. Then dictate these phrases which collocate with the verbs on the board, but not in the same order: *a phone call, the phone, wrong number, the answering machine, a message, down the phone*. Ss write them next to the correct word. Check their answers.

> **Answers:** make a phone call, answer the phone, call a wrong number, switch on the answering machine, leave a message, put down the phone/put the phone down

SPEAKING

1 Check the questions, then give Ss 3–4 mins to discuss them in pairs. In feedback, nominate Ss to give their answers.

VOCABULARY   COLLOCATIONS

2A First, check the meaning of the collocations. Ss then work alone and write *yes/no* next to each phrase.

B Model and drill the example conversation. Elicit and drill questions using the phrases in Ex 2A, e.g. *Have you arranged to meet friends/booked a table recently?* Ss then ask and answer the questions in pairs and make notes of their partner's answers. In feedback, nominate Ss to tell the class about their partner.

FUNCTION   MAKING A PHONE CALL

3A Check the rubric and play the recording. Ss write their answers and then compare them in pairs. Play the recording again if Ss have doubts. Then do feedback.

> **Answers:**
> Caller 1 wants to book a table.
> Caller 2 wants to change the date of tickets booked for a show.
> Caller 3 is inviting a friend for dinner.
> Caller 4 wants to cancel dinner.

B Give Ss time to read the notes. Check *new date*. **Stronger Ss** may be able to complete some of the answers before listening again. After listening, Ss compare answers in pairs. **Weaker Ss** may need to hear the recording again; pause after each answer (in bold in the audio script below) and elicit it.

> **Answers: 1** four, 9 o'clock   **2** King, 14 June   **3** 8.30, Saturday   **4** dinner

Unit 3   Recording 4

Conversation 1
A: Como's Restaurant.
B: Hello, I'd like to book **a table for four** on Saturday night. Around eight thirty if possible.
A: Let me just have a look. This Saturday?

B: Yes.
A: Saturday the fifteenth. Sorry, we're completely full on Saturday. There's nothing at all.
B: Ah, what about Sunday?
A: Sunday, Sunday. Um … the best I can do is a table at **nine o'clock**.
B: Nine o'clock? You haven't got anything earlier?
A: Nothing at all, I'm afraid.
B: OK, let's go ahead. **Nine o'clock.**
A: Can I take your name, please?
B: The table is for Jack Hopper.
A: Jack … hang on … can you repeat that, please? Did you say Jack Hopper?
B: Yes. H-O-double P-E-R.
A: OK, that's all booked. **Table for four, nine o'clock,** Sunday.
B: Great. Thank you.
A: Thank you.

Conversation 2
A: RSA Theatre. Jenny speaking. How can I help you?
B: Hello, I was wondering if you could help me. I've booked tickets for the show on the tenth of June, but I'd like to change the date.
A: OK, one moment. Can I just check? What's the name, please?
B: The tickets are booked in the name of **James King**.
A: Sorry, I didn't catch that. Did you say King?
B: **James King.**
A: OK, yes. Two tickets for June the tenth. What date would you like to change to?
B: What dates do you still have seats for?
A: There's nothing on the twelfth or thirteenth. There are two seats for the eleventh, but they're separate. We've got …
B: Sorry, can you slow down, please? Two seats for?
A: Sorry, two seats for the eleventh, but they aren't together. We can do you two seats together on the **fourteenth of June**.
B: **Fourteenth of June.** That's fine.
A: OK. I'll just go ahead and book that.

Conversation 3
A: Hello?
B: Hello, it's Mary here. Hello? Can you hear me OK? It's Mary here.
A: Oh hi, Mary. How are you?
B: Very well, thanks. And you?
A: Yeah, fine.
B: Are you doing anything on Friday? Because a few of us are going out for dinner.
A: Sorry, Mary, can you speak up, please? I'm at the station and I can't hear a thing.
B: Do you want to go for dinner on Friday?
A: Oh, that sounds nice.
B: There's going to be a few of us, Mohammed and Clare, and Robin.
A: That sounds like fun.
B: Are you free?
A: I think so.
B: Alright. **Eight thirty, Saturday. Pauly's.**
A: OK. **Pauly's on Saturday at eight thirty.**
B: That's right. Great. See you soon.
A: OK. Thanks for calling.

Conversation 4
A: Withertons. Who's calling?
B: Hello, this is Kim. Kim Brower. Can I speak to Alexandra Sanders, please?
A: I'm afraid she's not here at the moment.
B: Ah, do you know when she'll be back? I've tried her phone three or four times and left messages, but she hasn't called back.
A: She's visiting a customer. She should be back this evening. Can I take a message?
B: It's about dinner tonight. I've had to cancel because of work.
A: OK. I'll ask her to call you back.
B: Thanks.
A: Does she have your number?
B: It's 01823 2766.
A: Can you repeat that, please?
B: 01823 2766.

4 Check *caller/receiver*, then ask Ss to read the information and check if they need clarification of language there. Ss then complete the sentences and compare answers in pairs. In feedback, elicit/check and drill the answers. Highlight the use of *It's Andy* as *I am Andy* is a common error. Ss then work in pairs and take it in turns to read out the part of the caller/receiver. Monitor and help Ss with pronunciation.

> **Answers: 1** it's **2** Can **3** leave **4** here **5** take **6** back **7** for

5A Ss first read the phone conversations. Check *HR Manager*. Do question 1 as an example, then get Ss to do the exercise alone and compare answers in pairs, using the language in Ex 4 to help them. Elicit and drill the answers chorally and individually. Model the sentences first: beat the sentence stress and illustrate the intonation with your arms and hands, as if you were 'conducting'. This will prepare Ss for the next exercise.

> **Answers: 1** here **2** it's **3** See **4** speak **5** calling **6** isn't
> **7** message **8** back

B Ss should sit back to back and pretend to be talking on the phone. While they practise, monitor and help them with pronunciation.

▷ **LANGUAGEBANK 3.3** p132–133

Ss can refer to the information in the tables when they do the exercise.

Answers:
A: David speaking.
B: Hello, it's Mark Johnson.
A: How can I help you, Mr Johnson?
B: I'd like to speak to Sara Torres, please.
A: I'm afraid she's not here at the moment.
B: Can I leave a message?
A: Yes, of course.
B: Can you ask her to call me back?
A: No problem.
B: My number is 0276 765356.
A: Can you repeat that, please?
B: 0276 765356.
A: OK. Thanks for calling.
B: Bye.

LEARN TO **MANAGE PHONE PROBLEMS**

6A The extracts are from recording 3.4. Check problems a)–e) and do an example before Ss do the exercise. Don't check pronunciation in feedback – Ss will do it in Ex 6B.

> **Answers: b)** 3 **c)** 5 **d)** 1 **e)** 4

B Ss listen and repeat the phrases, focussing on the linking of *can* and *you*. Play the recording as many times as necessary until Ss are confident. Do individual repetition and correction as needed.

Unit 3 Recording 5

1 Can you slow down, please?
2 Can you hear me OK?
3 Can you speak up, please?
4 Can you repeat that, please?

7A Ss listen and write their responses. With **weaker classes**, Ss can just listen first and then listen again to write their answers. Ss compare answers in pairs. Do not confirm answers yet – Ss will check them in Ex 7B.

Unit 3 Recording 6

Conversation 1
My phone number is 765 9876 2135. OK?

Conversation 2
My full address is the one I gave you last week, the New York address.

Conversation 3
My phone number is 245 9888.

Conversation 4
I'll be taking the six forty-five from Houston and changing at Miami, and I'll arrive at about two.

B Ss listen to check their answers and correct them if necessary.

Answers:
1 Sorry, can you slow down, please?
2 Sorry, can you speak up, please?
3 Can you repeat that, please?
4 Can I just check?

Unit 3 Recording 7

Conversation 1
A: My phone number is 765 9876 2135. OK?
B: Sorry, can you slow down, please?

Conversation 2
A: My full address is the one I gave you last week, the New York address.
B: Sorry, can you speak up, please?

Conversation 3
A: My phone number is 245 9888.
B: Can you repeat that, please?

Conversation 4
A: I'll be taking the six forty-five from Houston and changing at Miami, and I'll arrive at about two.
B: Can I just check? Did you say two?

speakout TIP

Read the Speakout tip with Ss before doing Ex 8. Ask: *Why is this a good idea?* (Because it gives you more confidence and helps you feel more prepared.) Encourage Ss to use the Speakout tip in Ex 8 and in real life.

SPEAKING

8 Prepare Ss for the role-plays in two stages. First, divide the class into Students A and B. Student A reads the situations on p160 and Student B on p162. Check that Ss know all the language in the tasks. Put Ss in A/A and B/B pairs. Give them 4–5 mins to prepare. Monitor and provide support where needed. Then put Ss in A/B pairs, sitting back to back. They take turns to make a call and answer the phone. Monitor discreetly, making notes for feedback. Invite pairs to act out one of their conversations to the class. Record this if you have the facilities. Give feedback to Ss and do remedial work as necessary.

Homework ideas

- **Ex 8:** Ss write a phone conversation for one of the situations on p160 and 162.
- **Language bank** 3.3 Ex A, p133
- **Workbook** Ex 1–6, p19

RIO DE JANEIRO

Introduction

Ss watch an extract from a BBC travel programme about Rio de Janeiro. They then learn and practise how to talk about a perfect day out and write an invitation.

> **SUPPLEMENTARY MATERIALS**
> **Ex 6A:** photos of Pisa's main sights
> **Ex 7A:** photos of famous, popular cities

Warm up

Lead in and create interest in the lesson. Ss look at the main photo of the Sugarloaf Mountain in Rio. Ask, e.g. *What's the name of this mountain? Where is it? Why is it famous? Have you been there?/ Would you like to go there? Why/Why not?* Ss discuss their answers in pairs/groups. In feedback, check and discuss Ss' answers, using information from the Culture notes if necessary.

> **Culture notes**
>
> **The Sugarloaf Mountain** is a peak situated in Rio de Janeiro, Brazil, at the mouth of Guanabara Bay on a peninsula that sticks out into the Atlantic Ocean. Rising 396 metres above the harbour, its name is said to refer to its resemblance to the traditional shape of concentrated refined loaf sugar. It is known worldwide for its cable car and panoramic views of the city.

DVD PREVIEW

1 Give Ss 2–3 mins to discuss the questions in pairs. In feedback, discuss Ss' ideas with the class.

> **Culture notes**
>
> **Rio de Janeiro** is a huge seaside city in Brazil, famed for its Copacabana and Ipanema beaches, and the Christ the Redeemer statue atop the Sugarloaf Mountain, a granite monolith with cable cars to its summit. The city is also known for its sprawling favelas (shanty towns). Its raucous Carnival festival, featuring parade floats, flamboyant costumes and samba, is considered the world's largest.

2A Give Ss 2–3 mins to discuss the questions in pairs. If possible, put Ss together with others who know Rio de Janeiro. In feedback, discuss the answers with the class.

B Ss read the information and, using the photos to help them, make predictions in pairs. In feedback, elicit Ss' answers. They can check their predictions in the next exercise.

DVD VIEW

3A Check the questions and ask Ss to guess the answers in pairs. Elicit some answers in feedback, but do not confirm them yet – tell Ss they can check their answers after they watch the DVD.

B Play the DVD. Ss check their answers from Ex 3A and compare them in pairs. Play the DVD again if they don't agree about the answers. In feedback, elicit and check answers. Also check Ss' guesses from Ex 2B.

> **Answers:** 2, 3, 4, 6

> **Alternative approach**
>
> As the task is very visual, play the DVD with the sound turned off. Ss watch and check their answers. Play it again with the sound for Ss to check their answers.

4A Ss read the sentences first. Check new language, e.g. *sunshine, exotic, Frescoball*. Ss correct the sentences and compare their answers in pairs.

B Ss watch the DVD to check their answers from Ex 4A and tell you when to stop at each answer (in bold in the DVD script below). Replay each extract for Ss to read and listen to authentic English again.

> **Answers:**
> 2 You can view all the favelas from the ~~train~~ *cable car*.
> 3 The locals tell him to go to the ~~supermarket~~ *Amazon* to find exotic fruit.
> 4 The cashew nut tastes like a mixture of strawberries and ~~lemons~~ *chocolate*.
> 5 The men like to play frescoball ~~in the park~~ *on the beach*.
> 6 They play music with a local band ~~on the street~~ *in a pub/bar/club*.

> **Optional extra activity**
>
> Exploit the DVD for extra comprehension and attention to interesting detail. Pause it at suitable points and ask questions, e.g. *What's Rafael doing now? Where is he? What do you think is his favourite thing? What do you think about Rio de Janeiro?*

DVD 3 Going Local: Rio

R = Rafael   M = Man   W = Woman

R:	Welcome to Rio, home of sunshine, Samba and the Sugarloaf Mountain. But that stuff is for tourists. I want to find out what cariocas get up to when nobody's looking. My editor is sending me a series of challenges by SMS. To get by, I will ditch the guidebook and ask the locals for their help instead. Find the public transport with the best views. Public transport? With the, with the best views of the city.
M1:	É bonzinho, o teleférico ali.
R:	They're talking about a cable car. They say it's very cheap and the views are amazing.
M2:	**It's a new cable car here. You can view all the favelas here, the slums.**
M3:	I think you're gonna really like the views. You're gonna see the problems of poverty in Brazil. But I'm sure you're gonna like this view.
R:	One … two … one for you and one for me. Whoo-hoo! Wow! That is like a sea of houses. The city centre. This is the core of Rio de Janeiro. So, we're looking for 'exotic fruit'.
M4:	**It's difficult to find, you know, really exotic fruit. Maybe in the Amazon.**
R:	I'm afraid we're gonna have to go all the way to the Amazon to find exotic stuff.
W1:	Right over there.
R:	Right over there?
W1:	Yeah. Polly's succos.
R:	Uh huh. And what is that?
W1:	They have all kinds of juices with all different flavours.
R:	Que coisa é o?
W2:	Acai.
R:	Acai. This is the famous acai. Somebody else mentioned that. This is the place. This is the place we're looking for.
M5:	Fruta do Conde.
R:	Hmm, it's very nice. It's kind of um … it's very sweet …
M5:	That's the cashew nut. Everybody knows the cashew nut.

R: Amazing. It's soft, but it's difficult to chew. It's difficult to get a good bite. Now this is what I call exotic fruit. Very nice, very rich flavour. **I mean, it's something between strawberry and chocolate.**
'Beat a local at their own game.'

W3: So I don't know very well the places.

R: Where can I find a good place for me to, you know, to practise sport with the cariocas?

M6: OK. **The beach.**

M7: Frisbee.

M8: **Frescoball.**

M9: Surfing, but I like frescoball.

R: I got a message. 'Make music with the locals.'

M10: **The other side have a group to play** Samba. Listen. Listen.

R: **A nineties pub in Rio de Janeiro** … are we going to go, are we … are you serious?

W4: Trapiche Gamboa.

R: Trapiche Gamboa?

W4: Today we have Galote and Grupo Centelha playing.

R: Yes, this is the place. Wow! Look at this, Andy. People dancing and everybody singing. I really want to join these guys.

---

5 Ss can refer to Ex 3 and 4 as a prompt for ideas. Give them 5 mins to discuss the questions. They should make a list of things they'd enjoy and note next to them when/where they last did them. Ss can then work with another partner and exchange information. Elicit Ss' answers in feedback and find out which things were most common.

speakout a day in your city

Culture notes

Pisa is a city in Tuscany, Central Italy, on the right bank of the mouth of the River Arno on the Tyrrhenian Sea. It is the capital city of the Province of Pisa. Although Pisa is known worldwide for its leaning tower (the bell tower of the city's cathedral), the city contains more than 20 other historic churches, several palaces and various bridges across the River Arno.

6A Elicit what Ss know about Pisa: where it is, its main sights, etc. If you have photos of Pisa, use them here. If Ss don't know anything, it doesn't matter as they'll find out in the recording. Ss listen and do the exercise, and compare answers in pairs before feedback.

Answers: 2 b)   3 d)   4 e)   5 f)   6 a)

B Ss read the information and then listen to complete the sentences. Play the recording again, pausing at each answer (in bold in the audio script below) to elicit/check the key phrases. Drill the sentences and ask further comprehension questions, e.g. *What's the market like? What does Alessandro do in the evening?*

Answers:
1 We're going to …
2 It's going to be …
3 We're starting the day …
4 In the afternoon, we're planning to …
5 In the evening, we're …
6 Afterwards, for lunch, we're …

Unit 3 Recording 8

OK. I'm going to tell you about how to go local in Pisa, Italy. I'm going to take you on a tour that only the locals would know about. First of all, **we're starting the day with a coffee and a fresh pastry** from a little bar near the Vettovaglie market. I love this place because it's where all the locals who are selling on the market go to have their coffee. And the coffee is delicious. **We're going to spend the morning walking through the market** and the old part of the city near the university. **Afterwards, for lunch, we're going to one of the best restaurants I know.** It's called Le Bandierine and they specialise in home-made spaghetti and seafood, and we're going to have a fantastic meal there. **In the afternoon, we're planning to go a little outside Pisa** to San Rossore park. It's a beautiful place to walk, but they also have horse races there, so we can have some fun watching the horses. **In the evening, we're going back towards the Leaning Tower** for an early evening drink to look at the Piazza dei Miracoli as the sun goes down, when all the tourists have gone home. We'll finish the evening with a wonderful pizza from a restaurant on the other side of the city. I'm sure you'll love it. **It's going to be a day to remember.**

7A If you have photos of famous cities, use them to prompt ideas/support *weaker Ss*. Pair/Group Ss who want to talk about the same city together. Remind them to use the key phrases and the recording for ideas while they plan. ·

B Put Ss in new pairs/groups. They take turns to talk about their plans. Monitor and note down examples of good language and errors that need to be addressed in feedback later. Ss tell the class (or another group) about their plans. They listen and make notes about which plans are the best and why. In feedback, discuss Ss' plans and have a class vote on the best one(s). Give feedback on Ss' strengths and weaknesses now or at the beginning of the next lesson.

writeback an invitation

8 Ss use their ideas/notes from Ex 7 and the emails on p29 to write their invitations. Monitor and prompt Ss to self-correct. They give their emails to other Ss, who can then reply, also using ideas from p29.

Homework ideas

• **Ex 5:** Ss write their answers to the questions in this exercise.
• **Ex 8:** Ss write an invitation to have a perfect day in their town/city. They could put it on the class blog or send it to you.

LOOKBACK

Introduction

As well as revising and practising the language in the unit, use the Lookback exercises to provide you with an informal assessment of your Ss' speaking skills. Fluency practice is usually given in Ex B or C of each section. When assessing speaking skills, take these four areas into account: accuracy of grammar, range of vocabulary, fluency and pronunciation.

TIME OUT

1 Ss complete the sentences alone and then compare answers in pairs. In feedback, ask Ss to suggest verbs that collocate with the word/phrase that is not possible in each question, e.g. *go sightseeing, go to an art gallery*.

> **Answers: 1** sightseeing **2** an art gallery **3** a snack **4** a pub **5** a club

> **Optional extra activity**
>
> In pairs/groups, Ss write four similar sentences using the word webs on p28. They then give them to another pair/group to cross out the wrong words.

PRESENT CONTINUOUS/ BE GOING TO FOR FUTURE

2A Do the first sentence as an example to show Ss what to do. Give Ss 4–5 mins to write their sentences. Monitor and note down problems they're having with them in terms of word order. Give feedback and do remedial work if necessary, before Ss do Ex 2B. Model and drill the questions using contracted verb forms to prepare them for Ex 2B, e.g. *Who's cooking your dinner this evening?*

> **Answers:**
> 1 What are you doing tonight?
> 2 Are you doing anything special this weekend?
> 3 Who is cooking your dinner this evening?
> 4 When are you going on holiday?
> 5 Which city are you next going to visit/are you going to visit next?
> 6 What are you going to do after the lesson?

B Ss take turns to ask and answer the questions and note down their partner's answers. They then tell the class about their partner's plans/arrangements.

PLACES TO VISIT

3 Check the rubric and the example. Elicit one or two sentences before Ss work in pairs. Give Ss 4–5 mins for the exercise. Monitor and prompt Ss to self-correct.

QUESTIONS WITHOUT AUXILIARIES

4A Check the example. Ss read the prompts first. Elicit/Check what Ss know about the people and things mentioned there. (The answers are included in the answer key for Ex 4C, but don't check them until Ss do Ex C.) Give them 4–5 mins to write the questions. Monitor and assess how accurate the questions are. Do remedial work in feedback and/or use the information for assessment if required.

> **Answers:**
> 2 Who was an actor before he became US President?
> 3 Which 1975 Queen album includes the song *Bohemian Rhapsody*?
> 4 Who was a fourth great Renaissance painter, besides Leonardo, Michelangelo and Titian?
> 5 Which 'John' won an Oscar for his song *Can you feel the love tonight* from *The Lion King*?
> 6 Which Bob Marley song includes the words *Let's get together and feel alright*?
> 7 Which watery Italian city has an international art exhibition every two years?
> 8 Which member of the Dion family sold 200 million records before 2007?
> 9 Whose hit songs include *I'm like a bird*, *Promiscuous* and *Maneater*?

B Tell Ss that the answers here are also answers to the questions in Ex 4A. Ss can do the quiz alone or in pairs.

C Ss check their answers and then match them with the questions in Ex 4A. (See Ex 4A answer key.)

> **Answers: 2** Reagan **3** A Night at the Opera **4** Raphael **5** Elton **6** One Love **7** Venice **8** Céline **9** Nelly Furtado

MAKING A PHONE CALL

5A Ss first read the conversation. Ask: *What did you notice about it?* Elicit/Tell them that it's like a poem: the words at the end of each line rhyme with each other, e.g. *blue – you*. Ss then complete the phone call alone and check their answers in pairs. Do feedback and check the note for the meaning of the expression *get the sack*. Elicit more examples of rhyming words at the end of each line (*chow – now, back – sack*), but don't practise reading out the 'poem' yet – this is done in Ex 5C. Check the note for the meaning of the phrase *get the sack*.

> **Answers: 1** it's **2** can **3** like **4** here **5** back

B Explain first that the text is an answerphone message. Ss then complete the gaps with words from the box and compare answers in pairs. In feedback, nominate Ss to give the answers. Also elicit examples of words that rhyme at the end of each line, e.g. *Paul – all, meeting – eating, game – name, soon – moon*. Check the note for the meaning of the expression *pigs might fly*.

> **Answers: 1** this **2** busy **3** leave **4** message **5** call

C Ss first practise reading the poems out loud as a class. Do this two or three times as it will give them more confidence with their pronunciation. The rhyming words at the end of each line will also help Ss to focus on the rhythm of the poems. They then work in pairs and practise saying the poems. **Stronger Ss** might like to memorise them. In feedback, invite Ss to read out or recite the poems to the class.

> **Homework ideas**
>
> **Workbook** Review 1, p20–22

> **BBC interviews and worksheet**
>
> **What do you like doing in your free time?**
> This video consolidates and extends Ss' vocabulary of free time activities and exemplifies real usage of the present continuous for future.

OVERVIEW

4.1 HIDDEN TALENT

VOCABULARY | *make* and *do*
GRAMMAR | present perfect + *ever/never*
PRONUNCIATION | weak forms: *have*
LISTENING | listen to someone descibing how he used his hidden talent
SPEAKING | talk about hidden talents
WRITING | check your work and correct mistakes

4.2 SCHOOLS OF THOUGHT

VOCABULARY | education
READING | read an article about different schools
GRAMMAR | *can, have to, must*
PRONUNCIATION | weak forms: *have to*
SPEAKING | talk about rules in schools

4.3 WHAT SHOULD I DO?

VOCABULARY | language learning
READING | read replies to a website message
FUNCTION | giving advice
PRONUNCIATION | silent letters
LEARN TO | respond to advice
SPEAKING | give advice and make suggestions for language learners

4.4 INVENTIONS BBC DVD

DVD | watch an extract from a BBC documentary about developments that have changed the world
speakout | inventions
writeback | a forum post

4.5 LOOKBACK

Communicative revision activities

BBC INTERVIEWS

Are you learning anything at the moment?

In this video people describe what they are learning at the moment and the most difficult things they've ever learnt. The video also extends Ss' vocabulary of education and learning, and exemplifies real usage of the present perfect with *ever*. Use the video at the start or end of the unit.

HIDDEN TALENT

Introduction

Ss revise and practise the present perfect simple with *ever/never* in the context of hidden talents. They learn collocations with *make* and *do* and practise how to correct mistakes in their written work.

SUPPLEMENTARY MATERIALS
Resource bank p160
Language bank p134–135
Ex 1A: dictionaries

Warm up

Pre-teach/Elicit the meaning of the lesson title, *Hidden talent*. Ask: *What were you good/bad at when you were a child? What did you want to do when you grew up? Did you have any secret ambitions? Any hidden talents?* Ss discuss the questions in pairs/small groups and then as a class. Some Ss might have been good at, e.g. singing or football and had ambitions to be famous when they were young. If not, it doesn't matter as the questions lead in to the topic of the lesson.

VOCABULARY MAKE AND DO

1A Ss should be familiar with most of the vocabulary here except *do business*. First, do an example: elicit the meaning of *make a speech*, using the photos. Then elicit a definition, e.g. *talk in public*. Give Ss 2–3 mins to match the phrases with the photos. They can use dictionaries if necessary. Monitor to check Ss' progress. Check Ss' answers in feedback. They should then copy the list of phrases with *make* and *do* into their notebooks.

Answers: (top to bottom, left to right)
do a project with a big team, do well/badly in an exam, make a phone call, do business in another language, make a speech, make a meal

B Illustrate/Check the instructions for this exercise carefully. Ss first write down their own answers and then work in small groups and take turns to compare them. Monitor closely to check the accuracy of Ss' sentences. Prompt them to self-correct any errors if possible. Elicit answers in feedback and find out who in each group has made or done the most things overall.

GRAMMAR PRESENT PERFECT + *EVER/NEVER*

Watch out!
Ss make mistakes with both the meaning and form of the present perfect. This is because they may have the same form in their L1 but it's used in a different way (e.g. *I've seen it last week.*) and they may also confuse the form with the past simple (e.g. *Did you have seen that film?*). Check the form and concept of the two tenses thoroughly and give Ss as much contextualised practice as possible.

2A Check the meaning of *conference*. Ss then do the exercise and compare answers in pairs. Check answers in feedback.

Answer: the present perfect and past simple (and one example of the present simple)

B Check the concept of *general experience* in question 1, using an example, e.g. *I've ridden a camel.* Ask: *Is this sentence in the past or present?* (the past) *Do we know exactly when it happened?* (no) Ss then answer questions 1–3 and check in pairs before feedback. After checking their answers, write the first three lines of the conversation on the board. Draw Ss' attention to the abbreviated spoken form *No, never. Have you?* (instead of *No, I haven't. Have you ever made a speech … ?*).

> **Answers:**
> 1 **Questions:** Have you ever made a speech in public? Have you ever made friends with someone from another country?
>   **Form:** *have you (ever)* + past participle
> 2 **Sentences:** He met a woman from Chile in 2014. In fact, they got married a week ago!
>   **Verb tense:** past simple
> 3 No, never. Yes, I have. No, I haven't.

C Tell Ss to listen to the pronunciation of *have/haven't* carefully. In feedback, refer back to the sentences on the board from Ex 2B. Elicit/Underline the stressed words in each sentence: *Have you ever made a speech in public? No, never. Have you? Yes, I have.* Elicit/Tell Ss that *have* is stressed in short answers and pronounced /hæv/, but isn't stressed in questions, where it's pronounced /həv/. Ss can then listen and repeat the conversation, paying attention to the sentence stress and weak (unstressed) forms.

> ▷ **LANGUAGEBANK 4.1** p134–135
>
> *Stronger classes* can study the tables and notes at home when they do the exercises. Check the notes in class with **weaker Ss**, who then do Ex A–B.
>
> **Answers:**
> A 1 Have you ever ~~saw~~ *seen* the film *Titanic*?
>   2 Two days ago she~~'s been~~ *went* to a museum.
>   3 Unfortunately, we have ~~ever~~ *never* won the lottery.
>   4 Has *she ever* visited you?
>   5 I haven't ~~meet~~ *met* your brother.
>   6 In 2011, they~~'ve~~ travelled to Geneva.
>   7 ~~Have you seen~~ *Did you see* that TV programme last Wednesday?
>   8 He *has never* played a musical instrument.
> B 1 Have you ever done   2 's worked   3 visited
>   4 Has he made   5 haven't heard   6 ate

3A Check *snails* and do an example. Ss do the exercise alone and then compare answers in pairs. In feedback, recheck the concept of the two tenses. For each sentence, ask: *Do we know when? Is it important?*

> **Answers:** 1 was   2 Have you ever written   3 've never eaten
> 4 finished   5 Have you ever been   6 finished

B Elicit examples for question 1 that are true for Ss, using phrases with *make* and *do*. Monitor the accuracy of their sentences. In *mixed-ability classes*, **stronger** and **weaker Ss** could work together. Alternatively, pair **weaker Ss** and give them extra support.

C Ss find out if they have anything in common. In feedback, invite Ss to give their own/their partner's answers to the class. Correct as appropriate or prompt Ss to self-correct.

4A Give Ss 3–4 mins to write and check their answers on p127. Advise them to try to memorise 3–4 past participles a day, e.g. before they go to sleep/on the bus.

> **Answers:** keep – kept, make – made, drive – driven, do – done,
> fly – flown, come – come, cross – crossed, give – given, swim – swum,
> sleep – slept, lose – lost, win – won, pay – paid, grow – grown

B Check/Drill the example and write the phonemic symbols on the board. It's very useful to have a phonemic chart available nearby, on a wall or notice board. You can then refer to it easily to help Ss with their pronunciation. In feedback, check/drill the past participles. Ss could write them down with the phoneme for each pair of sounds (see phonemes in the answer key below).

> **Answers:** kept, slept /e/; made, paid /eɪ/; driven, given /ɪ/;
> done, won /ʌ/; flown, grown /əʊ/; come, swum /ʌ/; crossed, lost /ɒ/

C Check the words in the box and elicit one or two examples. In pairs, Ss write their questions while you monitor and prompt them to self-correct.

D Check/Drill the example conversation. Point out that with *yes* answers, Ss should add an extra piece of information. This time, monitor and make notes of problems Ss have with tenses for feedback.

LISTENING

5A Check the questions. Ask Ss to briefly describe the pictures, then play the recording. Get Ss to compare answers in pairs before feedback.

> **Answers:**
> 1 cooking
> 2 In his twenties; he started to make meals for his friends.
> 3 He started selling food to his colleagues and then opened a café in the office.

B Ask Ss to read the sentences and then play the recording again. With **weaker classes**, pause after each sentence (in bold in the audio script below) for Ss to check/complete their answers. Elicit answers in feedback and ask which sentences feature past participles (1, 5 and 6).

> **Answers: 1** enjoyed   **2** make   **3** sell   **4** do   **5** Have   **6** made

Unit 4 Recording 3

I = Interviewer   M = Mario

I: So Mario, can you tell us how you used your talent in your job?
M: Um, well, **I've always enjoyed cooking.** I come from a big Italian family and I learnt to cook by watching my mother in the kitchen.
I: But no one knew you could cook, right?
M: That's right, no one knew. I only cooked at home, but I did it well. **Then in my twenties, I started to make meals for my friends.** And, well, I was working in an office. And I brought food to office parties, that kind of thing.
I: Then you had an idea …
M: **I had the idea to sell my food at work.**
I: So your colleagues buy your food every day.
M: Yeah, I started selling it to friends and colleagues, and then to other people at work. I prepared all kinds of things: bread, pasta, cakes …
I: And then you made a decision.
M: Yeah, office work was OK, but **I wanted to do something more interesting.** So eventually, I asked the boss if I could open a café in the office.
I: And he was happy to …
M: He agreed. They gave me a room. Now I bring food there every day. We have chairs and tables. And now that's my job.
I: **Have you ever thought, 'Oh, I prefer my old office job** – This is too difficult'?
M: Never. I've never thought that because this is what I love doing: cooking and preparing different menus. Really, **it's the best decision I've ever made.**
I: And have you thought about expanding the business, maybe opening a restaurant one day?
M: I've thought about it, but it's a long way away!

SPEAKING

6A Elicit a few Ss' hidden talents or things they love doing. Ss could talk about and write them on the board. Prompt them to use ideas from the lesson or suggest other ideas, e.g. *writing stories/poems, playing a musical instrument*. Give Ss 2–3 mins to make notes alone/in pairs. Monitor and support them with vocabulary/accuracy.

B Monitor discreetly while Ss work in groups, and make notes of examples of good language and problems. In feedback, invite members of each group to tell the class about their partners' hidden talents. Write examples of Ss' errors and good language on the board. Ss discuss and correct them in pairs.

WRITING   CORRECTING MISTAKES

7A Check the rubric and give examples for each of the symbols. Ss then work alone and compare answers in pairs before feedback.

Answers:
My talent is that I can sing really well. I've always ~~like~~ *liked* (gr) music[.] (p) I sing all kinds of songs, including rock, pop and classical music[.] (p) I first discovered this ~~abillity~~ *ability* (sp) when I was young. I often listened to music and sang at the same time. I've ~~doing~~ *done* (gr) it many times at parties, in front of my ~~freinds~~ *friends* (sp), and in karaoke bars. There is no magic secret[.] (p) I just listen ~~carefuly~~ *carefully* (sp) and ~~am practising~~ *practise* (gr) on my own.

speakout TIP

Encourage Ss to use this tip and to get into the habit of always checking their work before they give it to you for checking.

B Ss write their paragraph. They should not write more than 75 words.

C Ss check and correct each others' paragraphs, using a different colour for corrections.

Homework ideas
- **Ex 7B:** Ss write the final draft of their paragraph or write a new paragraph about themselves/another person.
- **Language bank** 4.1 Ex A–B, p135
- **Workbook** Ex 1–6, p23–24

SCHOOLS OF THOUGHT

Introduction

Ss revise and practise *can, have to* and *must* for obligation in the context of education.

> **SUPPLEMENTARY MATERIALS**
> **Resource bank** p159 and 161
> **Language bank** p134–135
> **Photo bank** p154
> **Ex 3B and 5A:** dictionaries
> **Ex 7, optional extra activity:** sheets of A4 paper for Ss to make posters of their ideas (See notes below.)

Warm up

Lead in to the lesson. Ask: *Where did you go to school? Did you like it? Why/Why not?* Ss discuss the questions in pairs/groups. Elicit their answers and discuss the topic briefly with the class.

VOCABULARY EDUCATION

1 Check the meaning of the subjects in the box (use the Photo bank on p154 if necessary). Ss do the exercise in pairs and then compare answers with another pair before reporting back to the class about what they have in common, e.g. *We were all bad at maths, but were interested in IT.*

Culture notes

In England, education is compulsory until the age of 16. Those who want to study for advanced school-level qualifications (A-levels) either stay on at a **secondary school** with a **sixth form**, transfer to a local **sixth form college** or go to a **further education (FE) college**.

> ▷ **PHOTOBANK** p154
>
> Check the subjects in the photos and drill the pronunciation. Look at the diagram of State Education in England and check the meaning of *FE College* and *Sixth form*. Ss then discuss the questions in pairs. In **multilingual classes**, Ss might like to draw diagrams of their educational systems at home and share them with the class.

2A Ss complete the phrases and compare answers in pairs. Elicit/Check answers in feedback.

Answers: 1 study 2 play 3 make 4 do/take 5 give 6 wear

B Check the rubric and elicit examples before Ss do the exercise.

C Do an example. Elicit sentences based on Ex 2B, e.g. *I enjoyed art, but I didn't enjoy French. I've never studied online.* Ss then make sentences about their answers in Ex 2B and compare them in the same way.

READING

Culture notes

The Alternative School (also known as TAS) was set up in May 2007 in Barnoldswick in Lancashire, England, to offer an alternative educational curriculum for young people who are not engaging with mainstream education. They claim to offer every young person that they work with the chance to start again and feel included in an education programme where they aim to not only build self-esteem and confidence, but actively work to improve reading, writing, understanding, numeracy and ICT.

The flipped classroom is an instructional methodology and a type of blended learning that delivers instructional content, often online, outside of the classroom and moves activities, including those that may have traditionally been considered homework, into the classroom. In a flipped classroom model, Ss watch online lectures, collaborate in online discussions or carry out research at home and engage in concepts in the classroom with the guidance of the instructor.

The **Suzuki method** is an educational philosophy created in the mid-20th century by Shin'ichi Suzuki, a violinist who wanted to bring beauty to the lives of children in Japan after World War II. Although originally used with the violin, it has been adapted for other instruments – the flute, piano, etc.

3A Give Ss 3–4 mins to discuss the questions. In feedback, nominate Ss to give their opinion and reasons. Then have a class vote on whether a traditional approach to teaching is good or bad.

B Check the rubric and give Ss 2–3 mins to read the text quickly and match the topics with the paragraphs. In feedback, check answers and teach/check new vocabulary from the text for the next exercise, e.g. *mainstream, innovative, individual, 'open door' policy, approach, model, mother tongue, involved.* Ss could also use dictionaries.

Answers: a) 3 b) 1 c) 2

C First, elicit one idea Ss think is 'good' and 'bad' and discuss why. Then give Ss 4–5 mins to read the text more carefully and underline what they think is the best/worst idea. Ss compare answers in pairs, then discuss their reasons for their choices and decide whether any of the methods would work in their country. In feedback, elicit and discuss Ss' ideas and check if there is a consensus.

Optional extra activity

Ss work in pairs/groups and write 4–6 questions about the text to ask the class or other pairs/groups.

GRAMMAR CAN, HAVE TO, MUST

Watch out!

Due to both L1 and L2 (English) interference, Ss may confuse both the meaning and form of the modal verbs *can/must* with *have to*, e.g. *I can't to go./You don't can smoke here.* Highlight and check the meaning/form of the verbs carefully and provide thorough contextualised practice.

4 The sentences are from the texts in Ex 3. Check the table headings and the example: ask: *Is it possible for children to decide when they go to school?* (yes) *Is it allowed?* (yes) Ss then do the exercise alone and compare answers in pairs. Monitor while Ss work to check how familiar they are with the language and any specific problems you'll need to focus on in feedback. Draw the table on the board and invite Ss to write the verbs in the correct places. The class discuss if the answers are correct. During this process, check meaning and form. Ask concept questions for each sentence/verb, e.g. *Is it necessary/possible/allowed?* Double-check the meaning of *don't have to*, e.g. *You don't have to come to school every day, but you can if you want to.* Elicit more examples if necessary. (NB: Ss might ask about the verb form in question 6. With **weak classes**, don't explain that *must be involved* is in the passive. Just say it's the same as *You have to involve the parents, too.*)

Answers: not possible/not allowed: can't, mustn't; **necessary:** have to, must; **not necessary:** don't have to

Optional extra activity

Ss underline all the examples of *can/can't*, *have to/don't have to*, *must/mustn't* in the text in Ex 3 and match them with the categories in the table in Ex 4.

> **LANGUAGEBANK 4.2** p134–135

Weaker Ss should do Ex A and B in class. In Ex A, check *Hang it up!* In Ex B, check *log in* and *illegal.* Point out to Ss that in Ex B more than one answer may be possible.

Answers:
A 1 have to 2 can 3 can't 4 have to 5 can 6 mustn't
    7 can't 8 don't have to
B 1 can 2 don't have to 3 must/have to 4 can
    5 doesn't have to 6 can't/mustn't 7 has to/must
    8 can't/mustn't

5A Give Ss 1 min to read the text quickly for general understanding first. Check/Teach *home-schooled* and *qualifications* (or Ss can check in their dictionaries). Do question 1 as an example. Ss then complete the text and compare answers in pairs. Do not confirm answers yet – Ss will check them in Ex 5B.

B Play the recording for Ss to check their answers. In feedback, nominate Ss to answer. Recheck the concepts where needed.

Answers: 1 don't have to 2 don't have to 3 can 4 have to/must 5 can 6 have to/must 7 mustn't/can't 8 mustn't/can't 9 can't 10 can

C Point out to Ss that they should listen and notice the pronunciation of *have to* /hæftə/. Then play the recording.

D Play the recording again. Ss listen and repeat the sentences. While they are doing so, beat the sentence stress and intonation with your hands/arms, as if you were 'conducting' them. Pay particular attention to the pronunciation of *have to* /hæftə/ and the unstressed forms of *can/must* where appropriate.

Unit 4 Recording 4

 1 They don't have to wear a uniform.
 2 They don't have to wait for the school bus.
 3 You can choose which subjects you want to study.
 4 You have to work hard. You must work hard.
 5 But you can choose to work when you feel like it.
 6 You have to be at school at 8.30a.m. You must be at school at 8.30a.m.
 7 You mustn't wear trainers. You can't wear trainers.
 8 You mustn't use your mobile phone in class. You can't use your mobile phone in class.
 9 Some people think that children who study at home can't go to the exams and get the same qualifications.
10 But they can, and they do.

6 Elicit some examples from the text in Ex 3. Then give Ss 3–4 mins to write down their ideas for the questions in pairs. Monitor closely to provide support with language if necessary. Ss then compare their ideas with another pair and add to their own if possible. In feedback, invite Ss to give their opinions to the class.

Suggested answers:
Similarities: Students have to study. They can take exams/get qualifications.
Differences: Home-schooling: Students can study when they want to. At normal school they have to study when the school decides they should. At home they don't have to wear a uniform. At school they have to wear a uniform. At home they can use their mobile phones. At school they can't use their mobile phones. At school they have a variety of teachers. At home they probably only have one teacher (a parent).

Alterative approach

This could be organised as a debate: those in favour of home-schooling present their arguments to the class, and those against do the same. The class then votes for one or the other.

SPEAKING

7 First, check/teach *national anthem* and *get in* from the statements. Elicit some examples before Ss work in pairs to compare rules and customs in their own country. In **multilingual classes**, pair Ss of different nationalities/cultures so they can compare ideas and opinions. While Ss talk, make notes on their use of the language they've studied in this lesson and do any remedial work needed later. In feedback, invite each pair to present their comparisons and opinions to the class, then ask: *Which rules did you find surprising?*

Optional extra activity

If appropriate to your Ss, provide them with A4 paper, if you have any. Ss write two lists of their ideas for school rules: one for *can/have to/must* and the other for *don't have to*, etc. They display their posters around the classroom – or pass them round – for other Ss to compare and discuss.

Homework ideas

- **Ex 6:** Ss write a short paragraph about their opinion of home-schooling.
- **Ex 7:** Ss write about school rules/customs in their country and which are good/bad ideas.
- **Language bank** 4.2 Ex A–B, p135
- **Workbook** Ex 1–6, p25–26

WHAT SHOULD I DO?

Introduction

Ss learn and practise ways of giving/responding to advice, particularly in the context of language learning.

> **SUPPLEMENTARY MATERIALS**
> **Resource bank** p162
> **Language bank** p134–135
> **Ex 2A:** dictionaries
> **Ex 9:** audio/video recording facilities, if available

Warm up

Lead in to the lesson through the photos. First, ask: *What do you think is happening in the photos?* Ss discuss their answers in pairs and report back to the class. During/After the feedback stage, you could also ask other related questions, e.g. *Which of these activities have you done? When/Where?* You could also write on the board *It's never too late to learn* and ask Ss if they agree with the statement.

SPEAKING

> **Culture notes**
> '[What we have to learn to do,] we learn by doing' is a quote from Aristotle.
> The quote 'A little learning (knowledge) is a dangerous thing' was first used by poet Alexander Pope in *An Essay on Criticism*, 1709. It means that a small amount of knowledge can make people think they are more expert than they really are.
> The quote 'Anyone who stops learning is old, whether at twenty or eighty' is by Henry Ford (1863–1947), the founder of the Ford Motor Company.
> 'The best way to learn is to teach' is a quote from Frank Oppenheimer (1912–1985), an American physicist.

1A Check the quotes with Ss and elicit which photos they match. Then ask: *Do you have the same/similar sayings in your language?* Elicit examples. Discuss the first quote with Ss. Then give them 2–3 mins to make notes on the others.

B Ss compare their ideas in pairs/groups. In feedback, invite Ss from each pair/group to report back to the class. Find out what the majority opinion is.

VOCABULARY LANGUAGE LEARNING

2A Ss should be familiar with most of the words in bold, so allow them to match the definitions alone initially. They then compare answers in pairs and check new words in their dictionaries if necessary. In feedback, check answers and elicit other sentences using the words in bold.

> **Answers:** 1 b) 2 a) 3 e) 4 g) 5 c) 6 f) 7 d)

B Check the questions and give Ss 4–5 mins to discuss them. Monitor and notice Ss' answers, especially those for question 3. Nominate Ss to tell the class their own/their partner's answers. Discuss which Ss think are the most important/useful and elicit other ideas. This will give you important information about the language learning strategies your Ss are aware of and/or use outside the classroom. They'll learn more about them in Ex 3–6.

FUNCTION GIVING ADVICE

3A Give Ss 1–2 mins to read the message. Discuss which areas of English Zeynep might most need to improve: spoken, written, vocabulary, reading/listening skills, etc. Then give Ss 2–3 mins to note down three pieces of advice. They can use ideas from Ex 2A if necessary.

B Ss compare their answers in pairs and decide on the most useful ideas. In feedback, elicit their ideas and discuss which will help Zeynep the most.

4 Check the rubric. Ss read the replies again and discuss their answers in pairs. In feedback, elicit Ss' answers and write the three most useful ideas on the board.

5A Do an example and then give Ss 3–4 mins to write the replies in their notebooks. Monitor to check accuracy and invite Ss to write their answers on the board in feedback. Elicit/Underline phrases for giving advice (e.g. *I think you should …*) and drill the sentences.

> **Answers:** 1 think 2 Find a business website/Write them in a notebook 3 look them up 4 worry 5 don't, use 6 idea

B Ss discuss their answers in pairs. In feedback, refer to the sentences on the board from Ex 5A and elicit/check Ss' answers.

> **Answers:** 1, 3, 5 and 4, 6 have the same meaning.

C Check the instructions, then play the recording and ask Ss to listen and repeat. Elicit answers in feedback and drill the pronunciation of *should* if necessary.

> **Answer:** The letter *l* is silent in *should*.

> **Unit 4 Recording 5**
>
> should – you should – You should go online.
> shouldn't – you shouldn't – You shouldn't worry.
> should – should I? – Should I look it up?

6A Check the instructions, then play the recording. Ss discuss their answers in pairs before feedback.

> **Answers:** Students are too shy to speak in front of the class. They worry about making mistakes. They have problems listening to English. Native speakers speak really fast and it's difficult for students to understand them.

B Ss first read the information in the table: check *shy* and *body language*. Ss then complete the notes and compare answers in pairs. Do not confirm answers yet – Ss will check them in Ex. 6C.

> **Answers:** 1 making mistakes 2 prepare 3 groups 4 listening (to English) 5 hands 6 subtitles

C Play the recording again for Ss to listen and check. Check Ss' answers (in bold in the audio script below). With **stronger classes**, play the recording again, pausing to ask more detailed comprehension questions, e.g. *Why is it a good idea to use subtitles?*

D After Ss have discussed the questions in pairs, elicit their answers in open class. They can then offer advice to their partner about his/her language learning problems.

> **Optional extra activity**
> Ss work in pairs and choose one or two new learning strategies each to try out. They should decide which areas of English they need to practise more and also which strategies would be the most suitable/achievable for them.

Unit 4 Recording 6

G = Glynn   M = Magda

G: Magda, many of my students are too shy to speak in front of the class. They **worry about making mistakes**.

M: Yes, this is a common problem. Teachers should **give students time to prepare**. Tell them the question and give them a few minutes to think about what they'll say. They can take notes first.

G: That's a good idea.

M: Also, **let them practise in groups** before they speak in front of everyone. This'll give them confidence.

G: Yes, you're right. I do usually give them a chance to practise first. Now what about those **students who have problems listening to English**?

M: Problems listening. That's common, too.

G: Native speakers – for example, people from the UK or Australia or the States – speak really fast and it's difficult to understand them.

M: Yes. Students should practise listening to native speakers. Fortunately, if they have the internet, there are lots of opportunities. They can listen to the news and to podcasts. But even better is to go on YouTube and watch film clips. When we can see the people speaking, it makes it easier. We can **watch the mouth and the hands and the body language** and it helps us to understand.

G: And using subtitles? Some teachers say we shouldn't use them. Ever!

M: I'm not sure that's a good idea. Subtitles can be a real help. Students can see the differences between the spelling and the pronunciation of words. They can see which words are swallowed.

G: I suppose so.

M: For me, students should **use subtitles maybe the second time they watch**.

G: OK, and what about students' pronunciation? They have a lot of problems …

LEARN TO   RESPOND TO ADVICE

7A Ask Ss to read the extracts first, then play recording 4.6 again. Ss listen and write the responses. In feedback, elicit/drill the responses (underlined in the audio script above) in open pairs across the class.

Answers: 1 That's a good idea.   2 Yes, you're right.
3 I'm not sure that's a good idea.   4 I suppose so.

Optional extra activity

Ss listen again and read the audio script on p170. Ask: *Did it help you to listen and read at the same time? How?* Elicit specific examples from different Ss.

B Check the rubric and elicit Ss' answers.

Answers: 1 ✓   2 ?   3 ✓   4 ✗

▷ **LANGUAGEBANK 4.3** p134–135

Ss can refer to the information in the tables when they do Ex A and B.

Answers:
A a) That's a good idea.
   b) I think we should go out after the lesson.
   c) I'm not sure because I haven't got much money.
   d) Why don't we go out for a meal?
   e) OK, let's go to Butler's café for a coffee.
B b), a), d), c), e)

8A Ss cover the text and look at the pictures. Give them 1–2 mins to answer the question in pairs. They then check their answers with the text.

Suggested answers:
A The man eats too much.
B He watches too much TV.
C She's very fit and can run a lot, but he isn't fit and gets tired easily.
D They need to organise their shopping better.

B Ss can use language from Ex 5A and 7 to complete the conversations. Check their answers in feedback and drill the conversations. Ss then practise reading them out in pairs.

Answers: 1 you should work, a good   2 shouldn't spend, You're
3 Why don't, 'm not sure that's   4 it's a good, suppose so

9 Organise Ss into groups of three and number them A, B, C. First, read out one of the problems and elicit how to change it into their own problem using *I, my son*, etc. Ss then look at the relevant pages/texts. Give them 1 min to think about how to change them. Ss then take it in turns to explain their problem and get advice from their partners. Monitor and make notes of problems Ss have with the language of advice and give feedback afterwards. If you have recording facilities, record the role-plays. Ss watch them and then try to improve on their performance.

Homework ideas

- **Ex 6D:** Ss write about two new learning strategies they want to try out. They say why they chose them and what they'll do.
- **Ex 9:** Ss write advice for two of the problems.
- **Language bank** 4.3 Ex A–B, p135
- **Workbook** Ex 1–4, p27

INVENTIONS

Introduction

Ss watch an extract from the BBC documentary programme *Supersized Earth: The Way we Move*, which explores the developments that have changed the modern world. Ss then practise talking and writing about inventions.

> **SUPPLEMENTARY MATERIALS**
> **Warm up:** copies of a simple online technology quiz
> **Ex 3A/B:** dictionaries
> **Ex 6A:** photos of the inventors

Warm up

Lead in to the topic of the lesson by giving Ss a surprise technology quiz. The aim is to remind them, in a light-hearted way, how technology affects the world they live in. Tell Ss to put their books away and not talk during the quiz. Hand out the quiz and collect it after 5 mins. You can mark it later/at home. Ss discuss the questions in pairs and then as a class. Follow on immediately with Ex 1.

DVD PREVIEW

> **Culture notes**
>
> **The Wright brothers**, Orville and Wilbur, were two American brothers, inventors and aviation pioneers, who are credited with inventing and building the world's first successful airplane and making the first controlled, powered and sustained heavier-than-air human flight, on 17 December 1903.

1 Give Ss 2–3 mins to discuss the questions in groups. Elicit answers, then ask them to look at the photos at the bottom of the page and ask: *What is happening? Who are these people?* (the first flight/the Wright brothers). *What are they famous for?* If Ss don't know, provide them the information from the Culture notes above.

2 Give Ss 1 min to read the programme information and discuss their answer in pairs. In feedback, elicit the answer. Discuss it and check any unfamiliar words in the text if necessary.

> **Answer:** Dallas Campbell goes to the USA to try out a replica of the Wright brothers' glider and see if he can fly it.

3A If Ss don't have dictionaries, put **weaker**/**stronger Ss** together in pairs to work out the meaning of the phrases in bold. Don't do feedback until after Ex 3B, when Ss match the phrases with their meanings.

B Ask Ss to work in pairs. In feedback, check answers, then model and drill the pronunciation.

> **Answers:** **1** b) **2** d) **3** e) **4** a) **5** c)

DVD VIEW

4A Check the questions, then play the DVD. Ss note down their answers and compare them in pairs. Elicit answers in feedback.

> **Answers:** **1** The Wright brothers' first flight was in 1903. It was on a sand dune. They flew 120 feet (36 metres). This changed everything ('triggered a century of innovation'). They learned to ride the wind in a simple way. **2** yes

B Check *transform* in question 4. Ss then work alone/in pairs and underline the correct alternatives before watching the DVD again. Check Ss' answers (in bold in the DVD script below). Ask their opinions about statement 4: *Do you agree? Why/Why not?*

> **Answers: 1** 1903   **2** 120 feet   **3** a glider   **4** planet

> **Optional extra activity**
>
> Play the DVD again, pausing at suitable points. Ask questions about what Ss can see, e.g. *What are they doing now? Where are they? How is flying similar/different now?*

DVD 4 Supersized Earth: The Way We Move

D = Dallas Campbell   M = Man

D: Today billions of us can travel across the planet in a matter of hours. But that everyday miracle started in a rather humble way. On the seventeenth of December in **1903** on this very sand dune, two brothers made a journey that was going to change everything. They were trying out this radical new form of transportation that was going to give us the power to travel further than we've ever travelled before. And the distance they made on that day was extraordinary: **a hundred and twenty feet**. I know it doesn't sound very far, but that thirty-six metres triggered a whole century of innovation. Those two men were the Wright brothers, and the invention they're known for is the aeroplane. But it wouldn't have been possible without this: **the glider they built the year before**. Until they'd cracked how to ride the wind and steer through the breeze, no one could begin to conquer the skies. The Wright brothers achieved this in such a simple way that apparently, even I should be able to get the hang of it.

M: There you go.

D: The canard wing in front controls going up and down. Wow, look at that!

M: Put some weight in that harness. Good. There you go. Good reaction.

D: To turn, the Wright brothers banked the wings against the wind by twisting them.

M: You want to try shifting your weight?

D: OK, I'll try the other way.

M: There you go.

D: And this is … Oh God, yeah, yeah, yeah. And they put a rudder on the back.

M: Yeah, that's good correction.

D: This is an exact replica of their glider.

M: Excellent.

D: And I can just imagine how they must have felt.

M: Nose up. Excellent. Nose all the way up. Nose … Wow! It's this glider that makes all those aeroplanes that we fly today possible.

D: This was the moment we unlocked the secret to human flight. It launched a dramatic revolution in the way we move around the globe. **And that helped transform our planet.**

M: Now nose it up. Great flight. Great flight.

5 Give Ss 3-4 mins to discuss the question and any other information from the DVD they thought was interesting. In feedback, elicit ideas from different Ss.

speakout inventions

Culture notes

Johannes Gutenberg (1398–1468) was a German blacksmith, goldsmith, printer and publisher who introduced printing to Europe. His invention started the Printing Revolution and is widely regarded as the most important event of the modern period.

Alexander Graham Bell (1847–1922) was an eminent Scottish-born scientist, inventor, engineer and innovator who is credited with inventing the first practical telephone.

Thomas Alva Edison (1847–1931) was an American inventor and businessman. He developed many devices that greatly influenced life around the world, including the phonograph, the motion picture camera and a long-lasting, practical, electric light bulb.

Sir Timothy John Berners-Lee (born 1955) is an English computer scientist, best known as the inventor of the World Wide Web. He implemented the first successful communication between a Hypertext Transfer Protocol (HTTP) client and server via the internet in 1989.

6A If you have photos of the inventors, show them to the class and elicit their names. Then ask Ss to discuss the questions in pairs or small groups. Nominate Ss to give their answers in feedback. If necessary, provide the class more information about the inventors using the Culture notes above.

B Ss listen and write brief notes for their answers. After they've compared notes in pairs, play the recording again if they need to add more detail. Check key words, e.g. *antibiotics*, *painkillers*. Elicit and discuss Ss' answers.

> **Answers:** **1** medicines (aspirin, antibiotics), the car   **2** the internet   **3** the car

C Ss read the key phrases, then listen and tick the ones they hear. In feedback, play the recording again, pausing after each key phrase (in bold in the audio script below). Elicit/Drill the phrases.

> **Answers:** Ss should tick all the phrases except *In my opinion … , That's right* and *I agree.*

Unit 4 Recording 7

A: OK, well, **I think the most important** invention is probably the internet. **For me**, it's number one.
B: Uh huh.
A: It's opened up the world and we can get lots of information for free now. And it joins people together from all different cultures and countries.
B: **That's true, but** I think there are more important inventions. Really simple things that are so common we forget about them.
A: Like what?
B: Well, things like aspirin. It's not really an invention, I suppose, but can you imagine life without aspirin?
A: Umm, not really.
B: And all the other medicines we use.
A: Antibiotics to cure illnesses. That's true, actually. Painkillers.
B: And **another invention that I see as really important is** the car.
A: Oh yeah, **definitely**.
B: Before the car, travel was so slow it took days to get anywhere.
A: That's true. People went everywhere by horse, didn't they?
B: Yeah, and so the car opened up possibilities …

7A Ss discuss in pairs. They can use the ideas from Ex 6A or their own. They should rank their three inventions in order of importance (1–3) if possible. Provide support to Ss who need it or ask **stronger Ss** to work with **weaker ones**. Monitor and prompt Ss to correct errors of accuracy.

B Nominate Ss from each pair to report back to the class. The rest of the class tick the inventions that are the same or make a note of those they disagree with. When all pairs have reported back, Ss discuss the ideas they disagree with.

writeback a forum post

8A Elicit/Pre-teach *discovery*, *natural world* and *basic needs* from the forum post. Give Ss 4–5 mins to read the post, answer the questions and compare them with a partner. Nominate Ss to give their answers in feedback, and ask if they agree with the commenter's opinions. Encourage them to use the key phrases from Ex 6C when discussing this.

> **Answers:** The survey is about the top ten inventions in history. The commenter thinks the list includes important inventions, but also some strange choices (e.g. language and electricity aren't inventions). He's surprised the toilet and printing press aren't on the list. He's amazed the iPhone is on the list.

B Ss work in pairs/groups to decide on their top ten inventions. Individually, they then write a post about the inventions. Provide support where needed.

Homework ideas

Ex 8B: Ss write the final draft of their post.

LOOKBACK

Introduction

The notes below provide ideas for exploiting the exercises and activities, but your approach will depend on your aim, e.g. as a diagnostic test/assessment or for fluency practice/revision. For example, if you wanted to assess/test Ss' knowledge, then it would *not* be appropriate to monitor and help them.

MAKE AND DO

1A Check the example and give Ss 2 mins for the exercise before they compare answers in pairs. Check their answers and drill the questions, e.g. *Who in your family makes most of the meals?* Elicit Ss' answers in preparation for Ex 1B.

> **Answers:** **2** makes **3** does **4** makes **5** does **6** makes

B Give Ss time to prepare their answers before they work in pairs. Monitor while they ask/answer the questions and make notes of problems for assessment purposes or remedial work. To follow up and provide extended speaking practice, Ss can tell another student about their partner's family, e.g. *Alicia's husband makes most of the meals, but her daughter makes the most phone calls.*

PAST SIMPLE OR PRESENT PERFECT + EVER/NEVER

2A You could do this exercise as a real test of Ss' understanding of these two tenses. Give them 3–4 mins to write the completed sentences on a piece of paper with no help. In feedback, Ss swap papers and mark each other's sentences with a tick or cross as you give the answers. Ss write the result on their partner's papers, e.g. 4/6. Ss then correct their wrong answers. Recheck the answers before moving to Ex 2B.

> **Answers:** **1** Have you ever swum **2** Did you go
> **3** I've never visited **4** I didn't go out **5** I've lived **6** I ate

B If possible, put Ss in pairs with someone they don't know very well. In feedback, check who guessed both answers correctly.

C Ss prepare the questions alone. Monitor while they do this and prompt them to self-correct. Don't check the questions with the class, but assess how well they use the two tenses while they ask/answer the questions. In feedback, invite pairs to ask/answer their questions in front of the class. Tell the class to listen and write down follow-up questions to ask, e.g. *A: Did you go out last night? B: Yes, I did. A: Where did you go?/Who did you go with?* Give feedback on Ss' problems and do remedial work as needed.

EDUCATION

3A Check *particularly well* in question e). Give Ss 2–3 mins to match the questions. Check/Drill them before Ex 3B.

> **Answers:** **1** e) **2** c) **3** g) **4** d) **5** b) **6** a) **7** f)

B If possible, pair Ss with a partner they don't know very well in order to make the questions more authentic. Ss should take turns to ask a question and make a note of the answers. They can then report their partner's answers to the class in feedback.

CAN, HAVE TO, MUST

4A Ss could work in pairs and discuss what they think the answers are for questions 1, 2 and 5. Check answers and ask Ss to give reasons for their choice of verb.

> **Answers:** **1** must **2** can't **3** can't **4** don't have to **5** have to

B In a *mixed-ability class*, pair *stronger* and *weaker Ss* for this exercise. Alternatively, put *weaker Ss* together and help/prompt them with ideas. Try to check all Ss' work to ensure that their sentences are grammatically correct.

C Ss compare their sentences in pairs. In feedback, Ss read out their sentences. The rest of the class note down any new ideas and add them to their own. Discuss any facts that surprised Ss or that they found particularly interesting. Do remedial work as required.

LANGUAGE LEARNING

5A Give Ss 2 mins to complete the words before they compare answers in pairs. Check meaning and pronunciation in feedback.

> **Answers:** **1** re-read **2** online **3** subtitles **4** chatroom
> **5** memorise

B Ss take it in turns to ask/answer the questions. They should note down their partner's answers so that they can report back to the class in feedback. Monitor discreetly, making notes of Ss' performance. In feedback, Ss tell the class/group about their partner. Give feedback on Ss' problems if necessary.

GIVING ADVICE

6A Ss complete the tables and then check their answers on p43.

> **Answers:**
> **giving advice:** (I think) you should … , You shouldn't … , Why don't we/you … ?, I (don't) think it's a good idea to … , Find/Try/Go …
> **responding to advice:** That's a good idea., I suppose so., You're right., I'm not sure that's a good idea.

B Give Ss 3–4 mins to complete the conversation. *Stronger Ss* can write more. Pairs read out their conversations to the class. Prompt Ss to correct them where necessary.

C Ss rehearse their conversation and try to memorise it. Monitor and provide help with stress and intonation. Each pair acts out the conversation, then the class votes for the best one.

BBC interviews and worksheet

Are you learning anything at the moment?

In this video people describe what they are learning at the moment and the most difficult things they've ever learnt. The video also extends Ss' vocabulary of education and learning, and exemplifies real usage of the present perfect with *ever*.

5) travel

OVERVIEW

5.1 FANTASTIC FILM TRIPS

VOCABULARY | transport
READING | read about amazing journeys in films
GRAMMAR | past simple and past continuous
PRONUNCIATION | weak forms: *was/were*
SPEAKING | tell an anecdote

5.2 TRAVEL TIPS

VOCABULARY | travel items
PRONUNCIATION | stressed syllables
LISTENING | understand travel advice
GRAMMAR | verb patterns
SPEAKING | discuss travel
WRITING | write an email describing a trip or weekend away

5.3 YOU CAN'T MISS IT

VOCABULARY | tourism
READING | read a text about a man who works in three countries every day
FUNCTION | asking for/giving directions
LEARN TO | show/check understanding
PRONUNCIATION | intonation: questions
SPEAKING | ask for and give directions

5.4 FULL CIRCLE BBC ») DVD

DVD | watch an extract from a BBC travel programme
speakout | an award
writeback | an application

5.5 LOOKBACK

Communicative revision activities

BBC ») INTERVIEWS

Do you enjoy travelling to different countries?

In this video people describe what they like and don't like about travelling and whether they'd like to live in another country. The video also extends Ss' vocabulary of travel and holidays. Use the video at the start or end of the unit.

FANTASTIC FILM TRIPS

Introduction

Ss learn/practise the past simple and past continuous used to talk about interrupted past actions. They also learn vocabulary for transport and talk about journeys.

> **SUPPLEMENTARY MATERIALS**
> **Resource bank** p163–164
> **Language bank** p136–137
> **Photo bank** p155 (Ss may need dictionaries.)
> **Ex 3:** dictionaries
> **Ex 4:** a map of the world to show the places mentioned in the texts: Polynesia, Alaska, Australia

Warm up

To lead in to the lesson, play a word game such as *Hangman* to revise transport vocabulary, e.g. *bus*, *bike*, *coach*, *helicopter*, *lorry*. (See the Photo bank on p155 for more words.)

Write a word in blanks on the board, e.g. _ _ _ _ _ (*coach*). Ss work in pairs/teams and take it in turns to guess a letter. If the letter is in the word, write it in the correct place(s) on the board. Also write it underneath, to remind Ss it's already been used. If the letter isn't in the word, add a part of the body to the gallows (head, body, left arm, right arm, etc.). Ss continue guessing letters until they either guess the word or all the body parts are completed. Pairs/Teams get a point if they guess the word before the 'body' is completed. Play the game for 5–6 mins. Invite Ss to write the words (blanks) on the board themselves if appropriate.

VOCABULARY   TRANSPORT

1 Give Ss 2–3 mins to make a list of words from the Warm up and add others they know. They then check them in the Photo bank, Ex 1, p155. Check answers and elicit the stressed syllables in the words. Ss copy new transport words into their vocabulary notebooks and underline the stress. Then give Ss 3–4 mins to discuss question 2 in Ex 1, first in pairs and then as a class.

> ▷ **PHOTOBANK** p155
>
> **1** Ss can use their dictionaries to check any words they don't know.
> **2** Ss could discuss these questions together with question 2 in Ex 1 above.
>
> | **Answers:** |
> | --- |
> | **1** 1 F 2 M 3 K 4 L 5 N 6 G 7 H 8 B 9 E 10 J |
> | 11 I 12 D 13 C 14 A |

READING

Culture notes

Kon-Tiki (2012) is a historical drama film about the 1947 Kon-Tiki expedition. Legendary explorer Thor Heyerdal's epic 4,300-mile crossing of the Pacific on a raft in 1947 was his attempt to prove that it was possible for South Americans to settle in Polynesia in pre-Columbian times. Their only modern equipment is a radio and they must navigate using the stars and ocean currents. After three exhausting months at sea, they achieve their goal.

Into the Wild (2007) is a biographical drama survival film written and directed by Sean Penn. Christopher McCandless (Emile Hirsch), son of wealthy parents (Marcia Gay Harden, William Hurt), graduates from Emory University as a top student and athlete. However, instead of embarking on a prestigious and profitable career, he chooses to give his savings to charity, rid himself of his possessions and set out on a journey to the Alaskan wilderness.

The film *Rabbit-Proof Fence* (2002), based on the book *Follow the Rabbit-proof Fence*, stars three indigenous Australian (Aboriginal) actresses, Everlyn Sampi, Tianna Sansbury and Laura Monaghan, who play Molly, Daisy and Gracie. British actor Kenneth Branagh plays A.O. Neville, the man responsible for removing the girls from their families.

2 The questions here ask Ss to predict information about the photos and the texts they will read in Ex 3. However, first look at the photos and elicit briefly what Ss know about the films. Don't confirm any details about the films until after Ex 4. Check the questions and give Ss 3–4 mins to discuss the questions in pairs. In feedback, elicit Ss' predictions and write some of them on the board – but don't confirm if they are correct or not.

Suggested answers:

1 **A** raft   **B** bus, walking, car (people gave him rides)
  C none (walking)
2 **A** across an ocean   **B** into the wild   **C** across a desert

3 This is a jigsaw reading activity. It's important to set this up carefully to make sure Ss don't look at their partners' texts before they've all exchanged information about them. Check the rubric and questions, then put Ss in groups of three, A, B and C. Make sure they sit facing each other, not side by side, and don't show each other their books. Give them 4–5 mins to read their texts and make notes of the answers. Monitor closely and provide support where needed. Ss can use their dictionaries to check new words.

4 Give Ss 2 mins each to tell their group about their text while their partners take notes. In feedback, nominate Ss from each group in turn to answer a question about their text. Then check Ss' predictions from Ex 2. Discuss the films in more detail, using the Culture notes above if needed. Show Ss a map of the places in the texts if possible.

Answers:

1 **Kon-Tiki:** Thor Heyerdahl and five sailors/explorers;
  Into the Wild: a young man called Chris McCandless;
  Rabbit-Proof Fence: three Aborigine girls (Molly, Daisy, Gracie)
2 **Kon-Tiki:** to prove it was possible to travel from South America to Polynesia using only basic tools; **Into the Wild:** to experience life alone in the wilderness; **Rabbit-Proof Fence:** to get home
3 **Kon-Tiki:** across the Pacific Ocean; **Into the Wild:** the Alaskan wilderness; **Rabbit-Proof Fence:** 1,200 miles across the Australian desert

speakout TIP

Read the Speakout tip with Ss. Then give them 1–2 mins to find a sentence in their text and make a note of it in three or four words. Elicit some examples for each text and write them on the board.

5 While Ss discuss the questions, monitor and make notes of their ideas and language problems. Discuss the questions with the class and give feedback on Ss' problems. If Ss can't think of any other real-life journeys that have been made into films, ask them to think of any films they know which are about journeys.

Suggested answers:

2 Because they are true stories with an important message to pass on/celebrate.
3 **real-life journeys:** *Scott of the Antarctic* (1948) and *Touching the Void* (2003); **fictional journeys:** *Journey to the Centre of the Earth* (1959), *Easy Rider* (1969), *A Passage to India* (1984), *Central Station* (1998), *Around the World in 80 Days* (2004)

GRAMMAR   PAST SIMPLE AND PAST CONTINUOUS

Watch out!

Ss often tend to overuse the past continuous and say, e.g. *Last night we were in a restaurant and we were seeing a mouse.* It's important to check the use of the tenses carefully using clear examples in context and encourage self-correction at all stages of the lesson.

6A Ss do the exercise alone and then compare answers in pairs. While they do this, write the sentences on the board. In feedback, elicit/check Ss' answers and underline examples of the past simple and past continuous in the sentences on the board.

Answers:

1 **past continuous:** were sailing, was living, was raining
  past simple: crashed, wrote, decided
2 **a)** sail **b)** live **c)** rain
3 **a)** sail **b)** live **c)** rain
4 **background information: a)** were sailing   **b)** was living
  c) was raining
  main events: a) crashed   **b)** wrote   **c)** decided

B When Ss have answered the questions, check the concepts further: refer to sentence a) from Ex 6A on the board. Draw a timeline (see below or Language bank p136) to illustrate the continuous action (*were sailing*) and the completed action (*crashed*) (or long/short action). Ask: *Which action started first?* (were sailing) *Which was the short action?* (crashed) *Did the long action continue after?* (no)

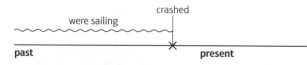

Answers: 1 past continuous   **2** past simple

C There's one example in each text and they all begin with *while*. Elicit the sentences and write them on the board. Underline *while* and ask: *What other question word could you use?* (when) *Is the meaning the same?* (yes) *Do you use* while *with the past simple or continuous?* (past continuous)

Answers:

Kon-Tiki: While others <u>were discussing</u> the theory, Heyerdahl <u>decided</u> to test it.
Into the Wild: While he <u>was travelling</u>, he met several people …
Rabbit-Proof Fence: … while they <u>were walking</u>, they <u>saw</u> the 'rabbit-proof fence' …

▷ **LANGUAGEBANK 5.1** p136–137

Ss can study the tables/notes in class or at home. They should refer to them when they do Ex A and B. In Ex A, teach *lawnmower* and *priest*.

Answers:
A 1 was living 2 decided 3 bought 4 began
  5 was travelling 6 helped 7 was driving 8 were fixing
  9 stayed 10 did, end
B 1 He was playing tennis when he hurt his leg.
  2 Sarah didn't like the job because it was boring.
  3 While they were travelling they met lots of other tourists.
  4 How did you know my name?
  5 Who were you dancing with in that nightclub when
    I saw you?
  6 I was swimming in the sea when I saw the shark.
  7 Did I pass my exam?
  8 The thief broke in while Jack was having breakfast.

7A Check the example and elicit as many *So …* sentences as possible. Ss work alone/in pairs. Give support where needed.

B While Ss compare their answers in pairs, monitor again and prompt them to self-correct any mistakes with the past simple and past continuous. For each question, nominate Ss to give the first sentence, then elicit all Ss' answers with *so*. Recheck the tenses using the rules in Ex 6A and 6B if necessary.

Answers:
2 I was waiting for a bus when I met my boss.
3 I was watching TV when I recognised my best friend!
4 I was walking home when I found $5,000 in a bag.
5 We were travelling by plane when a man with a gun stood up.
6 We were riding our bicycles when a cow walked across the road.
7 We were eating in a restaurant when we saw a mouse.
8 I was studying in my room when I heard loud music next door.

8A Play the recording, pausing after each sentence. Ss note down the consequence in the *So …* sentence, e.g. *went home* (underlined in the audio script below). They then discuss the similarities to their own answers in Ex 7A in pairs and report back to the class.

B Write *was* /wəz/ and *were* /wə/ on the board. Then play each sentence, pausing to elicit/highlight the sentence stress and weak forms of *was* and *were* (see verbs in italics in the audio script below). Drill the sentences chorally, then individually, to check sentence stress and weak forms.

Unit 5 Recording 1

1 *I was running* when it started to snow. So I <u>went home</u>! *I was running.*
2 *I was waiting* for a bus when I met my boss. So we <u>went for a drink.</u> *I was waiting.*
3 *I was watching* TV when I recognised my best friend! So I <u>called her.</u> *I was watching.*
4 *I was walking* home when I found $5,000 in a bag. So I <u>took it to the police</u>. *I was walking.*
5 *We were travelling* by plane when a man with a gun stood up. So we <u>hit him, took the gun and became heroes</u>! *We were travelling.*
6 *We were riding* our bicycles when a cow walked across the road. So we <u>stopped</u>. *We were riding.*
7 *We were eating* in a restaurant when we saw a mouse. So we <u>told the waiter and didn't pay</u>. *We were eating.*
8 *I was studying* in my room when I heard loud music next door. So I <u>went to complain and they invited me to their party</u>. *I was studying.*

9 First, read/check the example and the prompts with Ss. Give them time to think of five/six sentences and elicit another example before they work in pairs. During pairwork, write down sentences with examples of Ss' mistakes with the target language. In feedback, nominate pairs to say their sentences/respond across the class. This is a good time to do a correction slot. Write 5–6 sentences with Ss' mistakes on the board. Ss correct them alone and then compare answers in pairs. Check their answers and do remedial teaching as necessary.

SPEAKING

10A Check the questions and example. Give Ss 5 mins to write their answers in note form. *Weaker Ss* could work in pairs. Provide help with language Ss need.

B While Ss tell their stories in groups, make notes of problems for feedback. Check which stories Ss thought were the funniest/most interesting and invite Ss to tell them to the class. Do a correction slot as appropriate.

Homework ideas
• **Ex 10:** Ss write the story of their trip/journey.
• **Language bank** 5.1 Ex A–B, p137
• **Workbook** Ex 1–7, p28–29

TRAVEL TIPS

Introduction

Ss learn and practise the use of verb patterns and vocabulary for travel items in the context of journeys.

> **SUPPLEMENTARY MATERIALS**
> **Resource bank** p165
> **Language bank** p136–137
> **Photo bank** p155 (Ss may need dictionaries.)
> **Warm up:** photos of people on different kinds of holiday, doing different activities, e.g. sightseeing, eating/drinking in outdoor cafés, relaxing/swimming on beach, walking, camping, skiing, water sports, extreme sports, yoga/meditation, painting/craft-making, horse riding
> **Ex 8A:** a map of Poland
> **Ex 8C:** realia: advertisements with itineraries for weekend breaks/holidays to use as prompts for Ss' emails

Warm up

Show Ss the photos you've brought of different kinds of holiday/holiday activities. If you haven't got any photos, elicit ten different kinds of holiday and write them on the board. Ss work in pairs/groups, describe each type of holiday and then choose two they like and two they don't like. In feedback, elicit and discuss the three most/least popular types of holiday.

VOCABULARY TRAVEL ITEMS

1 Give Ss 2–3 mins to discuss their answers. **Stronger classes** could use the words in the box in Ex 2A.

2A Check the rubric and the words in the box. Ss should be familiar with all of them. If you have a **weaker class**, teach/check the words via the photos in the Photo bank, Ex 1 p155. Give Ss 3–4 mins to do the exercise: they must give reasons for their answers. In feedback, discuss Ss' reasons for their choices and find out what the consensus is.

> **Suggested answers:**
> 1 suitcase, digital camera, sunhat, souvenirs
> 2 notebook, waterproof clothes, walking boots, rucksack, money belt
> 3 suitcase, notebook, digital camera, map, binoculars, umbrella

> **Teaching tip**
>
> With **weaker classes**, it is a good idea to teach/check target vocabulary using the photos in the Photo bank where appropriate, before asking them to complete a vocabulary exercise.

B Ss should listen to the words first. Tell them that they should listen and notice the stress each time. They then listen, repeat and underline the stress in each word.

> **Answers:** suitcase, notebook, digital camera, souvenirs, waterproof clothes, dictionary, walking boots, sun hat, backpack, money belt, binoculars, map, umbrella

C Give Ss 3–4 mins to discuss the questions. While Ss work in pairs, monitor and make notes on their pronunciation for feedback. **Stronger classes** could do Ex 1 in the Photo bank first and incorporate the words there into this exercise.

> ▷ **PHOTOBANK** p155
>
> **1** Ss can use dictionaries to check words they don't know.
> **2** Do this exercise now or use it as revision in the next class.
>
> **Answers:**
> 1 1N 2O 3H 4K 5C 6P 7L 8I 9B 10J 11Q
>   12D 13A 14G 15R 16M 17F 18E

LISTENING

3A Ss listen and tick the items they hear in the box in Ex 2A.

> **Answers:** 1 dictionary 2 walking boots
> 3 digital camera, binoculars 4 sun hat, waterproof clothes
> 5 suitcase, souvenirs, backpack 6 money belt 7 notebook

B Elicit the answer for question 1. If Ss can't remember the information, give them a tip. Point out that they can work out what kind of word they need each time, e.g. question 2: there will be a noun or verb + -ing after love. Give Ss 3–4 mins to complete the sentences but do not confirm answers yet – Ss will check them in Ex 3C.

> **Answers:** 1 a few words of the language 2 walking 3 photos
> 4 a warm place 5 wild 6 money 7 remember

C Ss listen and check their answers, and then compare them in pairs. Play the recording again if necessary. In feedback, nominate Ss to give the answers (in bold in the audio script below).

> **Unit 5 Recording 3**
>
> 1 These days, we always expect to hear English in tourist areas. Most people working in tourism speak it, but I always want to talk to local people and many of them don't speak English. So **I try to learn a few words of the language**, especially 'please' and 'thank you', and I always take a small dictionary.
> 2 **I love walking** when I go on holiday … 'cause I think … I think you see more, so I always take a really good pair of walking boots.
> 3 I think a good digital camera is important when you travel. **I always take a lot of photos**. And I also take binoculars.
> 4 When I'm not travelling for work, **I usually spend my holidays in a warm place**, so I always take a sun hat. But when I go somewhere during the winter or rainy season, I always take waterproof clothes.
> 5 I think it's a good idea to buy a really good suitcase. And when you pack, leave enough space for souvenirs. On the other hand, **I enjoy travelling in wild places**, so often I take a backpack, not a suitcase. If you decide to go walking, a backpack is much easier to carry.
> 6 **It's best to avoid carrying too much money** because you don't want to look like a rich tourist! Because of this, I always take a money belt on holiday.
> 7 **I need to write things down to remember them** so I take a notebook and pen.

GRAMMAR VERB PATTERNS

> **Watch out!**
>
> It takes time for Ss to acquire confidence with verb patterns. It's important to encourage them to notice them in all contexts: reading/listening texts, exercises and their own speaking and writing.

4A Check the examples. Ss work alone and then compare answers in pairs. In feedback, tell Ss there are no fixed rules for verb patterns – they will learn them as part of the learning process.

> **Answers:** 4 seem to take 5 choose to go 6 enjoy travelling
> 7 decide to go 8 to avoid carrying 9 need to write

B Ss can refer to the sentences in Ex 4A when they do this exercise.

> **Answers:**
> **verb + -ing:** enjoy, avoid
> **verb + infinitive with to:** want, seem, choose, decide, need

C In feedback, elicit examples of sentences with *love/hate* in both forms, e.g. *I love to play/playing tennis.*

> **Answers:**
> **verb + -ing:** finish, imagine, hate, love
> **verb + infinitive with to:** hope, hate, would like, love
> **verbs which can go in both columns:** hate, love

> ▷ **LANGUAGEBANK 5.2** p136–137
>
> Check the table/notes with Ss, paying special attention to the verbs *love* and *hate*. Ss can refer to the notes when they do the exercises. *Weaker Ss* should do Ex A and B in class.
>
> > **Answers:**
> > **A** **1** to visit **2** living **3** drinking **4** to play **5** to have **6** swimming **7** to finish **8** reading
> > **B** Would you like ~~doing~~ *to do* something more exciting? Mad Dog Tours is perfect for people who hate ~~spend~~ *spending* time asleep on a beach. If you enjoy ~~to travel~~ *travelling* to strange places, if you don't mind ~~to stay~~ *staying* in cheap hotels and want ~~knowing~~ *to know* how the local people really live, we promise ~~helping~~ *to help* you. Cheap holidays are our speciality. If you choose ~~booking~~ *to book* your holiday with Mad Dog Tours, you can expect ~~living~~ *to live* your dreams!

5 Check the example. Ask: *Is there a difference between hope and expect?* (hope = when you want something to happen; expect = when you think something is going to happen) Ss discuss the question in pairs. Tell Ss to think about differences in the meaning of the verbs when they do the exercise. They work alone and then compare answers in pairs. *Weaker Ss* can refer to the table on p136. In feedback, check Ss' answers and elicit sentences using the verbs that don't fit, e.g. 1 *I enjoy flying long distances on a plane.*

> **Answers:** **2** imagine **3** needs **4** like **5** want **6** enjoy **7** expect **8** avoid

6A Elicit some examples for question 1. While Ss write, monitor and prompt them to self-correct. They can compare their answers, but try to check all Ss' sentences before they do Ex 6B. Also note if Ss have remembered that *hate* and *love* can be followed by both forms.

B Ss should work with a different partner for this exercise. They compare notes to decide what they have or don't have in common and prepare to report back to the class in feedback.

SPEAKING

7 Ss look at the photos and read the questions and examples. Ask, e.g. *Do you like looking at beautiful buildings? Do you put your photos on Facebook?* Give Ss 4–5 mins to discuss the questions and encourage them to use the verbs they've practised in the lesson. They should make notes of their partner's answers for feedback/homework. Note down mistakes Ss make with verb patterns. Ss could then compare their answers with another pair to find out what they have in common, and report their findings back to the class. Do a correction slot if necessary.

WRITING USING SEQUENCERS

8A Use a map of Poland if possible: elicit/show Ss where Warsaw, Kraków and Łódź are. Give Ss 2 mins to read the email before they discuss their answers in pairs. Check answers in feedback.

> **Answers:**
> **good things**: saw lots of interesting sights in Warsaw, had a beautiful day in Kraków, loved Łódź, met lots of friendly Poles
> **bad things:** rain in Kraków

B Check the example (*First*). Ss then underline the other four words/phrases and compare their answers in pairs. In feedback, check the meaning of *after a while* (after a period of time) and the use of commas after the last three sequencers. Ask: *Which words can't change places?* (*first* and *finally*) Practise further: ask: *What did you do this morning/yesterday/last Saturday?*

> **Answers:** Then, after a while, After that, Finally

C First, elicit brief details of Ss' recent holidays. If they haven't travelled recently, provide them with advertisements with itineraries of holidays from the newspapers/internet as prompts for the email. They could also use their ideas from Ex 10 p49. Give Ss 6–10 mins to write a draft of their emails, using the sequencers from Ex 8A. To build Ss' accuracy and confidence with their writing, encourage them to show each other their drafts and exchange ideas/advice. They then write a corrected final draft.

> **Optional extra activity**
>
> Ss exchange their emails from Ex 8C with as many classmates as possible. Alternatively, display them around the room on walls/tables so Ss can walk round and read them. In feedback, check which were the most interesting and why.

> **Homework ideas**
>
> • **Ex 8C:** Ss write another email about last weekend or another trip. They send it to you or a classmate or put it on the class blog.
> • **Language bank** 5.2 Ex A–B, p137
> • **Workbook** Ex 1–5, p30–31

YOU CAN'T MISS IT

Introduction

Ss learn and practise asking for and giving simple directions in the context of tourism. They also learn how to show and check understanding.

> **SUPPLEMENTARY MATERIALS**
> **Resource bank** p166
> **Language bank** p136–137
> **Warm up:** a map of Brazil, Argentina, Paraguay to show where the Iguaçu Falls are

Warm up

Use the photos to lead in to the lesson. Ss cover the texts and look at the photos. Ask: *Do you know this place?* Don't elicit or tell them more than the name: *the Iguaçu Falls*. Then ask the questions below (or write them on the board) and give the alternative answers. Ss discuss each answer in pairs and write it down (the correct answers are underlined below).

1 *The Iguaçu Falls are on the border of which countries?* Brazil, Peru, Argentina?
2 *How many falls are there – 275 or 157?*
3 *How high the highest fall – 64 or 82 metres?*
4 *Are they bigger or smaller than the Niagara Falls?*

Check answers and elicit anything else Ss know about the falls. Show them a map of the area if possible.

> **Culture notes**
>
> **The Iguaçu Falls** are located on the border of Brazil and Argentina. There are 275 waterfalls and some of them are 82 metres high. The Devil's Throat is the most impressive: water falls over a U-shaped cliff, 150 metres wide and 700 metres long. The Falls were nominated as one of the world's New7Wonders of Nature. **Foz do Iguaçu** is a Brazilian town near the falls.

VOCABULARY TOURISM

1 Check/Teach and drill new words in the box. Ss look at the photos and discuss the question in pairs. In feedback, nominate Ss to answer.

> **Answers:** boat trip, tourists, sightseeing, natural wonder

2A Give Ss 1 min to make predictions. They should cover the text. Check/Elicit their predictions and write them in note form on the board.

B Ss read the text and check their predictions against the information in the text. In feedback, ask: *Were your predictions correct? Why/Why not?*

> **Answers:** The man is a tour guide. He lives in Brazil, takes tourists to the Iguaçu Falls on both the Brazilian and Argentinian sides and then takes them shopping in Paraguay.

C Give Ss 3–4 mins to discuss their answers. They make a list of three/four reasons why they'd like the job or not and report back to the class in feedback. After they've done this, do a show of hands to find out how many Ss would like to do this job.

FUNCTION ASKING FOR/GIVING DIRECTIONS

3A Check the rubric and ask Ss to look at the map. Elicit where the tourist is. Play the recording. Ss listen and write the destinations on the map. Play the recording again if necessary. Check Ss' answers.

> **Answers: 1** Argentina (bottom) **2** Brazil (middle)
> **3** Paraguay (top)

B After Ss have listened to/read the audio script, elicit one or two examples. Then give them 5 mins to underline the phrases and compare answers in pairs. Check answers (in bold in the audio script below). Illustrate the meaning using the map.

Unit 5 Recording 4

1 To get to Argentina, **you wait at the corner** for the bus. **It takes you down** Avenida das Cataratas **and right** into Avenida Mercosul. **The bus goes straight on** for about twenty-five minutes. **Cross the bridge** and you're in Argentina.
2 To see the Iguaçu Falls on the Brazilian side, **you turn right and just go straight on down** Avenida das Cataratas and Highway 469 and the Falls are **in front of you. You can't miss them** – they're the biggest in the world!
3 To get to Paraguay, **you have to go left. You go along** the main road **through** the park **past** the trees. Then **you turn right** and **you're on** Avenida Kubitschek. Let's see. From there **you keep going until you reach** Highway 277. **Go left.** The bridge **is at the end of** the highway. **Cross the bridge** and you're in Paraguay.

4 Give Ss time to study the diagrams carefully and check the example. Then they label the pictures and compare answers in pairs. Check/drill them in feedback. Alternatively, Ss check them in the Language bank 5.3, p136.

> **Answers: B** go past the turning **C** go along the main road
> **D** take the first right **E** keep going until you reach (the border)
> **F** at the corner **G** go through the (centre of town)
> **H** cross the bridge **I** go straight on **J** in front of you

5A Check the rubric. Play the recording twice if necessary before you check Ss' answers (underlined in the audio script below).

> **Answers: 1** F **2** T **3** T

B Ss complete the notes alone/in pairs. After they've listened to check and compared their answers in pairs, do feedback (the answers are in bold in the audio script below).

> **Answers: 1** (about) ten, music **2** left, (about) fifteen, sign
> **3** left, restaurant, left

Unit 5 Recording 5

Conversation 1
A: Excuse me. We're trying to get to the carnival. Is this the right bus stop?
B: Yes, but you don't need the bus. It's very close.
A: Oh! Can we walk?
B: Yes, **it takes about ten minutes** from here. Just go straight on. **You'll hear the music!**
A: OK. Thank you very much.

Conversation 2
A: Excuse me, can you help me? I'm looking for the Plaza Hotel. Is this the right way?
B: Um … Plaza Hotel, Plaza Hotel. Yes, keep going, past the cinema and **take the first left**.
A: OK.
B: Then **keep going for about fifteen minutes** until you reach the end of the road. And **you'll see the sign** for the hotel. You can't miss it.
A: OK. Can you show me on the map?
B: Sure.

Conversation 3

A: Excuse me, we want to get to The Grand Motel. Is it far?

B: Um … sorry, I've no idea. Jim, do you know?

C: What?

B: The Grand Motel?

C: The Grand Motel? Yeah, it's just over there. Just go to the end of this street. **Go left** and go past the … um … there's a restaurant. **Go past the restaurant and it's on the left.**

A: On the left. So I need to go to the end of the street, turn left, go past the restaurant and it's on the left.

C: Yeah, that's it.

A: Thanks a lot.

▷ **LANGUAGEBANK 5.3** p136–137

Ss can refer to the information in the pictures/tables when they do the exercises.

> **Answers:**
> **A 1** h) **2** e) **3** d) **4** g) **5** a) **6** j) **7** i) **8** b) **9** c) **10** f)
> **B 1** along **2** reach **3** go **4** in **5** cross **6** take **7** through
>   **8** corner

LEARN TO **SHOW/CHECK UNDERSTANDING**

6A Ss listen to the extracts and then do the activity alone/in pairs. Nominate Ss to give the answers.

> **Answers:**
> **Extract 2**
> Excuse me, can you help me? (A)
> Is this the right way? (A)
> keep going (E)
> OK. (U)
> you'll see (E)
> You can't miss it. (E)
> Can you show me on the map? (A)
> **Extract 3**
> Is it far? (A)
> So I need to (U)

B Ss refer to the phrases in bold in the extracts in Ex 6A to find the answers to this exercise.

> **Answers: 1** Is this the right way?   **2** Keep going.
> **3** You can't miss it.

C Ss now practise the intonation in questions. Play the recording and drill the questions. Elicit answers in feedback.

> **Answer:** Words near the end of the question are said louder and with a higher voice. (They carry the information the speaker is asking for.)

Unit 5 Recording 7

1 Can you help me?

2 Is it far?

3 Can we walk?

4 Can you show me on the map?

5 Is this the right way?

---

7 Monitor while Ss practise to check/help them with their pronunciation. ***Stronger Ss*** could try to memorise/rehearse one of the conversations and act it out to the class.

SPEAKING

8 Prepare Ss for the role-plays in two stages. First divide the class into As and Bs. Student As read the situations on p161, and Student Bs on p163. Check if they have any doubts about language in the tasks. Put Student As in pairs, and Student Bs in pairs. Give them 3–4 mins to study their maps and prepare the questions they need to ask to get directions. Monitor and provide support where needed, especially with the pronunciation of the names. Tell Ss that the town hall and florists are on both maps. Then put Ss in A/B pairs, facing each other. They take turns to ask for directions and write the places on their maps. Monitor discreetly, making notes for feedback. In feedback, invite Ss to ask for/give directions in open pairs across the class. Give feedback and do remedial work as necessary.

Homework ideas

- **Ex 8:** Ss write a conversation asking for/giving directions based on the maps on p161 or 163.
- **Language bank** 5.3 Ex A–B, p137
- **Workbook** Ex 1–4, p32

FULL CIRCLE

Introduction

Ss watch an extract from the BBC documentary *Full Circle*, presented by Michael Palin of Monty Python fame. The series was made in 1995 and broadcast in 1997. Ss then learn and practise how to apply for an award and write an application.

> **SUPPLEMENTARY MATERIALS**
> **Warm up:** a map of South America and photos of famous places there if possible, e.g. Rio de Janeiro, the Sugar Loaf, Machu Picchu, Lake Titicaca, Perito Moreno glacier, Angel Falls
> **Ex 3A:** dictionaries
> **Ex 5B:** photos of Easter Island and its statues
> **Ex 6A:** Ss can use computer facilities to research places or bring photos of suitable places for an inspiring journey, e.g. Machu Picchu, Angkor Wat, Petra.

Warm up

Lead in and create interest in the lesson. Show Ss a map of South America and elicit the countries/capital cities. Ask: *What do you know about these countries? Have you visited any of them? What famous places can you visit there?* If you've brought photos, use them as prompts. Ss discuss their answers in pairs/groups. In *multilingual classes*, pair Ss with others who come from/know South America. Elicit/Discuss answers with the class.

DVD PREVIEW

> **Culture notes**
> **Michael Palin**, English comedian and actor, is well known as one of the Monty Python group. Since 1980, he's also become famous as a presenter of BBC travel documentaries, which are said to be responsible for the *Palin effect*: places he's visited have often become popular tourist attractions, e.g. Machu Picchu in Peru.
> **Arica**, the most northern city in Chile, is situated on the Pacific coast, 20 km from Peru and 319 km from La Paz, Bolivia.
> **La Paz** is located in the Andes at an altitude of 3,660 metres, the world's highest capital city. A small train takes passengers between the two cities.

1A Do this in open class. Nominate different Ss to share their experiences with the class.

B Ss look at the photos. Ask: *Do you know this man/the Andes?* Elicit Ss' answers but don't confirm details yet. Give Ss 2–3 mins to read the information and answer the questions. Elicit answers and give more information about Palin from the Culture notes if appropriate. Then ask further comprehension questions, e.g. *How far did Michael Palin travel?* (50,000 miles) *How long did it take?* (ten months) *What did he learn?* (how to cook eggs in a volcano and how to make music with horses' bones) *Where does he travel in this episode?* (across the Andes from Chile to Bolivia) Elicit/Discuss answers with the class.

> **Answers:**
> 1 Michael Palin is an actor and travel writer.
> 2 the seventeen countries on the Pacific coast
> 3 by train

DVD VIEW

2 Give Ss 1–2 mins to look at the list of problems, then play the DVD. Before class feedback, get Ss to compare answers in pairs.

> **Answers:** the air is thin and it's difficult to breathe; the train stops a lot because of animals/cars on the track; the train is very slow

> **Alternative approach**
> Put Ss in pairs: one student facing the screen and the other facing away from it. Play the DVD. Both Ss do the exercise and then compare their answers. Ss then swap places. They watch the DVD again and compare their answers. Check them in feedback.

3A Give Ss 3–4 mins to check the words/phrases they don't know in their dictionaries. They work alone/in pairs. Check their answers in feedback and drill the new language.

B Ss watch the DVD and number the sentences. Play it again to check/elicit Ss' answers (in bold in the DVD script below). Then ask: *Why was it the journey of a lifetime/the journey of everyone's dreams?* Give them 2–3 mins to discuss their answers in pairs or as a whole class.

> **Answers:** 2 c) 3 d) 4 b) 5 e) 6 f) 7 g)

> **Alternative approach**
> Exploit the DVD for extra comprehension and attention to interesting detail. Pause it at suitable points and ask questions, e.g. *Why is Michael Palin embarrassed?* (Because he's travelling with so many suitcases.) *How many suitcases does he have?* (45) *What was the rail bus built for?* (for the branch lines of Munich) *Where do they cook the food?* (a small galley on the train) *How does the woman feel?* (terrible) *Why did the train have to stop twice?* (Because there were llamas and then cars on the railway track.)

4 Ss discuss the questions in pairs/groups and make a note of their partners' answers. In feedback, find out how many Ss would like to make this journey and why.

DVD 5 Full Circle

M = Michael Palin W = Woman

M: **Twice a week, a railway service leaves Arica** for the Bolivian capital, La Paz.
This is going to take forever. Do you want a hand? Can I help? It's just … it's only two of you to do all this. **It's going to take two hours.** OK.
I've rarely felt quite as embarrassed at travelling with forty-five cases. **Some passengers are local**, some have come from countries far away. None have come quite as far as the train itself. We're to cross the Andes on a rail bus built for the branch lines of Munich thirty years ago.
From the world's tiniest galley, two of our three-man Bolivian crew produce the first of several hot dinners.
Three and a half hours after leaving the Pacific, we're at 10,000 feet and still climbing. Where the air is thin and simple things suddenly become difficult.
How are you feeling?
W: Terrible! Terrible!
M: Is it the altitude?
W: It's the air, it gives you the headache … nausea … and er … it's hard to breathe. You start to wheeze.
M: Six and a half hours and a few llamas after leaving Arica, **we've reached the Bolivian border**. We're entering the poorest country in South America.
Is it the journey of a lifetime?
W: It's the journey of everyone's dreams.

M: A few hours later, the lights of La Paz twinkle below us. As you can see, we've got a right of way problem here. This is the railway line and this is the road. And er … our conductor is trying to get people to clear out of the way. That's it. They've cleared them out, so we can go on. Getting to La Paz is not easy. To our enormous relief, the lights are still on at La Paz station, when our heroic vehicle finally pulls in. **We've crossed the Andes at 16.4 miles an hour.**

speakout an award

5A Ss read the text and answer the questions. In feedback, check *original* and *inspiring*.

> **Answers:**
> 1 €5,000 for the best idea for an original and inspiring journey anywhere in the world
> 2 receive training in film-making and record their experiences for a future programme

> **Culture notes**
>
> **Easter Island**, a Chilean territory, is in the South Pacific Ocean. It's a World Heritage Site due to the hundreds of monumental statues, called *moai*, built by the native Rapanui population between 400–1700AD. The population of the island is around 6,000 nowadays.

B Ss should make notes of their answers and then compare them in pairs. Play the recording again if needed. In feedback, elicit Ss' answers. Find out what they know about Easter Island and show them photos of it if possible.

> **Answers:**
> 1 Easter Island
> 2 She wants to experience the local culture, their music, food and way of life, and find out about their traditions and what they think of their history.

C Ss read the key phrases and tick the ones they hear. After they've compared their answers in pairs, play the recording again. Pause at each key phrase (in bold in the audio script below) to elicit/check the answers. Drill the sentences and ask further comprehension questions, e.g. *What's Easter Island like? How are they getting there?*

> **Answers:** Ss should tick all the phrases except *Some of the problems we're going to face include …* and *It should be an inspiring trip.*

Unit 5 Recording 8

OK, well, **we would like to go to** Easter Island. It is very isolated, very far from other places, and the nearest country is Chile, over two thousand miles away. We are going to travel there by plane and stay with different families and **the trip is going to take** three months. **We want to experience the local culture**, their music, food and way of life. So **our plan is to speak to the local people** about these things and to film them. **We hope to find out about their traditions** and to see what they think of their history. Well, finally, my husband and I always wanted to go to Easter Island. I read about it when I was a child and I saw pictures of these amazing stone heads on the island. So for us, **this is the journey of our dreams**.

6A Brainstorm places Ss would like to visit if they won the award and write them on the board. If computer facilities are available, Ss could research things to see/do there. Otherwise, prompt ideas/ support **weaker Ss** with photos of suitable places for an inspiring journey. Give Ss the necessary amount of time to prepare and make notes. Provide help where needed. Remind them to use the key phrases in their notes.

B Ss present their ideas to the class. The other Ss listen and note down ideas that are original/inspiring. At the same time, make your own notes with examples of good language and problems. In feedback, discuss Ss' presentations. The class votes for the winner of the award. Give feedback to Ss now or at the beginning of the next lesson.

writeback an application

7A Ss read the application and match the paragraphs with the headings. In feedback, ask Ss to justify their answers with, e.g. examples of goals/objectives and details.

> **Answers:** **1** c) **2** a) **3** b)

B Ss work alone/with the same partner as in Ex 6. They write a draft of their application, using the model in Ex 7A and their ideas from Ex 6. Encourage a collaborative approach to the process of writing to build Ss' confidence. They can show their drafts to each other/you and ask for and give opinions and advice. Ss write a final draft of the application when they're ready and send it to you or other Ss for a reply, or put it on the class blog.

> **Homework ideas**
> - **Ex 4:** Ss write their answers to the questions.
> - **Ex 7B:** Ss write a final draft of their application.

LOOKBACK

Introduction

As well as revising and practising the language in the unit, use the Lookback exercises to provide you with an informal assessment of your Ss' speaking skills. Fluency practice is usually given in Ex B or C in each section. When assessing speaking skills, take these four areas into account: accuracy of grammar, range of vocabulary, fluency and pronunciation.

> **SUPPLEMENTARY MATERIALS**
> **Ex 6C:** simple maps of your town/area, especially with *multilingual classes*

TRANSPORT

1A First, elicit one or two examples, e.g. *minibus: This type of transport is bigger than a car. It has four wheels and usually carries 10–15 people.* Ss write their sentences alone and check their answers in pairs. Monitor and assess Ss' understanding of transport vocabulary and the accuracy of their sentences. Provide extra support for **weaker Ss** and allow them to check vocabulary in the Photo bank on p155 if necessary. **Fast-finishers** should write more sentences. It's important that Ss' sentences are as accurate as possible for Ex 1B.

B Check the example and pair Ss with different partners from those in Ex 1A. Monitor and make notes of errors with the meaning and pronunciation of transport vocabulary. In feedback, nominate different pairs to read their sentences/respond across the class. Do corrections and remedial teaching if necessary.

PAST SIMPLE AND PAST CONTINUOUS

2A Check the example and use of the two tenses. Also check any unfamiliar words. Give Ss 2–3 mins to write full sentences. Monitor and note down problems they have with the two tenses for feedback. Check answers and, for each question, ask: *Why is the verb in the past simple/past continuous?*

> **Answers:** 2 were crossing, destroyed   3 ran, was raining
> 4 was wandering, met   5 were sailing, saw   6 was living, realised

B Give Ss 2–3 mins to answer the question and try to remember as much detail as possible about the films. Check their answers or allow them to check in their books on p48, 161 and 163.

> **Answers:** 1 Rabbit-Proof Fence   2 Kon-Tiki   3 Rabbit-Proof Fence
> 4 Into the Wild   5 Kon-Tiki   6 Into the Wild

3 Give Ss 1 min to note down where they were and what they were doing at the specific times yesterday. Drill the questions, e.g. *Where were you yesterday at 6 o'clock in the morning? What were you doing?* Highlight/Remind Ss of the weak (unstressed) form of *were*. They then work in pairs and take it in turns to ask and answer the questions, noting down their partner's answers. Monitor and make notes for feedback or assessment purposes. In feedback, Ss tell the class about their partner.

TRAVEL ITEMS

4A Check the example. Ss can do the exercise alone or you could make it into a team game. The first team to finish with the correct spelling *and* pronunciation of the words wins.

> **Answers:** 2 backpack   3 waterproof clothes   4 walking boots
> 5 sun hat   6 souvenirs   7 binoculars   8 notebook
> 9 digital camera   10 money belt

B Check the example and elicit one or two more ideas. Give Ss 3 mins to make as many different sentences as possible. Stop the activity after 3 mins and invite Ss from each pair to give one answer each. The pair with the most sentences wins.

VERB PATTERNS

5A First, do question 1 as an example. Give Ss 2–3 mins to write the answers and compare them in pairs before feedback.

> **Answers:** 1 to go   2 to visit   3 to have   4 to travel   5 travelling
> 6 flying   7 going   8 to have

B Elicit Ss' answers to question 1, e.g. *I always/never/hardly ever/often choose to go somewhere on holiday because a friend recommends it. I prefer to choose it myself./I never know where to go.* Give Ss 2 mins to decide which sentences are true for them and why/why not. Monitor and help them with vocabulary if necessary. Ss then exchange information in pairs. Monitor and assess the accuracy/fluency of their language. Do remedial work in feedback and/or use the information for assessment.

ASKING FOR/GIVING DIRECTIONS

6A Ss read the conversations. Elicit a mistake as an example before Ss work alone. Check answers and drill the conversations.

> **Answers:**
> 1 A: Is this the right way?   B: It's in on the right.
> 2 A: Is it far?   B: You can't miss it.
> 3 B: Keep going long along the main road. Then you'll see a sign and it's in front to of you.

B Monitor while Ss practise the conversations to assess and help them with their pronunciation. Invite pairs to read them to the class and do any remedial pronunciation work needed with sentence stress and intonation.

C If you haven't brought maps of your town/area in relation to the school or Ss' houses, they could draw simple ones to make the task clearer and provide authenticity. You can adapt the places mentioned in the instructions to your Ss' knowledge of the area around the school. Give Ss time to prepare for the role-play and monitor/support them as needed. During the activity (depending on your aim: revision or assessment), monitor and make notes on errors with the target language or assess Ss' speaking skills.

> **BBC interviews and worksheet**
> **Do you enjoy travelling to different countries?**
> In this video people describe what they like and don't like about travelling and whether they'd like to live in another country. The video also extends Ss' vocabulary of travel and holidays.

OVERVIEW

6.1 KEEPING FIT

VOCABULARY | health
READING | identify specific information in an article about types of exercise
GRAMMAR | present perfect + *for/since*
PRONUNCIATION | sentence stress
SPEAKING | talk about your lifestyle

6.2 THE FUTURE OF FOOD

VOCABULARY | food
LISTENING | listen to a radio interview with a food expert
GRAMMAR | *may, might, will*
PRONUNCIATION | intonation: certainty/uncertainty
SPEAKING | discuss food preferences
WRITING | write about food

6.3 HOW ARE YOU FEELING?

VOCABULARY | illness
LISTENING | listen to conversations between a doctor and her patients
FUNCTION | seeing the doctor
LEARN TO | predict information
PRONUNCIATION | difficult words: spelling v. pronunciation
SPEAKING | explain health problems

6.4 MONITOR ME BBC ⏵ DVD

DVD | watch an extract from a BBC documentary about health
speakout | create a health regime
writeback | health advice

6.5 LOOKBACK

Communicative revision activities

BBC ⏵ INTERVIEWS

What do you do to keep fit?

This video extends discussion of keeping fit and extends Ss' vocabulary of health and fitness. Use the video at the end of Lesson 6.1 or at the start or end of the unit.

KEEPING FIT

Introduction

Ss learn/practise the present perfect + *for/since* in the context of keeping fit. They learn health vocabulary and read/talk about other people's and their own health.

> **SUPPLEMENTARY MATERIALS**
> **Resource bank** p167–168
> **Language bank** p138–139
> **Photo bank:** p156 (Ss may need dictionaries.)
> **Ex 2B:** dictionaries

Warm up

Introduce the topic of the lesson. Ask Ss to write three things that make them feel healthy and three things that make them feel unhealthy. Elicit one or two examples for each category, e.g. *running, eating junk food*. Ss write their lists and compare them in pairs, to see what they have in common. Then ask: *Could you avoid things that make you feel unhealthy? Why/Why not?* Ss discuss their answers in pairs and then as a class.

VOCABULARY   HEALTH

1A Check unfamiliar words, e.g. *fizzy, caffeine*, and elicit examples of good/bad things. Then give Ss 1 min to do the exercise alone.

> **Suggested answers:** junk food (–), exercise classes (+),
> fizzy drinks (–), fresh fruit/vegetables (+), stress/worrying (–),
> alcohol (–), vitamins (+), running (+), caffeine (–), relaxing (+)

B Give Ss 4–5 mins to compare ideas and group the vocabulary under the headings. They should then think of at least three more words/phrases for each category. Elicit the words/phrases in feedback. Then invite Ss to write other words/phrases on the board. Correct/Drill pronunciation problems as they arise.

> **Answers:**
> **food/drink:** junk food, fizzy drinks, fresh fruit/vegetables,
> alcohol, vitamins, caffeine (additional: oily fish, eggs, juice)
> **exercise:** exercise classes, running (additional: playing football,
> playing tennis, swimming)
> **general habits:** stress/worrying, relaxing (additional: watching
> TV, listening to music, sleeping well)

C Check/Drill the questions and example. Give Ss 1 min to think about their answers before they work in pairs. In feedback, nominate Ss to ask/answer the questions in open pairs across the class. Give feedback/correct as needed.

> ▷ **PHOTOBANK** p156
>
> **1** Ss first check unfamiliar words in their dictionaries. They then match the photos with the words. Check answers, paying particular attention to pronunciation/word stress. Ss copy any new sports words into their vocabulary notebooks, underlining the stress.
> **2** Ss discuss the questions in pairs.
>
> > **Answers:**
> > **1B A** rollerblading   **B** badminton   **C** cycling   **D** basketball
> >   **E** cricket   **F** rugby   **G** squash   **H** yoga   **I** tennis
> >   **J** windsurfing   **K** surfing   **L** running   **M** horseriding

6
fitness

READING

2A Give Ss 2–3 mins to discuss the photos and answer the questions. Elicit Ss' answers and write them in note form on the board. This will give Ss a reason to read the text in Ex 2B.

> **Answers:** Towerrunning, PILOXING®, paddle boarding

> **Teaching tip**
>
> In real life, we never read anything without a reason or purpose: it helps us to focus on looking for specific details/information. It's also important to do this in the classroom.

B Give Ss 3–4 mins to read the article. You could ask them what they found out about each sport before they discuss the question. In groups or in open class, Ss then talk about which of the sports they would like to try and why/why not. After discussing the question, check unfamiliar words from the text. Alternatively, put Ss in groups of four. They look at one paragraph each and check 3–4 words/phrases in their dictionaries. They then 'teach' the words to the others.

C Give Ss 3–4 mins to answer the questions in pairs. Let them read the text again if necessary. Check answers in feedback.

> **Answers:**
> 1 It can help to make you feel happier and more relaxed.
> 2 Because there are lots of skyscrapers.
> 3 It uses music and dance like Zumba, power and speed like boxing, and builds strength like pilates.
> 4 At the end of the day (just before sunset) because the water is calm and it's beautiful.

GRAMMAR PRESENT PERFECT + FOR/SINCE

> **Watch out!**
>
> Ss may make mistakes with the use of *for/since*, e.g. *I've lived here since two years.* Check the difference in use carefully. Provide plenty of controlled practice and opportunities for self-/peer correction at all stages of the lesson.

3A Ss answer the questions alone, then compare answers in pairs. Elicit answers in feedback.

> **Answers:** 1 2014   2 yes   3 five years ago   4 yes

B Elicit and check answers further. Draw a timeline as below using a <u>true</u> example about your Ss, e.g. *You've been in this class since September/for six months.* Point to and exploit the timeline while you ask these questions: *Are you in this class <u>now</u>?* (yes) *When did you start?* (in September/six months ago) *How long have you been in this class?* (for six months/since September) *Which word is used with a period of time?* (for) *Which is used with a point in time?* (since) Elicit other phrases that Ss could use, e.g. *since last year, for two weeks.*

> **Answers:** 1 continues now   2 for, since

C Check the examples. Ss copy the table into their notebooks, complete it and compare answers in pairs. In feedback, draw the table on the board and invite Ss to write the answers in the correct column. They can then write 3–4 sentences about themselves (alone or in pairs) using *since/for* and the phrases in the table. Check/Correct their answers.

> **Answers:**
> **for:** a long time, two weeks/months/years, an hour or two
> **since:** July, Saturday, I left university, 2p.m., last night, I was a child/teenager

> ▷ **LANGUAGEBANK 6.1** p138–139
>
> Ss can refer to the notes when they do the exercises. **Weaker classes** should do Ex A and B in class. In Ex A, check *retired* in question 3.
>
> **Answers:**
> **A** 1 haven't done, since   2 haven't been, since   3 was, for
> 4 haven't seen, for   5 left, for
> 6 didn't see, haven't seen, since   7 since
> 8 hasn't driven, since
> **B** 1 since, came   2 bought, have lived, for
> 3 have known, for, met   4 moved, have been, for
> 5 haven't been, since   6 hasn't seen, since   7 since, started
> 8 has had, for

4A Ss do the exercise alone. Monitor and prompt them to self-correct. Elicit answers in feedback.

> **Answers:** 1 've done, since   2 've had, for   3 've known, since
> 4 've lived, for   5 've wanted, for

B Elicit answers to question 1 that are *true* for your Ss. Ss then compare answers in pairs; they should check both the form of the present perfect and the use of *since/for*. Again, monitor and prompt Ss to self-correct/correct each other. In feedback, elicit some answers and recheck the use of *since/for*.

5A Tell Ss there are eleven questions. Play the first two and check the example answers. Then elicit other possible answers. Play the remaining questions. Ss listen and write their answers. With **weaker classes**, play the recording first for Ss to familiarise themselves with the questions. Ss may need to hear the questions again after they've written their answers.

B Ask the first question and elicit Ss' answers. They then work in pairs. If they can't remember the questions, they just compare their answers. In feedback, elicit/give Ss the questions and nominate Ss to answer. Correct/Drill sentences as needed.

> **Unit 6** Recording 1
>
> 1 Do you live in a town or by the sea?
> 2 How long have you lived there?
> 3 How long have you lived in the house you live in now?
> 4 What is the name of your best friend?
> 5 How long have you known him or her?
> 6 Do you work or study?
> 7 How long have you worked or studied where you are now?
> 8 What hobby do you enjoy?
> 9 How long have you done it for?
> 10 Do you have a bicycle or a car?
> 11 How long have you had it?

6 Play the first question as an example. Write it on the board, elicit/underline the stressed words and drill it with the class. Ss then listen and write the other questions. They compare them in pairs and then listen again to underline the stressed words. In feedback, elicit the questions and drill them chorally and individually. Beat the stress and highlight the intonation with your hands/arms.

Answers:
2 How <u>long</u> have you <u>known</u> him?
3 How <u>long</u> have you <u>had</u> it?
4 How <u>long</u> have you <u>studied</u>?
5 How <u>long</u> have you <u>worked</u> there?

SPEAKING

7A Check the topics/photos first. Then check the example questions and elicit alternative ideas, e.g. *Do you live in a flat or a house?* Ss then write their own questions. Monitor and prompt them to self-correct and write accurate questions to use in Ex 7B.

Suggested answers:
hobbies/sport: Do you do (T'ai Chi)? How long have you done it?
possessions: Do you have (a watch)? How long have you had it?
work/study/school: Do you (work in an office)? How long have you (worked there)?

B First, check/drill the example conversation. Ss then ask and answer their questions in groups. Monitor and encourage them to find out as much information as possible and note it down. At the same time, make notes of problems Ss have with the present perfect and *since/for*.

C Give Ss time to prepare the information about their group, then nominate Ss to tell the class. Give feedback on Ss' performance as necessary.

Homework ideas

- **Ex 7:** Ss write sentences about their group using their notes.
- **Language bank** 6.1 Ex A–B, p139
- **Workbook** Ex 1–6, p33–34

THE FUTURE OF FOOD

Introduction

Ss learn and practise the use of *may*, *might* and *will* to talk about future possibilities/predictions in the context of food.

> **SUPPLEMENTARY MATERIALS**
> **Resource bank** p169
> **Language bank** p138–139
> **Photo bank** p157
> **Ex 6A:** a map of Colombia and photos of the dishes mentioned in the text (mondongo, peto)

Warm up

Lead in to the topic. Ss think of items of food/drink in as many different colours as possible, e.g. *yellow: pepper, banana; green: apple, peas; white: milk*. Give them 3 mins to make a list in pairs. Elicit/Write the colours Ss thought of on the board. Then elicit the names of food/drink to write next to the correct colour. Alternatively, Ss take turns to write the words on the board. Elicit the word stress and drill the pronunciation.

VOCABULARY FOOD

1A Ss use the food from the Warm up exercise and put it into the four categories, e.g. *fruit: apple*. Give them 3 mins to write their new lists and add other words they think of.

B Ss compare their lists and then check them in the Photo bank. They should add the names of food they didn't have to their lists.

> ▷ **PHOTOBANK** p157
>
> Elicit/Drill the names of food/drink that were new to Ss. They then discuss the questions in Ex 1 and 2. In feedback, find out which foods Ss eat a lot of and which they think are good for you.

C Check the food in the photos. Ask: *Where do these dishes come from?* (falafel: Egypt, sushi: Japan, paella: Spain, burrito: Mexico) *What's in them?* (falafel: fried onions, chickpeas or beans, spices; sushi: raw fish, rice; paella: meat or fish/seafood, rice, vegetables; burrito: minced meat, beans, chilli, tortilla) Ss then discuss the questions and make notes of their partner's answers for feedback. Check what Ss' favourite foods are and how often they eat food from other countries.

LISTENING

2A Ss look at the pictures, read the sentences and answer the questions in pairs, giving reasons if possible. In feedback, elicit Ss' answers and reasons. Then move on to Ex 2B.

B Ss listen and check their answers from Ex 2A.

> **Answers:** 1 T 2 T 3 T

C Read the Speakout tip with Ss and use it with Ex 2C. First, do an example. Ss look at question 1 and work out what type of word it is (noun). Elicit/Give Ss the word *groups*. Ss then do the exercise alone/in pairs, using the tip if they're not sure of the words. Ss listen to the recording again and check their answers (in bold in the audio script below). In feedback, elicit/check the meaning and pronunciation of each answer. In *stronger classes*, ask further comprehension questions related to each answer.

> **Answers:** 1 groups 2 farm 3 lab 4 seaweed 5 knife
> 6 information

speakout TIP

Encourage Ss to use this tip with Ex 2C and any time they come across words they don't know.

> **Unit 6 Recording 3**
>
> I = Interviewer   S = Sue
>
> **I:** Sue, what are the latest food trends?
> **S:** We have lots of interesting developments, and even possible solutions for world problems related to food.
> **I:** Great. So can you kind of …
> **S:** Well, the key question is always what to eat, and here **we may see some changes, things that you might not understand as food groups**.
> **I:** Can you give an example?
> **S:** An example is insects.
> **I:** As a food group?
> **S:** Well, in Latin America, Asia and Africa, people have eaten insects for thousands of years, but it's only now that we in the West are seeing what a good food source they are. **Insects are rich in protein, low in fat and easy to farm.**
> **I:** So spiders and ants may be on the menu?
> **S:** We might see them on menus in the West. Now, technology will also play a part in the future of food. **Scientists have already found ways to create meat in the lab.**
> **I:** Right, but it tastes awful, doesn't it?
> **S:** It tastes awful now, but maybe it won't in the future. And as well as meat made in a lab, **we're also looking at ways to make proteins out of things like mud and wood and also seaweed**.
> **I:** It seems incredible that mud might be something we can eat.
> **S:** Well, it's the same for seaweed, which again is easy to farm because it's everywhere. Um… **other developments on your kitchen table include an intelligent knife**.
> **I:** What's that?
> **S:** An intelligent knife will tell you all about the food it's cutting. So, say you cut a slice of meat, the knife will tell you how much protein and fat is in the meat, where it's from, how old it is.
> **I:** That's amazing!
> **S:** **Really giving people more information about their food.**

GRAMMAR MAY, MIGHT, WILL

> **Watch out!**
>
> Ss often use *will* to talk about future plans/arrangements instead of *be going to* or the present continuous, e.g. *I'll have dinner with Sue and Dave tomorrow night*, not *I'm having dinner … .* Here *will* is presented with *may/might*, which helps to avoid this problem in the practice exercises. However, it's important to be aware of this problem and clarify/correct the mistake consistently.

3A With books closed, write the sentences on the board and underline the words in bold in the book. Ss copy them down. Ask questions 1–3 and elicit/check answers. Elicit/Check the verb pattern: *may/might/will/won't* + infinitive without *to*. Then ask Ss to make the verbs in questions a) and b) negative, e.g. *We might not see them on menus./We may not see (any) changes* (NOT *mightn't* or *mayn't*). Ss then underline examples of the verbs in the sentences in Ex 2A.

> **Answers:** 1 d) 2 a), b) 3 c)

▷ **LANGUAGEBANK 6.2** p138–139

Read/Check the notes with Ss. They can refer to them when they do the exercises. **Weaker Ss** should do Ex A and B in class.

Answers:
A 1 e) 2 d) 3 a) 4 f) 5 b) 6 c)
B 1 I ~~don't will~~ *won't* know my exam results until August.
  2 Will you ~~to~~ go to university next year?
  3 Anna is very busy so she may not ~~comes~~ tonight.
  4 The traffic is heavy so they may ~~to~~ be late.
  5 Edson ~~mights~~ be the best player we have ever seen.
  6 I might ~~go not~~ *not go* to the exercise class today.
  7 We'll ~~to~~ be back at 6p.m.

B Ss listen to the sentences and note down their answers. Get them to compare answers in pairs before class feedback.

Answers: sentences 2 and 3

C Play the recording and elicit the answer. Then get Ss to practise the intonation by repeating the sentences.

Answer: *Will, might, may* and *won't* sound longer when the speaker is not sure.

Unit 6   Recording 4

1 In twenty years, food won't be much different from today.
2 Eating habits might change.
3 Fast food restaurants may change their menu.
4 People will always sit down for a family meal.

4A Check the example and ask: *Is it possible/probable/certain?* (possible) Ss then work alone and write the most suitable responses. Monitor and provide support.

Suggested answers:
2 You might lose weight.
3 It might be expensive.
4 You'll feel healthier.
5 It might not be open.
6 You might not like it.
7 You'll enjoy it.

B Check/Drill the example conversation. Ss then work in pairs. Monitor and encourage them to extend their responses. In feedback, nominate pairs to say a sentence/respond in open pairs across the class. Give feedback as needed.

SPEAKING

5A Check the rubric and statements. Discuss question 1 with the class. Ask: *Do you think it will happen?* Elicit *It might./No, I don't think it will.* Give Ss 4–5 mins to decide on their choices in pairs and write a response. They must be able to give reasons for their choices. Monitor closely and prompt Ss to self-/peer correct.

B Check the example. Pairs now work in groups and compare answers. While Ss talk, make notes on the use of the language and do remedial work as required in feedback. Invite members of each group to talk about one of their choices and discuss it with the class. Give feedback if necessary.

WRITING   SENTENCE STRUCTURE

6A Ss read the title and introduction to the blog. Check where Colombia is. Show Ss a map if possible and ask: *Have you ever eaten food from Colombia? What's it like?* If you've brought in photos of the dishes mentioned in the extract, use them here. Ss then read and discuss the questions. Check answers in feedback.

Answers:
1 In her late twenties, to continue her studies.
2 She missed Colombian food. There are lots of special dishes. In Colombia, people take their time preparing food. People say Colombians cook with love.
3 She tried food from many countries (Libya, Poland, Tunisia, Peru and Japan). Other international students made it.

B Read the two examples with Ss and elicit their answers.

Answers: The first example has three short sentences that don't connect together very well. In the second example, the three short sentences are linked with *when*. This makes it flow more smoothly, and easier for the reader to understand.

speakout TIP

Read and discuss the Speakout tip with Ss. They can look at their last piece of writing if they have it with them or do it later. It might be better to do Ex 6C first.

C Ss find the sentences and underline *and* and *also*. Elicit the sentences and do another example, e.g. *Last night I met some friends. We went to the cinema. We had dinner together.* Ask Ss to use *and* and *also* to connect them.

Answers: I missed my family *and* friends. I *also* missed Colombian food. It was wonderful *and* I tasted food from many countries: Libya, Poland, Tunisia, Peru, and Japan. I *also* made many good friends.

D Brainstorm Ss' responses to the topics, e.g. for cooking, they could say *I love/hate cooking, I can't cook, I'm a very good cook, I'd like to learn how to cook.* Ss then choose a topic and write a paragraph of 50–60 words. They can use the text in Ex 6A as a model. Monitor and support Ss while they write and encourage them to help each other. Ss then show their paragraphs to other Ss, who should find the different sentence lengths. Alternatively, nominate Ss to read out their paragraphs to the class. Ss should also respond to the paragraph and ask questions about it. Give feedback as required.

Homework ideas
- **Ex 6D:** Ss write a paragraph about a different topic from the box.
- **Language bank** 6.2 Ex A–B p139
- **Workbook** Ex 1–6, p35–36

HOW ARE YOU FEELING?

Introduction

Ss learn and practise language for visiting the doctor and talking about illness. They also learn how to predict language used in common everyday situations.

> **SUPPLEMENTARY MATERIALS**
> **Resource bank** p170
> **Language bank** p138–139
> **Warm up:** bilingual dictionaries
> **Ex 2A:** photos of (people with) the health problems/advice in bold in the exercise (or dictionaries)
> **Ex 6:** audio/video recording facilities if available

Warm up

Activate language connected to health/illness. Ask, e.g. *When was the last time you were ill/injured? What was wrong?/What happened? Did you go to the doctor? What medicine/treatment did you have? Did you take time off work? How long?* Give Ss 4–5 mins to answer the questions in pairs. They can ask you/each other for words they need or use bilingual dictionaries. They then report back to the class about their partners.

SPEAKING

1A Check the questions and elicit some initial answers. Ss then discuss the questions in pairs for 2–3 mins and report back to the class.

B Give Ss 2–3 mins to read the text and check their predictions from Ex 1A. In feedback, elicit the answers and ask: *Were your predictions correct?* Finally, teach/check useful language in the text, e.g. *be (less) likely to, in fact, even when, top reasons.*

> **Answers:**
> 1 women
> 2 Men don't like waiting.
> 3 They're fine/They don't need to go. They don't like waiting. Nobody told them to go. They don't want to talk about it. They don't have time.

C Allow Ss 2–3 minutes to discuss the questions. In feedback, elicit whether any Ss have used the excuses in the text and can think of any others.

VOCABULARY ILLNESS

2A If you have brought photos, you can use them here to teach/check the words/phrases in bold in the sentences. You can also use mime to check words Ss don't know (or they can use dictionaries). Ss then match the problems and advice alone and check in pairs. Tell them there might be more than one possible answer. Elicit/Discuss Ss' answers in feedback.

> **Answers:** 1 d) 2 c) 3 b) 4 a)

B Explain to Ss that the pronunciation of some words is different from the spelling and give an example, e.g. *cough.* Tell them that they are going to practise some of these words in this exercise, and play the recording for them to listen and repeat. Chorally or individually, drill any words that still cause difficulty.

Unit 6 Recording 5

1 headache – I've got a headache.
2 backache – I've got backache.
3 a cold – I've caught a cold.
4 flu – She caught flu.
5 a sore throat – I've got a sore throat.
6 a cough – I've got a bad cough.
7 temperature – He's got a high temperature.
8 medicine – Take some medicine.
9 antibiotics – Take some antibiotics.
10 painkillers – Take some painkillers.

C Check the example and give Ss 2 mins to discuss their answers. In feedback, find out who has the best remedy for these ailments.

FUNCTION SEEING THE DOCTOR

3A Check the rubric. Ss should take notes and focus on answering the two questions. They should try not to get distracted by unknown language. Ss listen, note down their answers and then compare them in pairs. Play the recording again for them to check/add to their notes. In feedback, check answers and teach/check new vocabulary, e.g. *painful.* During this stage, elicit more information about the conversations, e.g. ask: *Is the woman worried or under pressure? Does she have a healthy diet? How many cups of tea and coffee does she drink?*

> **Answers:**
> **Conversation 1**
> 1 The woman feels terrible. She gets headaches and feels sick. She can't sleep at night because her head hurts.
> 2 The doctor says she should stop drinking so much tea and coffee, only one small cup a day. She gives her some painkillers and says she should take two three times a day.
>
> **Conversation 2**
> 1 The man is worried about his foot. It hurts when he walks. It's very painful.
> 2 The doctor thinks it's broken and that he should go to the hospital for an X-ray.

Unit 6 Recording 6

Conversation 1

D = Doctor   W = Woman

D: Hello. I'm Dr Andrews. Now, what's the matter?
W: Well, doctor, I feel terrible. I get these headaches and I feel sick.
D: Oh. How long have you had this problem?
W: A few weeks now. And I can't sleep at night because my head hurts.
D: You can't sleep?
W: That's right.
D: And are you very worried or under pressure at the moment?
W: No, I don't think so.
D: Do you have a healthy diet?
W: Hmm. Quite healthy.
D: Do you drink tea or coffee?
W: Yes, I do.
D: How much?
W: Tea? Probably about eight cups, or ten.
D: A day?
W: Yes.
D: I see. And has that changed in the last few weeks?
W: Not really.
D: OK. Well the first thing is I think you should stop drinking so much tea and coffee. Try to drink just one small cup a day. I'll give you some painkillers for the headaches. Take two of these three times a day. I don't think it's anything to worry about, but if …

Conversation 2

D = Doctor   M = Man

D: Good morning. How can I help?
M: Well, <u>I'm worried about</u> my foot.
D: Your foot?
M: Yes. <u>It hurts when I walk.</u>
D: I see. Did you do anything to it? Did you have an accident?
M: Um. Well, sort of.
D: What happened?
M: I kicked a wall.
D: I see. When did you do that?
M: About a week ago.
D: OK. Did you go to hospital?
M: No.
D: Can I have a look?
M: Yes, of course.
D: Where does it hurt? Here?
M: Argh! Yes, there.
D: Can you move it?
M: Yes, a little, but <u>it's very painful</u>.
D: Hmm, I think it might be broken. It's nothing to worry about, but I think you should go to the hospital for an X-ray. I'll write you a note and if …

B Ss complete the sentences and then compare answers in pairs. Check and practise the pronunciation of the sentences in feedback.

Answers: **2** problem   **3** pills   **4** look   **5** hurt   **6** worry

C The sentences are extracts from what the patients say in the recording (underlined in the audio script above). Follow the same procedure as in Ex 3B.

Answers: **1** sick   **2** sleep   **3** worried   **4** hurts   **5** painful

D Ss listen again and check their answers from Ex 3C. Drill the phrases both chorally and individually. Prompt Ss to self-/peer correct during the individual repetition stage.

▷ **LANGUAGEBANK 6.3** p138–139

Ss should refer to the information in the tables when they do the exercise.

Answers: **1** What's the matter/problem   **2** I feel terrible   **3** How long have you had this problem   **4** Can I have a look   **5** very painful   **6** It hurts   **7** I'll give you

4 Elicit the answer to question 1. Ss work alone, compare their answers in pairs and report back to the class in feedback. With **stronger classes**, ask: *Why are the other two options* (*pain/sore*) *not possible?* (Because a verb is needed after the subject *My head. Pain* is a noun and *sore* is an adjective.) You could ask Ss to write sentences using *pain/sore*, e.g. *I've got a terrible <u>pain</u> in my leg/back. I've got a <u>sore</u> throat.* Elicit/Check them in feedback.

Answers: **1** hurts   **2** cold   **3** sick   **4** broken   **5** hurt   **6** worry   **7** give   **8** problem

LEARN TO **PREDICT INFORMATION**

5A Read the Speakout tip with Ss before they do the exercise. This should motivate Ss and give real purpose to the exercise. Then elicit the first two answers. Give Ss 2–3 mins to discuss and complete the answers. Monitor while they work to check how well they have remembered and can use the language. Do not confirm answers yet – Ss will check them in Ex 5B.

B Play the recording. Ss check their answers and then compare them in pairs before class feedback.

Answers: **1** matter   **2** cough   **3** terrible   **4** problem   **5** week   **6** look   **7** painful   **8** medicine

C Play the recording again. Ss repeat the phrases, paying close attention to the sentence stress and intonation.

Optional extra activity

Ss could practise reading the conversation in pairs. **Stronger Ss** could rehearse/memorise it and act it out to the class. Alternatively, Ss take turns to read out parts of the conversation to the class. Prompt other Ss to suggest pronunciation corrections after each pair has read the extract if appropriate. This should be done sensitively so as not to undermine Ss' confidence. Finally, relate this exercise back to the Speakout tip. Ask Ss to choose some words/phrases they think are the most useful for a visit to the doctor's. They work in pairs/groups and then report back to the class. Find out which words Ss found most useful.

speakout TIP

Encourage Ss to use the Speakout tip with Ex 5A and in real-life situations.

6 Divide the class into Ss A and B. They look at the relevant exercises on p161 and p163 and prepare their roles in A or B pairs. Monitor closely while Ss do this and provide support where necessary. Ss then work in A/B pairs and take turns to be the doctor and patient. Monitor and make notes of problems for feedback. Invite Ss to act out their role-plays to the class and give feedback on their performance as needed. Alternatively, record Ss doing their role-plays. Play the recordings in feedback and invite Ss to suggest corrections for language/pronunciation.

Homework ideas

* **Ex 6:** Ss write one of the conversations from p161 and 163 between the doctor and patient.
* **Language bank** 6.3, Ex A, p139
* **Workbook** Ex 1–4, p37

MONITOR ME

Introduction

Ss watch an extract from an episode of the BBC documentary series *Horizon*. They then plan a health regime and write a blog post giving health advice.

> **SUPPLEMENTARY MATERIALS**
> **Ex 1B:** dictionaries

Warm up

Introduce the topic of the lesson. Ss cover the text and look at the large photo on p64–65. Ask, e.g. *What are the people doing? Where are they? What are they wearing?* Elicit Ss' answers and teach new words using the photo.

DVD PREVIEW

1A Give Ss 2–3 mins to read the text and answer the question. Elicit answers in feedback.

> **Answers:** about new apps and technology that measures exercise, sleep, diet, etc., and how monitoring ourselves can improve our health

B Ss work in pairs and match the words with the meanings, using dictionaries if available. Elicit answers in feedback.

> **Answers:** 1 measure   2 monitor   3 app   4 healthcare

DVD VIEW

2A Ss watch the DVD and make notes while they watch. Elicit answers in feedback.

> **Suggested answer:** People are now able to monitor themselves (self-monitoring) and this might mean they can take care of their own health better. Hospitals and doctors might not need to monitor our health so much because we can do it ourselves.

B Check the rubric and any unfamiliar words in the questions, e.g. *heart, blood-alcohol level*. Monitor while Ss work in pairs. In feedback, elicit answers but don't confirm them yet – Ss will check them in Ex 2C.

C Play the DVD for Ss to check their answers. Pause after each answer to allow Ss time to check.

> **Answers:** 1 a), c), d), e)   2 a)   3 a), b), d)   4 a), b)

3 Ss discuss the questions in pairs. In feedback, elicit answers and ask Ss if there was any other information in the DVD they found surprising/interesting.

DVD 6   Horizon: Monitor Me

N = Narrator	B = Blain Price	K = Kevin Fong

N: Do you know how many steps you took today, how much food you ate, how many people you met, how many hours you slept? If you knew these things, it might make you healthier. The truth is, we can find this information easily. All we need is a phone and a few apps. And this might transform our health. Dr Kevin Fong wants to find out if monitoring ourselves every day and getting new information about our bodies will help us live longer, healthier lives. He's going to look at the latest technology, but he's not heading to a hospital or a doctor's surgery. He's come to a sports shop.
Wireless health and fitness technology: people will be using almost two hundred million of these apps in a few years' time. This is a revolution that takes monitoring out of doctors' hands, out of hospitals, and gives it to us. To find out more about this new world of medicine, he meets Blaine Price, a man who knows all about medical technology. Price is a technology expert, with a big box of toys.

B: Kind of a glorified pedometer, keeps track of how many steps you take, but it's a lot more than that. They'll monitor exactly when you took your steps, how active they were and intense they were and what time of day it was. Sleep is one that people are often interested in, so, this one, you wear it as a headband, so like this when you're asleep, and it measures a bit about your brain activity. It can tell you what phase of sleep you're in: deep sleep, light sleep, REM and so on. And if heart information is interesting to you, we've got a pulsoxymeter here.

K: Yeah, the sort of stuff I use in a hospital anyway.

B: Sure. And before you only could get it in a hospital. This is now very inexpensive and what it's doing is measuring cardiac rhythm and blood sats. Looks like I'm fairly healthy at ninety-eight or so.

N: From the comfort of our own homes, we can now measure exactly what our bodies are doing. There are now thousands of apps for our phones to track anything and everything about us. We can also measure a few other things, for example, your blood-alcohol levels and how high you jump. And we can do all this with a simple app.

speakout   create a health regime

4A Check the rubric and questions and any unfamiliar words in the notes, e.g. *machine operator, stress about sth, gain 6.5 kg.* Give Ss 3–4 minutes to answer the questions alone. Then get them to compare answers in pairs before feedback.

> **Suggested answers:**
> 1 **Marcin:** eats/drinks too much junk food and coffee, does no exercise, overweight; **Paulina:** sleeps only six hours, stressed, little energy; **Alvaro:** backache, no exercise, watches too much TV, unfit
> 2 **Marcin:** heart problems, more weight problems; **Paulina:** get too thin and weak, suffer from major stress; **Alvaro:** heart, weight, eye problems, worse backache

B Play the recording. Ss listen in order to find out which of the people in Ex 4A the expert is talking about. Elicit the answer in feedback and ask Ss if they agree with the advice.

> **Answers:** Alvaro

Unit 6   Recording 8

To get healthy, you need a combination of things. You need the right diet. You need to exercise. You need to sleep seven or eight hours. Then there are other things related to lifestyle: how many friends you have, how happy your relationships are. These are really important and they affect your general health. In this person's case, **there are some changes he can make. For example, he needs to** do some exercise. I understand that his back gives him problems, which is quite common in someone of his age. But he could really help himself by doing more activity. **He could try** going for walks or cycling. Also, six hours of TV every day is too much. **He should spend** some of that **time** exercising or seeing his friends. **He must lose weight**, so **maybe he could** eat less meat, perhaps once a day instead of twice. Now, some of these changes are related to the people around him. For example, if it's his wife who does the cooking, she'll need to …

C Ss read and check the key phrases. Play the recording again for them to tick the key phrases they hear. In feedback, play the recording again, pausing at each key phrase (in bold in the audio script above). Elicit/Drill the complete sentences.

> **Answers:** Ss should tick all the phrases except *It's a good idea to …*

Optional extra activity

Individually or in pairs, Ss read the audio script and write comprehension questions. They then exchange questions with other Ss/pairs and must answer them without looking at the audio script. The student/pair with the most correct answers wins.

5A Ss work in small groups and prepare their health regimes for Marcin and Paulina. Encourage them to use the key phrases and make notes. Monitor, checking accuracy and helping with vocabulary where necessary.

B Regroup Ss and ask them to compare their ideas, noting down any similarities/differences. In feedback, ask Ss to report back on their new groups' ideas. Take a class vote on which group(s) had the best ideas.

writeback health advice

6A Ss read the text and answer the questions. If time, get them to compare answers in pairs before feedback.

Answers:
1 In winter, he gets a cough or a sore throat and sometimes has a high temperature and bad headaches. He never sleeps for more than six hours.
2 He's heard it's a good idea to monitor his food and exercise, but he wants advice on what to do.

B Give Ss 8–10 mins to write their reply to Ahmed. Provide support where needed.

Homework ideas

• **Ex 5A:** Ss write a health regime for a family member/friend.
• **Ex 6B:** Ss write a final draft of the blog post.

LOOKBACK

Introduction

Lookback activities are designed to provide revision and communicative practice in a motivating way. This helps Ss and gives you the opportunity to assess their ability to use the language they've learnt in the unit. It's a good idea to monitor and assess individual Ss while they do the activities and compare their performance with their results in more formal tests.

HEALTH

1A Elicit a question for the first prompt, e.g. *Do you go to exercise classes?* Ss then work alone/in pairs to write the other questions. Monitor to assess how well Ss are using question forms and check/drill the questions in feedback as preparation for Ex 1B.

> **Suggested answers:**
> 1 Do you go to exercise classes?
> 2 Do you eat a lot of junk food or drink fizzy drinks?
> 3 Do you spend a lot of time relaxing?
> 4 Do you take vitamins?
> 5 Do you often go running?
> 6 Do you often feel stressed/spend time worrying about work?
> 7 Do you drink caffeine?
> 8 Do you eat a lot of fresh fruit and vegetables?

B Tell Ss that this is a survey and give clear instructions. Ask a question from Ex 1A and elicit answers from several Ss. Summarise or ask Ss to summarise the answers, e.g. *Three people in my group go to exercise classes.* Ss then work in groups and note down other group members' answers. They then prepare a summary of each answer for Ex 1C. Monitor and prompt Ss to correct any mistakes in their sentences. Make notes of persistent problems for remedial work after Ex 1C and/or for assessment.

C Ss from each group take turns to give a summary of each answer to the class. The other groups should note down how similar/different their own findings are in preparation for feedback. Ss could then prepare a summary of the similarities and differences in the class.

PRESENT PERFECT + FOR/SINCE

2A Elicit examples for question 1, e.g. *I haven't been to the USA since I was a child.* Give Ss 4–5 mins to write their sentences. Monitor and note down problems they're having in terms of the present perfect and the use of *for/since*. Give feedback on this before Ss do Ex 2B. Ss can correct their sentences if necessary before they do Ex 2B.

B Check/Drill the example conversation and encourage Ss to respond and expand their answers in a similar way when they work in pairs. Monitor and assess how well they do this, and give feedback afterwards.

FOOD

3 Give Ss 30 seconds to find the words. Elicit the words, but don't check meaning/pronunciation until after Ex 4A.

> **Answers:** onion, cream, pineapple, lemon, carrot, wheat, chicken, cake, oats, jelly, cheese, mussels

> **Optional extra activity**
>
> Individually or in pairs, Ss write another word snake using food and drink words and give it to a partner/another pair to find the words.

4A Give Ss 3–4 mins to put the words in the correct category. *Weaker Ss* could look at p60 or p157 if necessary. Elicit, check and drill the words in feedback.

> **Answers:**
> **desserts:** cake, jelly
> **dairy:** cream, cheese
> **fruit:** pineapple, lemon
> **vegetables:** onion, carrot
> **grains:** wheat, oats
> **meat/seafood:** chicken, mussels

B Ss add words they remember and then check their answers on p60 or p157. Alternatively, make this into a race between pairs/teams. Give Ss 3 mins to add as many words as possible. The pair/team with the most words wins.

MAY, MIGHT, WILL

5A Ss do the exercise alone/in pairs. Check answers and do remedial teaching as required.

> **Answers:** 1 f) 2 e) 3 a) 4 c) 5 b) 6 d)

B Check the example and elicit two more responses, e.g. *You'll love it! You may find it boring.* Monitor while Ss do the task and make notes of the appropriacy of their responses. In feedback, check Ss' answers in open pairs across the class. Invite other Ss to make corrections and/or suggest other answers. Write the most relevant problems you noted on the board in feedback. Ss correct them in pairs.

6 Elicit some example answers: encourage Ss to use *may, might, will, won't*, e.g. *I think there will be more jobs for young people in a few years' time.* Give Ss 6–8 mins to ask and answer the questions. Monitor their use of the modal verbs and do remedial teaching if necessary, after discussing Ss' answers as a class.

SEEING THE DOCTOR

7A Ss complete the questions individually, then compare answers in pairs before feedback.

> **Answers:** 1 broken 2 catch 3 feel 4 can 5 gave 6 have

B While Ss ask and answer the questions, monitor and note how well they are using language to talk about health problems. Give feedback and/or use your notes for assessment as required.

> **Homework ideas**
> **Workbook** Review 2, p38–40

> **BBC interviews and worksheet**
>
> **What do you do to keep fit?**
> This video extends discussion of keeping fit and extends Ss' vocabulary of health and fitness.

7 changes

OVERVIEW

7.1 LIVING THE DREAM

READING | read about living the dream
VOCABULARY | verbs + prepositions
LISTENING | listen to a radio programme about a woman who changed her life
GRAMMAR | *used to*
PRONUNCIATION | weak forms: *used to*
SPEAKING | talk about how your life has changed
WRITING | use paragraphs to write about a decision that changed your life

7.2 THE GREAT IMPOSTOR

READING | read and predict information in a story
VOCABULARY | collocations
GRAMMAR | purpose, cause and result
PRONUNCIATION | rhythm in complex sentences
SPEAKING | talk about why people tell lies

7.3 CAN YOU TELL ME?

READING | read about studying abroad
VOCABULARY | facilities
FUNCTION | finding out information
LISTENING | understand short, predictable conversations
LEARN TO | check and confirm information
PRONUNCIATION | intonation: checking information

7.4 A GREEK ADVENTURE BBC ◁))) DVD

DVD | watch an extract from the beginning of a BBC film about a family that moves to Greece
speakout | a new experience
writeback | a blog/diary

7.5 LOOKBACK

Communicative revision activities

BBC ◁))) INTERVIEWS

How has your life changed in the last ten years?

In this video people describe the best things about their lives, whether there is anything they'd like to change and how their lives have changed in the last ten years. Use the video at the end of Lesson 7.1 or at the start or end of the unit.

LIVING THE DREAM

Introduction

Ss learn/practise *used to* and verbs with prepositions in the context of life changes.

> **SUPPLEMENTARY MATERIALS**
> **Resource bank** p171–172
> **Language bank** p140–141
> **Warm up:** photos of famous people as they look now and as they looked in the past

Warm up

Show Ss recent photos of two famous people, e.g. Beyoncé and Lionel Messi. Ask: *What are they famous for? What are they like? What have they done recently?* Then show photos of the same people in the past. Ask: *What were they like then? What did they do? How have they changed?* Elicit statements, e.g. *Beyoncé wasn't famous then. Now she's a famous, successful artist.* Show/ Distribute more photos. Ss work in pairs and describe how the people have changed. Elicit/Discuss their answers. (NB: If you haven't got photos, Ss could talk about their country/town as it was ten years ago and as it is now. Give them prompts, e.g. *entertainment and leisure, transport, housing, health, shopping, education, employment/salaries, cost of living, politics.*)

VOCABULARY   VERBS + PREPOSITIONS

1A Check the title of the lesson and ask: *Are you living the dream? Do you know anyone who is? In what way?* Elicit and discuss Ss' answers. Then give them 3–4 mins to discuss the questions in pairs and report back to the class.

B Give Ss 2–3 mins to read the text and answer the question. Elicit Ss' answers (but wait until after Ex 2A to check the key vocabulary). Then ask: *Have you ever wanted to change your life?*

2A Check the example. Ss then do the exercise alone and compare answers in pairs. Check answers in feedback.

> **Answers:** **2** move to   **3** go back   **4** dream about   **5** wait for   **6** travel around   **7** get away   **8** look for

B Ss tick the sentences that are true for them. Give them 3–4 mins to discuss and compare their ideas in pairs. Ss then report back to the class about themselves and their partner, e.g. *I wouldn't like to move to another country, but Julia dreams about living by the beach in the Caribbean.*

speakout TIP

Read the Speakout tip with Ss. They copy the verb + preposition collocations into their notebooks, preferably with an example sentence. Take this opportunity to check how well Ss are organising new vocabulary. Ideally, they should create a separate section in their notebooks, to make it easier to access and review new words/phrases.

> **Optional extra activity**
>
> Check verb + preposition collocations from the text. Read out the text, pausing at each verb. Ss tell you what the correct preposition is, e.g. *Perhaps it's time to look _____ (for) something new.* Do this activity now or as a warmer/filler in the next lesson.

LISTENING

3A Invite Ss to speculate about the woman in the photo. Give them 1–2 mins to discuss in pairs, e.g. her age and job. Then, in open class, discuss the questions in the rubric. Elicit Ss' answers to the question *Why do you think she moved?* and write them on the board.

B Ss listen and check their ideas on the board. Check answers in feedback.

Answer: She moved because she felt her life was missing something, so she visited Scotland and fell in love with the country and the owner of a second-hand bookshop.

4A Ss first read the questions. Check *realise her dream*. Play the recording again, then give Ss 2–3 mins to answer the questions and compare answers in pairs.

Answers:
1 Yes, she had a dream job, an extraordinary network of friends, and loved the place where she was living.
2 She dreamed about working in a used bookshop by the sea/in Scotland.
3 She typed 'used bookshop, Scotland' into Google and discovered Wigtown, a town by the sea with lots of used bookshops.
4 No, she sent one email to a bookshop she liked the look of.
5 She felt sad that she wasn't in Scotland. She missed lots of things about Scotland and she was in love with the bookshop owner.
6 She loves the town, the people, the bookshop and being with the love of her life.

B Elicit initial responses to the questions before Ss discuss them in pairs. Encourage them to use the phrases with prepositions from Ex 1, particularly when they answer question 2. Note how well they do this while you monitor. In feedback, elicit/discuss Ss' answers. Give feedback on language you noted while monitoring.

Optional extra activity

Exploit the recording further. Play it again and pause it at suitable points to ask Ss for more specific details, e.g. *What was Jessica's job? How did she stay in touch with the bookshop owner?*

Unit 7 Recording 1

P = Presenter   J = Jessica

Part 1
P: Now, have you ever daydreamed about changing your life forever, about giving up your job and setting off for a distant country where you could find love and happiness? Well, Jessica Fox did just that and she's on the line now to tell us about her journey. Jessica, welcome to the programme.
J: Oh, thank you for having me. It's a pleasure to be here.
P: Now, you started your journey in Los Angeles. Tell me about your life there. What was your job? What sort of lifestyle did you have?
J: Ah, I was consulting for NASA and I was doing what I loved. I was living in a city that I adored and I had an extraordinary network of friends. There was, I can only describe it as like a … a … an abstract taste that I was missing. And so I really began … it was about a year … I began daydreaming of something quite different.
P: Did you have an actual vision of what the change might be?
J: I would often sit down in my studio and just dream of different things, and usually they turned into the screenplays I was writing, and this dream kept on coming back of working in a used bookshop by the sea. And I …
P: Working in a used bookshop by the sea?
J: In Scotland, yes.
P: In Scotland, right. Had you ever had any connection with used bookshops or Scotland before?
J: None, absolutely none.

Part 2
P: And so did you set about doing something to realise the dream?
J: Yeah, it happened quite quickly, actually. I typed in 'used bookshop, Scotland', into Google and Wigtown came up, Scotland's national book town of, I think, it was about sixteen bookshops and I thought, 'Oh my gosh, one of them, hopefully, will take me in,' for a kind of live/work exchange while I was on holiday and I could realise this dream of …
P: So, did you just send an email to these bookshops and ask them to take you in?
J: I sent one email to the first bookshop on the list, which was The Bookshop, and it was the largest used bookshop in Scotland, and within a couple of emails this sort of extraordinary, generous bookshop owner said, 'Yes, I host a lot of other artists. Come on over for the festival.'
P: And so you came over and you stayed at The Bookshop, and what sort of a bookshop was it? What sort of impression did it make on you when you first arrived?
J: I would describe it as, if Harry Potter had a bookshop, this would be it.
P: And what about the bookshop owner? Did you get on with him?
J: I did. You know, I was … I was here for a specific reason. I really wanted to get away from things, I wanted to write, so when I first met the bookshop owner I, it was just … it was a friendly, a kind of a friendly relationship I had with him. I didn't get to know him very much until towards the end of my stay.

Part 3
P: Your month ended and you went back to LA. Did you find yourself missing the shop and missing the owner?
J: Yeah, I loved the shop, I loved the town itself and the people there. And it took me a while to admit that it was actually most of all the bookshop owner that I was missing.
P: And how did you find out that he was missing you too?
J: We would correspond over email and Skype and I'd get lovely packages from him with things I missed about Wigtown.
P: Such as?
J: Such as, this is terrible, such as the biscuits, the digestive biscuits I absolutely adore, um, and a lot of the sweets and movies. I fell in love with Scottish films.
P: So your relationship deepened? Did you think, 'Well maybe I'm falling in love with this man'?
J: Yeah, and I think the reason why it took so long for me to admit was that it meant a radical life shift. And luckily, my job shifted at NASA; so suddenly, I had this freedom of being able to be anywhere in the world that I wanted. And I just thought, 'Well, why let all my characters in my movies have all the fun?' I really wanted to jump in and try this. This was a true challenge, an adventure.
P: So, tell me about your life now, living above the bookshop in Scotland.
J: Well, right now there's a heater underneath my legs – it is absolutely freezing – there is ice crawling up the windows, but it's very cosy, um, and the snow has just hit here, it's beautiful outside, and Wigtown remains, four years on, remains as charming as when I first came.
P: And how is it going with the bookshop owner?
J: Wonderful! You couldn't find a more beautiful place, and you couldn't find more excellent people, and you know … the love of my life is here so …
P: Jessica, it's been wonderful to speak to you.
J: Thank you so much for having me.

GRAMMAR USED TO

Watch out!

Ss may confuse the form and pronunciation of *used to*. They sometimes translate from their L1 and say, e.g. *I'm used to go*, or mix past simple forms, e.g. *I used to went*. Ss may also pronounce *used* with two syllables (/ju:sed/ instead of /ju:st/). It's important to check/drill the forms clearly and correct errors consistently in order to prevent fossilisation.

5A Write sentences a)–c) on the board. Underline the form in each sentence (*used to live, didn't use to work, did she use to dream*). Then ask concept questions 1–5 and elicit/check answers carefully. Model/Drill the sentences, highlighting the pronunciation of *used to*: /ju:stə/.

Answers: 1 yes **2** no **3** no **4** yes **5** the past

B Ss read the rules and discuss their answers in pairs. In feedback, do a personalised substitution drill to check the form and pronunciation of *used to* further. Give Ss prompts, e.g. *watch cartoons when you were a child*. Elicit/Drill *I used to/didn't use to watch cartoons when I was a child*.

Answers: 1 past simple **2** for an extended time

> ## ▷ LANGUAGEBANK 7.1 p140–141
>
> Ss can refer to the notes when they do the exercises. ***Weaker Ss*** should do Ex A and B in class. In Ex B, check *leather jacket*.
>
> **Answers:**
> **A 1** used to study **2** used to smoke **3** never used to argue
> **4** used to live **5** didn't use to like **6** Did, use to enjoy
> **7** used to go out **8** used to do
> **B 1** used to **2** didn't use to **3** used to **4** used to **5** used to
> **6** didn't use to **7** used to **8** did, use to

6A Ss work alone and then compare answers in pairs. Monitor and note any problems they have with the target language. Do not confirm answers yet – Ss will check them in Ex 6B.

B Play the recording, pausing after each sentence for Ss to make changes to their answers if necessary. Check answers with the class.

Answers:
1 When I was a child, I used to cycle to school ~~yesterday~~.
2 My brother always used *to* listen to heavy metal music.
5 We didn't ~~used~~ use to have any pets.
6 We used to go skiing in the holidays ~~last year~~.

C Ss listen and repeat the phrases. Highlight and drill the pronunciation of *use(d) to* /ju:stə/ and drill the sentences chorally and individually.

Unit 7 Recording 3

1 used to – I used to cycle to school – When I was a child, I used to cycle to school.
2 used to – used to listen – My brother always used to listen to heavy metal music.
3 used to – used to live – My family used to live in a different city.
4 used to – used to stay up – I used to stay up all night dancing.
5 didn't use to – didn't use to have any pets – We didn't use to have any pets.
6 used to – used to go skiing – We used to go skiing in the holidays.

D Elicit sentences for question 1 that are true for Ss. Give them 3–4 mins to do the exercise alone. They then compare answers in groups. In feedback, nominate Ss to tell the class about themselves/their partners, e.g. *When I was a child, I used to walk to school, but Marta used to cycle five miles every day.*

SPEAKING

7A Elicit some examples, e.g. *I didn't use to wear glasses. I used to live in a flat.* Ss then note down three things that used to be true about them ten years ago.

B Ss compare sentences and discuss how their lives have changed. Remind them to use *used to* when possible and monitor to see how successfully they do it. Ss should be prepared to tell the class about their partner. In feedback, Ss decide whose life has changed the most in the last ten years. Do remedial work on *used to* if necessary.

WRITING PARAGRAPHS

8A Check unfamiliar language in the sentences. Ss then order them and compare answers in pairs. They must be able to justify the order they decide on. Check answers in feedback.

Answers:
Paragraph 1
2 Before that, I was working for a company, but I didn't enjoy my job.
3 I've always thought that being a teacher would be really interesting.
4 So I went back to college and did a teacher training course.
Paragraph 2
2 For example, I had to work to earn money, and find time to do coursework.
3 So I used to study in the evenings.
4 Now, I have a teaching qualification, and I'm doing the job I've always wanted to do.

B Check the meaning of *support/conclude* and elicit the answers for paragraph 1. Ss then check paragraph 2 and discuss whether it follows the same pattern.

Answers:
In each paragraph:
1 Sentence 1 contains the main idea.
2 Sentences 2 and 3 support the idea.
3 Sentence 4 finishes/concludes the paragraph.

C Ss can use one of their examples from Ex 7 or invent a decision. With ***weaker classes***, elicit an example first, using the framework here. Give Ss 8–10 mins to write their paragraph. Monitor and support them where necessary. Also encourage them to read/comment on each other's work.

Homework ideas

• **Ex 8C:** Ss write another paragraph about themselves or someone they know.
• **Language bank** 7.1 Ex A–B, p141
• **Workbook** Ex 1–8, p41–42

THE GREAT IMPOSTOR

Introduction

Ss read a text about a famous impostor and revise/practise the use of linking words (*to, becauses, so*) to talk about purpose, cause and result.

> **SUPPLEMENTARY MATERIALS**
> **Resource bank** p173
> **Language bank** p140–141
> **Ex 1B:** dictionaries

Warm up

Revise vocabulary Ss need for the lesson. Dictate sentences 1–7 about Barney, but in the wrong order. Ss write them down and then number them in the correct order.

1 Barney committed a crime in 2010.
2 The police arrested him in 2011.
3 He escaped from the police station the next day.
4 They caught him again in 2012.
5 He went to prison.
6 He spent two years there.
7 They released him from prison in 2015.

Ss check their answers in pairs. In feedback, elicit the answers or ask Ss to write them on the board. Teach/Check the verbs in each sentence.

READING

1A Check the rubric and the dictionary definition. Ss then look at the photo and discuss the question in pairs for 1–2 mins. Elicit a few ideas from Ss in feedback.

> **Answers:** He pretended to be a naval officer (sailor), a US Marine (soldier), a lawyer, an engineer, a university professor, a doctor.

B Read part 1 of the story with Ss to illustrate what they have to do. Check the dates of the Korean War (1950–1953). Ss then guess the answer to the first question and read part 6 to find the answer. Give them 5–6 mins to read the rest of the text. They can use dictionaries to check unknown vocabulary if necessary. In feedback, ask: *How many correct guesses did you make?* Check the answers and ask further comprehension questions about each one. For example, for part 6 ask: *When did he pretend to be a doctor? Who did he pretend to be? Why did the soldiers love him?* Also teach new words/phrases, e.g. *bullet, perform an operation.*

> **Answers:** 1 a)   3 b)   4 c)   5 b)   6 c)

2 Check the questions and elicit one or two initial answers. Give Ss 3 mins to discuss them further. In feedback, elicit Ss' answers: use information from the Culture notes to enable them to expand on questions 1 and 2.

> **Culture notes**
> **Ferdinand Waldo Demara, Jr.** (1921–1982) was said to have a photographic memory and an extremely high IQ. This is how he memorised techniques from a textbook and performed operations. He is reported to have said that the things he did were like childish pranks; he didn't intend to hurt people.

Ss work in pairs/small groups and write four comprehension questions (**stronger Ss** could write more) about the text, e.g. *When was Demara born? When did he appear in a film?* Pairs/Groups then exchange questions and must answer them without looking at the texts. The pair/group with the most correct answers wins.

VOCABULARY   COLLOCATIONS

3A First, check vocabulary, e.g. *role, documentary, murder.* Ss find/underline the collocations in the story before class feedback.

> **Answers:** 1 f)   2 c)   3 e)   4 a)   5 d)   6 g)   7 b)

B Elicit/Help Ss with the first sentences in the story: *During the Korean War, Demara pretended to be a doctor on a ship. The soldiers loved him because he cured their illnesses.* Ss use the collocations in Ex 3A to help them tell the story in pairs. While they do this, monitor and provide support where needed. In feedback, Ss take turns to tell one part of the story. Prompt peer/self-correction during this stage.

speakout TIP

Read the Speakout tip with Ss. Advise them to write whole phrases in their vocabulary notebooks (such as the collocations in Ex 3A) where possible, rather than single verbs. Elicit some examples of words that collocate with *play/make*, e.g. *play football* (a game)/*the piano* (an instrument), *make a cake/a mistake.*

GRAMMAR   PURPOSE, CAUSE AND RESULT

> **Watch out!**
> Because of L1 interference, Ss frequently make mistakes with the use of *to* to talk about purpose, e.g. *I went to the shop for to buy a newspaper.* It's important to make Ss aware of this problem as early as possible. When teaching the form, ask Ss to compare it with their own language and notice the similarity/difference. Prompt them to self-correct and correct each other whenever they make this mistake.

4A Ss complete the sentences and compare answers in pairs. Move on to Ex 4B.

B Ss find and check their answers. In feedback, ask checking questions, e.g. *Why did he appear in a 1960 film? Why didn't he go to prison? What did the mother do when she saw the picture?*

> **Answers:** 1 to   2 because   3 so

C Give Ss 2–3 mins to find other examples in the story. In feedback, check Ss' answers. Then write these two sentences on the board:
1 Demara pretended to be Dr Joseph Cyr <u>to work</u> on a ship.
2 Demara pretended to be Dr Joseph Cyr <u>in order to work</u> on a ship.

Ask: *Do the sentences have the same or a different meaning?* (the same) Then ask Ss to find the sentence in the text (in part 6). Elicit and write it on the board. *Demara pretended to be Dr Joseph Cyr <u>so that he could work</u> on a ship.* Ask: *What's different?* Elicit/Underline *so that* and subject + *can/could* + verb (*he could work*). Ss will read about *in order to* and *so that* in the Language bank.

> **Answers:**
> **Part 4:** Instead the police released him and gave him extra money <u>to say</u> 'thank you' for his great work!
> **Part 5:** Demara became famous <u>because of</u> his great work as the ship's doctor …

▷ **LANGUAGEBANK 7.2** p140–141

Read/Check the notes with Ss if necessary. They can refer to them when they do the exercises. **Weaker Ss** should do Ex A and B in class. In Ex A, check *sales reps* and in Ex B check *wallet, attend a conference*.

> **Answers:**
> A 1 to 2 because 3 to 4 so 5 so 6 to 7 because 8 so
> B I usually get a newspaper *because* I want to know what's on TV, but today I read a strange story. An Englishman was feeling terrible *because* he was under pressure at work, *so* he decided to disappear. He went to a beach *to* go swimming (he said). Then he left his clothes there *so that* someone could find them. He also left his wallet with a photo and ID *so* the police knew who it was. The police went to his home *to* speak to him but he wasn't there. He was in Australia and had a different name! Three years later, he was caught when his cousin, who was in Australia *to* attend a conference, recognised him. Where were they? On a beach!

5A Do the first question as an example. Ss then work alone, underline the correct alternatives and compare them in pairs. Do not confirm answers yet – Ss will check them in Ex 5B.

B Play the recording for Ss to check their answers to Ex 5B. Point out that Ss should follow the words on the page with their finger as they listen. With **stronger classes**, before moving on to pronunciation work, you could ask Ss which sentences can be written with *in order to* or *so that* (*in order to* can be used with questions 1, 4, 6; *so that* with questions 1 and 6, e.g. *I'm doing an English course in order to improve my speaking. I'm doing an English course so that I can improve my speaking.*). Then play the recording again for Ss to listen and say the sentences at the same time.

> **Answers:** 1 to 2 because 3 so 4 to 5 because 6 to 7 so
> 8 because

C Discuss one or two of the sentences with the class. Then give Ss 3–4 mins to discuss in their pairs. In feedback, invite Ss to tell the class about their partners.

6 Check the examples and give Ss 2–3 mins to complete the exercise. While they do this, make notes on their use of the target language and do remedial work as needed in feedback.

> **Suggested answers:**
> I wanted to help people so I became a nurse.
> I went to the doctor because I felt sick.
> I liked travelling so I became a pilot.
> I went to university to get a Master's degree.
> I phoned my friend to invite her to a party.
> I cycled to work because I couldn't drive.
> I bought an iPod because I love listening to music.

> **Optional extra activity**
>
> Ss work with a different partner. They take it in turns to make sentences with the phrases in list A, but have to provide different answers, e.g. *I went to the cinema because I wanted to see the new James Bond film.*

SPEAKING

7A Discuss some answers to question 1 with the class. Then give Ss 3–4 mins to discuss their answers in pairs/groups.

B Ss read the situations. Check unfamiliar words, e.g. *CV, references, a designer bag*. Ss then discuss their answers in pairs. Remind them that they need to give reasons for their answers. To extend the practice, Ss could exchange opinions with another pair. Monitor and make notes on the strengths and weaknesses of the language they use. In feedback, invite pairs to discuss each situation with the class. Find out how far they agree. Give feedback as required.

> **Homework ideas**
> • **Ex 7B:** Ss write their response to each situation, giving reasons.
> • **Language bank** 7.2 Ex A–B, p141
> • **Workbook** Ex 1–5, p43–44

CAN YOU TELL ME?

Introduction

Ss learn and practise how to find out, check and confirm information about facilities in a language school/university.

> **SUPPLEMENTARY MATERIALS**
> **Resource bank** p174
> **Language bank** p140–141
> **Ex 3C:** copies of a plan/map of your school for Ss to describe
> **Ex 10:** audio/video recording facilities

Warm up

Lead in to the topic of the lesson: Ss discuss facilities in their town. Ask: *Is your town a good place for tourists and/or students?* Invite some initial responses and, if necessary, provide prompts of things Ss need to consider (places of interest and facilities), e.g. *museums, monuments, churches, parks, walks, hotels, pubs, cafés, library, internet cafés, art galleries, clubs, bookshops, cinema.* Ss discuss the question in pairs/groups. In **multilingual classes**, put Ss from different countries in different pairs/groups. In feedback, discuss Ss' conclusions about their town(s).

SPEAKING

1 Ss look at the photo. Ask, e.g. *What's this place? What can you see?* Ss then discuss the questions, first in pairs and then as a class.

2 Give Ss 2–3 mins to read the text, answer the question and compare their answers in pairs. In feedback, check answers and then ask further comprehension questions, e.g. *What do you think the Chinese saying means? Why is it difficult for foreign students when they arrive? What kind of things do they have to do?* Elicit and discuss Ss' answers.

> **Answer:** Chinese students find studying abroad hard at first, but then it gets easier and they think it's a great experience.

> **Optional extra activity**
>
> Ask Ss to find and underline four verb + noun collocations in the text, e.g. *read books, walk 1,000 miles, get easier, open a bank account, get a phone contract.*

VOCABULARY FACILITIES

3A Ss do the exercise alone and compare answers in pairs. In feedback, check answers and teach/check the meaning of the words. Elicit the stressed syllable in each word/phrase and drill the pronunciation. Ss write new words in their notebooks.

> **Answers:** 1 library 2 stationery shop 3 registration desk
> 4 cafeteria 5 accommodation/welfare office

B Check/Drill the example and elicit another one. Ss then take it in turns to ask and answer questions about the facilities. Check their answers in open pairs across the class: prompt self- and peer correction.

> **Suggested answers:** **study centre:** study by yourself, do your homework; **bookshop:** buy textbooks; **cafeteria:** have a coffee, eat something; **library:** borrow books, do research; **stationery shop:** buy pens, paper and notebooks; **main reception:** find out where to go; **classroom:** have a lesson; **photocopying room:** make photocopies; **lecture theatre:** listen to a lecture; **accommodation/welfare office:** discuss problems; **registration desk:** register for a new course

C Give Ss 3–4 mins to answer the questions in pairs. If possible, provide a map/plan of your language school (or Ss could draw one to facilitate their answers). In feedback, find out which facilities are most widely used.

FUNCTION FINDING OUT INFORMATION

4A Check the example and give Ss 3–4 mins to write the questions. Monitor and support **weaker Ss** if necessary. In feedback, check/drill the questions (in bold in the audio script below). **Stronger classes** could check their answers in Ex 4B.

> **Answers:**
> b) Where's the study centre?
> c) What time is/does the library open?
> d) Can you help me find my classroom?
> e) Where can I use the internet?
> f) Where can I buy a notebook?
> g) Where can I get a new student card?
> h) Can you tell me where to go (for information about …)?

B Ss listen, note down their answers and compare them in pairs. Play the recording again if they still have doubts.

> **Answers:** 2 b) 3 e) 4 c) 5 g) 6 d) 7 f) 8 h)

5 Give Ss time to read and check the statements before listening. Tell them to correct the false statements when they compare answers in pairs. Play the recording twice if necessary. In feedback, nominate Ss to answer with the corrected statements (see answers in italics in the audio script below).

> **Answers:** 1 T 2 T 3 T
> 4 F (The library is open from 9a.m. until 6p.m. every day.) 5 T 6 T
> 7 F (The stationery shop is downstairs.)
> 8 F (The welfare office is next to the bookshop.)

6A Point out/check the three headings for the questions/phrases here. Give Ss 3–4 mins to complete gaps 1–7 and compare their answers in pairs. Do not confirm answers yet.

B Ss check their answers in the audio script. In feedback, check answers (underlined in the audio script below) and elicit/drill the complete sentences from the recording, e.g. *Where can I get a new student card? I need to find out about my accommodation.*

> **Answers:** 1 Excuse 2 help 3 can 4 time 5 have 6 need
> 7 kind

Unit 7 Recording 5

Conversation 1
A: <u>Excuse me</u>, **where do I register for my course?**
B: Do you know where the main reception is?
A: Sorry?
B: *The main reception.*
A: Oh, yes.
B: *The registration desk is there.*
A: Thank you so much.

Conversation 2
A: Excuse me, **where's the study centre?**
B: *It's next to the cafeteria.*
A: The cafeteria? Where's that?
B: Follow me. I'll take you there.
A: Thank you. <u>That's very kind.</u>

Conversation 3
A: **Where can I use the internet?**
B: *You can use the computers in the library* or in the study centre.
A: <u>Do I have to</u> pay?
B: No.
A: So it's free for students.
B: Yes, that's right.

Conversation 4

A: Excuse me, **what time is the library open?**

B: *It's open every day, from 9a.m. until 6p.m.*

A: Did you say 'every day'?

B: Yes, that's right. Every day, from nine in the morning until six in the evening.

A: Thank you.

Conversation 5

A: Could you help me? **Where can I get** a new student card? I've lost mine.

B: OK. *If you go to the main reception, you can get a new one.*

A: Thank you.

Conversation 6

A: Excuse me, **can you help me find my classroom?**

B: Sure. What number is it?

A: 301.

B: OK. *You need to go up to the third floor. And it's on the right.*

Conversation 7

A: **Where can I buy** a notebook?

B: *There's a stationery shop downstairs.*

A: Sorry?

B: There's a stationery shop downstairs.

A: Thank you so much.

Conversation 8

A: Can you help me?

B: Yes, maybe.

A: I need to find out about my accommodation. **Can you tell me where to go?**

B: Accommodation? I think you have to go to *the welfare office, over there, next to the bookshop.*

A: Thank you.

▷ **LANGUAGEBANK 7.3** p140–141

Ss should refer to the information in the tables if necessary.

Answers:

1 Can you tell me where to ~~can~~ find a post office? Yes, there's one just behind ~~of~~ you!

2 I need to ~~be~~ find out about my accommodation. There's an accommodation office ~~on~~ downstairs.

3 Breakfast is in the restaurant from ~~on~~ 7 o'clock. Did you ~~to~~ say 7 o'clock?

4 Do you ~~is~~ know where the main reception is? Yes, I'll show ~~it~~ you. That's ~~you~~ very kind.

5 Is it ~~a~~ free to park my car here? No, ~~it's~~ you have to pay.

---

7 Elicit the answer to question 1. Ss then do the exercise alone and compare answers in pairs. In feedback, Ss read out the conversations in pairs. Prompt them to self-correct if they make mistakes and invite peer correction if necessary.

Answers:

1 A: Excuse ~~to~~ me, where's the bookshop?
   B: There's one around *the* corner.

2 A: What time ~~do~~ *does* the swimming pool open?
   B: During the week it opens ~~on~~ *at* eight o'clock.

3 A: Can *you* tell me where to get a student card, please?
   B: You need ~~going~~ *to go* to reception.

4 A: Where ~~I can~~ *can I* get a coffee?
   B: There's a cafeteria over there, next *to* the library.

---

8 Divide the class into two groups, A and B. They each check the relevant exercises and maps on p165 or p166 and work with another student from the same group (A or B) to prepare the questions they need to ask in Ex A. They also need to check the maps/information for Ex B. When they are ready, put Ss in A/B pairs. They take turns to ask and answer the questions. Monitor and make a note of problem sentences for feedback. Invite Ss to act out their conversations to the class. Give feedback on problems as needed.

Suggested answers:

A 1 A: Excuse me, what time do the shops open?
     B: At 10a.m. every day except Sunday.

  2 A: Excuse me, where's the nearest train station?
     B: It's over the bridge on the other side of the river.

  3 A: Excuse me, can you help me? I need to exchange some money. Can you tell me where to go?
     B: There's a money exchange next to the railway station.

B 1 A: Excuse me, where's the nearest coffee shop?
     B: It's next to classrooms 4 and 5, on the right.

  2 A: Excuse me, where can I buy an English dictionary?
     B: There's an English bookshop in the reception area.

  3 A: Excuse me, can you tell me what time the school closes?
     B: At 10p.m. from Monday to Saturday and at 1p.m. on Sunday.

LEARN TO **CHECK AND CONFIRM INFORMATION**

9A Ss read and listen to the extracts; tell them to pay attention to the intonation of the words/phrases in bold.

B Check the meaning of *repeat*, *checking question* and *rephrase*. Elicit the first answer as an example before Ss work alone/in pairs. In feedback, elicit and check answers.

Answers: a) extracts 2, 5 b) extracts 1, 4 c) extract 3

C Ss listen and repeat the words/phrases in bold in Ex 9A. Use your hands and arms to conduct/highlight the main stress and fall/rise of the intonation in each question.

Answer: The word is repeated as a question, so there is a fall/rise intonation after the stressed syllable.

10 Read and check the rubric and situation with the class. Give Ss 5–6 mins to work in pairs and plan/make notes about what they want to say. In *mixed-ability classes*, put *stronger* and *weaker Ss* together. They should prepare both A and B roles and rehearse both parts of the conversation. Monitor closely to provide support with accuracy and pronunciation where needed. Prompt Ss to self-correct any errors. Then put Ss in pairs with a different partner. They take turns to be A/B and role-play the situation. They may have to adjust some of the things they'd planned to say, depending on what their partner says. In feedback, invite pairs to perform the role-plays to the class. If you have audio/video recording facilities available, record the role-plays. Ss can watch and comment on them in feedback.

Homework ideas

- **Ex 10:** Ss write a conversation about a different situation, e.g. you lost your smartphone or you can't find the library.
- **Language bank** 7.3 Ex A, p141
- **Workbook** Ex 1–3, p45

A GREEK ADVENTURE

Introduction

Ss watch an extract from a BBC film about the famous Durrell family, who moved to Greece in the 1930s. They then learn and practise how to talk and write about a new experience.

> **SUPPLEMENTARY MATERIALS**
> **Warm up:** a map of Greece, showing the island of Corfu off the north east coast.

> **Culture notes**
> **Corfu** is a large Greek island in the Ionian Sea, off the north east coast of Greece. It has a long history of hospitality to foreign visitors and is a popular tourist destination for British people.

Warm up

Lead in and create interest in the lesson. Ss cover the text and look at the large photo on p74–75. Ask: *What's this place like? Where is it?* Elicit and discuss Ss' answers. If possible, show Ss a map of Greece/ the island of Corfu. Ask: *Would you leave your country and move to a place like this? Why/Why not? Why do you think people might move there?* Ss discuss their answers in groups and then with the class.

DVD PREVIEW

1 Check the rubric and give Ss 2–3 mins to discuss the questions in pairs. In feedback, Ss tell the class about their partner's answers. Discuss ways of communicating when you can't speak the language.

> **Suggested answers:** If you can't speak the language, you can use a dictionary/a phrase book, draw a picture of the object you want or mime an action to illustrate it, e.g. brush your teeth to show *toothpaste/toothbrush*.

> **Culture notes**
> The autobiography *My Family And Other Animals* is by famous naturalist and conservationist **Gerald Durrell** (1925–1995), who spent four years on Corfu with his family from 1935–1939. The book is the first of his Corfu trilogy, together with *Birds, Beasts, and Relatives* and *The Garden of the Gods*. His brother Lawrence (1912–1990) was also a famous author, best known for *The Alexandria Quartet*.

2 Check if Ss know the book/film *My Family And Other Animals*. If so, elicit what they know about it. Ss then read the text and answer the questions. In feedback, check Ss' answers and anything else they know about authors Gerald and Lawrence Durrell. Use the Culture notes if necessary.

> **Answers:** They move to Corfu, Greece, because they want to escape the wet, grey English weather.

> **Optional extra activity**
> Write on the board: *Who are the people in the photo?* Ss read the information again and discuss their answers in pairs. Tell them to use prepositions and details about the people's clothes to help them describe who the people are. Nominate Ss to answer in feedback. Check new words and elicit further information about them, e.g. ask: *How old is Gerry? Who's the eldest/an intellectual? Who loves animals?* Also lead in to the DVD extract. Ask: *What happens to the family in Corfu? Why are they delighted to meet Spiro? Who do you think Spiro is?*

> **Answers:** The man in the blue shirt on the left is Lawrence. The girl with blonde hair in front of him is Margot. The young man at the top of the stairs in the brown shirt is Leslie. The young boy in the front is Gerry. The older woman on the right in the red dress is their mother.

DVD VIEW

3A Check the rubric and elicit Ss' predictions. (NB: You could let Ss discuss in pairs/groups first.) Ss then watch the DVD to check their ideas. Elicit answers in feedback.

B Check the rubric and sentences about the DVD and pre-teach *customs officer*. Ss then watch the DVD, number the scenes and compare answers in pairs. In feedback, elicit Ss' answers and as much detail about each scene as they can remember, e.g. in scene 1, ask: *Why don't they feel well?* (Because Gerry, Margot and Leslie have colds and mother is tired.)

> **Alternative approach**
> Ss watch the DVD *without* sound first. They watch the actions/ events and should be able to put most scenes in order. Ss compare their answers and then watch the DVD again with the sound to check.

> **Answers:** 2 e) 3 b) 4 d) 5 c)

4A Check the rubric and quotes with Ss. They then complete the sentences and compare answers in pairs. Do not confirm answers yet – Ss will check them in the next exercise.

B Ss watch the DVD again and check their answers (in bold in the DVD script below). Pause after each answer and ask further comprehension questions to exploit the landscape, actions and events in the DVD to the fullest, e.g. for question 1, ask: *What did Lawrence's mother reply? Did the others want to pack up and go?*

> **Answers:** 1 sunshine 2 bathroom 3 place 4 Greek
> 5 language 6 take

DVD 7 My Family And Other Animals

La = Lawrence   G = Gerry   Ma = Margot   Mo = Mother   Le = Leslie
E = Estate agent   S = Spiro

La: Why do we put up with this climate? I mean, look at us! Gerry can't speak.
G: Uh?
La: Leslie can't hear.
Le: What?
La: Margot's got a face like a plate of red porridge.
Ma: Shut up!
La: And mother is beginning to look like an Irish washer woman.
Mo: I am not.
La: **It's August! We need sunshine.**
Mo: Yes, dear.
La: I've got a friend. Lives in Greece. Corfu. Says it's wonderful. Why don't we pack up and go?
Mo: I can't just go like that. We have a house here.
La: We'll sell up.
Mo: Don't be ridiculous, Lawrence. Gerry needs an education.
G: No, I'll be fine.
Mo: We can't just up and leave. That would be madness.
Mo: I'm sorry, but **you've shown us ten houses and none of them has a bathroom**.
G: Oh, not again.
E: Bathroom? What for you want a bathroom? You have the sea.
Mo: This is the cradle of civilisation. **They must have bathrooms. We'll find a place ourselves.** Uh … no, um, er … Taxi?
Le: **We don't actually speak Greek.**
Ma: We do plan to learn.
Mo: Can't you do something, Larry?
La: What?

S: Oi! **You need someone who talks your language?** Them's been worrying yous?
Mo: Ah … no, no.
S: Where you wants to go?
Mo: Eyes on the road.
S: **There. Villa with bathrooms.**
G: **We'll take it.**

5 Check the questions and elicit some initial answers. In *multilingual classes*, put Ss from the same countries in different pairs. Give Ss 4–5 mins to discuss the questions and make a note of their partner's answers for feedback. Find out who the most popular character is and why, and what the most common problems for tourists are.

speakout a new experience

6A Check the rubric. Remind Ss to focus on answering the three questions and not get distracted by unfamiliar language. Ss listen and make notes of their answers, and then compare them in pairs. Play the recording again if necessary. Nominate Ss to answer and elicit extra information if possible.

Answers:
1 Agata moved to the USA, but she didn't speak very good English.
2 She felt nervous when she had to speak to people.
3 She met some American girls and went out with them. Now her English is better, she feels more confident; she talks to people all the time.

B Ss read and check the key phrases. They then listen and tick the phrases they hear. In feedback, play the recording again, pausing at each key phrase (in bold in the audio script below). Elicit/Drill the complete sentences and ask further comprehension questions, e.g. *Where did Agata learn English? Why was it different in the USA?*

Answers:
The biggest problem was …
I felt very [nervous/shy/excited/…] when …
I couldn't …
Luckily, I met/made friends with …

Optional extra activity

Ss work in pairs/groups and retell Agata's story using the key phrases, e.g. *When Agata moved to the USA, her biggest problem was …*

Unit 7 Recording 8

Well, when I first arrived in the USA, it was a very interesting time for me. **The biggest problem was** that I couldn't really speak the language very well. I learnt English at school and at university in Poland, but it's very different when you are living in the country and you need to speak it all the time. **I felt very nervous when** I had to speak to American people, like in the shops or when you meet friends, and **I couldn't** understand what people were saying to me. It was terrible. I used to stay at home and watch loads of television to try and understand what people were saying. **Luckily, I made friends** very quickly **with** some American girls, so we used to go out together and that really helped me. After a few months my English was much better. I felt more confident. And now I talk to people all the time, but it was hard at the beginning.

7A Check the rubric/questions and give Ss 3–4 mins to make notes of their answers. Monitor and help them with language they need.

B Ss should make notes of one of their partners' experiences and prepare to report back to the class in feedback. Monitor and note down examples of good language and errors Ss make for feedback.

writeback a blog/diary

8A Ss read the text and answer the questions. Discuss Ss' answers and highlight the use of *used to* in the blog.

Answers:
1 yes
2 She misses her family and friends. When she first arrived, she used to get lost all the time.

B First elicit examples of what Ss could write, using the prompts given, e.g. *One thing that has really changed in my life is learning to drive. I decided to learn to drive so that I could be more independent. Before that I used to take buses everywhere.* Ss can use their notes from Ex 7 to write their blog/diary. Encourage them to read/comment on each other's work, while you provide support where needed. Ss can display their blogs in the classroom or pass them round for other Ss to read. Then discuss which experience Ss thought was the most unusual/interesting and give feedback on their performance.

Homework ideas

• **Ex 5:** Ss write their answer to question 2.
• **Ex 8B:** Ss write another blog/diary and put it on the school website/class blog.

LOOKBACK

Introduction
Use the Lookback section to monitor and assess Ss' understanding of the language covered in the unit.

> **SUPPLEMENTARY MATERIALS**
> Ex 3A: dictionaries

VERBS + PREPOSITIONS

1A Elicit/Check the answer to question 1. Ss then work alone and complete the exercise before comparing their answers in pairs. Monitor to assess how well Ss use the prepositions and do remedial work in feedback if necessary.

> **Answers:** 1 about 2 around 3 away 4 to 5 about 6 back

B Elicit and discuss Ss' answers to question 1. Give them time to prepare their answers before they ask and answer the questions in pairs. They should make notes of their partner's answers for feedback.

Optional extra activity
Ss write one sentence containing one of their partner's most interesting answers on a piece of paper, but leave their name blank, e.g. _____ *would like to travel around Nepal.* Collect the pieces of paper and redistribute them. Ss must then find the person their sentence is about by asking the relevant question, e.g. *Would you like to travel to Nepal?* They walk around the class asking their question or read out the question to the class. Monitor and make notes on Ss' strengths and weaknesses for feedback and/or assessment.

USED TO

2A Elicit the answer to question 1 to show Ss what to do and then give them 3–4 mins to write the questions. Check/Drill the questions before Ss do Ex 2B.

> **Answers:**
> 1 did you use to work hard at school?
> 2 did you use to eat fast food?
> 3 did you use to spend time with your grandparents?
> 4 did you use to get ill often?
> 5 did you use to have a special friend?
> 6 did you use to play any sport?
> 7 did you use to travel to school on public transport?
> 8 did you use to live in a different place?

B Elicit as many related questions as possible for question 1 in Ex 2A, e.g. *What subjects did you enjoy? What did you use to be good/bad at? Did you use to get good exam results?* Encourage Ss to use both *used to* and the past simple. **Stronger Ss** can work alone or in pairs with **weaker Ss**, depending on your aim (for revision/practice or for assessment). It's important that Ss' questions are accurate for Ex 2C, so monitor and support Ss.

C Check/Drill the example conversation, encouraging Ss to sound interested. While they work in pairs, monitor and assess their use of the target language and give feedback afterwards.

COLLOCATIONS

3A Ss work alone/in pairs and can check their answers on p71. In feedback, check answers. With **stronger classes**, elicit/check how the other alternative in each sentence could be used, e.g. *This hero rescued me.* Alternatively, Ss can use their dictionaries to check the verbs/find examples.

> **Answers:** 1 cured 2 saved 3 become 4 spends 5 for 6 spent 7 played 8 make

B Check the example. Give Ss 4–5 mins to write new sentences in pairs/teams. **Stronger Ss** could write more. Monitor, but don't help Ss while they work. In feedback, Ss take turns to read out their extra sentences to the class. The other Ss decide if the sentence makes sense and is grammatically correct. Ss get two points for appropriate/correct sentences, and one point for an appropriate but grammatically incorrect one.

PURPOSE, CAUSE AND RESULT

4A Ss read the two parts of the exercise first. Check *put my feet up*. Ss then do the exercise alone and compare answers in pairs. In feedback, check answers and prompt peer and/or self-correction where appropriate. Then do remedial teaching if necessary.

> **Answers:** 1 f) 2 g) 3 h) 4 a) 5 e) 6 d) 7 b) 8 c)

B Check the example. Do another one if necessary to illustrate the exercise further. Give Ss 1–2 mins to write the questions before they ask and answer them in pairs. Monitor and make notes of problems Ss have with the linking words. Write them on the board in feedback. Ss correct them in pairs.

FINDING OUT INFORMATION

5A Give Ss 3–4 mins to order the conversations and compare answers in pairs. In feedback, model/drill the sentences to remind Ss of the importance of sentence stress and intonation when asking for/checking information. This will prepare them for the practice in Ex 5B.

> **Answers:**
> **Conversation 1**
> 2 i) 3 e) 4 d) 5 f) 6 c) 7 g) 8 b) 9 h)
> **Conversation 2**
> 1 i) 2 b) 3 h) 4 g) 5 a) 6 d) 7 c) 8 f) 9 e)

B Ss practise reading the conversations and take turns to ask for information. Monitor and note Ss' pronunciation, particularly stress and intonation. In feedback, nominate pairs to act out a conversation and invite the other Ss to comment on their stress/intonation. Ask: *Did they sound polite?* Do remedial teaching/give further feedback if necessary.

BBC interviews and worksheet
How has your life changed in the last ten years?
In this video people describe the best things about their lives, whether there is anything they'd like to change and how their lives have changed in the last ten years.

OVERVIEW

8.1 TREASURE HUNT

VOCABULARY | money
PRONUNCIATION | pronouncing the letter 's'
READING | read the story of a treasure hunt
GRAMMAR | relative clauses
SPEAKING | talk about a project that people should invest in

8.2 PAY ME MORE!

LISTENING | listen to a discussion about salaries
GRAMMAR | *too much/many, enough, very*
VOCABULARY | multi-word verbs
PRONUNCIATION | multi-word verb stress
SPEAKING | talk about why you should earn more
WRITING | write an opinion piece

8.3 I'M JUST LOOKING

READING | read a questionnaire about shopping
VOCABULARY | shopping
LISTENING | listen to conversations in shops
FUNCTION | buying things
PRONUNCIATION | weak forms: *do you/can I*
LEARN TO | describe things
SPEAKING | describe items; go shopping

8.4 SOLEREBELS BBC)) DVD

DVD | watch an extract from the BBC news about an
        Ethiopian business
speakout | a money-making idea
writeback | a website entry

8.5 LOOKBACK

Communicative revision activities

BBC)) INTERVIEWS

How do you feel about shopping?

In this video people describe what they like and don't like about shopping, the best places to go shopping and what they've bought. The video also extends Ss' vocabulary of shops and shopping. Use the video after Lesson 8.3 or at the start or end of the unit.

TREASURE HUNT

Introduction

Ss learn/practise the use of relative clauses to describe people, places and things. They also learn and practise vocabulary to talk about money.

> **SUPPLEMENTARY MATERIALS**
> **Resource bank** p175–176
> **Language bank** p142–143
> **Photo bank** p158 (Ss may need dictionaries.)
> **Warm up:** copies of the matching activity (See notes below.)
> **Ex 1A:** dictionaries

Warm up

Lead in to the lesson with a light-hearted matching activity about nicknames for British/US money. If possible, photocopy these two columns of nicknames/definitions. Otherwise, write them on the board:

Column A: *1 a nickel   2 a dime   3 a quarter   4 a buck*
            5 a quid   6 a fiver   7 a tenner   8 a grand
Column B: *a) 5 cents   b) £5   c) £1,000   d) 10 cents*
            e) £10   f) 25 cents   g) £1   h) $1

Ss match the words in pairs. Check answers, then ask: *Do you have nicknames for money in your country?*

> **Answers:** **1** a) (US   **2** d) (US)   **3** f) (US)   **4** h) (US)   **5** g) (UK)
> **6** b) (UK)   **7** e) (UK)   **8** c) (UK)

VOCABULARY   MONEY

1A Ss read the questionnaire and tick the words in bold that they know. In pairs, they then discuss the meaning of the words in bold they *don't* know and check any they're not sure of in their dictionaries. In feedback, check and drill each word/phrase.

B Ss ask and answer the questions, noting down their partner's answers. In feedback, Ss tell the class about their partner. Discuss questions of particular interest, e.g. 5, 6, 9 and 10. (NB: Bear in mind that some Ss might not want to talk about their finances in class.)

C Give Ss 2 minutes to underline the examples of the letter 's' in the words. Encourage them to pronounce the different 's' sounds – they could do this in pairs, comparing their pronunciation. Play the recording for Ss to check their answers.

> **Answers:** ca**sh** /kæʃ/   note**s** /nəʊts/   coin**s** /kɔɪnz/
> inve**s**ted /ɪnˈvestɪd/   bill**s** /bɪlz/   po**ss**e**ss**ions /pəˈzeʃnz/
> trea**s**ure /ˈtreʒə/

D Follow the same procedure as in Ex 1C. In feedback, elicit answers and drill the words.

> **Answers:** mea**s**ure /ˈmeʒə/   earn**s** /ɜːnz/   tip**s** /tɪps/
> profe**ss**ion /prəˈfeʃn/   credit card**s** /ˈkredɪt kɑːdz/
> lend**s** /lendz/   impo**s**ter /ɪmˈpɒstə/   **s**ouvenir /ˌsuːvəˈnɪə/

▷ PHOTO**BANK** p158

1 Give Ss 2–3 mins to match the photos with the words and compare answers in pairs. They can use their dictionaries if necessary. In feedback, elicit/check and drill the words.
(NB: *ATM = automated teller machine*)

2 Ss prepare their definitions using dictionaries if necessary. Do feedback in open pairs across the class.

Answers:
1 1F **2**G **3**C **4**E **5**B **6**A **7**H **8**D

READING

Culture notes

The Fenn Treasure is a treasure reportedly worth $1m–$3m, hidden by art dealer and writer Forrest Fenn. According to Fenn, many people have claimed to have found the treasure, but no one has provided any evidence to him supporting their claim. As of 2015, Fenn has stated that to his knowledge, it is still not found.

2A Check language in the questions and give Ss 2 mins to discuss them in pairs. As question 2 asks Ss to predict information from the reading text, elicit Ss' predictions and note them on the board. Don't confirm them until feedback. Give Ss 3–4 mins to read the text to confirm the answer to question 2, then do class feedback. Finally, check vocabulary from the text.

Suggested answers:
1 *Raiders of the Lost Ark, Pirates of the Caribbean, The Treasure of the Sierra Madre, Three Kings*
2 The man expected to die and wanted to leave something behind for the public to search for, so he hid the treasure chest.

B Ss first read the rubric and prompts. Give them 3–4 mins to read the text again and discuss their answers in pairs. Elicit answers in feedback.

Answers:
2 The poem contained clues to help readers find the treasure chest.
3 When he releases new clues (every few months), more people come to look for the treasure, so this increases tourism in the area.
4 He has received over 13,000 emails from people who want more clues, and 18 marriage proposals.
5 He was in the Air Force before he opened an art gallery.

C Give Ss 2–3 mins to discuss their answers and compare them with another pair. Monitor and help where necessary. Elicit and discuss Ss' opinions in feedback.

Optional extra activity

In pairs, Ss write 5–6 true/false statements about the text. They then exchange with another pair, who must decide if the statements are true or false. Each pair collects back their statements and check their classmates' answers.

GRAMMAR RELATIVE CLAUSES

Watch out!

Ss tend to confuse the use of *who/which* for people/things, so highlight the difference clearly. Ss may also translate from their L1 and say, e.g. *He's the man that he sold me my car.* This error is connected to the use of defining/non-defining relative clauses, which is a more advanced language point and is not explicitly focused on here. Correct errors like these when they occur, but avoid any further explanation for now.

3 Ss do the exercise alone and then compare answers in pairs. Meanwhile, write the sentences on the board. In feedback, elicit/underline the relative pronouns *which, that, who, where* and the clause that follows. Elicit Ss' answers and check the rules carefully. Ask: *Is a poem a thing or a place?* (a thing) *Do we use* who *or* which? (*which*) *Are people a thing or a person?* (a person) *Do we use* who *or* which? (*who*) *Can we use* that *instead of* where? (No, we can only use *that* instead of *which* or *who*.)

Answers: 2 that **3** who **4** that **5** where

▷ LANGUAGE**BANK 8.1** p142–143

Ss can read the tables/notes in class or at home. However, draw their attention to the last point about the use of *the*, not *a/an*. In Ex B, teach *insurance* and *honeymoon*.

Answers:
A 2 which/that I sent you last week
3 restaurant where you can watch the chefs make your food
4 is a/the shop which/that sells cheap iPods and mobiles
5 accountant who/that helped me complete my tax form
6 where I learnt to do business
7 who/that invested the money was a criminal
B 2 who/that borrows $1,000,000 to buy a horse.
3 which/that sells insurance.
4 which/that she lends me.
5 who/that was working as a chef?
6 where we went on our honeymoon.

4A Check the words in the box and the example. Ss then work alone and compare answers in pairs before feedback.

Answers: 2 credit card **3** inventor

B Ss work alone to write definitions using relative pronouns and the prompts. Remind them to think carefully about which relative pronoun to use in each. Get Ss to compare answers in pairs and then give feedback.

Suggested answers:
1 It's a place where people look after your money. (bank)
2 It's a thing which/that you use to carry money and credit cards. (wallet)
3 It's a person who/that gives money to a product or business (to make more money). (investor)
4 It's a place where you go to borrow books. (library)
5 It's a thing which/that you use to watch films. (DVD player)

C Divide the class into two groups, A and B. They look at the relevant exercise on p164 or p167. Working in pairs with another student from the same group (A or B), Ss write the definitions of the words in their crossword. Monitor to provide support where necessary. Also prompt Ss to correct their sentences before the next stage. Then put Ss in A/B pairs. They take turns to ask for and give the definitions of the words. In feedback, nominate Ss to ask for and give definitions of their words in open pairs. Prompt them to self-correct/correct each other as needed.

Answers:

Student A

Down

  4 pieces of money which/that are made of metal, not paper
10 a person who/that owns something (he/she bought it or was given it)

Across

  6 a thing which/that you use to call someone
  8 a place where you find cars, houses, shops, etc.
11 money which/that you use to start a business and make more money
12 a person who/that acts in films or theatre

Student B

Down

  3 material which/that you use to make car tyres and chewing gum
  7 a place where you stay when you are travelling
  8 a person who/that fights for his country in wars
  9 a thing which/that grows in the earth and is usually green

Across

  1 a thing which/that we use to pay for something (not a credit card)
  5 a thing which/that you use to download and listen to music

SPEAKING

5A Check the rubric and any new vocabulary in the questions, e.g. *donations*. Ask Ss if they know who the people in their photos are and if not, introduce them (Oprah Winfrey, an American TV star; Richard Branson, an English businessman and investor; Muhammad Yunus, a Bangladeshi economist). Give Ss 4–5 mins to read the text and discuss the questions in pairs. Monitor and make a note of problems, particularly with language from this lesson. Elicit ideas from different Ss in feedback.

B Ss can discuss the questions in pairs or small groups. Give them 3–4 mins for this, and ask them to make notes. Monitor and make notes of any problems or good language for feedback. In feedback, nominate a student from each pair/group to report back on their projects. Then conduct a class vote on who had the best idea. Give feedback on any problem areas/good language as necessary.

Homework ideas

* **Ex 2C:** Ss write their opinion about the treasure hunt.
* **Ex 5B:** Ss write about their projects.
* **Language bank** 8.1 Ex A–B, p143
* **Workbook** Ex 1–6, p46–47

PAY ME MORE!

Introduction

Ss learn and practise the use of *too much/many, enough, very* and multi-word verbs. They read and discuss why certain people/ professions should earn the most money.

> **SUPPLEMENTARY MATERIALS**
> **Resource bank** p177
> **Language bank** p142–143

Warm up

Lead in to the topic of the lesson. Write this statement on the board: *Every job is important, so everybody should earn the same salary.* Ss work in pairs/groups. Give them 3–4 mins to agree/ disagree with the statement, giving reasons. Elicit/Discuss their answers in feedback.

LISTENING

1A Check the meaning of the jobs in the infographic and give Ss 2 mins to discuss the questions in pairs or small groups. In feedback, elicit Ss' answers and discuss their initial reactions to the information.

B Check the rubric and any unfamiliar words in the table, e.g. *nanny, funding.* Play the recording. Ss complete the table alone, then compare answers in pairs before feedback.

> **Answers: 1** children can be difficult, long hours, do extra work
> **2** working with children is important and (like teaching) it affects the future **3** firefighter **4** dangerous **5** research biologist
> **6** the whole world benefits

C Read the questions with Ss, then play the recording. Ss make notes as they listen, then compare answers in pairs before feedback.

> **Answers:**
> **1 a)** Speaker 3, the research biologist. He wants more money for the lab.
> **b)** Speaker 2, the firefighter. Firefighters save some (stupid) people who 'fell asleep with a cigarette in their mouth or forgot to switch off the oven'.
> **c)** Speaker 1, the nanny. Cleaning and cooking.

Unit 8 Recording 2

1 I work as a nanny, looking after children aged two, three, and five. I'm actually a live-in nanny. I live with the family. I came into the job with my eyes open. I knew it would be hard work because children can be difficult, though of course, they're fun, too. Also, we work long hours and too many of us do extra work like cleaning and cooking, when we should only look after the children. Nannies, particularly live-in nannies, aren't paid enough. Some of us need two jobs. We should earn enough just from being a nanny because working with children is a really important job. It's like teaching. It affects the future.

2 I'm a firefighter. It's one of the most dangerous jobs that exists. Really, it's too dangerous to be paid so little. People see us relaxed and calm and maybe we go and rescue a cat from a tree and people think, 'Oh they earn too much, their job is easy.' But when there's a serious fire, we have to be ready, even if it's just once a year. We risk our lives to save people, sometimes stupid people who fell asleep with a cigarette in their mouth or forgot to switch off the oven. You know, we save people, we save buildings, we save businesses. Anything and everything can burn down, and that's why we're so important.

3 I'm a research biologist. I work on finding solutions to some of the world's major problems, such as disease and hunger. The thing is, it's always difficult to get funding, to get enough money to actually do the research. Some of our projects are very expensive. They can

cost millions of dollars, and it can take years before you see results. So actually, I'm not asking for a bigger salary for myself, but I'd like more money for the lab. Too many scientists spend too much time applying for grants asking for money rather than actually doing their job in the lab. When things go well for us, the whole world benefits, so I think this work should be better funded.

GRAMMAR TOO MUCH/MANY, ENOUGH, VERY

> **Watch out!**
>
> It takes time for Ss to acquire confidence with quantifiers as most languages use them in different ways, e.g. they don't distinguish between countable/uncountable nouns, the word order is different. Ss will therefore make mistakes as part of the learning process, e.g. *There are too much cars/too many traffics in the streets. I'm not enough paid.* It's important to present the language clearly and correct errors at every opportunity.

2A Look at the example with Ss. They then work alone and compare answers in pairs. In feedback, elicit Ss' answers and check the meaning of the words in bold carefully.

> **Answers: 2** f) **3** e) **4** a) **5** c) **6** d)

B Ss look at the cartoons and describe them. Ask: *Why is it too much work but too many jobs?* (because *work* is uncountable and *jobs* is countable) Elicit Ss' answers and check them with the rules on the page. Check further: give Ss countable/uncountable nouns. They have to make a sentence with *too*, e.g. books/money: *I've got too many books. She spends too much money on clothes.*

> **Answers: 1** too many **2** too much

> ▷ **LANGUAGEBANK 8.2** p142–143
>
> Check the table/notes with Ss, paying special attention to the notes on the different uses of *enough*. Ss can refer to the notes when they do the exercises. **Weaker Ss** should do Ex A and B in class.
>
> **Answers:**
> A **1** The film was great. It was ~~too~~ *very* funny.
> **2** There aren't *enough* eggs ~~enough~~ to make a cake.
> **3** That child eats too ~~much~~ *many* sweets.
> **4** Do you earn *enough* money ~~enough~~ to pay the bills?
> **5** I spent too ~~many~~ *much* time on the first question.
> **8** There isn't enough ~~of~~ time to do this exercise.
> B **1** too much **2** enough **3** too **4** too many **5** very **6** too
> **7** too much **8** not enough

3 Do the first question as an example. Ss work alone and then compare answers in pairs. They should refer to the rules and examples in Ex 2 to check. **Weaker Ss** can also refer to the Language bank for help. In feedback, check answers carefully, referring back to the rules and examples in Ex 2.

> **Answers: 1** enough time **2** too much **3** very **4** too
> **5** too many **6** enough

4A Elicit examples for question 1. While Ss write their answers, monitor and prompt them to self-correct. Try to check all Ss' sentences before they do Ex 4B.

B Ss compare their sentences and find out what they have/don't have in common. They should prepare to report back to the class about themselves/their partner, e.g. *In my studies, I worry too much about my homework, but Juan doesn't worry about anything!*

VOCABULARY MULTI-WORD VERBS

5A Give Ss 3–4 mins to match the verbs with the definitions and compare answers in pairs. Check answers in feedback.

Answers: 1 a) 2 f) 3 d) 4 e) 5 b) 6 c)

B Ss discuss the sentences in pairs. In feedback, elicit answers and ask Ss to give reasons.

C Before Ss listen, ask them to read the sentences in Ex 5A to themselves. Then ask: *Which words are stressed in multi-word verbs?* Elicit the answer, then play the recording for Ss to check/confirm. If time, play the recording again for Ss to listen and repeat.

Answer: The particle (*up, back*, etc.) is stressed in multi-word verbs.

Unit 8 Recording 3

1 give up – I gave up my time.
2 give back – He gave back the money.
3 take up – It takes up hours of my time.
4 take over – He took over from his father.
5 turn down – I turned down the job.
6 turn into – It turned into a dream job.

6 Check the questions and elicit some examples. Give Ss 2–3 mins to note down their answers, while you monitor and provide support where needed. Ss then compare their ideas in groups. Monitor while Ss exchange information and note problems with the meaning/form of the multi-word verbs. In feedback, nominate Ss to share their ideas with the class. Prompt them to correct themselves/each other and give feedback as necessary.

speakout TIP

Read the Speakout tip with Ss and emphasise the importance of recording multi-word verbs in sentences. They should do this now with the verbs they've just learnt. Then elicit other verbs Ss know and write them on the board, e.g. *get up, go out, come back, get back*. Ss work in pairs and think of example sentences.

SPEAKING

7A First, elicit the names of the professions shown in the photos and write them on the board. Individually, Ss then make notes in answer to the questions.

Answers:
1 **A** security guard **B** teacher **C** maintenance worker
  D musician **E** nurse **F** soldier

B Ss compare their ideas in groups. They should summarise the differences and prepare to report back to the class, e.g. *Two of us think that teachers should earn more because they play a very important role in people's lives, but the other two think doctors should earn more.* In feedback, invite Ss from each group to tell the class about their opinions. Find out which profession Ss think should earn the most money and why. Give feedback on language problems Ss had now or in the next lesson.

WRITING ADDING EMPHASIS

8A Check the meaning of *emphasis*. Then check the rubric and the list of possible main ideas, and give Ss 2–3 mins to read the text and answer the question. In feedback, check the answer and any unfamiliar words in the text, e.g. *weak, support, newly qualified, working conditions*.

Answer: 3

B Ss read the text again and answer the questions in pairs. In feedback, check answers and elicit what type of words *extremely, very, fairly* and *really* are (adverbs). Elicit/Explain that these words are used to add emphasis.

Answers: 1 adjective 2 extremely 3 fairly

C Ss choose a job they want to write about. Give them 6–8 mins to write a 60–80-word paragraph. Monitor and support them with language they need. They might also want to draw/download a picture to illustrate their paragraph. Display Ss' opinion pieces around the class. They read them and choose the best one.

Homework ideas

- **Ex 7A:** Ss write their answer to one of the questions.
- **Ex 8C:** Ss write the final draft of their paragraph.
- **Language bank** 8.2 Ex A–B, p143
- **Workbook** Ex 1–6, p48–49

I'M JUST LOOKING

Introduction

Ss learn and practise buying and describing things in the context of shopping.

> **SUPPLEMENTARY MATERIALS**
> **Resource bank** p178
> **Language bank** p142–143
> **Ex 2B:** dictionaries
> **Ex 4, 5 and 6:** audio/video recording facilities
> **Ex 8A:** photos of unusual types of clothing, food and household appliances/equipment as prompts; dictionaries

Culture notes

People in the UK are changing the way they shop for food, clothes and consumer goods. Online shopping has become very popular because it's become safer to use credit cards online. People also want to avoid queues and save time and money. As far as food is concerned, there's a movement towards growing and eating 'real' food. People are more aware of their health and want fresh, ethically sourced ingredients rather than takeaway or ready-prepared meals. More and more people are growing their own vegetables again, as they did 30–40 years ago.

Warm up

Lead in to the lesson via the photos. Ask: *What are the people in each photo doing/buying? Are they enjoying it? Why/Why not?* Then ask Ss to think of two reasons why shopping in each of these ways is positive/negative, e.g. *quicker, cheaper.* Give them 3 mins to discuss this in pairs and report back to the class.

VOCABULARY   SHOPPING

1A Elicit/Check the meaning of the words in bold, then give Ss 2–3 minutes to read the questionnaire and match the words with the photos. Get them to compare answers in pairs before feedback.

> **Answers:** department stores (photo D)   markets (photo A)
> prices (photo E)   buy online (Photo B)   sale (photo C)

B Ss discuss the questions in pairs for 2–3 mins and compare their answers with another pair. In feedback, discuss Ss' answers in open class and find out what they have in common.

Optional extra activity

In pairs, Ss write extra questions for the shopping questionnaire (e.g. *Do you enjoy shopping online?*) and conduct a class survey.

FUNCTION   BUYING THINGS

2A Check the rubric and any unfamiliar words on the list, e.g. *hair/cleaning products, candle.* Ss listen to the conversations and underline the correct answers. Play the recording again if necessary and check Ss' answers in feedback.

> **Answers:** 1 we don't know   2 clothes   3 clothes
> 4 cleaning products   5 we don't know

B Give Ss time to read the phrases from the recording and ask about unfamiliar words/phrases, e.g. *fitting room, fit, in particular, PIN (Personal Identification Number).* Alternatively, they could use dictionaries to check new language. They then complete the phrases and compare their answers in pairs. Do not confirm answers yet – Ss will check them in Ex 2C.

C Ss listen again and check their answers (in bold in the audio script below). In feedback, play the recording again, pausing after each answer to elicit/check it.

> **Answers:** 1 me   2 of   3 on   4 for   5 cash   6 enter   7 here

Optional extra activity

Ss listen again and number *all* the phrases in Ex 2B in the order they hear them. They then check their answers in the audio script on p173.

Unit 8   Recording 4

S = Shop assistant   W = Woman   M = Man

Conversation 1
S: Can I help you?
W: No, thanks. I'm just looking.
S: OK, just let me know if you need anything.
W: Thanks.

Conversation 2
S: Hi there. **Are you looking for anything in particular?**
M: Yeah, do you sell those things that soldiers wear? Er … it's like a jacket.
S: Um, a type of jacket?
M: Yeah, a light green jacket with lots of pockets.
S: Ah, you mean a flak jacket?
M: Yes.
S: They're just on your left.
M: Ah, yes. Thank you. **Can I try this on?**
S: Of course.
M: Where's the fitting room?
S: Just over there.
W: Thanks.

Conversation 3
M: **Excuse me. Do you have one of these in a larger size?** It doesn't fit.
S: Is that the Large? I'll just go and check for you. I'm sorry. This is all we've got in stock at the moment. There are some other T-shirts over there on the other side. There might be some Extra Large sizes there.

Conversation 4
W: Hello. I was wondering if you've got any of that stuff you use for cleaning swimming pools.
S: Um … yeah, we usually sell a liquid cleaner. You pour it into the pool. There's one here.
W: Can I have a look?
S: Yep.
W: How much is it?
S: This one's twenty-eight pounds ninety-nine for a litre bottle.

Conversation 5
S: Hi. **Are you paying by cash or credit card?**
M: Credit card.
S: **Can you enter your PIN, please?** Thanks. Here's your card.
M: Thanks.
S: Thank you. Who's next, please?
W: Do you take Mastercard?
S: Yes, that's fine. **Can you just sign here, please?**

3 Write the questions from recording 8.5 on the board. Underline *Do you* and *Can I*, and ask Ss to listen to the questions and notice how *Do you … ?* and *Can I … ?* are pronounced. Play the recording. Then play it again for Ss to listen and repeat the questions. They should also pay attention to the sentence stress and intonation in each question. Correct and help Ss to sound natural. Prompt them to self-correct or correct each other if possible.

Unit 8 Recording 5

1 Do you sell pens?
2 Do you have one of these in red?
3 Can I try it on?
4 Can I try these on?

---

4 With *weaker classes*, play recording 8.4 again while Ss read it, if you think it will be helpful. Monitor while Ss practise the conversations, helping and prompting them to self-correct their pronunciation. *Stronger Ss* could rehearse/memorise one of the conversations and act it out to the class in feedback. If possible, record Ss reading the conversations and watch/invite comments on the recordings in feedback.

> **LANGUAGEBANK 8.3** p142–143

Weaker Ss can refer to the information in the tables when they do the exercise. *Stronger Ss* should cover them.

Answers: 1 help **2** on **3** fit **4** size **5** one **6** fitting **7** by **8** enter

5 Give Ss time to prepare for both the A and B roles. They should practise the complete conversation first, then swap roles and repeat it. Monitor and make notes on problems of accuracy and pronunciation for feedback. Alternatively, give Ss time to rehearse and then record them. Play the recordings and give feedback as needed.

6 First, divide the class into two groups, A and B. Group A read the information on p163 and Group B on p166. Put Ss in A/A and B/B pairs. Give them 3–4 mins to prepare, using the prompts. Monitor and provide support where needed. Ss then work in A/B pairs, facing each other, and role-play the situations. They could stand up, as if in a shop, if preferred. Monitor discreetly, making notes for feedback. In feedback, invite Ss to act out the role-plays to the class or record them if you haven't done so yet. Give feedback and do remedial work as necessary.

LEARN TO   DESCRIBE THINGS

7A Ss read the extracts from recording 8.4 and discuss the answers in pairs. Check them in feedback, asking Ss to give reasons.

Answers:
Those things that is used for countable nouns and *that stuff you use for + -ing* is used for uncountable nouns.

B Ss discuss the answers in pairs. Elicit/Drill the sentences in feedback. Point out that the phrases can be used with both countable and uncountable nouns.

Answers:
1 *It's a type of* pen.
2 *It's a kind of* oil that you use for cooking.

SPEAKING

8A Check the rubric and example and elicit a few examples of less common clothing, food and domestic products/appliances. Alternatively, use photos as prompts for this exercise if possible, e.g. *tie, glove, sandal, cucumber, onion, prawns, avocado, tin-opener, corkscrew*. Ss can work in pairs to choose their items. They can use dictionaries to find the words they need if necessary.

B Ss work with different partners and take turns to describe/guess the items. Nominate Ss to describe/guess the items in open pairs across the class in feedback.

Homework ideas
* **Ex 5 or 6:** Ss write a conversation in a shop based on one of these exercises.
* **Language bank** 8.3 Ex A, p143
* **Workbook** Ex 1–5, p50

SOLEREBELS

Introduction

Ss watch an extract from the BBC News about the company soleRebels. They then talk about a money-making idea and write an entry for a competition.

> **SUPPLEMENTARY MATERIALS**
> **Ex 2B and 4:** dictionaries

> **Culture notes**
>
> **soleRebels** was founded in 2004 by Bethlehem Tilahun Alemu and has become one of Africa's most recognizable footwear manufacturers. Today, shoes under the soleRebels brand are sold in over 30 countries around the world and through various e-commerce sites like Amazon and Endless. soleRebels also sells its products through its own e-commerce site.

Warm up

Lead in and create interest in the lesson via the photos on p84–85. Ask: *Where's the woman in the photo on page 85? What do you think the two women in the photos do? What do you think the connection between them is?* Let Ss discuss in pairs/small groups for 1–2 mins, then briefly discuss in open class.

DVD PREVIEW

1 Check the rubric and elicit some initial answers. Ss then discuss the questions in pairs. In feedback, elicit Ss' ideas.

2A Check the rubric and give Ss 4–5 mins to read the text and discuss the questions in pairs. Check answers in feedback. Do not do vocabulary work here – Ss will look at vocabulary from the text in Ex 2B.

> **Answers:** soleRebels is a fair trade shoe company that makes shoes from recycled materials. It has been very successful.

B Ss read the definitions and match them with the words. Elicit/Check meaning and pronunciation in feedback. Ss can then ask you about other unfamiliar words in the text, e.g. *local, cool, tyres, fast growing, powerful, newsreader*. Alternatively, they could check the words in their dictionaries.

> **Answers:** **1** unemployed **2** talent **3** entrepreneur
> **4** opportunities **5** fair trade **6** recycled

DVD VIEW

3A Play the DVD and give Ss 2 mins to discuss the questions in pairs. Elicit answers in feedback.

B Ss read the fact file and work out what type of word is needed for each gap. Give them 1–2 mins to discuss their answers in pairs. Elicit answers but do not confirm them yet – Ss will check them in Ex 3C.

C Ss watch the DVD again and check their answers. In feedback, check answers (in bold in the DVD script below) and play the relevant sections of the DVD again if Ss have problems.

> **Answers:** **1** tyres **2** five **3** bought **4** five **5** London
> **6** poverty

> **DVD 8** BBC News: soleRebels
>
> **P = Presenter B = Bethlehem**
>
> **P:** Now, if you've ever wondered **what happens to all those old tyres**, well, here is one use for them. We're at the home of soleRebels and the pun is entirely intended because **what they make here is a rather special kind of shoe**. The other part of the process is that **they use home-spun cotton fabric**. This is the beginning, with these ladies here doing the spinning. It's an ancient skill but they're using it in a modern way. Now, the thing about private sector companies like this is that they are breathing new life into Ethiopia's once faltering economy. **Nine years ago, when the company began, there were just five workers here.** Today, that number is a hundred and twenty and much of that success is down to one woman. And her name is Bethlehem Tilahun Alemu. And she's here with us. She's also on Forbes' list of one hundred most powerful women in the world. Congratulations on that.
> What are you proudest of?
>
> **B:** Thank you. Er, we're proud that we created job opportunities here, and **we're paying five times than the other companies are paying locally, in Ethiopia**. And, we're doing that by just giving, by empowering our own people and giving, give them to chance to work here.
>
> **P:** And your shoes can be bought all around the world?
>
> **B:** **Yes, people can buy our product everywhere because we're a global brand now.** People can buy it online, in different module cities. **We do have flagship stores, including Taiwan, Japan, Sweden and Austria … and we're about to open in London, also.**
>
> **P:** And here we have a finished product: a rather funky shoe. I can just see myself reading the news in one of these. The important thing about a company like this is that **it's helped to reduce the number of people living in poverty** by about a third. And for a country like Ethiopia, that is a win-win.

---

4 Ss look at the expressions in bold in the extracts and answer the questions in pairs. Encourage them to use their dictionaries if necessary. In feedback, elicit answers and check/drill the expressions.

> **Answers:** **1** It's old. **2** It's weak. **3** They're fashionable.
> **4** Yes, it is.

5 Elicit an initial answer to the question. Ss then discuss in pairs and report back to the class. Ask Ss if they know any other companies with similar principles.

speakout a money-making idea

6A Ss read the summary and then listen and underline the answers. Play the recording again if they still have doubts. Elicit/Check answers in feedback.

> **Answers:** **1** bags **2** material **3** markets **4** doesn't need
> **5** website

B Ss listen and match the key phrases with the sentence endings. *Stronger Ss* could do the matching task first, then listen and check. In feedback, play the recording again. Pause at each key phrase to elicit/drill the complete sentence (in bold in the audio script below). Ask further comprehension questions, e.g. *What do they use to make the bags? Do they make one particular type of bag? Why don't they need a lot of money to start the business?*

> **Answers:**
> Our business is called … 2
> Our idea is to … 4
> To be successful, we need to … 5
> We plan to … 6
> The best thing about the company is … 3

Unit 8 Recording 6

Our business is called Ragbags. Our idea is to make beautiful bags out of recycled material, so old jeans and clothes that you would normally throw away. **We hope to make money by reusing old material and turning it into different types of bags;** all types of bags: shopping bags, beach bags, handbags, whatever you need. So, you can either buy one of our ready-made bags or if you have some material that you really like, we can make one especially for you. **To be successful, we need to make sure the bags are really good quality and look wonderful.** We don't need a lot of money to start the business because we'll make the bags at home. **We plan to sell Ragbags at markets, in local shops and also online.** We'll have a website with lots of beautiful photos, where people can choose their designs and colours and then order their wonderful bag. And **the best thing about the company is that you will have an amazing bag**, made from your own favourite recycled material. Each bag will be unique, one of a kind, **and we'll have fun making them too**. It's a win-win.

7A Read/Check the rubric and questions. Ss discuss hobbies/interests they have for 2–3 mins. Elicit/Discuss some ideas for making money briefly and decide which are workable. Ss then work in groups and make notes of their ideas in more detail, using the checklist of questions. Provide help where needed.

B Remind Ss to use the key phrases as well as their notes from Ex 7A. While they prepare the presentation, monitor and prompt them to correct their notes if necessary. They should decide which part of the presentation each of them will present to the class and rehearse what they'll say.

C While Ss present their ideas, the rest of the class listen and note down interesting/useful ideas. Monitor discreetly and make your own notes with examples of good language and problems. In feedback, Ss discuss the presentations and vote for the best idea. Give feedback as needed.

writeback a website entry

8A Ss read the advertisement for the competition. Check *entrepreneur* and ask: *How much will the winner receive? What's the money for?* Ss then reread the entry and answer the question in the rubric. In feedback, check the answer and the meaning of *a fair price*. Ask: *Why is this different, do you think?*

Answer: They will pay fair prices to the people making the clothes in their own country.

B Ss work alone/in pairs with partners they worked with for Ex 7. They write a draft of their entry, using the model in Ex 8A and their ideas from Ex 7. Encourage them to show their drafts to each other and ask for/give opinions and advice. Ss write a final draft of the entry when they're ready. They can email it to you or other Ss to be 'judged'. Alternatively, display Ss' entries around the classroom. Divide the class into different groups of 'judges'. They read the entries and decide which one most deserves to win.

Homework ideas

Ex 8B: Ss write a final draft of their competition entry or write an entry for a different idea.

LOOKBACK

Introduction

Lookback exercises are designed to provide you and your Ss with an informal assessment of the language and skills covered in the unit. However, you might want sometimes to make them into a more formal test. In this case, set aside a lesson for Ss to do all the exercises with no help from you or their books. Monitor the speaking activities and make notes of Ss' performance (Ex 1B, 2C, 5B). At the end of the lesson, check answers formally, awarding marks where relevant (Ex 1A, 2A, 3, 4, 5A). Assess Ss' speaking skills from your notes and give them marks out of 20 (five marks each for fluency, accuracy, pronunciation, interaction).

MONEY

1A Read the first two lines of the poem with Ss. Ask: *What is the poem about?* Elicit Ss' answers/predictions. Then elicit the two rhyming words at the end of each line (*thin/win*). Tell Ss that rhyming words like these will help them complete the poem. Give them 1–2 mins to do this.

B Elicit/Check answers after Ss have compared them in pairs. Then ask: *What happened to Brenda Bones?* Elicit answers for the whole story, e.g. *First, she paid her bills. Then she …. After that she ….* Check/Teach new language during this stage, e.g. *super-size, hot air balloon, crash.* (Cameroon is in central/west Africa.) Read the poem aloud with Ss to give them confidence. Do this twice or more if necessary. They then practise reading it in pairs, saying alternate lines. Monitor and prompt them to correct mistakes with their pronunciation. In feedback, invite Ss to read the poem to the class. Ask: *What did Brenda learn? Do you agree?*

Answers: 1 bills   2 invest   3 lent   4 cash   5 borrowed
6 coins   7 tips   8 earn

RELATIVE CLAUSES

2A Check the example and ask: *What other word can you use here? Why?* (*which* for things) Tell Ss that they can sometimes use *who/that* in the exercise. Give them 3–4 mins to write the complete sentences and compare them. Monitor and note down problems with relative clauses for feedback. Check answers. Ask: *Where could you also use which?* (in question 2 and also in question 4 and 6 + *in*)

Answers:
2 Pasta is the food *that* I eat most often.
3 My mother is the person *who/that* has helped me the most.
4 The town *where* I grew up is really beautiful.
5 My brother and sister are the only people *who/that* understand me.
6 The restaurant *where* I usually have lunch is expensive.

B Elicit one or two examples, e.g. *Saturday is the day of the week that I like best. Monday is the day of the week that I hate most.* Then give Ss 3–4 mins to rewrite the sentences. Monitor to provide support and encourage Ss to self-correct.

C Check the example conversation. Ss then work in pairs and compare and respond to each other's statements in the same way. Monitor and make notes for feedback or assessment. In feedback, nominate Ss to say their sentences/respond in open pairs. Give feedback as needed.

TOO MUCH/MANY, ENOUGH, VERY

3 Look at picture A and elicit sentences about the problem, e.g. *There are too many people in the lift. There isn't enough space in the lift. The lift is very/too crowded.* Ss work alone/in pairs. Give them 4 mins to write as many sentences as possible about the other three pictures. Elicit/Check answers in feedback. Ss with the most correct sentences win.

Suggested answers:
A There are too many people in the lift. There isn't enough space in the lift. The lift is too/very crowded.
B It's too/very cold. The woman isn't wearing enough clothes. There's too much snow. Her clothes aren't warm enough.
C There's too much water in the bath. The bath is too/very full.
D The plant doesn't have enough water. The earth is too/very dry.

MULTI-WORD VERBS

4 Check the example. Ss then do the exercise in pairs, taking it in turns to ask the questions. Elicit/Check answers in feedback.

Answers: 2 turned into   3 gave, back   4 took up   5 turned, down
6 took over

BUYING THINGS

5A Do an example. Give Ss 5 mins to write out the conversations and then compare answers in pairs. In feedback, check answers. To prepare Ss for Ex 5B, elicit the main stress in each sentence. Also remind Ss of the pronunciation of the weak forms and word linking in *Do you … ?* and *Can I … ?* Drill selected sentences to illustrate this.

Answers:
1 **A:** Can I help you?
  B: I'm just looking.
2 **A:** Can I help?
  B: Do you sell gardening tools?
  A: I'll just check.
3 **A:** Are you looking for anything in particular?
  B: Do you have one of these in red?
4 **A:** How is it?
  B: It doesn't fit. Do you have one of these in a bigger size?
  A: I'll have a look. Here you are.
  B: Thanks. It fits OK.
5 **A:** Who's next? Are you paying by cash or credit card/credit card or cash?
  B: Credit card, please.
  A: Can you just sign here, please?
6 **A:** Excuse me. Can I try this on?
  B: Yes, certainly, sir.
  A: Where's the fitting room?
  B: It's on the left.

B Monitor while Ss practise the conversations to assess/help them with their pronunciation. Invite pairs to read them to the class. Do remedial pronunciation work with sentence stress, weak forms and linking if necessary.

BBC interviews and worksheet
How do you feel about shopping?

In this video people describe what they like and don't like about shopping, the best places to go shopping and what they've bought. The video also extends Ss' vocabulary of shops and shopping.

OVERVIEW

9.1 GREEN LIVING

VOCABULARY | nature
LISTENING | listen to a radio programme about green ideas
READING | read about great green ideas
GRAMMAR | comparatives/superlatives
PRONUNCIATION | stressed syllables
SPEAKING | talk about green issues
WRITING | write about your views on the environment

9.2 INTO THE WILD

VOCABULARY | the outdoors
READING | understand an article about an experience in the wild
GRAMMAR | articles
PRONUNCIATION | word stress, weak forms: *a* and *the*
SPEAKING | give your views on life in the city or the country

9.3 IT COULD BE BECAUSE …

VOCABULARY | animals
LISTENING | listen to people discussing quiz questions
FUNCTION | making guesses
PRONUNCIATION | silent letters
LEARN TO | give yourself time to think
SPEAKING | talk about different animals

9.4 THE NORTHERN LIGHTS BBC))) DVD

DVD | watch an extract from a BBC documentary about the Northern Lights
speakout | an amazing place
writeback | a travel blog

9.5 LOOKBACK

Communicative revision activities

BBC))) INTERVIEWS

How do you feel about being in the countryside?

In this video people describe how they feel about the countryside, nature and wildlife. The video extends Ss' vocabulary on nature, the outdoors and animals. Use it at the start or end of the unit.

GREEN LIVING

Introduction

Ss revise the comparative/superlative forms and vocabulary to describe nature in the context of the environment.

> **SUPPLEMENTARY MATERIALS**
> **Resource bank** p179–180
> **Language bank** p144–145
> **Photo bank** p158 (You may need maps of Ss' countries.)
> **Warm up:** copies of the list of activities (See notes below.)
> **Ex 1B:** a map of the world

Warm up

Prepare Ss for the lesson. Write the list of activities below on the board (or photocopy them for Ss): *have a picnic in the park, take a boat trip on the river, walk in the mountains, go horseriding in the countryside, swim in a lake, watch the sunset on a beach, go surfing in the ocean, drive a 4x4 in the desert.* Ask: *Which of these activities would you most like to do this weekend? Why?* Elicit one or two answers. Then give Ss 1–2 mins to put the activities in order of importance for them. Ss then compare their lists in pairs and give reasons for their choices.

VOCABULARY NATURE

1A Check the vocabulary in the questions. Then elicit a sample conversation, e.g. *A: Have you ever swum in an ocean? B: Yes, I've swum in the Atlantic and Pacific Oceans. A: Really? Where exactly? B: I've swum on both sides of the Atlantic.* Ss discuss the questions in pairs and report back to the class.

B Read the word box and check *mountain range* in the example. Show Ss a map of the world if possible and elicit examples for each item. Give Ss 2–3 mins to think of or find more examples. In feedback, invite Ss to answer, and show the places on the map if available.

> **Suggested answers:**
> **mountain ranges:** Alps, Himalayas, Blue Mountains
> **lakes:** Michigan, Toba, Baikal
> **waterfalls:** Angel, Niagara, Victoria
> **rivers:** Nile, Amazon, Yangtze, Mississippi
> **deserts:** Sahara, Kalahari, Gobi
> **oceans:** Atlantic, Pacific, Arctic, Indian, Antarctic
> **rainforests:** Amazon, the Congo Basin Forest of Central Africa

C Ss discuss the question in pairs. If they can't think of any cities now, you could ask them to do some research at home, then discuss their ideas in the next lesson.

> ▷ **PHOTOBANK** p158
>
> **1** Check *glacier* and *coastline*. Give Ss 4–5 mins to discuss their answers in pairs/groups. In **multilingual classes**, provide maps of Ss' countries if possible.

LISTENING

2A Ask Ss to look at the photos and give them 2 mins to discuss what's happening, in pairs or small groups. Elicit answers in feedback, but do not confirm them yet – Ss will check them in Ex 2B.

B Ss listen to the programme and check their answers to Ex 2A.

> **Answers:**
> 1 In photo A people are building a school out of plastic bottles.
> 2 In photo B people are generating energy for the nightclub by dancing on a special dance floor.
> 3 Photo C shows people in the Seoul River Park, which used to be a motorway.

C Ss discuss the question in pairs. Play the recording again if necessary. Elicit answers in feedback and any other details Ss remember about the programme.

3A Ss read the summary. If you have a map of the world, show the places mentioned in the summary. Ss underline the four mistakes and compare their answers in pairs. Do not confirm answers yet – Ss will check them in Ex 3B.

B Play the recording again, pausing at each mistake to elicit the correct answer (in bold in the audio script below).

> **Answers:**
> The Hug it Forward project uses plastic *bottles* to build schools.
> Club Surya is in *London*. The dancers produce *60 percent* of the energy the nightclub uses.
> Dr Kee Hwang's idea was to take down *the main highway* to reveal the river below.

C Ss discuss the questions in groups. Elicit their opinions and reasons in feedback.

Unit 9 Recording 1

Hi and welcome to *Green Ideas*. Now, the problem with some of the traditional ways of saving the environment is that they can be really boring. So today we're looking at ideas for protecting the environment that are a bit different, and we think they sound fun.

Our first project is called Hug it Forward. This great project started in Guatemala, where communities decided to work together to **build schools out of old plastic bottles**. In the first project, over one thousand eight hundred kids from the region filled ten thousand plastic bottles with bits of plastic, food wrappers and other rubbish found on the streets. They then used the bottles as bricks to help build a school. By the time they had finished, they had a new school and the area was a lot cleaner too! Now the idea is spreading, and around the world more communities are using the bottle school technology to build their own schools. What a fantastic idea!

And here's an idea for those of you who enjoy going out clubbing. **The Surya nightclub in London** was one of the first eco-friendly nightclubs in the UK. The club has a special dance floor which uses the movement people make when they dance to generate energy. **The dancers manage to produce sixty percent of the energy that the club uses for light and music.** The owner of the eco-club had another great idea. If you walk or cycle to the club, rather than using a car or public transport, you get free entry. I love it.

And our final idea for today is the story of the Seoul River Park. It's getting more and more difficult to find green spaces in cities, so when **Dr Kee Hwang had a 'crazy' idea to take down the city's main highway and uncover the river that flowed below**, to make a green park, most people thought he was mad. They told him that his idea would create traffic chaos and would be a disaster for the area. But Dr Hwang went ahead with the project, and created the five-point-eight-kilometre green river park. It's a place where the residents of Seoul can walk, relax and really enjoy the city. And do you know what? People are happier and there's a lot less traffic chaos than before! It just shows that sometimes even the craziest ideas can work.

GRAMMAR   COMPARATIVES/SUPERLATIVES

> **Watch out!**
>
> The short/long comparative and superlative forms in English often cause problems for Ss as their L1 probably won't make this distinction. Ss tend to mix up the forms, e.g. *The most bigger problems are because of climate change.* It is therefore very important to highlight form clearly and give Ss adequate spoken and written practice in *full sentences*. Monitor and correct errors consistently to prevent fossilisation.

4A Ss should be familiar with the basic comparative/superlative forms, so give them 1–2 mins to read the sentences, complete the rules and compare their answers in pairs. Check answers in the rules, referring to sentences 1–5. With **weaker classes**, read the sentences and rules with Ss and elicit other examples, e.g. *shorter, bigger, friendlier, more important, more/less time.*

> **Answers:**
> short adjectives: *-er, -ier*
> longer adjectives: *more, more, less*

B Follow the same procedure as in Ex 4A for the superlative form.

> **Answers:**
> short adjectives: *-est*
> longer adjectives: *most*

> ▷ **LANGUAGEBANK 9.1** p144–145
>
> Read/Check the tables and notes with Ss, especially the irregular forms and use of *as … as*. Ss can refer to the tables when they do Ex A/B. (NB: *CVC = consonant-vowel-consonant*)
>
> **Answers:**
> A 2 longer, than   3 noisier   4 more interesting than
>   5 more expensive than   6 more dangerous than
>   7 hotter than   8 more exciting than   9 less cold
> B 2 You're the best friend I've ever had.
>   3 That's the most boring film I've ever seen.
>   4 This is the shortest day of the year.
>   5 That's the longest run I've ever done.
>   6 This is the oldest building I've ever seen.
>   7 That's the hardest job I've ever done.

5A Check the rules for the examples in the table. Ss then complete it and compare answers in pairs. Do not confirm answers yet – Ss will check them in Ex 5B.

B Ss listen and check their answers. Check the form/spelling of the answers using the rules in Ex 4.

> **Answers:** higher, the highest; healthier, the healthiest; more difficult, the most difficult

C Play the recording twice. Ss listen and underline the main stress. Check answers and highlight the unstressed *than* in sentences 2–4. Ss listen again and repeat chorally/individually. Prompt self- or peer correction of pronunciation mistakes.

> **Answers:**
> 2 It's <u>hotter</u> than I <u>expected</u>.
> 3 The food is <u>cheaper</u> than at <u>home</u>.
> 4 It's more <u>dangerous</u> than I <u>thought</u>.

6A Do an example. Ss complete the exercise alone and then compare answers in pairs. Tell them that more than one answer is possible in two sentences.

Answers: 1 the greenest **2** warmer than **3** the nicest
4 healthier than **5** the furthest **6** bigger than
7 less friendly/friendlier than **8** the most/least polluted

B Ss prepare their answers before they work in pairs. Monitor and note how well they use comparative/superlative forms. Discuss Ss' answers and give feedback on persistent mistakes.

SPEAKING

7A Read/Check the survey with Ss and elicit one or two answers to the question in the rubric. While Ss work, monitor and check the accuracy of Ss' questions before Ex 7B.

Suggested answers: Do you plant trees/turn off lights and electrical appliances/take showers, not baths/reuse plastic bags?

B First, Ss should make a note of their own answers to the questions. Monitor and support Ss with language they need during this stage. They then take turns to answer/discuss each question and make a note of the *yes/no* answers. Make notes of good use of comparatives/superlatives and mistakes. Each group reports the results of their survey back to the class. Find out who the 'greenest' group/person is and why. Finally, give feedback on Ss' performance as needed.

WRITING   SIMILAR SOUNDING WORDS

8A Do question 1 as an example and ask: *Why do people often spell these words wrongly?* (because they sound the same) Then elicit the difference in meaning between *you're* and *your*. Ss then do the exercise alone and compare answers in pairs. In feedback, check answers and elicit other words Ss know that have the same sound but a different meaning (homophones).

Answers: 1 your **2** wear **3** two **4** write **5** see **6** their

B Give Ss 1 min to read the text and ask: *What does the writer do to protect the environment?* Ss then underline and correct the six mistakes. After checking answers, tell Ss to check their written work for mistakes before they give it to you.

Answers:
I think everyone should recycle. I've done this since I was a child and it's not difficult. Children need to be educated about the ~~write~~ *right* way to look after the world we live in. I use a bicycle to get to work every day, and I get very angry when I ~~sea~~ *see* people use a car to drive round the corner to the shops. ~~Their~~ *There* are lots of small things we can do to help the environment like turning off the television when ~~your~~ *you're* not watching it, using plastic bags for ~~you're~~ *your* rubbish, and recycling, ~~two~~ *too*.

C Ss work alone/in pairs to choose the topic they want to write about. Give them 10 mins to write their comment in 70–100 words. Monitor and support them with language where necessary. In feedback, Ss can work in groups and read out their comments or read them to the class. Alternatively, they can put them on the class blog for other Ss to respond to.

Homework ideas
- **Ex 8C:** Ss write a final draft of their comment or write a comment about a different topic from Ex 7A.
- **Language bank** 9.1 Ex A–B, p145
- **Workbook** Ex 1–8, p51–52

INTO THE WILD

Introduction

Ss revise and practise the use of articles in the context of nature and the outdoors.

SUPPLEMENTARY MATERIALS
Resource bank p181
Language bank p144–145
Ex 2A, 4 and 5A: dictionaries

Warm up

Lead in to the topic of the outdoors. Ask: *Which would you choose for a two-week holiday: a walking/camping holiday around the countryside or a beach holiday in a hotel? Why?* Ss discuss their answers in pairs/groups and report back to the class. Find out which kind of holiday is most popular with your Ss.

VOCABULARY   THE OUTDOORS

1 Check the rubric/questions and elicit examples of wild places. Give Ss 3–4 mins to discuss the questions in groups and prepare to report back to the class, e.g. *Two of us like wild places, but three of us don't.* They should also give reasons for their answers.

2A Do the first question as an example: ask Ss for a definition of *rural area* in question 1. Tell them to try to work out the meaning of *rural* from the context if they don't know the word. If they can't, they should check the meaning/pronunciation in their dictionaries. Don't ask for examples of the words here as Ss will talk about the sentences in Ex 2B. Give Ss 3–4 mins to discuss/find out about the words and check their answers in feedback.

Suggested answers:
1 a place in the countryside
2 a place in the countryside which is very pretty
3 natural features that you can see that are very pretty
4 land which is protected by the government because it is very pretty and people can visit it
5 a building/place used for the study and protection of animals and plants that people can visit
6 a hot, wet area of very tall trees
7 natural parts of the land such as mountains or lakes
8 clean air found in areas which are not polluted

B Find out if sentence 1 is true for your Ss. If so, elicit/discuss their reasons for this. Ss then work alone and decide which sentences are true for them, making notes of the details, e.g. *The north of my country has an area of natural beauty called the Lake District. It's very popular with tourists.* Ss then work in pairs/groups and take turns to give their answers. In **multilingual classes**, put Ss from the same countries/areas of the world in different groups. Invite Ss to tell the class about sentences that are true for them. Give feedback on errors with the new vocabulary.

C Ss write the words in bold in their notebooks. Play the sentences several times: Ss listen and underline the main stress in each word. In feedback, elicit the pronunciation and stressed syllables in the collocations.

Answers: 2 natural beauty   **3** beautiful scenery   **4** national park
5 wildlife centre   **6** tropical rainforest   **7** geographical features
8 fresh air

Teaching tip

In pronunciation exercises, use finger highlighting to help Ss with word stress. Say a word naturally first, e.g. *natural beauty*. Then hold up the fingers of one hand and ask: *How many syllables in 'natural beauty'?* Elicit/Say *five*. Ask: *Where's the stress?* Elicit/Say *on the first and fourth syllables*. At the same time, point to the thumb and fourth finger. Say the word again naturally, beating the stress, and drill it chorally and individually.

D Ss listen and repeat the sentences chorally and individually. Prompt them to self-correct or correct each other where necessary.

READING

Culture notes

The Amazon rainforest, covering much of north-western Brazil and extending into Colombia, Peru and other South American countries, is the world's largest tropical rainforest, famed for its immense biodiversity. It's crisscrossed with thousands of rivers, the biggest being the Amazon river.

3A Teach/Check *anaconda*. Put Ss in pairs and give them 2 mins to discuss the title and predict what happened in the story. Elicit their ideas and note them on the board if necessary.

B Give Ss 2–3 mins to read the story and check their predictions from Ex 3A in pairs. In feedback, discuss which predictions were correct/incorrect. Ss will deal with unknown vocabulary in the next two exercises. Elicit what Ss know about the Amazon rainforest.

Suggested answers: When Marisa was visiting a tribe in the Amazon, she was tested by the medicine man. She was taken to a clearing in the forest and asked to close her eyes. Then a large anaconda snake was placed on her shoulders. She was terrified, but she tried to breathe to stop her fear. The anaconda relaxed and she passed the test.

4 Check *hold a ceremony*. Give Ss 4–5 mins to write their answers and check them in pairs. Ss can check new words in their dictionaries, but only essential words they need for their answers.

Answers:
1 In the Amazon, in Peru.
2 She planned to stay with a tribe for a short while.
3 She enjoyed helping the women prepare food, playing with the children and learning about the plants they use for medicine.
4 To say *thank you* to Marisa for coming and to welcome her into the tribe.
5 She was terrified.
6 The man told her to breathe, so she did, and the snake relaxed and rested its head on her arm. She passed the test.

5A Ss find/underline the words in the story. Do question 1 together. Ask: *What do you think* howling *means from the context?* Elicit answers, then tell Ss to check the word in their dictionaries. Give them 4–5 mins to complete the exercise using their dictionaries. In feedback, elicit/check the pronunciation, part of speech and an example sentence from the dictionary.

Suggested answers:
1 making a long, loud crying sound
2 warm and wet
3 a space with no trees
4 looking at something for a long time without moving your eyes
5 stopped moving and stayed very still because you were afraid
6 go down into the ground

Teaching tip

It would be good to focus on the usefulness of dictionaries at this point. Ask: *What other information can you find out about a word in your dictionary?* Elicit *part of speech, pronunciation, example sentence.* Encourage Ss to become more autonomous and use their dictionaries more often.

B Ss cover the text and look at the picture and the words in Ex. 5A. Elicit ideas about how to start the story, e.g. *Marisa was on a jungle trip in Peru.* They then practise retelling the story in pairs. In feedback, nominate Ss to take turns telling different parts of the story (in chronological order). The rest of the class listen and add/correct details where appropriate.

GRAMMAR ARTICLES

Watch out!

Articles cause confusion for learners because either they're used in a different way in their L1 or they're not used at all. However, there are patterns in the use of articles which help, e.g. *no article before plural nouns.* Patterns like these are revised in this lesson. It's particularly important that Ss learn, keep a record of and practise phrases with articles as fixed/semi-fixed phrases.

6 Ss read the rules and examples. Check the answer to question a) as an example. Ss then work alone and compare answers in pairs before feedback. In feedback, elicit Ss' answers and check each rule carefully. Elicit more example sentences for each rule or read further examples in the notes in the Language bank on p144.

Answers:
1 a) a huge anaconda snake   b) with a guide
2 c) in the Amazon in Peru   d) The snake was very hungry
3 e) in Peru   f) tropical birds

▷ LANGUAGEBANK 9.2 p144–145

Ask Ss to read the notes and tick the ones that are the same as in Ex 6 on p91. Then check the other notes/examples. Ss can refer to the notes when they do the exercises. **Weaker Ss** should do Ex A and B in class. In Ex A, check *whale, bat, blood, squirrel, eagle.* In Ex B, check *escaped.*

Answers:
A 1 – 2 the 3 – 4 the 5 a 6 – 7 an 8 the 9 an
10 the
B I was feeling bored so I went for *a* walk. The trees were green and *the* sky was blue. It was *a* beautiful day. Suddenly I heard a strange noise, like *an* animal. But I knew it wasn't *a* cat because cats don't sound like that. *The* sound continued for a minute or more. I went home and switched on *the* TV to watch the local news. The newsreader said, 'Some animals have escaped from *the* city zoo.'

7A Check the example. Ss complete the exercise alone and then compare answers in pairs. They can refer to the rules and examples in Ex 6 or the Language bank to check. Do not confirm answers yet – Ss will check them in Ex. 7B.

B Play the recording for Ss to check their answers. In feedback, refer Ss back to the rules and examples in Ex 6/the Language bank. Then drill the sentences chorally and individually, paying particular attention to the pronunciation of *a* and *the.*

Answers:
2 I was one of many tourists in ~~the~~ South America.
3 A guide met us at the airport. The next day, *the* same guide took us hunting.
4 On *the* second day, the guide took us to a river.
5 I sometimes make a programmes in Britain.
6 In my job, I can explain *the* natural world to millions of people.
7 I hate ~~the~~ insects in general, but especially mosquitoes.
8 I had *a* camera in my bag.

C Play the recording, pausing after each sentence to allow Ss to write down the sentence. Get them to compare answers in pairs before feedback.

Answers:
1 I met wonderful people in the Amazon.
2 The birds we saw were amazing.
3 I've got a brilliant idea.
4 We need to put up a tent.
5 We took photos of the beautiful scenery.

8 First, elicit details about the picture and teach *bow, arrow, gravity.* Ask: *Why are the men running away?* Elicit some ideas. Give Ss 1–2 mins to read the text and check their ideas. Discuss the answer in feedback and check new words, e.g. *hunting, jumped up, missed, fortunately, gravity.* Then elicit the answer for gap 1 and ask: *What's the rule?* (no article with the names of states) Ss complete the text alone and compare answers in pairs. They must identify the correct rule. Monitor and prompt them to self-correct if possible. Check answers in feedback.

Answers: 1 – 2 – 3 – 4 a 5 the 6 the 7 – 8 a

SPEAKING

9A Give Ss 1–2 mins to read the comments. To check comprehension, ask: *What's wrong/good about country life?* Ss then discuss the question in pairs. In feedback, elicit answers briefly as Ss will expand on their answers in Ex 9B.

B Elicit an example of one advantage/disadvantage of living in the country/a city. Ss then discuss in pairs/groups and think of reasons for each advantage/disadvantage. Monitor and provide language Ss need if necessary. Elicit Ss' ideas in feedback.

C In pairs, Ss take turns to talk about their preferences. Monitor and note down examples of good language/problems they have. In feedback, invite Ss to tell the class about their partner. Find out how many people prefer country/city life. Give feedback on language problems Ss had, now or in the next lesson.

Homework ideas
* **Ex 9C:** Ss write two paragraphs explaining why they are a city/country person.
* **Language bank** 9.2 Ex A–B, p145
* **Workbook** Ex 1–4, p53–54

IT COULD BE BECAUSE …

Introduction

Ss learn/practise making guesses and giving themselves time to think in the context of talking about animals.

SUPPLEMENTARY MATERIALS

Resource bank p182

Language bank p144–145

Photo bank p159 (Ss may need dictionaries.)

Warm up: copies of the fable (See notes below.)

Ex 3A: a photo of a gerbil

Ex 6B: photos of a swift and a python

Ex 9B: photos of an elephant, an eagle, a dog, a chameleon, a shark, a camel a fly

---

Warm up

Lead in to the topic of the lesson. Use the fable below for a *running dictation* (or dictate it yourself). Place several copies on the walls around the room. Ss work in A/B pairs. Student A, the 'runner', runs to read the text and memorises as much of it as possible. He/She then runs back and dictates as much of the text as he/she can remember to Student B, the 'writer'. This continues over several turns, until the text is complete. When they have finished dictating the text, check it with the class or give Ss a copy to check themselves. Then ask: *Do you know this story/fable? What's the message?* (Don't believe everything people tell you!/Don't trust people who flatter you!)

The Fox and the Crow

One day, a fox saw a crow in a tree. It was holding a big piece of cheese in its mouth. 'I must have that cheese,' thought the fox. So he said, 'Good morning, Miss Crow. You're looking very well this morning. I'm sure your voice is more beautiful than any other bird. Please sing for me.' The crow was very proud, so she opened her beak to sing. Of course, the cheese fell out and the fox ate it!

VOCABULARY   ANIMALS

1A First, elicit/check the names of the animals in the photos on p92 (rat, seal, dog). Then teach/check language in the word webs, e.g. *wild, jaguar, insect, bee, domestic*. Ss copy the word webs into their notebooks and complete them with words they know. In feedback, draw the word webs on the board and invite Ss to complete them.

Alternative approach

Do the exercises in the Photo bank with Ss (see below) *before* they do Ex 1. Ss can then add the words they learn to the word webs.

Suggested answers:

wild: monkey, lion, cheetah

insect: mosquito, fly, butterfly

domestic/farm: cat, guinea pig, hamster, cow, pig, sheep, chicken

reptile: crocodile, lizard, alligator

B Elicit one or two examples and give Ss 2–3 mins to do the exercise. In feedback, go through the alphabet, eliciting the names of animals for each letter.

▷ **PHOTOBANK** p159

1 Check the headings. Ss can use dictionaries if necessary. Check answers in feedback.

2 Ss discuss the questions in pairs and then report back to the class.

Answers:

1   **B** dolphin   **C** whale   **E** lion   **F** tiger   **G** leopard   **I** crocodile   **J** snake   **L** spider   **M** fly   **N** butterfly   **O** pigeon   **P** penguin   **Q** eagle   **R** ostrich   **S** chimpanzee   **T** monkey   **U** gorilla   **W** elephant   **X** cow   **Y** camel   **Z** bear

---

speakout TIP

Read the Speakout tip with Ss and ask them if they already have a *study buddy* or regularly practise their English with other learners. If not, discuss why it's a good idea and discuss other ways of practising their English together.

LISTENING

2 Give Ss 2–3 mins to discuss in groups and note down their answers to the questions using verbs, e.g. *talk, cook, run*. Discuss Ss' ideas in feedback.

3A Ss look at the photos and read the title. Ask: *What's the quiz about?* Elicit Ss' answers. Then give them 2–3 mins to do the quiz in pairs. They should discuss/guess which might be the best answer to each question. Check/Teach *gerbil* using a photo if possible.

B Ss compare/discuss reasons for their answers and may modify them if they wish. They will check the answers in Ex 4.

4A Ss listen and make a note of the answers to the quiz questions. They then compare answers in pairs.

B Ss listen again and check their answers (in bold in the audio script below). Play the recording again, or relevant parts of it, if Ss still have doubts. Nominate Ss to answer in feedback.

Answers:

1   Rats are used to rescue people. They can move in small spaces and they have a good sense of smell, so they can find people.

2   Abandoned dogs are taken to prisons and then the prison inmates take care of them until the dogs are adopted.

3   Dolphins are used to protect areas of water. They can detect swimmers who shouldn't be there.

4   Gerbils can smell people's adrenaline when people are excited, scared or angry. The airport security bosses hoped the gerbils would smell terrorists or other criminals in airports.

5   Seals can dive deep down into freezing water. Scientists can attach research equipment to the seals' bodies.

Optional extra activity

Ss work alone/in pairs. They read the audio script and write 4–6 questions to ask other Ss. Ss ask/answer their questions in groups (as a team game) or across the class.

Unit 9 Recording 7

A: Why do we use rats after an earthquake? I'm not sure. It might be to help find people or other animals?

B: **Yeah, they're used to rescue people. They can move in small spaces and they have a good sense of smell, so they can find people.**

A: Why do some prisons use abandoned dogs? Mmm, let me think. It could be as prison guards. Maybe they use the dogs to guard the prisoners? Actually, no, it can't be that because they'd be trained dogs, not abandoned dogs. I don't know.

B: OK. It says: it was a programme that started some years ago. **Abandoned dogs are taken to prisons and then the prison inmates take care of them until the dogs are adopted.**

A: Why does the army use dolphins? It's definitely not to attack people because dolphins are kind of nice. Um, it's hard to say. I really don't know.

B: **Dolphins are used to protect areas of water. They can detect swimmers who shouldn't be there.** A light is attached to the dolphin's nose. The dolphin bumps into the swimmer and the light falls off its nose. This tells the army where the swimmer is.

A: Why did airport security plan to use gerbils in the 1970s? Perhaps they can smell drugs or something like that?

B: **Gerbils can smell people's adrenaline. When someone is excited, scared or angry, adrenaline is released by the body. The airport security bosses hoped the gerbils would smell terrorists or other criminals in airports.** In the end, the idea was abandoned because gerbils didn't know the difference between terrorists and people who were just scared of flying.

A: Why do we use seals for research in the ocean? Er, that's a good question. It might be because they can live in very cold temperatures.

B: **They can dive deep down into freezing water. Scientists can attach research equipment to the seals' bodies**, and this doesn't stop the seals from diving and swimming.

FUNCTION MAKING GUESSES

5A Do the first question as an example. Ss then complete the table and compare answers in pairs. In feedback, elicit answers, then drill the phrases/sentences.

Answers:
It's possible: It could be, It might be, Maybe, Perhaps
It's not possible: It can't be, It's definitely not

B Read the question with Ss and elicit their answers.

Answers: *Could* has a silent 'l'. In *might*, 'gh' are silent.

C Ss listen and repeat the sentences at least twice. Then drill the sentences chorally and individually, prompting Ss to correct themselves/each other.

Unit 9 Recording 8

1 It could be. It could be you!
2 It might be. It might be us!
3 It can't be. It can't be them!

D Drill the phrases chorally and individually.

▷ **LANGUAGEBANK 9.3** p144–145

Ss refer to the information in the tables when they do the exercise. Check *common*.

Answers: 1 e) **2** g) **3** h) **4** a) **5** b) **6** f) **7** c) **8** d)

6A Ss should do the exercise alone as the answer to the question and the language are sometimes closely related.

B Ss compare answers in pairs and then check them on p164. In feedback, check the language questions in Ex 6A and the answers from p164. Find out how many questions Ss answered correctly. Show Ss photos of a *swift* and a *python* (or draw them on the board).

Answers: 1 can't be **2** is definitely not **3** Maybe it's **4** It can't be **5** Maybe it's **6** It's definitely not **7** Perhaps it's **8** might be

LEARN TO GIVE YOURSELF TIME TO THINK

7 Ss read and complete the extracts from recording 9.7. Get them to compare answers in pairs before feedback.

Answers: 1 sure **2** think **3** say **4** That's

8A Do an example. Ss then correct the other mistakes and compare answers in pairs. Elicit/Check and drill the sentences in feedback to prepare Ss for Ex 8B.

Answers:
1 A: Er, let me ~~to~~ think.
   B: Well, I'm not ~~much~~ sure, but I think it's the cheetah.
2 A: Um, that's *a* good question.
   B: It's hard *to* say, but …

B Remind Ss about the pronunciation points in Ex 5B and 5C. Monitor while they practise, and help with pronunciation where needed. **Strong Ss** could memorise the conversations and act them out to the class in feedback.

SPEAKING

9A Check the rubric and extend part B's example. Elicit, e.g. *It could/might be a hippo./Yes, maybe it's a hippo./No, it can't be because …* . Give Ss 3–4 mins to speculate and discuss why the parts are special. Monitor and make notes on language problems for feedback later.

B Ss work with another pair and compare their answers before checking them on p164. In feedback, show Ss photos of the animals if you have them. Check how many answers Ss guessed correctly. Also ask what they learnt.

Homework ideas
• **Ex 3/4:** Ss write a paragraph about one of the animals described in the quiz.
• **Language bank** 9.3 Ex A, p145
• **Workbook** Ex 1–4, p55

THE NORTHERN LIGHTS

Introduction

Ss watch an extract from the BBC documentary *Joanna Lumley In The Land Of The Northern Lights* (2008). They then learn/practise how to talk about an amazing place and write a travel blog.

SUPPLEMENTARY MATERIALS

Warm up: photos of actress Joanna Lumley, e.g. in the TV series *Absolutely Fabulous* or *The Avengers*; photos of the Northern Lights if possible

Ex 1A: a map showing Norway and the Svalbard archipelago

Ex 5A: photos and a map of Fish River Canyon and Namibia

Culture notes

The Northern Lights, or *aurora borealis*, most often occur from September to October and from March to April. This natural phenomenon is the result of an interaction between the Earth's magnetic field and solar wind. The Lights are most visible close to the North Pole because of the long periods of darkness and magnetic field.

Joanna Lumley (born 1946) is an English actress, best known for her role as Patsy in the BBC TV comedy series *Absolutely Fabulous* (*Ab Fab*). She's also famous as a human rights and animal welfare activist. She was born in India and her family moved to Malaysia when she was two. In the programme, she travels up through Norway to Tromso, and then to Svalbard, an archipelago in the Arctic Ocean. It's the most northerly permanently inhabited place on Earth with temperatures of minus 30˚C.

Warm up

Lead in and create interest in the lesson. Ss look at the big photo on p94–95. Ask: *What does the photo show? What are the green lights?* Elicit/Discuss Ss' answers, using the Culture notes if necessary, and show more photos of the Northern Lights. Then look at the photo of Joanna Lumley and show more photos of her if possible. Ask: *What do you know about her? Where's she from? What's she famous for?* Elicit what Ss know and discuss – use information from the Culture notes above if necessary.

DVD PREVIEW

1A Ss discuss the questions in groups for 2–3 mins. In feedback, elicit Ss' answers. Show the map of Norway with Tromso, Svalbard, etc. For question 2, ask: *Would you like to go to this place? Why/Why not?*

B Give Ss 2 mins to read and answer the question in pairs. In feedback, discuss Ss' answers. Ask: *Why did she dream of being somewhere cold?* Also check/teach *get the chance to* and *sled*. Ss can discuss/predict the answer to the question at the end of the text.

Answer: When she was young, she dreamed of being somewhere cold and seeing the Northern Lights.

DVD VIEW

2A Ss watch the DVD and discuss the question in pairs. In feedback, elicit Ss' answers and any initial responses to the DVD extract.

B Ss read the information and complete the sentences in pairs. In feedback, check answers (in bold in the DVD script below) and elicit other information they can remember about each answer.

Answers: 1 snow   2 people   3 books   4 dogs   5 lights

3A Ss read the sentences and match the words in bold with the definitions. Encourage them to look for clues in the context which will help them decide on the correct definition. Ss finish the exercise alone and compare answers in pairs. Check these in feedback.

Answers: b) not definitely good or bad   c) difficult to find   d) amazing   e) necessary   f) happy to wait (maybe for a long time)

B Ss watch again and order the sentences. After they've compared answers in pairs, play the DVD again, or the relevant parts of it, if necessary. In feedback, check Ss' answers (underlined in the DVD script below). With **stronger classes**, you could ask more detailed comprehension questions related to each answer, e.g. *What did she miss when she was a child? What sort of books did she read? What were they about?*

Answers: 2 c)   3 e)   4 b)   5 f)   6 d)

Optional extra activity

Play the DVD again for Ss to watch/enjoy. Invite comments and questions from them as they watch or at the end. Elicit what the Northern Lights look like and how Ss would feel if they saw them.

DVD 9 **Joanna Lumley In The Land Of The Northern Lights**

J = Joanna Lumley   T = Tura Christiansen   K = Kjetil Skøglie

J: The far north. Fairytale mountains. It's just fabulously beautiful. The land of the magical Northern Lights is somewhere I've longed for all my life. As a little girl I lived in the steamy heat of tropical Malaysia. I used to yearn to be cold. **I'd never even seen snow.** But my storybooks were full of snow queens, and now I'm entering that world. This is the journey I've always dreamt of making. **I feel I've come into another world now; no people except you and us.** And if we're very lucky, we might see the elusive Northern Lights. **I pack up things that are going to be essential on every trip.** So in here I've got, for instance, oil-based pastels; and **I've got a lovely little drawing book**, but I've got coloured pages so that you can draw in different colours; **a lovely old guidebook** – it's called *The Land of the Vikings*. It's got beautiful old maps. Look at that. But if it wasn't for one item in my case, I wouldn't be on this journey at all. **This is the book:** *Ponny the Penguin*. This is when I first heard of the Northern Lights. And there was this picture, which haunted me, of a sort of rippling curtain and a little tiny penguin. This is not your average taxi rank at the station. **I'm in the hands of Tura Christiansen and his team of eleven sled dogs.** Good morning. I'm Joanna.
T: Tura.
J: Tura. How nice to see you, Tura.
T: Yes.
J: These are wonderful dogs.
T: They like to … to, er …
J: They like to run?
T: Yes.
J: The weather near Tromsø is uncertain. **But local guide Kjetil Skøglie promises me we'll track down the lights even if it takes till morning.** I can't see anything, Kjetil.
K: No it's … it's nothing yet. You just have to be patient.
J: OK, so I just wait here.
K: Yeah, you just wait here.
J: Yeah.
K: Good luck.
J: Thanks, Kjetil. I stand in the pitch black by the side of the fjord and wait. Look – much brighter there. Oh, something's happening there. Oh … Look up here! Look what's happening here! Look at that! Look at this! And it just keeps changing and changing. I can't believe I'm seeing this. It's fantastic and it's coming back again. I have been waiting all my life to see the Northern Lights. I'm as happy as can be. This is the most astonishing thing I have ever, ever seen.

---

4 Elicit some initial answers to the questions. Ss then discuss them in pairs and report back to the class about their partner.

speakout an amazing place

Culture notes

Fish River Canyon in Namibia, Africa, is a gigantic ravine about 160 km long, up to 27 km wide and almost 550 m deep in places.
The Grand Canyon in Arizona, USA, is 446 km long, from 6.4 to 29 km wide and 1.83 km deep in places.

5A Check the rubric and questions before Ss listen. They compare answers in pairs and listen again if they haven't understood and still have doubts. Elicit answers in feedback. Show Ss a map and photos of Namibia and Fish River Canyon if you have them and discuss details from the Culture notes.

Suggested answers:
1 Fish River Canyon is in Namibia, Africa.
2 It is the second biggest canyon in the world. It is silent.

B Ss listen again and tick the key phrases they hear. In feedback, play the recording again. Pause at each key phrase (in bold in the audio script below) and elicit/drill the complete sentence.

Answers:
What did you think of it?
It was [amazing/frightening/wonderful] … !
The first thing you notice is [how big it is/how quiet the place is] …
The best thing about it was … [the silence/how beautiful the place was] …
Would you like to go back?

Unit 9 Recording 9

A: OK, the most beautiful place I've been to. Well, a few years ago I went to Fish River Canyon.
B: Where?
A: Fish River Canyon. It's the second biggest canyon in the world.
B: After the Grand Canyon?
A: After the Grand Canyon.
B: Where is it?
A: It's in Namibia, in Africa.
B: Wow. And **what did you think of it?**
A: **It was amazing. The first thing you notice is how big it is**, of course.
B: Of course.
A: It just goes on and on as far as your eye can see. But **the best thing about it was the silence**.
B: Right.
A: It was so amazingly quiet. We went there in August and there weren't many tourists and it was just so quiet.
B: **Would you like to go back?**
A: I would love to go back. One day!
B: One day.

6 Check the questions and give Ss 2–3 mins to make notes of their answers. Monitor and prompt Ss to correct their notes if necessary. Provide help where needed.

7A First, demonstrate the activity. Elicit example sentences using the key phrases, e.g. *The highest place I've ever been to is Mont Blanc in Switzerland. It was amazing! The best thing about it was the light.* Give Ss 3–4 mins to prepare what they'll say using the key phrases. Monitor and help with language where necessary. Ss then take turns to talk about their experiences in pairs.

B Ss work with another pair/group. First, they take turns to talk about their experiences. Then they discuss which were the most interesting/exciting/dangerous. Monitor discreetly and note examples of good language and problems.

C Ss talk about their partners, experiences while the rest of the class note down the most interesting/exciting/relaxing places. The class then decides which place was the most interesting/exciting/relaxing of all. Give feedback as needed.

writeback a travel blog

8A Check the rubric and give Ss 3–4 mins to read the blog and answer the questions. After checking answers, check/teach *trekking*, *humid* and *watch tower*.

Answers:
She visited China. She enjoyed walking along the Great Wall of China. Although it was hot, humid and hard to walk and climb the steps, the views were spectacular and she was proud of what she had achieved.

B Check the rubric and questions. Ss choose a place they talked about in Ex 6 (or another place of their choice) and decide if they want to work alone/with a partner from Ex 7. They write a draft of their travel blog, using the model in Ex 8A and the key phrases. Encourage Ss to show their drafts to each other and ask for/give opinions and advice. Monitor while they do this, providing support as needed. Ss can put the final draft of their travel blog on the class blog. Alternatively, display Ss' entries around the classroom for the class to read/discuss.

Homework ideas

Ex 8B: Ss write a final draft of their travel blog, adding photos if possible.

LOOKBACK

Introduction

Lookback activities are designed to provide revision and communicative practice in a motivating way. This helps Ss and gives you the opportunity to assess their ability to use the language they've learnt in the unit. It's a good idea to monitor and assess individual Ss while they do the activities, and compare their performance with their results in more formal tests.

NATURE

1A Give Ss 2 mins to answer the quiz questions alone.

B Give Ss 2 mins to compare their answers in pairs and check them on p164. In feedback, check which pair had the most correct answers. Also ask: *Which was the easiest/most difficult question?*

Alternative approach

Give Ss 3–4 mins to work in pairs/teams and discuss the questions together. Check each team's answers and give a point for each correct one. The team(s) with the most correct answers win(s).

COMPARATIVES AND SUPERLATIVES

2A Do an example with *hot* and write the comparative and superlative forms on the board. Ss then write the correct forms for the other adjectives. Monitor and note down persistent errors Ss make and focus on them in feedback. Elicit/Check Ss' answers, including the spelling, and do remedial work if necessary.

Answers: hot, hotter, the hottest; good, better, the best; lovely, more lovely, the most lovely; cheap, cheaper, the cheapest; high, higher, the highest; boring, more boring, the most boring; healthy, more healthy, the most healthy; long, longer, the longest; exciting, more exciting, the most exciting; fast, faster, the fastest; old, older, the oldest; cold, colder, the coldest

B Check the examples. Ss then take it in turns to test each other in pairs. In feedback, nominate Ss to ask and answer in open pairs across the class, and prompt other Ss to correct if necessary.

3A Do question 1 as an example. Ss then complete the answers alone and compare them in pairs. In feedback, nominate Ss to answer, giving reasons for their choice of form, e.g. *hard* is a one-syllable adjective, so it ends with *-est*.

Answers: 1 the most organised 2 the hardest 3 the longest 4 the youngest 5 the tallest 6 the most 7 the fastest 8 the furthest/farthest

B Elicit the answer to question 1 as an example. Ss then do the exercise in groups, taking it in turns to ask the questions. Elicit/ Check answers in feedback. Find out if the groups have the same names in their answers to each question. Ensure that sensitive Ss don't feel uncomfortable during this exercise.

Optional extra activity

Use the Photo bank on p159 for this exercise. Put Ss in pairs/ groups and number them 1, 2, 3, etc. Select the names of two/ three animals from the photos and say their names. Team 1 must make a comparative sentence (if you give them two words) or a superlative sentence (if you give them three), e.g. *shark, dolphin: A shark is more dangerous than a dolphin. shark, dolphin, whale: The shark is the most dangerous animal./The whale is the biggest/heaviest.*
Ss get two points if they give a correct meaningful sentence and one point if only the comparative/superlative forms are correct.

ARTICLES

4 Do question 1 as an example. Ask: *Why do we use* the? (because it's a superlative form/there's only one: *the nearest*) Ss can check in the Language bank if they know the correct answer but can't say exactly why. They then work in pairs and use the Language bank for each question if necessary. Check answers in feedback.

Answers:
1 Excuse me, where's *the* nearest bank?
2 This city is big, but it doesn't have *an* airport.
4 Hi. Would you like *a* drink?
5 Where's *the* money I lent you?
7 She goes to *a* small school in the centre of London.
8 We missed the bus and waited an hour for *the* next one.
9 My sister is working in *the* United States at the moment.
10 Is there *an* internet café near here?

5 Ss work alone and then compare answers in pairs. They can check their answers in the Language bank if necessary. Elicit, check and correct Ss' answers in feedback.

Answers: 1 animals 2 the sky 3 a journalist 4 the lion 5 Argentina 6 the first day

ANIMALS

6A Give Ss 2 mins to find the nine words. Stop the activity after 2 mins. Invite Ss to write the answers on the board. The student with the most correctly-spelt words wins.

B Give Ss 2–3 mins for this. If time, you could then put them in new pairs and get them to describe a different animal to their new partner.

Answers:

C	R	O	C	O	D	I	L	E	E
H	O	A	O	B	O	C	D	T	F
I	T	G	W	H	L	L	J	U	K
M	B	L	M	N	P	I	G	R	O
P	I	P	Q	R	H	S	T	T	U
A	T	V	W	W	I	X	Y	L	Z
N	A	B	H	S	N	A	K	E	C
Z	D	E	A	F	F	H	I	J	A
E	A	G	L	E	D	I	O	E	N
E	E	Y	E	L	I	P	M	S	O

MAKING GUESSES

7A Do A as an example. Encourage Ss to make as many sentences as possible with *could/might be* or *can't be*. While they guess the others in pairs, monitor to check how well they are using the target language and give feedback after Ex 7B.

B Ss check their answers on p165. Give feedback as needed.

Homework ideas

Workbook Review 3, p56–58

BBC interviews and worksheet

How do you feel about being in the countryside?
In this video people describe how they feel about the countryside, nature and wildlife. The video extends Ss' vocabulary on nature, the outdoors and animals.

OVERVIEW

10.1 TOP CITIES

READING | read about the best cities for young people
VOCABULARY | describing a city
LISTENING | listen to conversations about different cities
GRAMMAR | uses of *like*
PRONUNCIATION | sentence stress
SPEAKING | discuss qualities of different places
WRITING | use formal expressions to write an email

10.2 CRIME AND PUNISHMENT

READING | read an article about crime and punishment
VOCABULARY | crime and punishment
GRAMMAR | present/past passive
PRONUNCIATION | weak forms: *was/were*
SPEAKING | discuss alternative punishments to fit the crimes

10.3 THERE'S A PROBLEM

VOCABULARY | problems
LISTENING | listen to people complaining
FUNCTION | complaining
LEARN TO | sound firm, but polite
PRONUNCIATION | sentence stress
SPEAKING | talk about problems in a school

10.4 MARY'S MEALS BBC ◗ DVD

DVD | watch an extract from a BBC documentary about an internet sensation
speakout | an issue
writeback | a web comment

10.5 LOOKBACK

Communicative revision activities

BBC ◗ INTERVIEWS
How do you feel about city life?

This video extends and consolidates Ss' vocabulary of describing a city and extends discussion on the advantages and disadvantages of city life. Use the video at the end of Lesson 10.1 or at the start or end of the unit.

TOP CITIES

Introduction

Ss revise and practise different uses of *like* as a verb and preposition. They learn vocabulary to describe a city and practise writing a formal email.

> **SUPPLEMENTARY MATERIALS**
> **Resource bank** p184
> **Language bank** p146–147
> **Ex 1A:** a world map and photos of well-known cities not on the list on p165, e.g. Madrid, Berlin, Cape Town, Buenos Aires, São Paulo, Moscow, Bangkok
> **Ex 3A:** a world map

Warm up

Lead in to the topic of the lesson. Ask: *What do you like about your town/city? Is it a nice place to live in? Why/Why not?* If necessary, write prompts for Ss on the board, e.g. *friendly, safe, clean, attractive, good facilities/nightlife/places to eat and shop, transport, interesting events.* Elicit some examples, then give Ss 4–5 mins to discuss the questions in pairs/groups. In **multilingual classes**, put Ss from different countries in different pairs/groups. In feedback, discuss Ss' answers and find out what Ss like/don't like about their town/city.

SPEAKING

> **Culture notes**
> **Dubai** is a state on the Arabian Gulf, one of the seven United Arab Emirates and the most populated/expensive.
> **Prague** is the capital of the Czech Republic and an important industrial centre. It is known for its Old Town Square, which has colourful baroque buildings and Gothic churches.
> **Melbourne** is the second largest city in Australia and the capital of the state of Victoria in the south-east of the country. It is an important business, industrial and cultural centre.

1A If you've brought photos of well-known cities, use them as prompts for the discussion. If not, elicit some examples of the best cities to live in. Give Ss 3–4 mins to discuss their choices in pairs, using the prompts from the Warm up. In feedback, discuss Ss' answers and write their suggestions on the board.

B Ss read the text and then check the list of cities on the board against the list on p165. In feedback, ask: *How many are the same/different? Do you agree with those on the list?* Elicit/Discuss Ss' answers.

VOCABULARY DESCRIBING A CITY

2A Read/Check unfamiliar words in the sentences, then give Ss 2–3 mins to answer the question alone or in pairs. Elicit and discuss reasons for their answers.

> **Answers:** 1+ 2– 3– 4+ 5+ 6– 7– 8+ 9+ 10+ 11– 12–

B Play the recording. Ss listen to the sentences, mark the stressed words, then compare answers in pairs before class feedback.

Answers:
3 There's a <u>lot</u> of <u>traffic</u>.
4 It has <u>beautiful buildings</u>.
5 The <u>people</u> are <u>friendly</u> and po<u>lite</u>.
6 There's a <u>lot</u> of <u>crime</u>.
7 It's very pol<u>luted</u>.
8 There are nice <u>parks</u> and <u>green</u> spaces.
9 It has good <u>shopping</u> and <u>night</u>life.
10 There are <u>lots</u> of things to <u>see</u> and <u>do</u>.
11 It's ex<u>pensive</u> to <u>live</u> there.
12 It's very <u>crowded</u>.

C Play the recording again for Ss to listen and repeat, paying attention to sentence stress. Drill the sentences chorally and individually.

D There are six positive sentences. Give Ss 3–4 mins to decide on the three most important ones in pairs, giving reasons for their choices. Ss then compare their ideas with another pair and should try to come to an agreement on the three most important things for a city. In feedback, discuss Ss' answers. They should agree on/ vote for the top three factors.

LISTENING

3A First, elicit what Ss know about the cities in the photos. If possible, elicit their locations on a world map. Check the rubric and play the recording. Ss should make notes of the positive/negative things mentioned, and compare answers in pairs. In feedback, elicit as much detail as possible about the three cities.

Answers:
Speaker 1: Melbourne – great city, friendly and fun; lots of things to see and do; very arty; lots of cafés and street art, music; good nightlife; good public transport; good atmosphere; great location; fantastic beaches
Speaker 2: Dubai – one of the world's fastest growing cities; lots of people, very crowded; great shopping; good nightlife; lots of bars and clubs; not a lot of crime; streets are very safe; traffic is terrible; everybody drives a car; petrol is cheap; lots of cheap taxis, so you don't have to drive
Speaker 3: Prague – one of the best cities in the world; so beautiful, like the city of your dreams; beautiful buildings and squares; old streets wonderful to walk along; full of culture, music, restaurants and bars; very cold in winter – a lot of snow; sunny in the summer, so you can sit outside in the cafés or walk up to the castle; very special city; people are very friendly

B Ss read the questions first. **Stronger Ss** might be able to write some of the answers before they listen. Play the recording again. Ss write their answers and compare them in pairs. In feedback, play the recording. Tell Ss to say *Stop!* at each answer (in bold in the audio script below).

Answers: 2 Prague   3 Dubai   4 Melbourne   5 Dubai   6 Prague

4 Give Ss 3–4 mins to read and underline the phrases. Tell them the words are not always exactly the same. Elicit/Check the phrases in feedback (underlined in the audio script below). Then ask: *Which of the three cities would you like to live in?* Ss discuss the question in pairs, groups or as a class.

Suggested answers: See the underlined phrases in the audio script below.

Unit 10 Recording 2

Conversation 1

I = Interviewer   D = Daniela

I: Daniela, so you live in Melbourne, right?
D: Yeah, that's right.
I: Well, Melbourne has been voted one of the best cities to live in for young people. So what do you think? Do you like living in Melbourne?
D: I love it! Melbourne <u>is a really great city</u>. It's very friendly and fun. Umm … <u>there're lots of things to see and do</u>.
I: OK, so you can go out a lot?
D: Yeah, <u>it's very arty</u>, there are **lots of cafés and street art**, music … and <u>the nightlife is really good</u>. People like to enjoy themselves in Melbourne.
I: That's great. And what about getting around? What's the public transport like?
D: <u>Public transport is really good</u>, actually. It's quite cheap and it's efficient. **You can go everywhere by tram and sometimes it's even free.**
I: So, what do you like best about living in Melbourne?
D: I think it's probably the atmosphere. Also, <u>it's a great location</u>. It's really close to some fantastic beaches, so there's surfing. <u>It's got everything</u>, really. <u>It's a great city</u>.

Conversation 2

I = Interviewer   R = Rick

I: Rick, you've lived in Dubai for … what, four years, right?
R: Yeah, four years.
I: So what's it like, living in Dubai?
R: Well, I read that Dubai is one of the world's fastest growing cities, so <u>there are a lot of people</u> and <u>it's very crowded</u>. It's a great city for shopping and going out. And <u>it has really good nightlife</u>, with **lots of bars and clubs**.
I: Is it a safe city?
R: Yes, <u>there isn't a lot of crime</u>. <u>The streets are very safe</u>. But one of the biggest problems is the traffic. Everyone drives a car here – petrol is still cheap, so <u>the traffic's terrible</u>. **One good thing is the taxis though. There are lots of them and they're cheap**, so you don't have to drive.

Conversation 3

I = Interviewer   M = Matt

I: What about Prague? What's Prague like, Matt?
M: I've always loved Prague. <u>I think it's definitely one of the best cities in the world</u>.
I: What do you like best about living in Prague?
M: I think it has to be the city itself. <u>It's so beautiful. It's like the city of your dreams</u>, **with beautiful buildings and squares**. The old streets are wonderful to walk along. <u>It is full of culture, music, bars, restaurants</u> …
I: What about the weather? What's the weather like in Prague?
M: Yeah. OK, when I arrived in Prague, it was minus seven degrees. So, obviously, it gets very cold in the winter, and <u>there is a lot of snow</u>. But, in the summer, the sun shines and you can sit outside in the cafés or **walk up to the castle**. <u>It's a very special city and the people are so friendly</u>.

GRAMMAR   **USES OF *LIKE***

Watch out!

Ss often translate from their L1 and say, e.g. *How is your city?* or confuse the forms in English, e.g. *How is it like your city?* Highlight/Check the two forms clearly and correct errors at all stages of the lesson.

5A Ss match the questions with the answers and compare answers in pairs before feedback.

Answers: 1 b)   2 c)   3 a)   4 e)   5 d)

B Write questions 1 and 3 on the board. Elicit Ss' answers and underline *be like* and *do you like* in the sentences. Ask: *Which questions ask for a description/an opinion?* (questions 1, 2 and 4)

Answers: **1** 3, 5 **2** 1, 2, 4

▷ **LANGUAGE**BANK 10.1 p146–147

Ss can refer to the tables/notes when they do the exercises. In Ex B, check *peaceful*.

Answers:
A 1 What's your new job like?
2 Do you like my new dress?
3 What is tapas like?
4 What's the weather like there?
5 Do you like living in the country?
B 1 d) **2** b) **3** c) **4** e) **5** a)
C 1 I like ~~listen~~ listening to music.
2 ~~How~~ What is the flat like?
3 Did you like it?
4 What's he like ~~he~~?
5 What's ~~like~~ the weather *like*?
6 ~~Are~~ Do you like speaking English?

6A Do the first question as an example and check the rule. Ss then do the exercise alone and compare answers in pairs. Do not check answers at this stage – Ss will check them in the next exercise.

B Ss listen and check their answers. Recheck the rules in feedback. Play the recording again for Ss to listen and repeat the questions.

Answers: **1** it like **2** you like **3** What's, like **4** do you like

C Elicit example questions for question 1. Ss then write their own. Monitor and help Ss with accuracy, prompting them to self-correct.

D Look at the example conversation and do one more example for question 1 with a strong student. Monitor while Ss take turns to ask and answer their questions. Again, prompt Ss to correct their mistakes. In feedback, nominate Ss to ask and answer their questions in open pairs across the class. Encourage them to correct each other's errors. Do remedial work if necessary.

SPEAKING

7A Elicit/Discuss some cities Ss know well, including those Ss talked about in the Warm up. Give Ss 4–5 mins to write their notes. Help them with language if they need it.

B In *multilingual classes*, put Ss from the same country in the same groups. Monitor discreetly while Ss describe their chosen cities, making notes of examples of good language and problems. They should discuss/agree on *one* city which should be in the top ten places to live in the world. In feedback, nominate Ss from each group to tell the class about the city they've chosen to be in the top ten, giving reasons. The class then vote for one of them. Write examples of Ss' errors and good language on the board. Ss discuss and correct the errors in pairs.

WRITING USING FORMAL EXPRESSIONS

8A Give Ss 2–3 mins to read the email and answer the questions. Check answers in feedback.

Answers: She's writing to ask for more information about the Bed and Breakfast. She wants to know:
1) if it is possible to travel easily into the town centre by public transport and how much it costs.
2) if it's safe to walk home in the evening.
3) if she can get a discount if she stays for the whole month.

B Give Ss 1 min to reread the email quickly and answer the question. Discuss the answer in feedback.

Answers: The language is formal. You can notice expressions like *Dear Sir/Madam, Yours faithfully*, etc.

C Check the rubric and example. Ss underline the formal expressions in the email and complete the table. Get them to check answers in pairs before feedback.

Answers: I am writing to ask for … ; I would like to … , I would like to know if … , … if it is possible to … ; I look forward to hearing from you.; Yours faithfully

D Give Ss 3–4 mins to prepare notes for their emails. Ss then write their email alone. While Ss write the first draft, monitor and provide support. When they have finished, encourage them to show their work to a partner before they write a final draft.

Homework ideas
- **Ex 8D:** Ss write a final draft of their email (and put it on the class blog or send it to you).
- **Language bank** 10.1 Ex A–C, p147
- **Workbook** Ex 1–9, p59–60

CRIME AND PUNISHMENT

Introduction

Ss learn and practise the use of the present and past passive forms in the context of crime and punishment.

> **SUPPLEMENTARY MATERIALS**
> **Resource bank** p183 and p185
> **Language bank** p146–147
> **Photo bank** p159 (Ss may need dictionaries.)
> **Ex 2C:** dictionaries

Warm up

Lead in to the topic and language of the lesson. Write examples of 'modern' crimes on the board, e.g. illegal downloading of music/films/books from the internet, DVD piracy. Ask: *What do you think of this crime? Is it serious? Do you think material on the internet should be free for everybody? Should people who commit this crime be punished? How? Should they go to prison or get a fine?* Give Ss 3–4 mins to discuss the questions in pairs/groups, then discuss as a class.

SPEAKING

1A Ss read the words in the box. Don't check meaning until they've tried to match them with the photos. In feedback, elicit/teach the words Ss know/don't know and drill the pronunciation. Ss copy the words into their vocabulary notebooks and underline the main stress (see answer key below).

> **Answers: A** murder **B** speeding **C** drink driving **D** graffiti

> **Optional extra activity**
>
> Ss rank the crimes in the box in order of seriousness. They first decide on the order alone, making notes of their reasons. They compare their answers in pairs and must persuade each other to agree on the same order. They then work with another pair and do the same thing. Monitor and help Ss with language they need. In feedback, elicit each group's order and write it on the board. Ss should then discuss/come to an agreement on the same order as a class.

B Check the rubric and elicit some examples. Ss discuss in groups for 3–4 mins and report back to the class. In **multilingual classes**, put Ss of different nationalities in the same pairs/groups.

READING

2A Check the rubric and the title of the text. Give Ss 4–5 mins to read the introduction and answer the questions in pairs. In feedback, nominate Ss to answer. Check *fine/prison sentence*.

> **Answers:**
> 1 He stole books from a bookshop.
> 2 He was sent to read stories and books to hospital patients.
> 3 Giving punishments that fit the crime, e.g. not prison sentences.

B Check the example and elicit other alternative sentences for this crime. Ss then discuss for 4–5 mins and note down their ideas. Elicit/Check all answers in feedback. Ss should make notes and vote for the best alternative sentences for each crime.

C Give Ss 4–5 mins to read and check the ideas mentioned there. They should use dictionaries to check essential vocabulary. In feedback, nominate Ss to talk about the ideas from Ex 2B that were mentioned. Check new words if necessary.

D Check the rubric and elicit an example for each opinion, e.g. *I think it's a great idea because it helps criminals to learn from their crimes.* Give Ss 3–4 mins to discuss. Monitor and support Ss with language they need if necessary. In feedback, nominate Ss from each pair to take turns to tell the class about an advantage/disadvantage. The class then discuss/vote on whether alternative sentencing is a good idea or not.

> **Optional extra activity**
>
> In groups, Ss discuss alternative sentencing for more serious crimes, e.g. *murder, bank robbery, kidnapping*.

VOCABULARY CRIME AND PUNISHMENT

3A Check the example. Give Ss 3 mins to write and compare their answers in pairs. In feedback, check/drill the words.

> **Answers: 2** prison sentence **3** writing graffiti
> **4** community service **5** theft **6** shoplifter **7** fraud
> **8** shoplifting **9** fine

B Give Ss 2 mins to complete the table and check their answers in pairs before class feedback.

> **Answers:**
> **criminal:** shoplifter
> **crime:** writing grafitti, theft, fraud, shoplifting
> **punishment:** prison sentence, community service, fine

speakout TIP

Read the Speakout tip with Ss. Elicit other examples from the lesson so far, e.g. *punish/punishment, crime/criminal*.

> ▷ **PHOTOBANK** p159
>
> **1** Ss can use their dictionaries if they have difficulty matching the words. In feedback, elicit/check and drill the answers.
> **2** Give Ss 3–4 mins to write sentences. Check them in feedback.
>
> > **Answers:**
> > **1 People: 1** B, D, E, F, G **2** A, E, (C) **3** B **4** A
> > **Verbs: 5** D **6** F **7** G **8** E **9** C
> > **2** (Suggested answers) Criminals break in and shoot people. Police officers arrest criminals, help victims and investigate crimes.

GRAMMAR PRESENT/PAST PASSIVE

> **Watch out!**
>
> Ss usually find the passive form easy to understand, but may make mistakes with the form, e.g. *He didn't was arrested. The thief was never catched.* They may also use the passive when the active would be more appropriate, e.g. *The money was stolen by me.* vs *I stole the money.* It's important to check the form/use of the passive carefully and provide appropriate practice in natural contexts.

4A Ss complete the tables alone and then compare answers in pairs. In feedback, elicit and write the passive sentences on the board. Underline the form: *be + past participle*. Refer Ss to the irregular verbs table on p127 and remind them to review the past participle forms as often as possible.

> **Answers:**
> **present passive:** A man *is caught* stealing books from a bookshop.
> **past passive:** The man *was sent* to read stories.

B Check the rubric and read the sentences in Ex 4A again. Elicit the answer to the question and complete the rule.

Answers:
The *active* sentences say *who* does the actions.
Rules: to be

C Give Ss 3–4 mins to find and underline other examples of the passive in the article and compare answers in pairs. In feedback, elicit the examples and check form/meaning. E.g. ask: *Are they in the present or past passive? Do we know who caught the man/boys/ shoplifter?* (no) *Is it important?* (no) Then ask: *What do we say if we want to say who did the action?* Elicit/Teach and write on the board: *The shoplifter was caught by the manager/police. She was sent by the judge to speak to shop owners.*

Answers:
Two boys **were caught** writing graffiti …
… the boys **were told** to do community service.
A shoplifter **was caught** shoplifting …
She **was sent** to speak to shop owners.
… he **was told** to spend several weeks painting local schools …

5A Ask Ss to listen and pay attention to how *was* and *were* are pronounced in the sentences. Elicit the answer in feedback.

Answers: *Was* and *were* are pronounced as weak forms in the passive.

B Play the recording again for Ss to repeat the sentences. Then chorally and individually drill the sentences.

> ## ▷ LANGUAGEBANK 10.2 p146–147

Ss can refer to the tables/notes when they do the exercises.
Weaker Ss should do Ex A and B in class. In Ex B, check *snails*.

Answers:
A **1** is served **2** was given **3** aren't caught **4** was written
  5 are shown **6** are arrested **7** wasn't told **8** were sent
B **1** Snails are eaten by the French.
  2 *Crime and Punishment* was written by Dostoyevsky.
  3 I was asked some questions by a journalist.
  4 All of our programmes are produced by Alejandro Ledesma.
  5 Most of the roles in that film were played by Alec Guinness.
  6 The best chocolate is made by Swiss companies.

6A Check the example. Ss write the sentences alone and then compare answers in pairs. In feedback, nominate Ss to write the answers on the board, using contracted verb forms.

Answers:
2 My real name is James, but I'm called Jim by my friends.
3 On my tenth birthday, I was taken to Disneyland.
4 These days, people in my company are paid a bonus every December.
5 When I was younger, I was helped by many teachers.
6 On our first day, all the new students are shown around the school.
7 Even now, I'm told that I look like my mother.
8 When we were young, all the children in my family were expected to become doctors.

B Check the example and elicit similar examples which are true for your Ss, e.g. *When I was a child, I was taught to be polite.* Give Ss 4–5 mins to write personalised sentences and then compare them in pairs. Monitor and help Ss with language they need and prompt them to self-correct. Ss then compare their sentences with a different partner and find out what they have in common. In feedback, they should tell the class about their similarities/ differences, e.g. *I'm told I look like my mother, but Hiroshi is told he looks like his uncle.*

SPEAKING

7A Give Ss 1–2 mins to read the texts, and ask: *What crimes did the people commit?* Check answers (1 writing graffiti 2 sailing illegally 3 playing loud music late at night 4 stealing eggs). Refer Ss back to the alternative sentencing in the article in Ex 2. Elicit how the sentencing in the cases there fitted the crimes. Give Ss 2–3 mins to think of alternative punishments for the crimes here. Monitor closely to provide help with ideas and vocabulary where needed.

B Ss compare and discuss their ideas in groups. They should prepare a presentation to the class and decide who is going to talk about which crime. Groups then take it in turns to present their ideas, while the class make notes of the ones they like. At the same time, make notes on Ss' use of the target language for feedback/ remedial work later. When Ss have finished their presentations, the class discusses/votes for the best idea for each crime.

C Ss turn to p161 and read about the alternative sentences given for the crimes. Have a brief class discussion on whether they agree with the sentences.

Optional extra activity

In groups, Ss role-play the 'trial' for one of the crimes. Each student chooses his/her role: the judge, the lawyers for the prosecution/defence and the criminal(s); there could also be witnesses for the prosecution/defence. Ss choose the crime they want to role-play and then prepare/rehearse their roles. Provide support where needed. Ss then act out their role-plays to the class.

Homework ideas

- **Ex 7:** Ss write an article about the arrest and sentencing of the criminals in one of the crimes.
- **Language bank** 10.2 Ex A–B, p147
- **Workbook** Ex 1–7, p61–62

THERE'S A PROBLEM

Introduction

Ss learn and practise ways of complaining about problems and how to sound firm, but polite. They also practise how to complain politely in an email.

SUPPLEMENTARY MATERIALS
Resource bank p186
Language bank p146–147
Ex 1A: dictionaries
Ex 7: audio/video recording facilities

Warm up

Lead in and prepare Ss for the lesson. Write/Dictate these questions: *When did you last make a complaint about something? What was the problem? Who did you complain to? What did you say? How did the other person respond? Were you happy with the result of the complaint? Why/Why not?* Elicit answers to the first two questions, e.g. *Two months ago. My neighbours were having very noisy parties every weekend.* Ss work in pairs/groups. They take turns to ask and answer the questions and make notes of their partners' answers. In feedback, Ss report back to the class.

VOCABULARY PROBLEMS

1A Ss first look at the photos. Elicit a brief description of each one. Ss then read the phrases and check the words in bold. They could use dictionaries to check unfamiliar words. In feedback, check answers and the meaning of the words in bold.

Answers:
Definitions
1 delay: a period of time when you have to wait for something to happen
2 litter: waster paper, cans, etc. that people leave on the ground
3 service: the help that people who work in a restaurant, etc. give you
4 faulty: not working properly
5 loudly: not quietly, noisily
6 crashing: stop working suddenly (for computers)
7 stuck in a traffic jam: not able to move in a long line of cars, etc. on a road
8 spam: unwanted emails
Photos
A 5 B 6 C 1 D 2 E 7

B Check the rubric and example. Ss then work in pairs and choose three things from Ex 1A that most annoy them. Check answers in feedback and find out which single thing most annoys the class.

FUNCTION COMPLAINING

2A Check the rubric. Tell Ss to focus only on the two questions and not get distracted by the other information. They listen, note down their answers and then compare them in pairs. In feedback, check answers (in bold in the audio script below) and play the relevant parts of the recording again if Ss have problems.

Answers:
1 **Conversation 1:** in a hotel
  Conversation 2: in a restaurant
  Conversation 3: at a train station
2 **Conversation 1:** air conditioning doesn't work
  Conversation 2: slow service and an extra charge on the bill
  Conversation 3: train delays

B Ss read the questions first. They then listen, make notes of their answers and compare them in pairs. Monitor to check if they need to listen again to add more details to their notes. In feedback, check answers (underlined in the audio script below). Ask: *Why is the problem of the snow so surprising?* Teach *kidding* (a colloquial word for *joking*).

Answers: 1 look into it right away and send someone up
2 polite 3 (about) twenty minutes 4 another hour
5 it's a very busy time of year 6 for over an hour
7 because the cause of the delay is the wrong type of snow

3A Check the example. Ss do the exercise and then compare answers in pairs. Check answers after Ex 3C.

Answers: 1 problem 2 work 3 look 4 sorry 5 nothing
6 over

B Give Ss 3–4 mins to complete the exercise and compare answers in pairs. Check answers after Ex 3C.

Answers: 2 C 3 R 4 R 5 R 6 C

C Ss now check their answers to Ex 3A and 3B in the audio script. Elicit and check answers in feedback.

Unit 10 Recording 5

Conversation 1

G = Guest R = Receptionist

G: Oh hello. Could you help me? **There's a problem with the air conditioning.**
R: Oh yes?
G: I've just tried to switch it on, but it doesn't work.
R: Is it completely dead?
G: Completely. Absolutely nothing.
R: OK, we'll look into it right away. I'll send someone up. It'll be about five minutes, OK?
G: Thanks.
R: You're welcome. And sorry about that.

Conversation 2

D = Diner W = Waitress M = Manager

D: I'm afraid I have a complaint. Could I speak to the manager, please?
W: Yes, of course.
M: Good evening, sir. I understand there's a problem.
D: Yes. I'm afraid I have a complaint.
M: Oh?
D: Well, we got here at eight. And then **we waited about twenty minutes for a table**.
M: Right.
D: This is for a table we'd booked for eight, OK? Then **we waited another hour for our meal**.
M: Right.
D: One hour. Then when the bill arrived, they put this **extra charge** on it.
M: An extra charge? That's probably the service charge.
D: Well, could you check this for me, please?
M: Yes, that's service.
D: Well, to be honest, I don't want to pay this.
M: Of course not. Well, sir, I am really sorry about that. It's a very busy time of year.

Conversation 3

W = Woman M = Man

W: Excuse me. Do you work here?
M: Yes.
W: Do you know when the next train will be arriving? I mean, I've been here for over an hour.
M: I'm sorry, but there's nothing we can do at the moment. **Everything is delayed.**

W: And you don't know when the next train is coming?
M: No.
W: Or why there's a delay?
M: Snow.
W: What?
M: Snow on the track. It was the wrong type of snow.
W: What do you mean 'the wrong type of snow'? You're kidding, right?

▷ **LANGUAGEBANK 10.3** p146–147

Ss can refer to the information in the tables to help them with this exercise.

Answers:
Conversation 1
A: Excuse me. I'm afraid I have a complaint.
B: What's the problem?
A: The shower doesn't work.
B: We'll look into it right away.
Conversation 2
A: Excuse me. Could you help me?
B: Yes.
A: There's a problem with the internet connection.
B: I'm sorry but there's nothing we can do at the moment.
Conversation 3
A: Excuse me. Could I speak to the manager?
B: Yes.
A: I've been here for over an hour.
B: I'm really sorry about that.

4 Ss read the sentences first. Check *appointment*, *flight delay*, *faulty engine*. In feedback, elicit and drill the complaints/responses.

Answers: 1 d) 2 a) 3 b) 4 c)

LEARN TO **SOUND FIRM, BUT POLITE**

5A Give Ss 1–2 mins to discuss their answers in pairs. Check them in feedback.

Answers: We use the expressions to introduce a complaint.

speakout TIP

Read the Speakout tip with Ss and briefly discuss the questions in open class.

B Ss listen to the sentences, underline the stressed syllables and compare their answers in pairs. Play the recording as many times as necessary for Ss to be sure. For feedback, write the sentences on the board and elicit/underline the stressed words (see answer key below). When Ss listen again to repeat, show them how the voice rises on the stressed words in polite intonation by using your hands/arms, as if you were conducting an orchestra. Again, play the recording several times until Ss are confident. Then do individual repetition and correction as needed.

Answers:
1 Could you help me?
2 I'm afraid I have a complaint.
3 Excuse me, could I speak to the manager?

6 Check the word box and do an example. Ss work alone and then compare answers in pairs. In feedback, elicit/drill the answers. Ss can then practise reading the conversations in pairs to help prepare them for Ex 7. Monitor and help Ss with their pronunciation while they practise.

Answers:
1 A: Excuse me. Could I *speak* to the manager?
  A: There's a *problem* with the TV in my room. It *doesn't* work.
2 A: Excuse me. I ordered room service over an hour *ago*. Can you look *into* it, please?
3 A: *Could* you help me? I'm *afraid* I have a complaint.

7 Set up the role-play carefully. First, divide the class into As and Bs. Student As look at p165 and Student Bs at p166. They check the instructions and ask for clarification if necessary. They then work in pairs to prepare for the role-play. Monitor closely and support Ss where needed. Then put Ss into A/B pairs for the role-play. Monitor and make notes of how well they use the target language for feedback later. Invite pairs to act out their role-plays to the class. Ss must listen and decide which pair was the most firm, but polite. If possible, record Ss' role-plays.

SPEAKING

8A Check the rubric and sentences with Ss. Then give them 2 mins to work alone and decide which they find most annoying.

B Prepare Ss for this role-play in the same way as in Ex 7 above. They should refer to the language in the previous exercises for help. Provide support while they do this, especially with polite intonation. During the activity, monitor discreetly, making notes of both good language and errors for feedback.

Homework ideas
• **Ex 8B:** Ss write an email complaining about something that happened to them.
• **Language bank** 10.3 Ex A, p147
• **Workbook** Ex 1–4, p63

MARY'S MEALS

Introduction

Ss watch an extract from the BBC documentary *Mary's Meals*, about a school girl who used a blog to raise money to help feed school children in Malawi. They then learn and practise how to talk about an issue they feel strongly about and write a web comment about it.

> **SUPPLEMENTARY MATERIALS**
> **Warm up:** various photos of (students having/being served) school meals
> **Ex 2B:** dictionaries

Warm up

Introduce the topic of food and revise some food vocabulary. Show Ss the photos and distribute them to pairs/groups of Ss. Elicit *school meals* and give pairs/groups 1–2 mins to list the food they can see in each photo. Elicit answers in feedback and write them on the board. Ask Ss which of the meals they think looks more appetising/healthier. Elicit answers from a few Ss, then move on to Ex 1.

DVD PREVIEW

1 Look at the questions and give Ss 2–3 mins to discuss them in their pairs. Elicit a few answers from different pairs, then refer Ss to the photos at the bottom of p104–105. Elicit a brief description of each, then ask: *Do you think they get free school meals? Why/Why not?*

2A Check the rubric and questions and give Ss 3–4 mins to read the programme information and find the answers. Elicit answers in feedback.

> **Answers:**
> 1 She started the blog because she wasn't happy with her school meals.
> 2 She heard that in some parts of the world, some children went to school hungry. She decided to use the blog to raise money for hungry children.

B Ss complete the exercise alone, then compare answers in pairs. Encourage them to use dictionaries to check any unfamiliar words. Check answers in feedback.

> **Answers:** 1 raise money   2 charity   3 banned
> 4 an internet sensation   5 score

DVD VIEW

3A Check the rubric. Ask: *What is Mary's Meals?* (a project/charity Martha used to raise money) Ss watch the DVD to find out what Mary's Meals did with the money Martha raised. In feedback, elicit and discuss the answer (in bold in the DVD script below).

> **Answers:** They used the money to build a new kitchen in a school in Malawi, to feed nearly 2,000 children every day.

B Ss read the words and numbers in the box. Check *grow vegetables* and *raise sheep* and give Ss 3–4 mins to do the exercise alone before they compare answers in pairs. Do not confirm answers yet – Ss will check them in Ex 3C.

C Ss watch the DVD again to check their answers (underlined in the DVD script below). Remind Ss to focus on the words and numbers in the box and not get distracted by unknown language or other details in the clip. If Ss haven't been able to check/correct all their answers, play the DVD, or the relevant parts of it, a third time. Alternatively, play the DVD again in feedback, pausing at each answer for Ss to check.

> **Answers:**
> **grow vegetables/raise sheep:** Martha's family grow their own vegetables and raise sheep.
> **school dinners:** Martha thought of school dinners for her blog because she wasn't happy with her own and always came home hungry, so she wanted to do something about them.
> **£100,000:** Martha raised more than £100,000 for the charity Mary's Meals.
> **100,000 people:** This is the number of people that saw Martha's school meal photos in the first week.
> **2,000 children:** This is the number of children that are fed every day by the charity Mary's Meals.
> **kitchen:** The charity used the money to build a new school kitchen in Malawi.
> **Hollywood:** Martha and her family received offers from Hollywood after her story went worldwide (but she chose to visit the children in Malawi).

4 Look at the rubric and questions. Check *achievement* and let Ss discuss in pairs. Then elicit answers from different Ss and discuss briefly in open class.

DVD 10 Mary's Meals

P1 = Presenter 1   P2 = Presenter 2   L = Laura Vicker   M = Martha
Ma = Man

P1: A nine-year-old girl has travelled to Malawi to see how money she raised by blogging about her school dinners is being spent.

P2: Yes, Martha Payne from Argyll in Scotland became an internet sensation. You'll remember the local council banned her from posting photographs of her school meals on her blog.

P1: So, Martha went on to raise more than a hundred thousand pounds for a charity which helps provide meals for children in Malawi. Laura Vicker travelled there with her.

L: Food is important to nine-year-old Martha Payne. It's family time. It's also a chance to create. All of the family bake, grow their own vegetables and raise sheep. But when Martha went to school, her lunches didn't always impress. So much so, she started her own blog, called *NeverSeconds*.

M: We thought of school dinners because I always came home hungry and we've always wanted to do something about them, but we've never actually been bothered to.

L: Word spread over social media and in just over week, a hundred thousand people had viewed Martha's photos of her food. And Martha started to wonder if the blog could help others.

M: Someone made a comment on the blog saying, 'Why are you complaining? At least you're having school meals.' So then we thought about the people who didn't have school meals and decided to raise money.

L: **And this is what that money went towards: a school kitchen in Malawi run by the charity Mary's Meals. It will feed nearly two thousand children every day.**

Ma: This little building here was the temporary kitchen. And for five months, we used … that … the community used that. **And now we've managed to … through Martha's efforts, we've managed to raise enough money to build this kitchen.**

L: It has given this community a reason to celebrate. And Martha is the centre of attention. At first, she was a little overwhelmed by such a welcome, such a thank you. But she managed to put the finishing touches to a kitchen she helped create.

M: It was quite nerve-racking because everyone was singing, and staring at me.

L: Were you a bit overwhelmed?

M: Yeah.

L: Are you a bit more relaxed now? How do you feel now?

M: Happy.

L: <u>Martha and her family had offers from Hollywood, TV companies and publishers after her story went worldwide.</u> Instead, this is where they wanted to come, to see the effect that a simple blog, written by a nine-year-old could have on the lives of others. Laura Vicker, *BBC News*, in Malawi.

P1: Amazing story, isn't it?

P2: What an achievement for nine-year-old Martha Payne. Well done!

speakout an issue

5A Ss read the word box. Check the meaning/pronunciation of *issue* and any other words Ss have doubts about. Ss then listen and tick their answers. Check them in feedback.

> **Answers:** 1 imported food   2 activities for teenagers

B Ss read the summaries, then listen again and complete them. Give them 1 min to check their answers in pairs. Play the recording again if Ss don't agree on the answers or they haven't completed all the gaps. Ss will check their answers in Ex C.

> **Answers:** 1 food   2 grow   3 teenagers   4 sports centres

C Ss read the key phrases first. Check *get fed up with*. Then give them 3–4 mins to read audio script 10.7 and do the exercise. In feedback, check answers to Ex 5B. Then check the key phrases (in bold in the audio script below) and ask more detailed comprehension questions, e.g. *Where do the apples in supermarkets come from? Why are teenagers 'just on the streets, causing problems'?*

> **Answers:** Ss should tick all the phrases.

Unit 10 Recording 7

1 **One thing that really annoys me** is the fact that we import so much food from overseas, rather than growing our own food here in this country. So you go to the supermarket and you can buy strawberries in the middle of winter, and I suppose that's OK. But then you try to buy an apple, and the apples are from New Zealand, and you think, 'Well, that's just crazy.' I mean, **I don't understand why we need to** fly apples all over the world when we could just grow them here in this country. It really makes me angry. It would be so much better for the environment if people bought food locally. So, I'd like to start a campaign to encourage people to buy and eat local food. Perhaps I could start a website or publish articles in newspapers to try to get people to stop buying food that comes from all over the world.

2 **I get** really **fed up with the fact that** there's nothing for teenagers to do in this town. **I just think it's really difficult** because people complain that teenagers are just on the streets, causing problems. But actually, there isn't really anywhere else for them to go. There are no sports facilities or clubs where they can spend time together and have some fun. **And another thing is** we get a lot of crime because there're too many bored teenagers around. I'd like to raise money to build sports centres and youth clubs where teenagers can go to enjoy themselves or do sports or learn something. **I think** there **should** be more things for teenagers to do, and they should be better and cheaper.

6A Ss discuss their chosen issues and make notes of their answers to the questions. Monitor and provide support or language Ss need if necessary.

B While Ss work in groups, monitor and note down examples of key phrases Ss use well or not. In feedback, first find out about the issues Ss talked about and then if they agreed with other people's ideas or not. Give feedback on Ss' use of key phrases.

writeback a web comment

7A Give Ss 3–4 mins to read the comment and answer the questions. Then elicit the answers and teach/check unfamiliar words, e.g. *clear it away, collect/drop litter*.

> **Answers:**
> 1 rubbish/litter left on the streets and beaches
> 2 She feels angry and thinks that people should be fined if they litter the streets/beaches.

B With **weaker classes**, first elicit a few examples for the prompts. Ss can use an issue from Ex 6A or B. Provide support where needed.

> **Homework ideas**
> - **Ex 4:** Ss write their answer to question 2.
> - **Ex 7B:** Ss write about another issue they feel strongly about, using the prompts.

LOOKBACK

Introduction

If you have a **stronger class**, it's a good idea to ask Ss to write their own versions of some of the discrete-item test types, e.g. gap fills for vocabulary/grammar, jumbled words for vocabulary, word ordering in sentences, questions/answers to match, sentences with a mistake to correct. See the optional extra activity after Ex 2A as an example of what Ss can do. Use Ex A/B test types in the Lookback sections for more ideas. Ss can write one or two short tests in pairs/groups and then give them to another pair/group to answer. Ss usually find this kind of activity quite rewarding as it is not only competitive but also shows them how much language they know.

> **SUPPLEMENTARY MATERIALS**
>
> **Ex 1B:** photos of famous cities/buildings in your Ss' country/countries (or other countries)
>
> **Ex 5B and 6:** audio/video recording facilities

DESCRIBING A CITY

1A Ss can do this exercise as a race between pairs/teams. The first to finish with all the correct answers wins.

> **Answers:** 1 traffic 2 buildings 3 polite 4 transport 5 crime
> 6 streets 7 nightlife 8 expensive

B In **monolingual classes**, Ss could describe the place but not mention its name. The other person must guess where it is. Alternatively, display photos of famous cities/buildings as prompts. Ss take turns to describe a place and their partner has to guess which it is.

USES OF *LIKE*

2A Give Ss 2–3 mins to rewrite the sentences and compare answers in pairs. Check answers in feedback.

> **Answers:**
> 1 What's ~~do~~ the weather like today?
> 2 What food do you ~~to~~ like most?
> 3 What's your capital city ~~it~~ like?
> 4 What do you like about where ~~do~~ you live?
> 5 What's ~~about~~ the food in your country like?
> 6 What ~~like~~ are the people like where you live?

> **Optional extra activity**
>
> Ss work in pairs and write 4–5 more sentences with an extra word, using the different forms/uses of *like*. They exchange sentences with another pair and correct each other's sentences.

B In **multilingual classes**, put Ss of different nationalities together. While Ss ask and answer the questions, monitor and note down problems they have with the use of *like*. Give feedback and do remedial work on this or use the information for assessment.

> **Optional extra activity**
>
> Ss write two or three more questions each, with *like* as a verb/preposition – they can choose any topic they like. They then ask and answer their questions in pairs or groups.

CRIME AND PUNISHMENT

3 Give Ss 3–4 mins for the exercise and to compare answers in pairs. As a follow up, Ss write new sentences with the words, e.g. *She was given a five-year prison sentence for theft.* Alternatively, Ss write their sentences but leave a gap for the word. They give their sentences to another student/pair to complete.

> **Answers:** 1 prison sentence 2 community service 3 shoplifter
> 4 theft 5 fraud 6 fine 7 thief 8 writing graffiti

PRESENT/PAST PASSIVE

4A Ss do the exercise without any help. Check answers after Ex 4B.

> **Answers:** 1 b) 2 d) 3 f) 4 e) 5 c) 6 a)

B Ss discuss their answers and decide if they are true/false. In feedback, check answers and elicit what Ss know about *penicillin* and the other names/places in the exercise.

> **Answers:** All are true except 3 (The answer is Alexander Fleming. Ian Fleming wrote the James Bond books.) and 5 (Hawaiian, not Australian, sportsmen).

COMPLAINING

5A Do an example first. Ss then do the exercise alone and compare answers in pairs before feedback. Monitor and assess how well Ss can use the language. Do remedial work in feedback if necessary.

> **Answers:** 1 afraid 2 into it 3 have 4 doesn't

B Monitor and assess Ss' pronunciation while they practise. Encourage them to memorise the conversation and rehearse it. Help them with their pronunciation. Invite pairs to act out the conversations to the class. If you have recording facilities available, record Ss and use the recordings for feedback or assessment.

6 Check the situations carefully. With **weaker classes**, put Ss in A/A and B/B pairs first, to prepare their roles. Monitor closely and prompt/help them if necessary (depending on your aim: fluency practice or assessment). While Ss do the role-plays, record them if possible, for feedback or assessment. Otherwise, invite one or more pairs to act out one of the role-plays to the class. Give feedback as required.

> **BBC interviews and worksheet**
>
> **How do you feel about city life?**
>
> This video extends and consolidates Ss' vocabulary of describing a city and extends discussion on the advantages and disadvantages of city life.

11 technology

OVERVIEW

11.1 KEEPING IN TOUCH

VOCABULARY | communication
LISTENING | listen to people talking about how they keep in touch
GRAMMAR | present perfect
PRONUNCIATION | sentence stress
SPEAKING | talk about things you've done/would like to do
WRITING | improve your use of pronouns

11.2 MAKE A DIFFERENCE

VOCABULARY | feelings
READING | read an article about social media
GRAMMAR | real conditionals + *when*
PRONUNCIATION | weak forms: *will*
SPEAKING | talk about future consequences

11.3 I TOTALLY DISAGREE

VOCABULARY | internet terms
READING | read about wasting time
LISTENING | listen to a discussion about the internet
FUNCTION | giving opinions
LEARN TO | disagree politely
PRONUNCIATION | polite intonation

11.4 IS TV BAD FOR KIDS? BBC ᴰ)) DVD

DVD | watch an extract from a BBC documentary about giving up television
speakout | technology
writeback | a web comment

11.5 LOOKBACK

Communicative revision activities

BBC ᴰ) INTERVIEWS
How do you feel about technology?

This video extends discussion on technology and consolidates Ss' vocabulary of communication and the key phrases from Lesson 11.4. Use the video at the end of Lesson 11.4 or at the start or end of the unit.

KEEPING IN TOUCH

Introduction

Ss revise/practise the present perfect with *just*, *already* and *yet* in the context of communication. They also learn how to use pronouns for back-referencing to avoid repetition in their writing.

> **SUPPLEMENTARY MATERIALS**
> **Resource bank** p188
> **Language bank** p148–149
> **Ex 8C, optional extra activity:** simple texts containing a variety of pronouns (See notes below.)

Warm up

Lead in to the topic with a game of *Chinese whispers*. Organise Ss into large groups of at least six: they need to be able to whisper to each other without being overheard. Then check the lesson heading, *Keeping in touch*. Give one student in each group a sentence on a piece of paper, e.g. *The large black dog bought a new mobile phone.* The student whispers the message to the person on his/her right, who then whispers it to the next person, and so on. They mustn't say the message more than once. The last person in the group writes the message they heard on the board. It will probably not be exactly the same as people often don't catch the exact words they hear, which can be very amusing. Discuss this in feedback.

VOCABULARY   COMMUNICATION

1 Check the rubric and language in the quiz. Do an example to check instructions. In pairs, Ss then take turns to ask and answer the questions and complete the quiz. They then work with another pair to compare answers and exchange information. Ss should find out how often they use the different ways of communicating. In feedback, elicit answers from each group and find out which of the activities the class does most/least often.

LISTENING

2A Check the rubric. Ss then listen, write their answers and compare them in pairs. Elicit/Check answers in feedback.

> **Answers: Speaker 1:** text messages   **Speaker 2:** Skype
> **Speaker 3:** a blog   **Speaker 4:** social networking sites

B Ss listen again and note down the benefits and negative points the speakers mention (in bold in the audio script below). Get Ss to compare answers in pairs before feedback. With *stronger classes*, ask further comprehension questions, e.g. *Who does the girl text? Who sets up the computer for the man?*

> **Answers:**
> **Benefits**
> **Speaker 1:** quick and cheap; texts are quiet
> **Speaker 2:** can see his grandchildren; it's free
> **Speaker 3:** a great way to tell people about your travel experiences; you can put up photos of the people you meet and the places you visit; as soon as you write the blog, people all over the world can read it
> **Speaker 4:** found friends she hadn't seen for years and it was great to get in touch again
> **Negative points**
> **Speaker 1:** gets annoyed when you're talking to someone and they're texting someone else
> **Speaker 2:** internet sometimes crashes during the phone call or he can't see the picture properly
> **Speaker 3:** can't do it if they can't find an internet café
> **Speaker 4:** keeps checking it when she should be working

C Check the statements, then give Ss 3–4 mins to discuss them in groups. In feedback, elicit ideas and discuss briefly in open class.

Unit 11 Recording 1

1 I use my phone for everything. I text most of the time because **it's quick and cheap**, so I text my friends and my boyfriend. I like texts because **they're quiet** – nobody knows what you're saying. My mum used to call me all the time to check that I'm OK, but now she can text me, which is much better. **I get really annoyed when you're talking to someone though, and they're texting someone else.** I think that's really rude.

2 I use the internet a lot. I use Skype to keep in touch with my family because my daughter lives in France, so I don't see her very often and the phone is expensive. With the internet, **I can see my grandchildren** – it's wonderful. My son sets up the computer for me. I haven't learnt how to do that yet. **And sometimes it crashes during the phone call, which is annoying, or I can't see the picture properly.** But usually it's fine. Generally, I think technology is wonderful. When I was younger, we only dreamed of having video phone calls, but now it's possible and **it's free.**

3 We use a blog. **It's a great way to tell people about your travel experiences.** We've been to so many places already and it's nice to tell people about them. **And you can put photos there of the people you meet and the places you visit. The best thing is that as soon as you write the blog, people all over the world can read it.** The only problem we have is when we can't find an internet café.

4 I've just started to use networking sites like Facebook. **I found some friends I haven't seen for years and it was great to get in touch again.** The only problem is that I keep checking it when I should be working.

GRAMMAR **PRESENT PERFECT**

Watch out!

Ss are familiar with the present perfect, but may have problems with the meaning of the adverbs *just, yet* and *already* and their position in a sentence, e.g. *I've just done it three days ago. Has he yet come?* Check the meaning carefully and monitor/correct word order consistently.

3A Ss can do the exercise alone and then compare answers in pairs. In feedback, elicit the answers, but move on to Ex 3B to check the meaning of the words in bold.

Answers: **1** c) **2** a) **3** b)

B Ss complete the rules alone and then compare answers in pairs. With **weaker Ss**, read and elicit the answers as a class. In feedback, check the meaning of each adverb using the sentences in Ex 3A, e.g. for sentence 1, ask: *Can you do it yourself?* (no) *Did you expect to learn it before now?* (yes) *Is the sentence positive or negative?* (negative) Then elicit/check the position of each adverb in the sentences (see Language bank 11.1 on p148). If possible, elicit personalised examples for each adverb, e.g. *We haven't had lunch yet. I've already got 500 friends on Facebook.*

Answers: **1** yet **2** just **3** already

▷ **LANGUAGEBANK 11.1** p148–149

Stronger classes can study the tables and notes at home when they do the exercises. Otherwise, read/check the notes with Ss. ***Weaker Ss*** should do Ex A and B in class. In Ex A, check *lift* and *confirmation.*

Answers:

A **1** already **2** yet **3** just **4** already **5** yet **6** already
  7 just **8** already/just
B **1** Yes, I've *just* finished it ~~just~~.
  2 No, Imelda hasn't called ~~yet~~ us *yet.*
  3 We've (*already*) been ~~already~~ there (*already*).
  4 Well, ~~just~~ she's *just* run five miles.
  5 I'd love to come out, but I haven't finished ~~yet~~ my work *yet.*
  6 Yes, but ~~already~~ I've (*already*) seen it three times (*already*)!

4A Check the example. Ss then do the exercise alone and compare answers in pairs. Monitor and prompt them to self-correct. Recheck the meaning of the adverbs and their position in the sentences in feedback.

Answers:

2 I haven't done any sport yet this week.
3 My best friend has just had a baby.
4 I've (*already*) had a holiday this year (*already*).
5 I haven't finished my studies yet.
6 I've (*already*) seen the new James Bond film (*already*).
7 I've just moved house.
8 I've (*already*) paid for my next English course (*already*).

B Check the example and elicit Ss' answers for question 2 in Ex 4A. Monitor and support them while they write. Encourage Ss to read/check each other's sentences for accuracy as it's important for them to use correct sentences in Ex 4C.

C Ss work with another partner to compare their answers. In feedback, nominate Ss to tell the class one thing about their partners, e.g. *Maria's already been to the gym three times this week.*

5 First, elicit information about the cartoon, e.g. *She's working on the computer.* Ss then write six sentences alone and compare answers in pairs. Check answers in feedback.

Answers:

She's already called her mother.
She's already checked her email.
She hasn't written the/her blog post yet.
She hasn't uploaded the/her photos yet.
She's already texted Jim.
She hasn't updated her webpage yet.

6A Play the recording and pause after each sentence to allow time for Ss to write down the sentences. Get Ss to compare answers in pairs before feedback.

Answers:

1 I've <u>been</u> there al<u>ready</u>.
2 I <u>haven't met</u> her yet.
3 We've <u>just</u> seen a <u>film</u>.
4 They've al<u>ready gone</u>.
5 We haven't <u>finished</u> yet.
6 He's just <u>spoken</u> to her.

B Play the recording again and ask Ss to listen and repeat. Drill the sentences chorally and individually. In feedback, ask Ss to underline the word stress in the sentences (see answer key above).

SPEAKING

7A First, check the phrases in the box and elicit examples for question 1, *e.g. I've already created my own webpage.* Give Ss 4–5 mins to take turns answering the questions. Encourage them to show interest in their partner's answers and extend the conversation. Monitor closely and note how well they use the adverbs. In feedback, elicit Ss' answers and prompt them to self-correct.

B Elicit examples of things Ss need/want to do this week. Then give them 2–3 mins to write their lists.

C Check the example conversation. Monitor discreetly while Ss work in pairs, making notes of examples of good language and problems. In feedback, write examples of Ss' errors and good language on the board. Ss discuss and correct the errors in pairs.

speakout TIP

Read the Speakout tip with Ss and elicit other things they could do to improve their English. They then write five things they want to do in their notebooks. Tell them you will check how many things they've done in a month's time. Make a note of this in your diary!

WRITING PRONOUNS

8A Elicit an example answer. Ss then work alone and compare answers in pairs before feedback.

Answers:
It's big – Izmir   Most of **them** – my new friends
they're new – my new friends
Our course – my new friends and my (course)
looking forward to **it** – the course   haven't met **him** – Ahmed
he sounds nice – Ahmed   near **there** – the city centre

B Elicit the answer and emphasise how important the use of pronouns is in writing.

Answer: to avoid repetition of words

C Ss read the travel blog first. Elicit/Check where Bucharest is (the capital of Romania, which borders on Hungary in Central Europe). Then give Ss 3 mins to rewrite the blog and compare answers in pairs before feedback.

Answers: Alecia and I have finally arrived in Bucharest, and ~~Alecia and I~~ *we* love ~~Bucharest~~ *it*. We thought we should update you on ~~Alecia's and my~~ *our* tour. Last month we were in Hungary. We had a really good time ~~in Hungary~~ *there*. We met a man called George, who was very friendly. ~~George~~ *He* took us to some wonderful lakes and castles, and we really enjoyed ~~the lakes and castles~~ *them*. The other news is that we have decided to stay ~~in Bucharest~~ *here* for at least two years. We think ~~living in Bucharest~~ *it* will be a wonderful experience for ~~Alecia and I~~ *us*.

Optional extra activity

Ss work alone. Give them a simple text from a newspaper/magazine or tell them to look at a text they've seen before in a previous unit/the Communication bank. Give them 3–4 mins to find/underline the pronouns and draw a line to the word(s) they refer to. Ss then compare answers in pairs. Tell them to practise noticing the use of pronouns in all the texts they read.

Homework ideas

- **Ex 8C:** Ss write a travel blog about a place they've visited recently. They then underline all pronouns in the text which avoid repetition.
- **Language bank** 11.1 Ex A–B, p149
- **Workbook** Ex 1–8, p64–65

MAKE A DIFFERENCE

Introduction

Ss revise and practise real conditionals + *if/when* in the context of social media.

SUPPLEMENTARY MATERIALS
Resource bank p187 and p189
Language bank p148–149
Warm up: photos of and information about Facebook, the film *The Social Network* and Facebook's founder, Mark Zuckerberg (See Culture notes below for more information.)

Culture notes

Facebook is one of the world's most successful online social networking sites and is headquartered in Menlo Park, California. Its website was launched on 4 February 2004, by Mark Zuckerberg with his college roommates and fellow Harvard University students Eduardo Saverin, Andrew McCollum, Dustin Moskovitz and Chris Hughes.

The film *The Social Network* (2010) follows the story of Facebook and some of the personal and legal complications that occurred in recent years.

Warm up

Introduce the topic of the lesson. If you've brought photos of/information about Facebook, the film *The Social Network* and Mark Zuckerberg, use them as prompts here. If not, write *Facebook*, *Mark Zuckerberg* and *The Social Network* on the board and ask: *What do you know about them? What type of website is Facebook? Do you know the man? Have you seen the film? What happens in it?* (NB: The aim is for Ss to describe, not evaluate, social media as they do this in Ex 1 below. Avoid asking, e.g. *What do you think of social media/Facebook?*) Ss discuss the questions in pairs or groups first, then in open class.

VOCABULARY FEELINGS

1A Give Ss 2–3 mins to answer the questions in pairs. Discuss their answers in feedback. Teach/Provide adjectives/phrases to describe their opinions of social media e.g. *a waste of time, entertaining, useful.*

B Ss read and check the opinions. Teach/Check *sharing information* and *learning tool*. Elicit Ss' reactions to the first opinion. Then give them 2 mins to think about the other opinions and discuss their answers in pairs. In feedback, elicit Ss' reasons for their answers and find out which opinion is the closest to their own.

C Check the rubric and the example. Tell Ss to find the word *bored* in the opinions and look at the words before and after it. This will illustrate how the context helps them to work out the meaning of the word. Then give Ss 3–4 mins to match the definitions with the other words. In feedback, check answers and drill the pronunciation of each word.

Answers: **2** confused **3** lonely **4** excited **5** uncomfortable
6 amazed **7** worried **8** nervous

D Check the rubric and example. Give students time to think about their answers before they work in pairs. Monitor while they work to check how well they are using the vocabulary. In feedback, asks Ss to tell the class about their partner's answers, e.g. *The last time Paula was worried was before her maths test!*

READING

2A First, look at the photos. Ask: *What can you see in the photos? What is the woman doing? What are the symbols?* Elicit some answers, then check the rubric and questions. Give Ss 3–4 mins to read the introduction to the article and discuss their answers in pairs. They should cover the rest of the text while they do this. In feedback, elicit Ss' answers and write their predictions for question 2 on the board. Don't confirm them yet. Ss will check answers in Ex 2B.

B Give Ss 3–4 mins to read the article and check their predictions on the board. In feedback, refer to the predictions on the board and elicit/discuss which of them were correct.

C Check the questions. Give Ss 4–5 mins to do the exercise in pairs. In feedback, elicit and discuss Ss' answers, and teach/check unfamiliar/useful words, e.g. *online communities, toy ovens, campaign, bullying.*

Answers:
1 They can.use social media to quickly organise demonstrations and protests against government decisions. They can also use media to show the world what is happening.
2 She wanted to get the company to sell toy ovens designed not just for girls, but for boys too. In less than a month, the company changed the packaging of the ovens.
3 A Canadian man wanted to raise some money to give the bus driver a holiday, but he raised so much money that Karen Klein decided to start a foundation to help others.

D Give Ss 3–4 minutes to discuss the questions in pairs. Elicit their opinions in feedback and ask other Ss if they agree or not.

GRAMMAR REAL CONDITIONALS + WHEN

Watch out!

Unlike many other languages, English doesn't use subjunctive forms in conditional sentences. In real (first) conditional sentences referring to the future, Ss often make the mistake of using *will* in the *if/when* clause, e.g. *If/When I will see you, I'll tell you.* It is important to highlight the use of a present tense in *if/when* clauses, and provide sufficient practice and feedback.

3A Ss should first read the sentences. Give them 3–4 mins to do the exercise alone and then compare answers in pairs. While they are working, write sentences a)–d) on the board. Refer to these in feedback: elicit Ss' answers and underline the verb forms in the sentences. Check the concept of *if/when* sentences. Point to sentence a) and ask: *Will you use social media?* (maybe) *Will you find people who will help you?* (yes, if you use social media) Then point to sentence c) and ask: *Will people see what's happening?* (yes) *Will they be shocked?* (yes) If appropriate, ask Ss how they would say these sentences in their own language(s) and elicit any similarities/differences.

Answers:
1 the future
2 The present simple is used after the *if/when* clause, and *will/won't* is used in the main clause.

B Check the meaning of *consequence*, *likely* and *certain* before Ss do the exercise. Elicit answers in feedback and refer back to the concept questions in Ex 3A.

Answers: **1** future **2** likely **3** certain
4 can be at the beginning or the end of the sentence

▷ **LANGUAGEBANK 11.2** p148–149

Read/Check the notes with Ss if necessary. Highlight the use of modal verbs in main clauses. **Weaker Ss** should do Ex A and B in class. In Ex A, check *pay rise* and *get time off work*. In Ex B, check *behave badly*.

Answers:
A 1 'll leave, finish   2 miss, 'll take   3 see, 'll ask
4 won't have, leaves   5 ask, won't give   6 'll cook, do
7 is, 'll go   8 'll go, gets
B 1 If you ~~will be~~ *are* in the office tomorrow, we'll talk about it then.
4 We'll ask the doctor when we ~~will~~ get to the hospital.
5 If Theo behaves badly in class, the teacher *will* speak to his parents.
6 They'll move into the house as soon as Mark ~~will finish~~ *finishes* building it.

4A First, give Ss 1–2 mins to read the sentences quickly. Check *petition, elections, protesting, product* and *reviews*. Ss then complete the sentences and compare their answers in pairs. Do not confirm answers yet – Ss will check them in Ex 4B.

B Ss listen and check their answers, making corrections if necessary. In feedback, check answers and then focus on the pronunciation of *will*. Play the first sentence again and elicit/drill the pronunciation of the contracted form *I'll*.

Answers: 1 give, 'll send   **2** sign, 'll have to   **3** see, won't be
4 gets, will, leave   **5** aren't, will start   **6** see, 'll be   **7** is, won't write
8 change, will, buy

C Ss listen and repeat the sentences chorally and then individually. Prompt them to correct their pronunciation. To follow up, Ss could take turns to say one sentence each around the class.

Unit 11 Recording 4

1 'll – I'll send you the photo – If you give me your details, I'll send you the photo.
2 'll – the company'll have to respond – If people sign the petition, the company'll have to respond.
3 won't – they won't be surprised – When your friends see the video, they won't be surprised.
4 will – will you leave your job? – If the situation gets worse, will you leave your job?
5 'll – people'll start protesting – If there aren't elections soon, people'll start protesting.
6 'll – I'll be in the Canaries – When you see this picture, I'll be in the Canaries!
7 won't – people won't write bad reviews – If the product is really good, then people won't write bad reviews.
8 will – will you buy one? – If they change the design, will you buy one?

Optional extra activity

Do a chain drill around the class. Start off with, e.g. *If I win the lottery, I'll take a trip around the world.* Choose a student to continue with *If I take a trip around the world, I'll …* Continue the activity until Ss can't think of any more sentences.

5A Do an example and give Ss 3–4 mins to write their sentences. Monitor and prompt them to make any necessary corrections.

B Ss compare and discuss their answers in pairs. Elicit some interesting/unusual answers in feedback.

6A Check the rubric/questions and put Ss in groups. While Ss prepare their plan, provide help to those who need it. **Weaker Ss** could work together.

B Groups now present their ideas to the class, who listen, make notes and tell the group about the possible consequences of their campaign (using real conditionals + *if/when*). Make notes on the use of the target language and do any remedial work needed afterwards. In feedback, conduct a class vote on which group had the best campaign.

Homework ideas

- **Ex 6:** Ss write 80–100 words about their or another group's social media campaign.
- **Language bank** 11.2 Ex A–B, p149
- **Workbook** Ex 1–8, p66–67

I TOTALLY DISAGREE

Introduction

Ss learn and practise ways of giving opinions and disagreeing politely, in the context of using the internet.

> **SUPPLEMENTARY MATERIALS**
> **Resource bank** p190
> **Language bank** p148–149
> **Warm up:** copies of the survey sheet (See notes below.)
> **Ex 1:** bilingual dictionaries
> **Ex 8C:** video/audio recording facilities

Warm up

Lead in to the lesson with a *Find someone who …* activity asking what Ss use their computers for. Prepare a survey sheet using 8–10 items from this list: *chat with friends, buy things, play games, surf the internet, read/write emails, listen to the radio, watch films/TV, check spelling, write documents, check information in a dictionary/encyclopaedia, do research for work/studies, write programs, organise your finances, find entertainment, earn money.* Use this sample for your survey sheet:

Activity	Name	How often?
watch films/TV	Maria	rarely
check spelling	Frank	sometimes

Make a copy of the worksheet for each student in your class. In class, hand them out and ask, e.g. *Do you use the computer to watch TV?* If the answer is *yes*, ask: *How often do you do it?* Elicit *sometimes, always, not very often*, etc. Ss then walk round the class (or work in groups) and ask/answer the questions. In larger classes, they should try not to write information about the same person more than twice. In feedback, elicit information about each activity, e.g. *Maria rarely uses the computer to watch TV.* (NB: If you don't have a survey prepared, Ss can work in groups and find out the five most common things their partners use the computer for.)

VOCABULARY   INTERNET TERMS

1 Check the words in the box, or Ss could check words they're not sure of in bilingual dictionaries. Give them 3–4 mins to ask and answer the questions in pairs or groups. Discuss their answers in feedback and find out which things Ss use most/least.

READING

2A Look at the photo with Ss and ask: *What's the boy doing? Why?* Elicit answers and then encourage them to speculate on the questions in the rubric. Give them 2 mins to read the article to find out. Discuss their answers in feedback and teach/check *distracted, get off the internet, get on with life.*

B Check the questions. Give Ss 3–4 mins to read the text again and underline/note down their answers before comparing them in pairs. In feedback, nominate Ss to answer, quoting the relevant information from the text.

> **Answers:**
> 1 It's difficult for people to concentrate on Friday afternoons, so they waste time on the internet.
> 2 the internet and social media
> 3 up to eight days a month
> 4 The internet can be bad for relationships because it can cause arguments if one partner spends too much time using their computer or mobile device.

3 Put Ss into A/B pairs for the discussion. Monitor discreetly and notice how well Ss use the language of giving opinions, agreeing and disagreeing, as they will learn/practise this in Ex 4–8. They should be able to use a wider range of more appropriate language by then. In feedback, invite pairs to give their reasons for their opinions to the class. Discuss the points Ss made and find out which opinion Ss hold most strongly.

FUNCTION   GIVING OPINIONS

4 Check the rubric and statements. Ss then listen, complete the exercise alone and compare answers in pairs. Play the recording again if there is strong disagreement. Otherwise, elicit/check answers.

> **Answers:** 1 T 2 T 3 F 4 T

5A Ss read the statements. Check the meaning and pronunciation of *an addict, be addicted to, addictive.* Ss tick their answers and compare them in pairs. Do not confirm answers yet – Ss will check them in Ex 4B.

B Play the recording again. Tell Ss to say *Stop!* at each answer they ticked (in bold in the audio script below).

> **Answers:** 1, 4, 5, 6

Unit 11 Recording 5

M1 = Man 1   M2 = Man 2   W = Woman

M1: I use the internet all day at work and I still get my work done.
M2: Yeah, me too.
M1: I'm sorry, but I really don't see what the problem is.
W: I think the problem is that lots of workers spend all day surfing the internet and wasting their time instead of doing their work.
M1: Hmm.
W: **And students at university are failing their degrees because they spend all their time checking Facebook and watching videos that friends send them.**
M2: Yes, that's true, but … um … I don't think, you know, I don't think that the problem is the internet. You know, I think the problem is with the websites like Facebook.
M1: Yeah, definitely, like YouTube.
M2: Some companies and universities stop you from using certain websites. And in my opinion, that's OK.
W: **But it's so easy to waste time.** I don't think you should use the internet when you're trying to work, unless you need it for your work, for research or something.
M1: I'm not sure about that. **Going on the internet sometimes gives you a break. It's like having a cup of coffee or talking to someone in the office.** People should use the internet as much as they like.
W: I don't think so …
M2: Yes, that's right. I think it's good. I run a small business and my staff use the internet as much as they want to. I don't check what they are doing. They do all their work and they are happy. I don't think it's a waste of time at all. It's the same as going to a bookshop …
W: No, but …
M2: … or looking through a pile of magazines.
W: I'm afraid I totally disagree. **The problem is that people are addicts. People aren't addicted to reading books, but the internet is different. People spend too much time in front of their computer or their phone.** They choose the internet over sports and going out. They forget how to live in the real world, and I think it's a real problem.

6A Check the headings and elicit possible answers. Check the meaning of *totally*. Ss then listen to phrases from audio script 11.5, complete the phrases in the table and compare answers in pairs. In feedback, write the headings on the board, elicit the answers and write (or invite Ss to write) them in the correct column.

Answers:
agreeing: That's *right*, *That's* true
disagreeing: I totally *disagree*, I'm not *sure* about that
giving an opinion: I *think*, I *don't* think

Unit 11 Recording 6

Yes, that's right. I think it's good.
Yes, that's true.
I'm afraid I totally disagree.
I'm not sure about that.
I think it's good.
I don't think it's a waste of time at all.

B Ss find the phrases from Ex 6B and one additional phrase for each column in audio script 11.5 (underlined in the audio script above). They work alone first, then compare answers in pairs before feedback.

Answers:
agreeing: Definitely.
disagreeing: I don't think so./I'm sorry but I (really) don't see …
giving an opinion: In my opinion, …

▷ **LANGUAGE**BANK 11.3 p148–149

Ss can refer to the tables/notes to help them with the exercises. In Ex B, check *hunt animals*.

Answers:
A 1 I'm *sorry*, but I don't think there is enough money for that.
2 I don't *think* we should spend too much time discussing this.
3 I have to say I think *that's/you're* right.
4 I'm afraid *I* totally disagree.
5 Make them pay fines? I'm not sure *about* that.
6 In *my* opinion, we should start from the beginning.
B 1 I think **2** not sure about **3** I'm afraid **4** totally disagree
5 my opinion **6** Definitely

7A Ss read the conversations first. Check unfamiliar words and do an example. Give Ss 2–3 mins to correct and compare their answers in pairs before you check them.

Answers: 1 I think *so* too. **2** That's true.
3 I'm not sure by *about* that. **4** So definitely.
5 I am totally disagree. **6** I don't think *so*.

B Elicit/Discuss Ss' opinions of the first statement. Prompt them to use phrases they learnt in Ex 6, e.g. *In my opinion, everybody should learn at least two other languages. Yes, I totally agree./ No, I don't think so.* Before they work in pairs, give them time to make notes of their own opinions, and reasons for them.

LEARN TO DISAGREE POLITELY

8A Do question 1 as an example. You may wish to read the Speakout tip with Ss now. Then elicit the introductory phrase used in question 1A: *I'm sorry, but …* Ss then finish the exercise alone and compare answers in pairs. Do not check answers yet – Ss will check them in Ex 8B.

B Play question 1A/B as examples. Ask: *Which sounds more polite? Why?* (A sounds more polite. First of all, because the speaker uses a softening introductory phrase. More importantly, her voice is softer/gentler and the pitch of her voice on the stressed syllables is lower. The person in B speaks more loudly/aggressively and his voice on the stressed syllables is higher/louder.) Play the rest of the recording. Ss listen, note down their answers and compare them in pairs. Play the recording again. Stop after each pair of sentences and elicit/check answers.

Answers: 1 A **2** B **3** A **4** A **5** B

C Ss listen again and repeat both the polite and the impolite responses. Encourage them to copy the intonation and extend/ soften their voice range accordingly (see the stressed words in the audio script below). Play the recording as many times as necessary until Ss are confident. Ss then practise in pairs. Monitor and help Ss with their pronunciation. If you have recording facilities, Ss can record the phrases and compare their pronunciation with the recording. This will help them to become more aware of their pronunciation.

Unit 11 Recording 7

1 **A:** I'm <u>sorry</u>, but I <u>really</u> don't see what the <u>problem</u> is.
  B: I <u>really</u> don't <u>see</u> what the <u>problem</u> is.
2 **A:** I <u>disagree</u>.
  B: I'm not <u>sure</u> about <u>that</u>.
3 **A:** I <u>don't</u> think it's a <u>waste</u> of time at <u>all</u>.
  B: It's <u>not</u> a <u>waste</u> of <u>time</u>.
4 **A:** That's <u>true</u>, but I <u>don't</u> think the <u>problem</u> is the <u>internet</u>.
  B: The <u>problem</u> is <u>not</u> using the <u>internet</u>.
5 **A:** I <u>totally</u> disa<u>gree</u>.
  B: I'm a<u>fraid</u> I <u>totally</u> disa<u>gree</u>.

speak**out** TIP

Read the Speakout tip with Ss before Ex 8B or at the end of Ex 8.

SPEAKING

9A Check the rubric and statements with Ss. Elicit sample answers to the first one. Then give Ss 4–5 mins to work alone and make notes of their opinions. They should include examples of language for giving opinions from Ex 6. Monitor and support *weaker Ss*.

B Demonstrate what Ss have to do. Elicit an opinion and prompt other Ss to agree/disagree using phrases from Ex 6 and 8. Ss then work in groups and compare their ideas in the same way. Monitor discreetly, making notes of how well Ss use the language they've practised in the lesson. Note down examples for feedback. In feedback, elicit opposing opinions for each statement.

Homework ideas

• **Ex 9:** Ss write their opinion for each statement.
• **Language bank** 11.3 Ex A–B, p149
• **Workbook** Ex 1–4, p68

IS TV BAD FOR KIDS?

Introduction

Ss watch an extract from the BBC documentary series *Panorama*, which explores the effect TV has on families and children. Ss then learn and practise how to talk about technology and write a comment about it on a website.

Warm up

Lead in to the lesson. Read the title of the lesson and write two prompts on the board: *TV is good for kids because …/TV is bad for kids because …* . Elicit a sample answer for each one, e.g. *TV is good for kids because there are lots of educational programmes and documentaries.* Ss then work in pairs and complete each sentence with at least three reasons. In feedback, elicit/discuss their answers. Then ask: *Do you think TV is bad for kids? Yes or no?* Ss vote for their answer with a show of hands.

DVD PREVIEW

1 Check the rubric and word box. Give Ss 2–3 mins to discuss the questions in pairs. In feedback, invite them to tell the class about their partner. Find out which things Ss think save or waste time.

2A Ss read the text. Check *concentrating, meaningful conversations.* They then discuss their answers in pairs and decide what they'll write. Elicit some answers for each gap. Ss then check them on p166. In feedback, ask: *Which answers surprised you? Why?*

> **Answers:** 1 4   2 60   3 3.5, 12   4 1   5 3.5, 1,600

B Check the rubric and elicit some answers before Ss discuss in pairs/groups. They should make a note of what they have/don't have in common and report back to the class in feedback.

3 Give Ss 1 min to read the programme information and answer the questions. In feedback, elicit Ss' predictions and note them on the board. Ss will check them in Ex 4. Also teach new vocabulary, e.g. *do an experiment, survive.*

DVD VIEW

4 Ss watch the DVD and focus on checking their predictions on the board with how the children/parents reacted to the experiment. After watching, give them 1 min to compare answers in pairs. Then elicit/discuss how the children and parents reacted to the experiment and compare this with Ss' predictions. Which were correct/incorrect?

Alternative approach

Ss could watch the DVD without the sound first. Tell them to pay careful attention to the faces/expressions of the parents and children, the activities they do, etc. This should give them information about their answers from Ex 3. Elicit/Check their answers as above and play the DVD again with sound.

Answers:

1 The children watched less TV but seemed to enjoy playing games and spending more time with their parents.
2 The parents found the experiment very positive. There was a lot more laughter in the house. They laughed a lot and were more of a family.

5 Ss read the sentences. Check *microwaves.* They then watch the DVD again, write their answers and compare them in pairs. *Stronger classes* could write their answers before they watch the DVD. In feedback, play the DVD and tell Ss to say *Stop!* when they hear/see the answers (in bold in the DVD script below).

Answers:

1 T
2 F (They went to a primary school in Manchester.)
3 F (They took the TVs, computers and computer games.)
4 T
5 T
6 F (They watched less TV.)

DVD 11 Panorama

N = Narrator   J = Jeremy Vine   Ja = James   MrB = Mr Breem
MrsB = Mrs Breem   MrsR = Mrs Roper   B = Boy

N: Television. Are our children watching too much? And what is the effect of TV on family life? Is it time to switch off for good?

J: **It makes our kids fat**, teaches them to be violent and rots their brains. If, as some argue, TV, computer games are guilty of all of that, then surely they should be banned or at least severely rationed. But hang on, if the kids were unglued from the screen, could we, the parents, cope?

N: Eighty-four percent of children over five have a television in their bedroom. At the age of eight, the average child watches thirty-two whole days of television. What would life be like without the TV?

J: **This is Park Road Primary School, on the outskirts of Manchester.** A very friendly place, as we are about to see. This is Year 3 in here. Hi there!

Kids: Hello.

J: Seven and eight years old. James, what are you studying?

Ja: Numeracy.

J: Numeracy. Well, they have agreed to take part in our experiment to see what happens when televisions and computers are removed from their lives. And just over here on the wall, we've got cameras to record the impact of what goes on.

N: The experiment looks at children's progress in school. However, **Jeremy and his team also go into their homes and remove the screens, the telly, the PC, the games, everything but the microwave.** In exchange, **they get one new piece of electrical equipment: a camera, to film what happens. Without the TV, it's clear the parents will have to work a lot harder.** They and the children will move their bodies, they'll play board games, they'll mime, they'll get into shape, they'll rediscover old games, they'll even draw pictures and paint. Anything and everything but the screen. Life for these families has to change. But is it a change for the better or the worse? After ten days of the experiment, Jeremy talks to the parents. What changes were there at home?

J: You know, we were looking for results in the classroom, and we found them in the home, and that was the big thing for us. Does that … ? Mr Breen … Is your … ?

MrB: Um … I think we definitely found it very positive.

MrsB: Well, it was … it's just there was a lot more laughter in the house. We were having a good laugh, um … and we kind of, you know, we were more of a family.

J: Anyone else got, got rules here, as a result of this? The Ropers, you got any rules now?

MrsR: What's our rule?

B: **Erm, there's not really any TV in the morning apart from the news …**

MrsR: Yeah.

B: … on a school day.

J: OK.

MrsR: Yes, on a school days. Yes.

MrB: I think most people have done that, haven't they? We definitely don't have any TV …

MrsB: We started doing that beforehand. We all have …

6 Give Ss 3–4 mins to answer the questions. In feedback, elicit/discuss Ss' answers. Find out how many Ss think the experiment was a good idea, and why/why not.

speakout technology

7A Check the rubric and teach *gadget*. Ss listen and write their answers, then compare them in pairs. Play the recording again if Ss don't agree/have all the answers. Nominate Ss to answer in feedback.

Answers:
Speaker 1: essential: smart phone, microwave, laptop; not essential: television, DVD player, digital camera, tablet
Speaker 2 essential: smart phone, TV, DVD player, laptop; not essential: tablet, digital camera, microwave

B First, read and check the key phrases with Ss. They then listen, tick the answers and compare them in pairs. In feedback, play the recording again, pausing at each key phrase (in bold in the audio script below). Elicit/Drill the complete sentences in feedback.

Answers: Ss should tick all the phrases except *It's good/important because …* and *It's very useful.*

Unit 11 Recording 8

1 OK – smart phone? **That's essential. I love it. I use it all the time**, for everything. I talk to people, chat, text, take photos. **I couldn't live without** my phone. Microwave? That's essential. I don't have lots of time for cooking, so I use the microwave a lot. Television? Not essential. I don't watch much television. DVD player, no … not essential. Digital camera? Not essential. I use my phone. So, what else? Er … laptop? **That's essential**, really. I use my laptop for work, so yes, I need that. Tablet? Hmm, I guess it's not essential.

2 Which are essential? All of them! Goodness! Right. Smart phone? Essential. **I don't go anywhere without** my phone. **I need it in case** there's an emergency and I have to call someone. Or if there's a problem with one of the children. Yes, I definitely need my phone. TV? **That's essential**, really. **I couldn't live without** my television and DVD player. Um, laptop? Well, I need a computer, really, so yes, that's essential. Tablet. Well, no, that's not essential. Digital camera? **I suppose I don't need** that. Someone else can take the photos! What else? Microwave? No. **I can live without** that.

C Elicit some examples using the key phrases. Then give Ss 4–5 mins to make notes. Monitor and provide support with language where needed.

D While Ss compare answers in groups, monitor and make notes of language problems, especially with the key phrases. In feedback, find out which gadgets are the most popular. Then do a correction slot: write problem sentences on the board. Ss correct them in pairs.

writeback a web comment

8A Check the questions. Give Ss 3 mins to answer them and compare their answers in pairs. In feedback, elicit Ss' answers and teach/check new words in the text, e.g. *interact, humans*.

Answers: Shantanu thinks technology is bad because it makes people lonely. Jake thinks technology is good because it allows us to find out what is happening in the world.

B Elicit sample answers using the framework provided. Give Ss 3–4 mins to write their own comment and read it to other Ss. Ss discuss the similarities/differences in their opinions.

Homework ideas

Ex 8B: Ss write a different comment for the website/class blog responding to the statement: *TV is very bad for children/people.*

LOOKBACK

Introduction

The main aim of the Lookback exercises is to give Ss fluency practice of the language they've learnt in the lesson. Fluency practice is usually provided in Ex B of each section, and provides the opportunity for you to assess your Ss' speaking skills. When doing this, you need to consider four things: accuracy of grammar, range of vocabulary used, fluency and pronunciation. For a balanced assessment, give Ss marks out of five for each area, making a total of 20 marks.

COMMUNICATION

1A Ss complete the words alone and check their answers in pairs. In feedback, elicit the words and check the meaning/pronunciation.

> **Answers:** 1 mobile phone   2 web page   3 SMS, text message
> 4 links   5 blogs   6 chat

B Elicit Ss' answers to question 1. Give them 2–3 mins to ask and answer the other questions in pairs, and make notes. In feedback, nominate Ss to tell the class about their partner.

PRESENT PERFECT

2A Ss first read sentences 1–6. Draw a circle on the board and do an example. Elicit short one-word answers to question 1 and write them randomly in the circle. Ss then draw a circle in their notebooks and write their answers to the questions in it. Remind them to write them *randomly*, not in order.

B First, check the example conversation, and drill it if necessary. Tell Ss they should use the present perfect in their first question, and then ask further questions to show interest and extend the conversation. While Ss work, monitor to check they are doing the exercise correctly. Take notes on their performance for remedial work if required. Invite/Nominate pairs to act out their conversations in feedback and prompt self-/peer correction.

FEELINGS

3A Check the example and the words in the box if necessary. **Weaker Ss** could check them in Ex 1C, p110. Give Ss 3–4 mins to do the exercise. Monitor and prompt them to self-correct.

B Check the rubric and elicit sample answers, e.g. *I feel nervous when I have to do an exam, so I study hard to give me confidence/go to bed early the night before/breathe deeply before the exam starts/take my lucky charm with me.* Give Ss time to prepare their answers, and provide help with language if needed. Ss then work in pairs and take turns to exchange details of what they do in each situation. Monitor and make notes of their performance for feedback and/or assessment. Elicit some examples in feedback and find out who has the best ideas/advice.

REAL CONDITIONALS + WHEN

4A Do an example and check vocabulary, e.g. *ladder*. Give Ss 2–3 mins to do the exercise and compare answers in pairs. In feedback, elicit answers and check the form/use of real conditionals in the sentences.

> **Answers:** 1 e)   2 c)   3 f)   4 a)   5 d)   6 b)

B Read the rubric and check the meaning of *superstitions*. Give Ss 5 mins to answer the questions in pairs. In **multilingual classes**, pair Ss from different countries. They should note down examples of superstitions in their partner's countries. In feedback, nominate Ss to tell the class about their partner's answers. Find out which superstitions are universal/unique.

5A Check the example and elicit another one to demonstrate the activity clearly. Give Ss 1–2 mins to write their sentences. Monitor to ensure they are accurate.

B Check/Drill the example. Ss then take turns to read out their sentences and extend the conversation. In feedback, nominate Ss to act out their conversations to the class. Give feedback on their use of real conditionals as needed.

> ### Optional extra activity
>
> Play the *consequences* game in groups of ten. Write on the board: *If you go on holiday next year, where will you go?* Elicit Ss' answers. Then give Ss one sheet of A4 paper each. They all write their answer to the question at the top of their paper. They then fold the paper over the answer and pass it to the student on their right. Then ask: *Who will you go with?* Ss write their answer, fold the paper over it again and pass it on. Follow the same procedures with the following questions: *Where will you go if you have lots of money? When will you go? How long will you stay? Where will you stay? What will you take with you? What will you do there? What will you bring back? How will you feel when you get home?* Finally, collect the folded papers up and redistribute them to different Ss. In their groups, they unfold the papers and read out the series of answers. These are usually very amusing.

GIVING OPINIONS

6A Do conversation 1 as an example. Ss then write the sentences in order and check their answers in pairs. In feedback, nominate Ss to read parts A/B in open pairs across the class. Prompt Ss to correct themselves/each other when necessary.

> **Answers:**
> 1 I'm afraid I totally disagree.
> 2 I'm not sure about that.
> 3 In my opinion, all drugs should be legal.
> 4 That's right. I think so, too.
> 5 Do you think the next government will be better?
> 6 I don't think so.
> 7 That's true. I agree.
> 8 I totally disagree.

B Check/Drill the example conversation and remind Ss how to use polite intonation. Give them time to prepare their responses. They should also rehearse the polite intonation in each conversation. Monitor and help Ss with their pronunciation where needed. Then in pairs, they take it in turns to give and respond to each opinion. Monitor discreetly, making notes of Ss' performance, especially their pronunciation/intonation. In feedback, elicit/discuss Ss' opinions and do remedial work as required.

> ### BBC interviews and worksheet
>
> **How do you feel about technology?**
> This video extends discussion on technology and consolidates Ss' vocabulary of communication and the key phrases from Lesson 11.4.

OVERVIEW

12.1 CAUGHT ON FILM

VOCABULARY | film
READING | read a magazine article about writing a blockbuster
GRAMMAR | reported speech
PRONUNCIATION | contrastive stress
SPEAKING | talk about your favourite film

12.2 A LUCKY BREAK

READING | read a magazine article about internet fame
SPEAKING | talk about being famous
VOCABULARY | suffixes
PRONUNCIATION | word stress
LISTENING | listen to people talking about fame
GRAMMAR | hypothetical conditionals present/future
WRITING | write about a famous person

12.3 WHAT CAN I DO FOR YOU?

VOCABULARY | collocations
READING | read a text about concierges
LISTENING | listen to people making requests
FUNCTION | requests and offers
PRONUNCIATION | polite intonation: requests
LEARN TO | ask for more time
SPEAKING | make requests and offers

12.4 BILLION DOLLAR MAN BBC ◎ DVD

DVD | watch an extract from a BBC documentary about Lewis Hamilton
speakout | dreams and ambitions
writeback | a web comment

12.5 LOOKBACK

Communicative revision activities

BBC ◎ INTERVIEWS

Would you like to be famous?

This video extends discussion on the advantages and disadvantages of being famous. People also describe which famous people they'd like to meet. Use the video at the end of Lesson 12.2 or at the start or end of the unit.

CAUGHT ON FILM

Introduction

Ss learn/practise reported speech and film vocabulary in the context of film extras and film quotes.

> **SUPPLEMENTARY MATERIALS**
> **Resource bank** p191–192
> **Language bank** p150–151
> **Warm up:** cinema listings of films being shown this week

Warm up

Lead in to the topic of the lesson. Dictate/Write these questions on the board: *What's on at the cinema this week? Which one(s) would you like to see? When? Where? Why?* Put Ss in pairs/groups and give each one a copy of the film listings for this week. Ss ask and answer the questions, using the listings. They should then try to decide on a film they could all go to and make arrangements for a day/time/place. In feedback, elicit/discuss Ss' answers/arrangements. (NB: If you haven't got any listings, elicit what Ss know about current films in their area using the questions above.)

VOCABULARY FILM

> **Culture notes**
>
> *Mandela: Long Walk to Freedom* (2013) is a British-South African biographical film directed by Justin Chadwick, starring Idris Elba and Naomie Harris. The film is based on the 1995 autobiographical book *Long Walk to Freedom*, by apartheid revolutionary and former South African President Nelson Mandela.
>
> *Iron Man 3* (2013) is a superhero film featuring the Marvel Comics character Iron Man. It is the sequel to 2008's *Iron Man* and 2010's *Iron Man 2* and stars Robert Downey Junior and Gwyneth Paltrow.
>
> *The Zero Theorem* (2013) is a British science fiction film directed by Terry Gilliam and stars Christoph Waltz, Lucas Hedges, Mélanie Thierry and David Thewlis. The story centres on Qohen Leth (Waltz), a computer genius working on a formula to determine whether life holds any meaning.
>
> *The Lego Movie* (2014) is a computer animated adventure comedy film and features the voices of Chris Pratt, Will Ferrell, Elizabeth Banks, Will Arnett, Nick Offerman, Alison Brie, Charlie Day, Liam Neeson and Morgan Freeman.

1A Look at the film posters with Ss and elicit what they know about each film (see Culture notes above). Elicit what type of films they are if possible. Give Ss 2 mins to match the films with the film types and compare their answers in pairs. In feedback, check the meaning/pronunciation of each type.

> **Suggested answers:** *Iron Man 3*: an action film, a blockbuster; *The Zero Theorem*: a science fiction film, a drama, a thriller; *The Lego Movie*: a comedy, a cartoon

B Check the questions. Ss then ask and answer them in pairs and compare their answers with another pair. In feedback, elicit Ss' opinions of the films on the page and find out what the most popular type of film is in the class.

READING

2A Check *formula* and give Ss 2 mins to discuss the questions. In feedback, elicit and write their answers to question 2 on the board.

B Give Ss 2–3 mins to read the text quickly and find an answer to question 2 from Ex 2A. Tell them not to worry about unfamiliar words at this stage. In feedback, refer to the answers on the board and check which Ss guessed correctly. You may need to check words in the text which are relevant to the answers, e.g. *myths, settings, opponents, structures*.

Answers: Blockbusters have a 'formula': they use myths, amazing settings, strong heroes and opponents, a three-part structure and big set pieces.

3 Ss read the definitions first and ask for clarification of unfamiliar words if necessary. Invite other Ss to explain these words if possible. Give Ss 4–6 mins to do the exercise alone and then compare answers in pairs. In feedback, check answers and elicit the pronunciation/word stress.

Answers: 1 myth 2 setting 3 opponent 4 structure 5 scene 6 studio

Optional extra activity

Ss work in pairs and write 4–6 comprehension questions about the text, e.g. *Why are myths useful for blockbuster films? How many parts does a typical blockbuster have?* They exchange questions with another pair and answer them.

4 Ss discuss the questions in groups. In feedback, nominate Ss from different groups to share their ideas with the class.

GRAMMAR   REPORTED SPEECH

Watch out!

The rules of form in reported speech are quite complex, so it's important not to expose Ss to too much information at first. In this lesson, Ss learn only four tense/verb changes: present/past simple, present/past continuous, *will/would, can/could*, and two reporting verbs, *say* and *tell*.

To help Ss acquire the rules of form, give them extensive controlled practice and feedback.

5 Check the rubric and questions. Ss answer the questions alone and compare answers in pairs. Meanwhile, write the third and fourth examples of direct/reported speech on the board. In feedback, refer to these sentences as you elicit/check Ss' answers. Check the reporting verbs. Ask: *Which verb has an object: said or told?* Elicit *told* and the objects (*Steve, Hermione*), and elicit other examples, e.g. *me, you, him/her, it, us, them,* [name]. Finally, teach Ss that habits in the present simple don't change in reported speech. Elicit an example of a habit, e.g. *I have cereal for breakfast every day* and ask Ss to change it to reported speech, e.g. *Olga said she has cereal for breakfast everyday.*

Answers:
1 The verb tenses change from the present to the past in reported speech.
2 say, tell

▷ LANGUAGEBANK 12.1 p150–151

Stronger classes can study the tables and notes at home, and refer to them when they do the exercises. Otherwise, check the tables and notes with Ss, especially the use of *say/tell*. ***Weaker Ss*** should do Ex A and B in class. In Ex A, check *invisible* and *remind*. In Ex B, check *lecture*.

Answers:
A 1 She told me (that) her favourite film was about an invisible man.
2 He said (that) he didn't like westerns.
3 She told us (that) they were actors.
4 He said (that) the film wasn't really about fashion.
5 He told me (that) he worked for a film studio.
6 We told her (that) that director was famous.
7 She said (that) she wrote thrillers.
8 He said (that) the scene reminded him of another film.
B 2 I'm home by 6.00p.m. every day.
3 I don't want to do my homework.
4 We are busy.
5 I don't understand the lecture.
6 I don't like flying.
7 I go back to China every summer.

6A Check the example. Ss then rewrite the paragraph alone and compare answers in pairs. Monitor and prompt them to self-correct. Recheck the tense changes and use of reporting verbs in feedback.

Answers: He said/told me (that) he loved his job, but he didn't like playing criminals. He said/told me (that) he lived in Hollywood, where he worked as a waiter.

B Play the recording and give Ss 1 min to discuss the question in pairs. Elicit answers, then play the recording again for Ss to listen and repeat, copying the stress pattern each time.

Answer: The speaker uses stress to emphasise certain words and thereby changes the meaning.

C Play the recording and ask Ss to read the audio script on page 176 while they listen. Elicit the answer in feedback and drill the different stress patterns, chorally and individually if required. Play the recording again if Ss are still unsure.

Answer: The people or the jobs are stressed according to what the speaker wishes to emphasise each time.

Unit 12 Recording 2

He told me he was an <u>actor</u>, not a <u>dancer</u>!
He told <u>me</u> he was an <u>actor</u>, but he told <u>John</u> he was a <u>doctor</u>!
<u>He</u> told me he was an actor, but his <u>wife</u> said he was a <u>waiter</u>!

7A This exercise checks the use of *said/told* and is also a light-hearted quiz about well-known films, many of which Ss will be familiar with. It would, however, be a good idea to reassure Ss that they are not expected to know all the films, or the answers. Check the meaning of *film quotes* in the title of the quiz and do the first question as an example. If Ss don't know who said the quote, tell them they'll find out later. Give them 2–3 mins to complete the gaps and choose their answers. They can then compare and discuss answers in pairs/groups.

Answers: 1 told   2 said   3 said   4 told   5 said   6 told

Culture notes

Quote 1: Dorothy Gale is a young Kansas girl who falls asleep and finds herself in a fantasy world in the musical *The Wizard of Oz* (1939). She says this line when she 'wakes up' in Oz with Toto, her dog. She adds, 'We must be over the rainbow.'

Quote 2: Gordon Gekko (played by Michael Douglas), a ruthless and greedy corporate raider, says this line in the 1987 film *Wall Street*. Gekko has become a symbol in popular culture for unrestrained greed, often in fields outside corporate finance.

Quote 3: This is a quote from the horror film *Frankenstein* (1931), starring Boris Karloff as the Monster and Colin Clive as Doctor Henry Frankenstein. The most famous line from the film comes from Henry Frankenstein in the creation scene. With the monster's hand slowly rising from the lab table, exhibiting its first signs of life, Henry Frankenstein utters these words.

Quote 4: This is from the film *Apollo 13* (1995). The original phrase pronounced by the astronaut Jack Swigert (Kevin Bacon) and then repeated by Jim Lovell (Tom Hanks), 'Houston, we've had a problem,' was altered to the present tense in the film script. Swigert and then Lovell used the phrase to report a major technical fault in the electrical system of one of the Service Module's oxygen tanks.

Quote 5: This line was famously delivered by Greta Garbo in the American drama film *Grand Hotel* (1932). She speaks these words in the film, first pathetically to her maid and manager, then as a plaintive cry and, finally, as a futile declaration to a stranger. The stranger becomes her lover and she is no longer alone.

Quote 6: This is the last line of the World War II romantic drama *Casablanca* (1942). Police officer Captain Louis Renault and night club owner Rick Blaine (Humphrey Bogart) have just helped Isla Lund (Ingrid Bergman) and her husband escape to Paris and Rick has killed a German officer. Renault suggests they go to join the Free French fighters. Rick replies with this line.

B After Ss have checked their answers on p166, elicit more information about the quotes, using the Culture notes above if necessary. Ask, e.g. *What do you know about this film? Who was in it? When/Where did this quote come in the film?* Also discuss the other films if Ss know/want to talk about them.

Answers: **1** b) **2** b) **3** b) **4** a) **5** a) **6** a)

C Check the example and give Ss 3–4 mins to do the exercise in pairs. In feedback, elicit the answers and check the verb changes made.

Answers:
2 He said (that) greed was good.
3 He said (that) it was alive.
4 He said (that) they had a problem.
5 She said (that) she wanted to be alone.
6 He said (that) he thought that was the beginning of a beautiful friendship.

SPEAKING

8A First, read/check the phrases with Ss. Give them 3–4 mins to think about and note down their answers before they do Ex 8B. If they find it difficult to think of a film, they can use one from Ex 7. **Weaker Ss** could work together. Monitor and provide support where needed.

B In pairs, Ss take turns to describe their films. Remind them to take notes for Ex 8C. Monitor discreetly while Ss work, and make notes of examples of good language and problems.

C Give Ss 2–3 mins to rewrite their notes and put them in reported speech. They then take turns to talk about their partner's answers in groups. Monitor and make notes on problems Ss have with reported speech. Nominate Ss to tell the class about their partners in feedback. Find out if any particular film was chosen more than once. Write examples of Ss' errors and good language on the board. Ss discuss and correct them in pairs.

Homework ideas
- **Ex 2:** Ss write a description of one of the films or a film they know well.
- **Ex 8B/C:** Ss write what their partner said about his/her favourite film.
- **Language bank** 12.1 Ex A–B, p151
- **Workbook** Ex 1–5, p69–70

A LUCKY BREAK

Introduction

Ss learn and practise hypothetical conditionals, and also study word patterns with suffixes.

> **SUPPLEMENTARY MATERIALS**
> **Resource bank** p193
> **Language bank** p150–151
> **Ex 3B:** dictionaries
> **Ex 9C:** internet facilities, if available

Warm up

Lead in to the topic of the lesson. Ask: *Have you ever been in the local/a national newspaper or on TV? Why? When? How did you feel? Did you like it?* Give Ss 3–4 mins to discuss the questions in pairs/groups. If they haven't been in the newspapers/on TV themselves, they could talk about someone they know who has. In feedback, discuss Ss' answers.

VOCABULARY SUFFIXES

1 Check the rubric and give Ss 3–4 mins to discuss in pairs. In feedback, elicit/discuss Ss' answers and find out what Ss think are the top three positive/negative things about being famous.

> **Suggested answers:**
> **positive:** you're always in newspapers/magazines; companies want you to advertise their products; you have famous friends/(a) lovely home(s); you can buy expensive things; you can talk to politicians to try and change the world
> **negative:** photographers/the paparazzi follow you and take your photograph wherever you go; you and your family have no privacy; being recognised by everyone in the street can be annoying; people constantly judge celebrities

2A Ask the question in the rubric and elicit Ss' answers. Then ask them if they recognise the girl and cat if the photos and if not, encourage them to guess why they might be famous. Give them 2 mins to read the article and check. In feedback, check the answer and teach *grumpy*.

> **Answer:** an ordinary person who becomes famous because of the internet

B Check the questions and give Ss 3–4 mins to discuss them in pairs. In feedback, check and discuss Ss' answers in open class. Also ask if they agree with the Andy Warhol quote in the text (*In the future, everyone will be famous for fifteen minutes.*).

> **Answers:**
> 1 In the past you often needed to be a successful actor, footballer or musician to be famous. Nowadays you can become famous through the internet, not just by using your talent.
> 2 You can become famous by posting a photo, a video or a blog.

3A Check the example with the suffix *-ful*. Ss then copy the table into their notebooks and find the other words in the text. Do not confirm answers yet – Ss will check them in Ex 3C.

> **Answers:** **-ous:** famous **-ion:** invention **ity:** celebrity
> **-er/-or/-ian:** footballer, actor, musician

B Ss work alone/in pairs to do the exercise, using dictionaries if available. They will check their answers in Ex 3C.

> **Answers:** **-ful:** helpful, wonderful **-ous:** adventurous, dangerous
> **-ion:** celebration **-ity:** popularity
> **-er/-or/-ian:** photographer, politician

C Ss listen and check that their answers are in the correct suffix columns. They then listen again to underline the main stress (underlined in the audio script below). In feedback, play the recording again, pausing after each word for Ss to repeat it. Drill each word chorally and individually if necessary.

> **Unit 12** Recording 3
>
> successful, helpful, wonderful
> famous, adventurous, dangerous
> invention, celebration
> celebrity, popularity
> footballer, photographer, actor, musician, politician

D Give Ss 2–3 mins to think of other words. Elicit/Add them to the correct column on the board.

> **Suggested answers:** **-ful:** painful **-ous:** ridiculous
> **-ion:** education **-ity:** familiarity **-er:** teacher **-or:** instructor
> **-ian:** electrician

LISTENING

4A Check the rubric and give Ss 3–4 mins to discuss the questions in pairs. In feedback, find out what Ss have in common.

B Check the words in the box. Ss listen and write the answers, then check them in pairs. Play the recording again if students don't agree. Elicit answers in feedback (in bold in the audio script below).

> **Answers:** 2 a politician/president 3 a footballer/sportsperson
> 4 a singer/dancer 5 a writer 6 an actress
> 7 a scientist/inventor 8 –

5A Ss first read the sentences and then listen and complete them. While they check their answers in pairs, monitor to see if they have the correct answers. If not, play the recording again and then check answers with the class (underlined in the audio script below).

> **Answers:** 1 time 2 change 3 World 4 sing 5 writer 6 rich
> 7 lives 8 happy

B Check the example and elicit Ss' opinions. Give them 3–4 mins to decide which speakers they agree with. Elicit and discuss their answers in feedback.

> **Unit 12** Recording 4
>
> 1 If I could be famous for anything, it would be art. I love painting and if I had more time, I would love to **paint** seriously. If I could have a painting in a museum, I'd be really happy.
> 2 I'd be a famous **politician**. If I was a politician, I would try to change the world. To stop all these wars and do something to help poor countries. You know, I think it's terrible how most politicians don't seem to worry about things like that.
> 3 If I could do anything, um … I think I'd be a famous **footballer** or something like that. Imagine if you scored a goal for your country in the World Cup, that would be such a good feeling. You would remember something like that forever.
> 4 I'd love to sing. If I could be famous for anything, I think I'd be a **singer**. Or a **dancer**. I'd love to be a famous dancer. I'm terrible at both of those things – I can't sing or dance! I guess that's why we have dreams, isn't it?

5 I would love to be a famous **writer** or poet, like Shakespeare. I think it's a wonderful thing to be able to write a book that people all around the world want to read. To be able to speak to people in that way. Yes, <u>I'd like to be remembered as a great writer.</u> But I don't think that'll happen.

6 If I could be famous for anything, well, let me see … oh, for being beautiful! That would be good. **One of those beautiful actresses** who wins at the Oscars. <u>If I was famous, I would be rich, live in a big house and have all those clothes.</u> Oh yes, that would be nice.

7 If I could be famous for anything, it would be for **inventing something like a medicine or a cure for cancer**. Not for being an actor, or a musician. <u>If I invented something that made people's lives better, that would be good.</u>

8 What would I want to be famous for? Hmm … I wouldn't like to be famous. <u>If I was famous, I wouldn't be happy.</u> No, I prefer just being me, thank you.

GRAMMAR HYPOTHETICAL CONDITIONALS

Watch out!

Conditional forms in English are relatively easy compared to many other languages as they don't use the subjunctive. It might be useful to point this out to Ss. However, they often confuse hypothetical (second) conditional forms in the main clause/*if* clause and say, e.g. *If I would have more time, I would learn other languages.* (NB: This is common usage in US English.) To help Ss with this problem, provide sufficient practice and feedback.

6A Ss refer to Ex 5A to complete the table, then compare answers in pairs. In feedback, copy the table on the board and elicit Ss' answers.

Answers: 1 had **2** wouldn't **3** was

B Read the rules with Ss and elicit/check their answers. Also point out that the order of the *if*/main clause can change. Write an example on the board and show the position of the comma when the *if* clause is used first.

Answers: 1 imaginary **2** unlikely

> **LANGUAGE**BANK 12.2 p150–151

Read/Check the notes with Ss, especially the use of *were* for giving advice. In Ex A, check *trains were running.* In Ex B, check *mess.*

Answers:
A 1 c) **2** f) **3** a) **4** d) **5** b) **6** e)
B 1 would go, were **2** sold, would, buy **3** would help, could
4 had, would call **5** had, would ask **6** lived, would see
7 Would, be, didn't work **8** didn't, make, would be

7 Do an example. Ss then underline the correct answer and check in pairs. In feedback, check the form and rules of hypothetical conditionals again.

Answers: 1 was **2** worked **3** would feel **4** had **5** didn't
6 didn't have **7** would use

8A Check the example. Give Ss 2–3 mins to write the questions and compare them in pairs. Check/Drill the questions in feedback.

Answers:
2 If you could have dinner with any two living people, who would you choose?
3 If you could do any job, what would you do?
4 If you had more time, what would you do?
5 If you could change one thing about yourself, what would you change?

B Elicit Ss' answers to the first question. While they work in pairs, make notes of problems they have with the target language. In feedback, nominate Ss to tell the class about their partners. Do remedial work if necessary.

WRITING PARAGRAPHS

9A Check the rubric and give Ss 3–4 mins to do the exercise and compare answers in pairs. In feedback, check answers and ask Ss what they learnt about Jack Monroe.

Answers: 1 c) **2** a) **3** d) **4** b)

B Check the meaning of *achievements* and *rise to fame*. Elicit the correct heading for each paragraph.

Answers: 1 Introduction **2** Childhood and education
3 Rise to fame **4** Achievements

speakout TIP

Read and discuss the Speakout tip with Ss before they do Ex 9C.

C If internet facilities are available in your school, Ss could do research for their profile. Otherwise, use the profile of Aung San Suu Kyi on p167. Ss should use the model in Ex 9A and the Speakout tip to help them. Monitor to support Ss and prompt them to correct their writing. Ss can display their final drafts around the classroom or put them on the class blog.

Homework ideas
*   **Ex 9C:** Ss write a final draft of their profile or write another profile.
*   **Language bank** 12.2 Ex A–B, p151
*   **Workbook** Ex 1–9, p71–72

WHAT CAN I DO FOR YOU?

Introduction

Ss learn/practise requests and offers in the context of dealing with a personal concierge. They also learn collocations related to the topic and how to ask for more time.

> **SUPPLEMENTARY MATERIALS**
> **Resource bank** p194
> **Language bank** p150–151
> **Ex 2B:** photos of *The Lion King* musical, the red carpet at the Oscars ceremony, the Rolling Stones, Madonna, Jennifer Lopez, Bill Clinton
> **Ex 9B:** audio/video recording facilities

Warm up

Lead in to the topic of the lesson. Ask/Write these questions on the board: *If you could be a millionaire for one day, where would you go? What would you do? Would you invite other people? Who?* Elicit some initial answers and tell Ss to write down 4–6 things they would do. Encourage them to be imaginative. Ss then work in pairs/groups and take turns to exchange information. In feedback, discuss Ss' answers and find out who had the most original ideas.

VOCABULARY COLLOCATIONS

1A Check the example. Ss work alone and then compare answers in pairs. In feedback, check answers and elicit other examples that collocate with the verbs, e.g. *recommend a good film/book*.

> **Answers:** 2 rent   3 book   4 invite   5 recommend   6 organise

B Ask: *What can you see in each photo?* Elicit details and teach/check useful vocabulary, e.g. *It's a table for two (in a restaurant). A chauffeur's opening the door of a car. A singer's performing at a concert; he's on the stage.* Then elicit collocations from Ex 1A to match each photo.

> **Answers: A** get tickets for a concert
> **B** organise a private tour/rent a car for the day   **C** book a table for two

C Model/Drill the question *How often do you get tickets for a concert?* Do a substitution drill using the collocations from Ex 1A: *How often do you rent a car/book a table/invite someone to dinner?*, etc. Ss then ask and answer the questions in pairs and report back to the class about their partner.

READING

2A Read/Check the rubric and definition. Elicit one or two things Ss think a personal concierge can do. Then give them 2–3 mins to discuss and write a list of others. In feedback, elicit Ss' ideas and write them on the board.

B Give Ss 3 mins to read the text and underline what a personal concierge does. Ss discuss and compare the answers to their ideas on the board. In feedback, use photos of the people/places mentioned as prompts if possible. Elicit the things Ss have underlined and check them with their ideas on the board. Discuss their reactions to the 'amazing' things a personal concierge does. Also check *red carpet at the Oscars, former* and *client*.

> **Answers:** book a table at the world's top restaurants, get the best seats for a popular musical, find you a private plane, organise a red carpet at the Oscars, get twenty tickets for a Rolling Stones concert, fly your favourite tea from one country to another, find rare birds, organise dinner with an ex-US President

FUNCTION REQUESTS AND OFFERS

3A Check the rubric. Ss listen, note down their answers and compare them in pairs. In feedback, check answers (in bold in the audio script below). Also check *adaptor plug*.

> **Answers:**
> 1 to go to a restaurant, possibly with traditional food
> 2 to go to a local food market; to take a taxi
> 3 to borrow an adaptor plug
> 4 to get two tickets for a show (*Cats*)

B Ss read the sentences first, then listen again and complete them. Check/Drill the answers in feedback (underlined in the audio script below).

> **Answers:** 1 like   2 Could   3 Would   4 possible   5 want   6 able
> 7 Shall

C Read/Check the rubric and questions with Ss and elicit an example of a request/offer. Give them 3 mins to answer the questions before they compare answers in pairs. In feedback, elicit and check Ss' answers.

> **Answers:** a) requests: 1, 2, 4, 6; offers: 3, 5, 7   b) 1   c) 4, 6   d) 2

> **Optional extra activity**
>
> **Stronger classes** could read the audio script and underline more examples of requests/offers.

Unit 12 Recording 5

Conversation 1
A: Hello.
B: Hello.
A: How can I help you?
B: **I'd like to go to a local restaurant. Maybe something with traditional food.** <u>Could you recommend somewhere?</u>
A: Yes, of course. Hang on. We have a list on a map.
B: Ah, OK.
A: OK? So here's the hotel. And if you want to walk, you can go to this one here.
B: OK.
A: This is a reasonably priced restaurant which serves mainly …

Conversation 2
A: Hello.
B: Hello. How are you?
A: Fine, thanks. What can I do for you?
B: I read that there's **a local market in the area**. Is it a food … ?
A: The food market. Yes, it's a bit of a walk. Maybe thirty minutes.
B: Oh, that far?
A: <u>Would you like me to call</u> **a taxi?** It's about a five-minute drive.
B: **That would be wonderful.**
A: OK, just a moment. I'll see if there's one waiting.
B: Thank you very much.

Conversation 3
A: Good morning.
B: Morning. **I forgot my adaptor** for the laptop. It's from the United States. **Would it be possible to borrow one** <u>from the hotel?</u>
A: An adaptor plug? Of course. <u>Do you want me to send one up to your room?</u>
B: Yes, please.
A: Can you give me a moment? I'll ask at the desk. It's just for a laptop?
B: Yeah, that's right. A US laptop. I just forgot the adaptor.
A: OK, no problem. What's your room number?
B: Fourteen.
A: Room fourteen. OK.
B: Thanks a lot.

Conversation 4
A: Hello.
B: Hello.
A: How can I help you?
B: **I want to see a show this evening. *Cats*.**
A: Oh yes. *Cats*.
B: **Would you be able to book two tickets for us?**
A: Hold on. Let me just check where it's playing. OK, here we are. Yes, shall I book the tickets for you? Do you have any preference about the seats?
B: Any seats. Two together.
A: Two together, yes. OK, and it starts at 7 o'clock. So you should have plenty of time, and if you'll just wait here while I …

▷ **LANGUAGEBANK 12.3** p150–151

Ss can refer to the tables for help with this exercise. Check *plumber*.

Answers:
Conversation 1
A: *Could* you recommend … ?
B: Would you like *me* to show you … ?
Conversation 2
A: I'd like *to* eat out tonight.
B: OK. Do you want *me* to choose the restaurant?
B: OK. And *shall* I book a table for two?
Conversation 3
A: Would you be *able* to get me a good plumber?
B: *No* problem.
A: Would *it* be possible to do it today?
B: Yes, *of* course.

4A Do an example with Ss. Monitor while they write the sentences to check how well they have understood the target language. Check answers in feedback.

Answers:
1 I'd like to try some local food.
2 Could you recommend a good nightclub?
3 Would you be able to book three tickets?
4 Would it be possible to rent a car?
5 Shall I buy your ticket?
6 Do you want me to book a table?
7 Would you like me to call the manager?

B First, check *print out*, *daily rates* and *box office* with **weaker classes**. Otherwise, do it in feedback. Give Ss 2 mins to match the responses and check in pairs. Elicit/Ask Ss to justify their answers by giving you key words, e.g. in answer 1b), *local food, restaurants*.

Answers: 1 b) 2 c) 3 d) 4 a) 5 g) 6 e) 7 f)

5A Check the example and give Ss 2–3 mins to write their own requests. Monitor and help them with accuracy in preparation for Ex 5B.

B Check the example and elicit the offer of help in B's response. Tell Ss to make similar offers in their responses. Monitor while Ss work and make notes of good use of the target language and problems. In feedback, invite pairs to act out their conversations to the class. Do a correction slot using your notes.

C Ss listen, noticing the rising and falling intonation in the requests. Explain that this is how to sound polite when making requests: their voice should start high, then become lower.

D Ss listen again and repeat. Drill the phrases chorally and individually if required, paying close attention to the polite intonation.

Unit 12 Recording 6

Could you recommend a restaurant?
Would you be able to book a table for me?
Would it be possible to rent a car?
Could you recommend somewhere to visit?

LEARN TO ASK FOR MORE TIME

6A Look at the example. Then give Ss 2 mins to underline three more phrases and compare answers in pairs. Elicit/Check them in feedback.

Answers: Just a moment. Can you give me a moment? Hold on.

B Read the rubric and elicit/check Ss' answers.

Answers: The phrases are informal. *Can you give me a moment?* is the most formal.

7 Do an example for conversation 1, using language from Ex 6. Ss work alone and then compare answers in pairs before feedback.

Answers:
Conversation 1: Hang *on*.
Conversation 2: Can you give *me* a moment?
Conversation 3: *Just* a moment.
Conversation 4: Hold *on*.

SPEAKING

8 Divide the class into As and Bs. They read their roles on p165 and p167. Ss first prepare their roles in pairs while you monitor and provide support. They then work in A/B pairs and do the role-plays. Make notes of their performance for feedback.

9A Ss write one of their conversations in pairs using the information provided in the rubric. Monitor to check they do this and prompt them if necessary. Also support them while they rehearse their conversations for Ex 9B.

B If you have recording facilities, use them here to record Ss' role-plays for feedback.

Homework ideas
• **Ex 9:** Ss write another conversation from p165 and p167.
• **Language bank** 12.3 Ex A, p151
• **Workbook** Ex 1–5, p73

BILLION DOLLAR MAN

Introduction

Ss watch an extract from a BBC documentary about Formula 1 driver Lewis Hamilton. They then learn and practise how to talk/write about their dreams and ambitions.

> **SUPPLEMENTARY MATERIALS**
> **Warm up:** photos of people doing extreme sports, e.g. rock climbing, surfing, skydiving, snowboarding, scuba diving, skiing, F1 racing
> **Ex 1:** photos of famous contemporary Formula 1 drivers

Warm up

Lead in and create interest in the lesson. Elicit the names of 6–8 extreme sports, as listed in the Supplementary materials box above, and write them on the board. If you have photos of these sports, use them as prompts. Ask: *Which are the most dangerous/exciting sports? Which have you done? Which would you like to try?* Give Ss 3–4 mins to discuss their answers in pairs/groups. Ss could put the sports in order of most dangerous/exciting.
Elicit/Discuss Ss' answers in feedback and find out which sports Ss would most/least like to try.

DVD PREVIEW

1 Give Ss 3–4 mins to discuss the questions. If possible, use photos of famous F1 drivers from their countries/worldwide as prompts for question 1. In feedback, elicit what Ss know about F1 drivers and check/teach language to describe what type of people they are, e.g. *ambitious, brave/courageous, talented, excellent driving skills, very fit, able to concentrate.* Elicit/Drill the pronunciation of the longer words and write them on the board.

> **Culture notes**
>
> British F1 champion **Lewis Hamilton** was born in 1985. He began driving remote-controlled cars in 1990. His father bought him a go-kart in 1993 and worked very hard to support his son's racing career. In 1998, Lewis joined McLaren's young driver programme. He first drove in Formula 1 in 2007 and won the F1 World Championship in 2008 and 2014. The BBC documentary *Lewis Hamilton: Billion Dollar Man* was first broadcast in November 2008.

2 First ask Ss to look at the photos of Lewis Hamilton. Ask: *What do you know about him?* Elicit Ss' answers. They then read the text to check their ideas and answer the questions in the rubric. In feedback, check Ss' answers to the questions. They will find out more about Hamilton in the DVD.

> **Suggested answer:** The programme is about Lewis Hamilton. You might learn about Lewis Hamilton's childhood/early life and his development as a racing driver.

DVD VIEW

3 Check the questions and the ideas in the box, then play the DVD. Ss note down their answers and then compare them in pairs. Play the relevant sections of the DVD again if necessary. In feedback, nominate Ss to give the answers. Elicit/Discuss Ss' initial impressions of the DVD.

> **Suggested answers:**
> **who he is now:** Hamilton is a world famous F1 driver, model, celebrity and winner, loved by many.
> **F1 facts:** F1 is a glamorous sport that takes place in some of the world's richest locations. It involves fame, money and glory.
> **early days as a racer:** Hamilton started racing electric cars as a six-year-old; then he progressed to go-karts. He won four British go-karting championships.
> **teenage ambitions:** As a teenager, he wanted to be F1 champion by the age of twenty.
> **route to F1:** He joined F3, was the best driver, moved up a level (where he stayed for two years) and then joined F1.

4A Ss read the notes first. Check *go-karts* and '*the big guys*' either here or in feedback if you have a **stronger class**. Tell Ss to think about the type of word that could complete each gap e.g. noun, verb. Ss then complete the notes and compare answers in pairs. Do not confirm answers yet – Ss will check them in Ex 4B.

B Ss watch the DVD and check their answers to Ex 4A. Monitor while Ss are watching/checking their answers to see if they need to watch the DVD again. Elicit/Check answers in feedback (in bold in the DVD script below).

> **Answers:** 1 winner 2 cars 3 F1/Formula One 4 four
> 5 lots of money 6 F3/Formula Three 7 managers 8 two

> **Optional extra activity**
>
> Exploit the context and language of the DVD further. Play it again, pausing at suitable points. Ask questions about what Ss can see/hear, e.g. *What's Lewis doing? Where is he? How long is the Formula 1 season? Where does it take place? What was he like when he was seven/a teenager?*

DVD 12 Lewis Hamilton: Billion Dollar Man

N = Narrator   M = Man   P = Presenter   L = Lewis Hamilton
NR = Newsreader

N: This is Lewis Hamilton, **Formula One driver, model, celebrity, winner**. Journalists love him. Fans love him. Formula One loves him. He's got it all. This is the story of how an ordinary young man went from this … to this. Formula One is all about speed. In this world, only the fastest survive. The season lasts from March to October, and it takes place in some of the world's richest locations. It's the sport of millionaires and heroes. Speed on the track, money in the bank, fame and glory. And nobody does it better than Lewis Hamilton, the billion dollar man. A hero today. But where did it all start?

M: **Cars like these** are getting ready to compete in the World Championships. Someone who's preparing for those very same championships is Lewis Hamilton, who is **only seven years old**. So **how long have you been racing cars for already**, Lewis?

L: **About a year.**

P: So you must be pretty good at it. Is it easy to do?

L: No.

P: What do you have to do then?

L: This is the brake.

P: That's the brake. Oh, you need the brake.

L: And these are the turns for steering.

P: That's your steering wheel, right and left. OK, now, um, d'you think I'd be able to have a go?

L: Yes.

P: You sure? They're under starter's orders for the Blue Peter mini Grand Prix. Three, two, one, go.

L: **The reason I want to be a Formula One driver** is because it's got a lot of speed in it. When I saw the ultra-speed that they were doing it was amazing because you don't actually think about it when you're watching on TV and my kart feels really powerful when I'm in it, but imagine being in a Formula One car. It must be very powerful that.

NR: **Lewis Hamilton has won four British go-karting championships.** Now he says he wants to be world Formula One champion by the time he's twenty.

L: My ambition is to get to Formula One. Definitely. **Um, I enjoy the speed. Um, I like to be with all the big guys, and I'd like to be making lots of money.**

N: **After go-karting, Lewis moved on to Formula Three**, which is two levels below Formula One. Formula Three is fast, dangerous and full of young, ambitious drivers. **The best of the drivers are seen by Formula One managers.** And Lewis, of course, was the best. **After two years of winning everything**, he moved up to the next level and then to Formula One. And the rest is history.

5 Give Ss 3–4 mins to discuss the questions in pairs/groups. In feedback, elicit/discuss them.

speakout dreams and ambitions

6A Check the rubric/questions and *inspire, special skill, achieve a dream*. Ss then listen and tick the answers, and then compare them in pairs. Elicit/Check them in feedback.

Answers: 1, 2, 5

B Ss discuss what Marianna said in more detail. Play the recording again if Ss need more information. In feedback, elicit answers (in bold in the audio script below) and Ss' reasons for them.

Answers:
1 She grew up by the sea.
2 She wanted to work on a boat.
5 Yes. She got a job as a cleaner on a big cruise ship.

Unit 12 Recording 7

I grew up by the sea. My father and my uncle are fishermen, and as a child I used to spend all my time on the beach. Every morning I watched the fishermen come in with their nets full of fish, and these men seemed so free and happy. So, I had this idea that **I wanted to work on a boat**. But the problem was, it was a very male profession. Only men did it and fishermen didn't accept that women could go fishing. They thought we should stay at home and clean the house, do the cooking, have babies. I always asked my father to go on the boat with him and he always said, 'No, stay at home and help your mother.' Anyway, it's a long story, but eventually, I became a cleaner in a hotel. **And then one day I had the chance to work as a cleaner on a ship, one of the big cruise ships.** It's a great job and I've done it for the past six years. It's a dream come true because I spend a lot of time at sea. My next dream is to have a houseboat and actually live on the water. We'll see. I can make it happen!

C First, check the rubric and key phrases. Elicit sample answers to the questions in Ex 6A. Give Ss 4–5 mins to write their notes. Monitor closely to provide support where needed.

D Ss work in pairs and take turns to talk about their dreams and ambitions. They should make notes of similarities in their answers. Monitor and make notes on Ss' performance for feedback later. In feedback, Ss report back to the class about their group. Find out which ambitions the class shares now.

writeback a web comment

7 Give Ss 2–3 mins to read the text and answer the questions. Check Ss' answers and check *sociology*.

Answers:
1 He wanted to be a teacher.
2 He wants to go back to college, do some management courses and open his own school.

8 Ss write a web comment in answer to the three questions, using their notes from Ex 6. Provide support if needed.

Homework ideas

- **Ex 6D:** Ss write about their own or a partner's dreams and ambitions for a website or class blog.
- **Ex 8:** Ss write a final draft of their web comment.

LOOKBACK

Introduction

With **stronger classes**, you could exploit the last Lookback section in a slightly different way. Put Ss in pairs/groups and ask: *Which areas of the language here do you feel most/least confident about? Which would you like to do first?* Give Ss 15–20 mins to do the sections they choose. Monitor and provide support as needed, while you also assess Ss' performance. In feedback, check Ss' answers as far as possible or give them a copy of the answer key for them to check their own work. Ask: *Why did you choose these sections? How well did you do them? What did you learn?* Discuss Ss' answers.

FILM

1A Check the words in the box (unless you want this exercise to be a test). Ss then complete the text alone and compare answers in pairs. In feedback, elicit/check Ss' answers.

Answers: 1 horror films   2 setting   3 opponent   4 scene
5 blockbuster   6 studio

B Give Ss 3–4 mins to prepare and make notes. **Weaker Ss** could refer to p118–119 for help. Monitor and take notes for feedback and/or assessment. In feedback, find out how many Ss chose the same film.

REPORTED SPEECH

Culture notes

Quote 1: *Oliver* (1968) is a British musical drama, based on Charles Dickens' novel *Oliver Twist*. Oliver, a nine-year-old orphan, was a resident of a workhouse where the conditions were dreadful. He says this line to his master, asking for more food.

Quote 2: This is the opening line of the American crime drama *The Godfather* (1972). Italian Amerigo Bonasera says this line as he shares his story with Vito Corneone (Marlon Brando), the patriarch of a Mafia crime family in New York, asking for his help and explaining that he has tried to live his life like an American.

Quote 3: This is part of the opening voiceover in *The Piano* (1993), a romantic drama about Ada McGrath (Holly Hunter), a mute piano player, and her daughter. In this voiceover, Ada explains that she primarily communicates through the music she plays on her piano.

Quote 4: This is the catchphrase of police detective Roger Murtaugh (Danny Glover) in the *Lethal Weapon* series of buddy cop action films. Murtaugh, who is considering retirement, repeatedly says this line when he is faced with dangerous situations on the job.

Quote 5: *Blue Velvet* (1986) is an American neo-noir mystery film. Jeffrey Beaumont (Kyle MacLachlan), an innocent young man, says this line as he discovers that a dark underworld exists beneath the surface of his seemingly quiet hometown.

Quote 6: *Grand Hotel* (1932) is an American drama film about a group of very different individuals staying at a luxurious hotel in Berlin. Dr Otternschlag, a World War I veteran and permanent resident of the hotel, says this line, after which a great deal transpires.

2A Do the first question as an example and find out what Ss know about the film *Oliver!* Give them 4–5 mins to write their sentences and compare answers in pairs. Monitor and note down problems they have with reported speech. Nominate Ss to answer and give feedback/do remedial work as needed.

Answers:
1 wanted some more
2 believed in America
3 heard was not her speaking voice, but her mind's voice
4 was too old for this
5 was a strange world
6 came. People went … nothing ever happened

B Ss discuss the question in pairs, then compare answers with another pair. In feedback, discuss Ss' answers.

SUFFIXES

3A Give Ss 3–4 mins to do the exercise and then compare answers in pairs. In feedback, check the meaning/pronunciation of each word. Drill the questions if necessary.

Answers: 1 dangerous   2 wonderful   3 celebration   4 famous
5 politician, musician   6 successful

B Give Ss time to prepare their answers. They then take turns to ask and answer the questions in Ex 3A. They should note down their partner's answers. In feedback, Ss tell the class about their partner, using their notes. Do remedial work as required.

HYPOTHETICAL CONDITIONALS PRESENT/FUTURE

4 Ss read the sentences first. If necessary, check *upset, scarf, ideal partners* and *desert island*. Give Ss 4–5 mins to complete the sentences and compare answers in pairs. Check answers and do remedial work if needed.

Answers: 1 didn't have to, would take   2 would be, lost
3 were able to, would, choose   4 would be, didn't argue
5 wouldn't say, knew   6 lived, would be

5 Do the example with Ss around the class, each one adding a new 'consequence' for as long as possible. Ss then do the exercise in pairs. Monitor and make notes of Ss' problems for feedback. In feedback, invite pairs to act out their longest exchange to the class. Find out who has the longest.

REQUESTS AND OFFERS

6A Ss underline the correct alternative and then compare answers in pairs. In feedback, elicit/drill the answers.

Answers: 1 to see   2 me to buy   3 able to   4 recommend
5 I call you   6 like to visit

B Check the rubric. Give Ss time to choose their three things from the box or use their own ideas. Encourage them to be imaginative.

C Check the example conversation and the meaning of *whereabouts*. Give Ss time to prepare how they want to make their requests and provide support if necessary. Ss should take turns to be the concierge. Monitor and make notes of their performance for feedback and/or assessment. In feedback, invite pairs to act out their conversations to the class. Do remedial work as needed.

Homework ideas

Workbook Review 4, p74–76

BBC interviews and worksheet

Would you like to be famous?

This video extends discussion on the advantages and disadvantages of being famous. People also describe which famous people they'd like to meet.

PAGE	UNIT	PHOTOCOPIABLE	LANGUAGE POINT	TIME
147	1	Love story	**Vocabulary: relationships** • review vocabulary of relationships • practise structured story telling using the past simple	30–35
148	1	Heads and tails	**Grammar: question forms** • practise forming questions • practise speaking skills by talking about free time activities using the present simple and the past simple	25–30
149	1	Talk about it!	**Grammar: past simple** • practise speaking skills using the past simple	30–35
150	1	Party time!	**Functional language: making conversation** • practise functional language for making polite conversation	30–35
151	2	What do I do?	**Vocabulary: jobs** • review vocabulary of jobs, work and the workplace • practise speaking skills in the context of a guessing game	20–30
152	2	Grammar maze	**Grammar: present simple and continuous** • practise the present simple and present continuous • practise speaking skills by asking and answering questions	30–40
153	2	How often do you …?	**Grammar: adverbs of frequency** • use adverbs of frequency to talk about habits and free time activities • practise speaking skills in the context of a game	20–30
154	2	I can't stand cheese!	**Functional language: expressing likes/dislikes** • practise functional phrases for expressing likes and dislikes	20–30
155	3	Time out target practice	**Vocabulary: time out** • review vocabulary to talk about going out • review letters and spelling	20–30
156	3	Bank holiday weekend	**Grammar: present continuous/*be going to* for future** • use the present continuous and *be going to* to make future arrangements • practise speaking skills by accepting and refusing invitations	30–40
157	3	Is it art?	**Grammar: questions without auxiliaries** • use questions without auxiliaries to complete a text about Banksy • practise speaking skills by asking and answering questions	20–30
158	3	Who's calling?	**Functional language: making a phone call** • practise functional language for making and receiving phone calls	25–35
159	4	Collocation football	**Vocabulary: *make* and *do*; education** • review collocations with *make, do, give, play, study, tell* and *wear* • practise speaking skills by talking about education and school	15–25
160	4	Have you ever …?	**Grammar: present perfect + *ever/never*** • use the present perfect and past simple to talk about life experiences • review the past participles of irregular verbs	25–35
161	4	Class rules	**Grammar: *can, have to, must*** • use *can, have to* and *must* to write rules for the class • practise speaking skills by discussing rules and obligations	25–35
162	4	Save our school!	**Functional language: giving advice** • practise functional language of giving advice and responding to advice for schools	30–40
163	5	Getting around	**Vocabulary: transport** • review vocabulary of types of transport • practise speaking skills by describing types of transport	20–25
164	5	Missing money	**Grammar: past simple and past continuous** • use the past simple and past continuous to talk about a crime	20–30
165	5	20 things about you	**Grammar: verb patterns** • use verb patterns to talk about yourself	20–30
166	5	Tipton tour	**Functional language: asking for/giving directions** • practise functional language for asking for and giving directions around a town	25–30
167	6	A healthy city	**Vocabulary: health** • review vocabulary of health • practise speaking skills – agreeing and disagreeing	20–30
168	6	How long …?	**Grammar: present perfect + *for/since*** • use the present perfect + *for/since* to talk about sports stars	25–30
169	6	Predictions	**Grammar: *may, might, will*** • use *may, may not, might, might not* and *will/won't* to talk about future predictions	25–30
170	6	Where does it hurt?	**Functional language: seeing the doctor** • practise functional language for visiting the doctor	20–30

RESOURCE BANK

Photocopiable activities index

PAGE	UNIT	PHOTOCOPIABLE	LANGUAGE POINT	TIME
171	7	Another life	**Vocabulary: verbs + prepositions** • use verbs with prepositions to talk about life changes • practise speaking skills – sharing personal information	20–30
172	7	Did you know ...?	**Grammar: *used to*** • use *used to* to describe past states and habits of famous people and things • practise speaking skills in the context of a quiz	20–30
173	7	I went home to ...	**Grammar: purpose, cause and result** • use *to*, *because* and *so* to express purpose, cause and result in the context of a game	25–35
174	7	Career change	**Functional language: finding out information** • practise functional language for finding out information in the context of changing careers	25–30
175	8	Amazing money	**Vocabulary: money** • review vocabulary for money • practise speaking skills by doing a quiz	20–30
176	8	Four guesses	**Grammar: relative clauses** • use relative clauses to describe familiar and successful things and places for a guessing game	30–40
177	8	Let's celebrate!	**Grammar: *too much/many, enough, very*** • use *too much/too many*, *enough/not enough* and *very* in the context of planning a party	30–40
178	8	Can I help you?	**Functional language: buying things** • practise functional language for shopping and buying things	20–30
179	9	It's a cheetah!	**Vocabulary: animals** • review the names of animals in the context of a game	20–25
180	9	Compare it!	**Grammar: comparatives/superlatives** • use comparatives and superlatives to make comparisons in a board game	25–30
181	9	Race to the South Pole	**Grammar: articles** • practise recognising incorrect article use in a text about an explorer	20–25
182	9	It might be ...	**Functional language: making guesses** • practise functional language for making guesses and speculating about objects	20–25
183	10	Crime crossword	**Vocabulary: crime and punishment** • review vocabulary of crime and punishment	20–30
184	10	What's it like?	**Grammar: uses of *like*** • use *like* for descriptions, opinions and positive and negative attributes in a snakes and ladders game	30–35
185	10	I don't believe it!	**Grammar: present/past passive** • use the passive in the context of discussing surprising facts • revise irregular verb forms	30–40
186	10	Excuse me ...	**Functional language: complaining** • practise functional language for making and dealing with complaints in a variety of situations	30–35
187	11	Dominoes	**Vocabulary: feelings** • practise recognising adjectives to describe feelings	25–30
188	11	Who am I?	**Grammar: present perfect (+ *just, yet, already*)** • use the present perfect and *just*, *already* and *yet* in a guessing game	25–30
189	11	Conditional wheels	**Grammar: real conditionals + *if*** • use the real conditional to make sentence chains	30–35
190	11	Gadgets	**Functional language: giving opinions** • practise functional language for giving opinions and disagreeing politely about new ideas	30–40
191	12	Noughts and crosses	**Vocabulary: film** • review vocabulary of films in the context of a game	15–25
192	12	Star interview	**Grammar: reported speech** • practise speaking skills in the context of an interview • use reported speech to repeat information from an interview	30–40
193	12	Three in a row	**Grammar: hypothetical conditionals for present/future** • use the hypothetical conditional to describe imaginary situations in a game	35–40
194	12	All in a day's work	**Functional language: requests and offers** • practise functional language for making requests and offers	30–35

1 Match pictures A–H with the words and phrases in the box. Some pictures are used more than once.

didn't have a girlfriend *A*   fell in love   met   argued   got married   accepted got back together   got divorced   proposed to her   got on well

2 Put the pictures in order to make a story.

When did you last	buy something expensive?
When did you last	go on holiday or have time off?
What is	your favourite book?
What is	your favourite sport?
Were you	feeling happy yesterday?
Were you	at home last night?
Do you have	a best friend?
Do you spend	a lot of money?
How often do you play	or watch sport?
How often do you cook	for other people?
Where do you go	out with friends?
Where do your	family live?

Talk about a journey you took. 1

Talk about the last time you met your friends. 1

Talk about your best holiday. 5

Talk about your first English lesson. 2

Talk about an easy subject at school. 4

Talk about what you last saw at the cinema. 4

Talk about your first bike or car. 4

Talk about your first day at school. 3

Talk about the last time you cried or laughed a lot. 2

Talk about the last time you worked or studied hard. 3

Talk about your favourite toy when you were a child. 5

Talk about how you met your best friend. 6

Talk about a difficult subject at school. 3

Talk about the last present you bought. 2

Talk about the last party you went to. 5

Talk about what you cooked/ate yesterday. 1

Role card 1

Tom from Scotland

Family	wife: Elizabeth
Occupation	actor
Recreation	going shopping and cooking
Education	parents – at home
Task	Find out who is an architect.

Role card 6

Jenny from New Zealand

Family	no husband, one child
Occupation	chef
Recreation	playing golf and travelling
Education	went to school in Japan
Task	Find out who comes from Scotland.

Role card 2

Sarah from Australia

Family	boyfriend: Brad
Occupation	dancer
Recreation	driving fast cars and riding horses
Education	went to a school for actors and dancers
Task	Find out who went to school in Japan.

Role card 7

Andrew from Northern Ireland

Family	wife: Angela and a pet crocodile
Occupation	singer
Recreation	running and making cakes
Education	went to an expensive private school
Task	Find out who has ten pets.

Role card 3

Joe from Wales

Family	wife: Maria, five children and ten pets
Occupation	doctor
Recreation	gardening and having barbecues
Education	went to school in Canada
Task	Find out who is a lawyer.

Role card 8

Laura from the United States of America

Family	husband: John
Occupation	architect
Recreation	reading and playing the guitar
Education	Harvard University
Task	Find out who went to Bath University.

Role card 4

Annie from Ireland

Family	husband: James
Occupation	TV presenter
Recreation	playing football and learning languages
Education	Bath University
Task	Find out who likes fishing.

Role card 9

Evan from England

Family	wife: Kate
Occupation	businessman
Recreation	boxing and fishing
Education	went to eleven different schools
Task	Find out who likes making cakes.

Role card 5

David from England

Family	married twice, three children
Occupation	fire fighter
Recreation	karate and painting
Education	didn't go to school very much
Task	Find out who is a dancer.

Role card 10

Rachel from South Africa

Family	three sisters
Occupation	lawyer
Recreation	swimming and having barbecues
Education	went to school in Cape Town
Task	Find out who has three children.

START

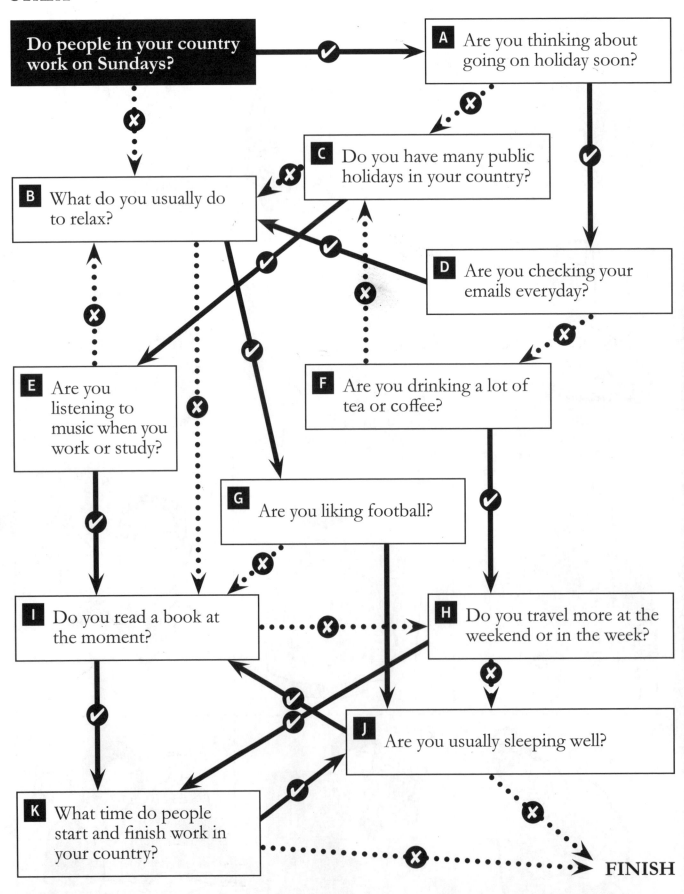

Do people in your country work on Sundays?

A Are you thinking about going on holiday soon?

C Do you have many public holidays in your country?

B What do you usually do to relax?

D Are you checking your emails everyday?

E Are you listening to music when you work or study?

F Are you drinking a lot of tea or coffee?

G Are you liking football?

I Do you read a book at the moment?

H Do you travel more at the weekend or in the week?

J Are you usually sleeping well?

K What time do people start and finish work in your country?

FINISH

Read the questions. If the grammar is correct, follow the black arrow. If the grammar is incorrect, follow the dotted arrow to the next box.

Write the order here: Start ___ ___ ___ ___ ___ ___ ___ ___ ___ ___ ___ **Finish**

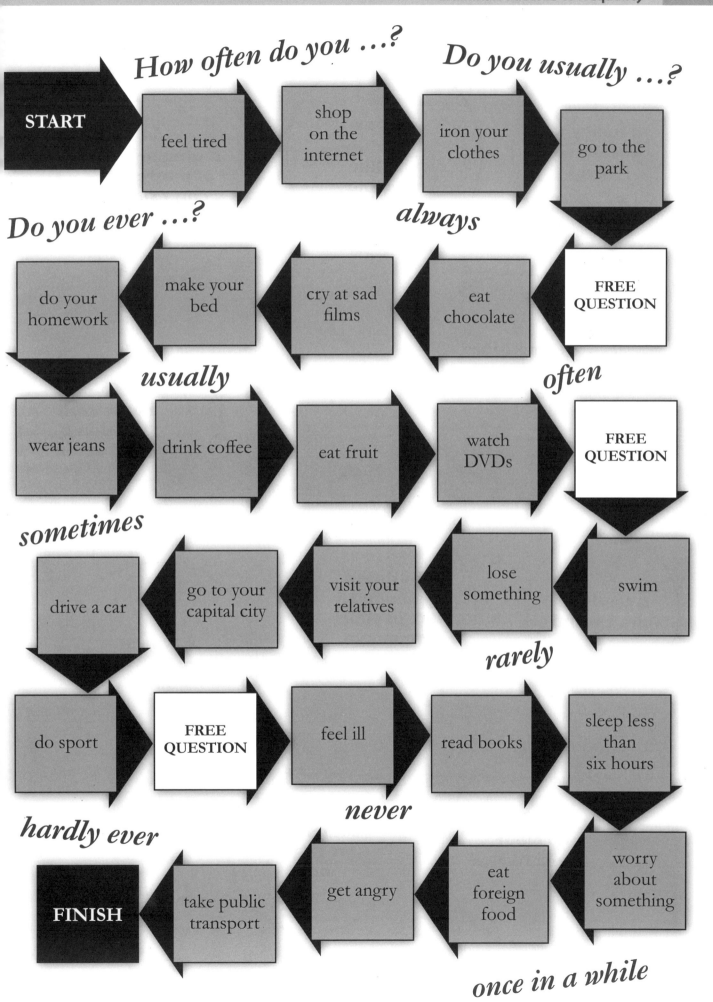

How often do you ...?

Do you usually ...?

START → feel tired → shop on the internet → iron your clothes → go to the park

Do you ever ...?

always

do your homework ← make your bed ← cry at sad films ← eat chocolate ← **FREE QUESTION**

usually

often

wear jeans → drink coffee → eat fruit → watch DVDs → **FREE QUESTION**

sometimes

drive a car ← go to your capital city ← visit your relatives ← lose something ← swim

rarely

do sport → **FREE QUESTION** → feel ill → read books → sleep less than six hours

never

hardly ever

FINISH ← take public transport ← get angry ← eat foreign food ← worry about something

once in a while

I CAN'T STAND CHEESE!

Functional language: expressing likes/dislikes

Write the name of …

1
a food you
absolutely
love

_____

2
an item
of clothing
you like
wearing

_____

3
a song or type
of music you
can't stand

_____

4
something
about learning
English you
don't like

_____

5
a smell you
absolutely
love

_____

6
housework
you don't
mind doing

_____

7
a food you
can't stand

_____

8
a building
you don't
like in your
hometown

_____

9
a type of
weather you
hate

_____

10
a colour
you like

_____

11
something
on TV you
hate

_____

12
a sport you
are keen on

_____

Student A

Put these words somewhere in the grid:

| nightclub | actor | concert | exhibition | hang out | comedy | indoors | band |

	1	2	3	4	5	6	7	8	9	10
A										
B										
C										
D										
E										
F										
G										
H										
I										
J										

> Miss!

> Hit 'a'!

> You've hit my (concert)!

Student B

Put these words somewhere in the grid:

| outdoors | waterfront | sightseeing | chess | live music | gallery | cards | bar |

	1	2	3	4	5	6	7	8	9	10
A										
B										
C										
D										
E										
F										
G										
H										
I										
J										

> Miss!

> Hit 'a'!

> You've hit my (band)!

The *London* Guide:

The best of what's on in London this Bank Holiday

Art/Dance/Culture	Cinema/Theatre	Special events	Sport
Art Exhibition See the work of the great artist Salvador Dali at The National Gallery. All weekend from 10a.m. until 5p.m. £15	**Shakespeare at Night** See *Romeo and Juliet* outside at Regent's Park Theatre. Saturday, 7p.m. until 11p.m. £30	**International Food Fair** Taste food from all over the world and meet famous chefs in Brick Lane. All weekend from 10a.m. until 5p.m. £15	**Brazil v Argentina** Two great football teams and both here in London! It will be a great match at Wembley Stadium. Saturday, 3p.m. £30
Russian Ballet See the world's best ballet dancers in Covent Garden. Saturday/Sunday, 7.30p.m. until 10p.m. £30	**Horror Film Day** See lots of famous horror films and meet actors, directors and monsters in Covent Garden. Saturday, 1p.m. until 11p.m. £15	**Rock Concert** See the best London and international rock bands in Hyde Park. Saturday, 1p.m. until late Free	**Extreme Sports Fair** Watch and try extreme sports at the ExCeL Exhibition Centre. All weekend from 11a.m. until 5p.m. £25
French Circus See the world's best circus in Camden Town. Everyday from 7p.m. until 10p.m. £25	**Star Wars Film Fair** Meet some of the actors, thousands of fans and watch the films inLeicester Square. Sunday, 11a.m. until 5p.m. £15	**Street Carnival** A celebration of London's different cultures: music, food, dancing and lots more in Notting Hill. Sunday, 12p.m. until late Free	**Fun Run** Run 5 km from Buckingham Palace to the Tower of London with thousands of people or just watch! Sunday, 10a.m. until 4p.m. Free

Saturday 27	
morning	9a.m. breakfast with Sarah at The Corner Café
afternoon	
evening	

Sunday 28	
morning	
afternoon	
evening	

Monday 29	BANK HOLIDAY
morning	
afternoon	
evening	

Worksheet A

**Ask your partner questions to find the missing information in your text.
Use the words in brackets.**

Banksy is a ¹_____ (who). He is probably the most famous one in the world. He became famous in the early 2000s, but we know very little about him. We know he was born in 1974, in Bristol, UK and lives and works in Shoreditch, London. Perhaps his real name is ²_____ or _____ (what). There are no photos of Banksy because he doesn't want people to know who he is.

Banksy makes 'street art' and it is in many countries, including ³_____ , _____ and _____ (where). His art is successful because it's powerful, it's simple and often funny. Animals such as ⁴_____ and _____ (which) are often in his pictures, as well as people like police officers, soldiers and children. However, a London council painted over one of Banksy's famous paintings in 2009 because they thought it looked like graffiti.

Banksy's art now sells for hundreds of thousands of dollars and he sells art to many famous people. In 2007 ⁵_____ and _____ (who) spent $2 million on his work. His most successful exhibition was in Bristol in 2009. There were over 8,500 visitors every day. However, his parents don't even know what he does. They think his job is painting houses!

Worksheet B

**Ask your partner questions to find the missing information in your text.
Use the words in brackets.**

Banksy is a famous graffiti artist. He is probably the most famous one in the world. He became famous in the early 2000s, but we know very little about him. We know he was born in ¹_____ (when), in Bristol, UK and lives and works in Shoreditch, London. Perhaps his real name is Robert or Robin Banks. There are no photos of Banksy because ²_____ (why).

Banksy makes 'street art' and it is in many countries, including USA, Australia and Israel. His art is successful because it's ³_____ , it's _____ and often _____ (why). Animals such as rats and monkeys are often in his pictures, as well as people like police officers, soldiers and children. However, ⁴_____ (who) painted over one of Banksy's famous paintings in 2009 because they thought it looked like graffiti.

Banksy's art now sells for hundreds of thousands of dollars and he sells art to many famous people. In 2007 Brad Pitt and Angelina Jolie spent $2 million on his work. His most successful exhibition was in ⁵_____ (where) in 2009. There were over 8,500 visitors every day. However, his parents don't even know what he does. They think his job is painting houses!

Role card 1A

You booked a General English course for two weeks at The English School.

The course starts next Monday, but you want to change it to a course one month later.

Phone the school.

Role card 1B

You are a receptionist at The English School.

There are courses available next month.

Students who change courses must pay an extra £50.

Role card 2A

You work for HBS and you are Mrs Forster's secretary.

Mrs Forster is busy – she is in a meeting.

Ask if you can take a message.

Role card 2B

You need to phone a company called HBS for your job.

You want to speak to Mrs Forster.

If you can't speak to her, you would like her to call you back.

Phone the company.

Role card 3A

You are at home and you are bored. You want to do something with your friend.

You would like to go to the cinema or see a play.

Ask your friend for ideas.

Phone your friend.

Role card 3B

You are at home and you are bored. You want to meet a friend.

The weather is nice and so you would like to do something outside.

Role card 4A

Your uncle owns a restaurant called The Borough Lounge (spell this to your friend).

The phone number is 020 87973 2047.

It is best to phone in the afternoon when the restaurant is not busy.

Role card 4B

You are looking for a job in a restaurant as a waiter/waitress.

Your friend's uncle owns a restaurant, but you can't remember the name of the restaurant.

You need the restaurant's telephone number.

Phone your friend.

GOAL A		START		GOAL B

Worksheet A

1 I am really healthy, I <u>make</u> a lot of sport. ✗
   (play/do)

2 I studied English online, but it was quite boring. ✓

3 I need to <u>do</u> a very important decision. ✗
   (make)

4 At my school, I studied French and Spanish. ✓

5 When I arrived at this school, I did a test. ✓

6 I can play a musical instrument. ✓

7 At school I <u>made</u> a project on Roman history. ✗
   (did)

8 I once <u>did</u> a meal for six friends. ✗
   (made)

9 We didn't wear a uniform at school. ✓

10 My company <u>makes</u> business with many foreign customers. ✗
   (does)

Worksheet B

1 I am so nervous when I <u>do</u> speeches. ✗
   (give)

2 I am studying a lot because I am <u>making</u> an exam soon. ✗
   (doing/taking)

3 When I was a child, I played card games with my grandparents. ✓

4 I <u>do</u> a lot of mistakes when I write in English. ✗
   (make)

5 My father did really badly at school. ✓

6 After the lesson, I need to <u>do</u> a phone call. ✗
   (make)

7 I was in a play at school and gave an amazing performance. ✓

8 It was hard for me to make friends at school. ✓

9 I am not doing anything this weekend. ✓

10 I'm a really bad student, I never <u>make</u> my homework. ✗
   (do)

HAVE YOU EVER …?

Grammar: present perfect + *ever/never*

Find someone who …	Name
1 has _____ (swim) with dolphins.	
2 has _____ (keep) a pair of shoes for more than ten years.	
3 has _____ (do) a test online.	
4 has _____ (drive) a lorry.	
5 has _____ (win) some money.	
6 has _____ (grow) vegetables.	
7 has _____ (fly) in a helicopter.	
8 has _____ (make) a birthday cake for someone.	
9 has _____ (buy) an animal.	
10 has _____ (lose) their passport on holiday.	
11 has _____ (give) a present to a teacher.	
12 has _____ (not pay) a bill.	
13 has _____ (sleep) outside, but not in a tent.	
14 has _____ (catch) a train from one country to another.	
15 has _____ (write) a letter to a newspaper.	
16 has _____ (meet) someone famous.	

The class contract

The students

- The students don't have to switch their mobiles off in class.
- The students must arrive ten minutes before lessons start.
- The students mustn't sit in the same place everyday.
- The students can talk when the teacher is talking.
- The students can't sit next to who they want.
- The students can eat and drink during the lesson.
- The students must stand up when the teacher enters the class.
- The students have to bring the teacher a cake on Fridays.

The teacher

- The teacher doesn't have to mark the students' homework.
- _____
- _____
- _____
- _____
- _____
- _____
- _____

Signed _____ and _____ (students)

Signed _____ (teacher)

St William's Grammar School

Many students arrive late for school and they are tired in lessons.

New Wood Senior School

The students steal books from the library and vandalise computers during lunchtimes.

Oxbridge Comprehensive

The students don't eat the school lunches and say they are hungry in the afternoon.

East Village College

You want students to start wearing a uniform. You want something smart, but also comfortable.

Forest Green School

The school sports teams always lose and a lot of students don't want to do sport.

The Edward Long School

The school's exam results are bad. Many students leave school with few qualifications.

Foxbury School

The school needs money for a new computer lab. You asked the government, but they didn't help.

Manchester High School

The students often text their friends in class and don't listen to the teacher.

Crossword A

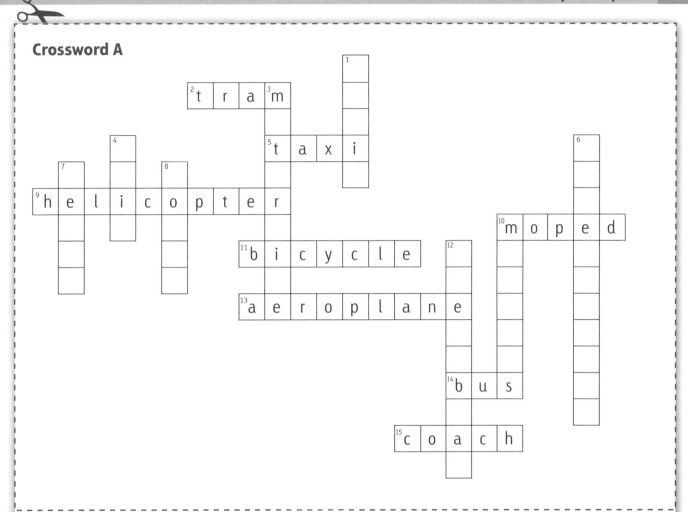

Crossword B

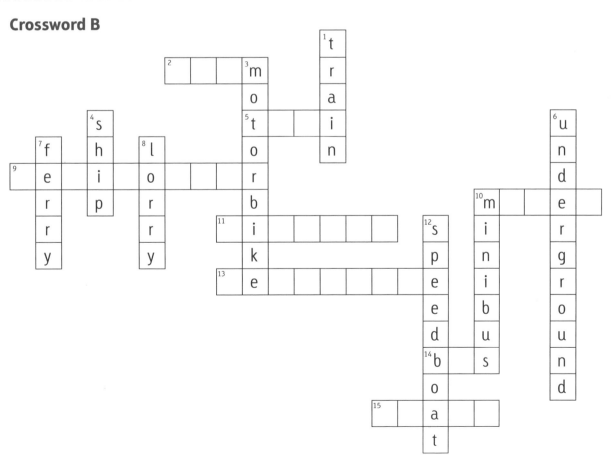

Role card 1

Detective Inspector Dick Brown

You know the following information:

- The train was travelling from London to Manchester. It left London at 6p.m. and arrived in Manchester at 8.15p.m.
- The money was stolen between 7p.m. and 7.30p.m.
- There were only five passengers on the train.
- At 7.30p.m., when Chris Hinds realised his money was missing, he stood up and shouted, 'Somebody stole my money!' That's when the train driver called you.

Interview the other passengers and find out:

- what time the other passengers got on the train
- where they were going
- what everyone was doing between 7p.m. and 7.30p.m.
- what everyone did after they heard Chris Hinds say his money was missing
- any other questions you need to ask.

After you've spoken to the other passengers, decide who you think did it.

Role card 2

Richard Cagney, 36

You are Shirley Cagney's husband. You both got on the train at 6p.m. and were travelling to Manchester to visit your wife's mother. You stole the money because you were having problems with your business and you didn't want your wife to know.

Between 7p.m. and 7.30p.m., you were sitting with your wife and reading the newspaper. At 7.15p.m. you told your wife you were going to the toilet, but on the way you stopped because you saw Chris Hinds with his bag open and his wallet inside. You asked him where the toilet was, but then fell over and took the wallet.

Prepare the following information before the detective speaks to you:

- What will you tell the detective you were doing between 7p.m. and 7.30p.m.?
- What did you do when you heard Chris Hinds shout?

Role card 4

Jack Brown, 25

You got on the train in London at 6p.m., and were travelling to Manchester to play in a football match. You were sitting in the same carriage as Chris Hinds. You were looking at him because you thought you knew him – he looks like someone you went to school with.

At 7.15p.m. you saw a man in a suit come into the carriage and talk to Chris Hinds. You didn't hear what they said, but you saw the man in a suit fall onto the chair.

Prepare the following information before the detective speaks to you:

- What were you doing before you heard Chris Hinds shout?
- What did you do when you heard Chris Hinds shout?

Role card 3

Shirley Cagney, 29

You are Richard Cagney's wife. You both got on the train at 6p.m. and were travelling to Manchester to visit your mother. Between 7p.m. and 7.30p.m., you were sitting with your husband and reading a book. Around 7.15p.m., you saw Susan Wright come running out of the carriage Chris Hinds was in. She was looking nervous.

Prepare the following information before the detective speaks to you:

- What did you do when you heard Chris Hinds shout?

Role card 5

Susan Wright, 31

You got on the train at 6.45p.m., and were travelling to Manchester to visit your friends. You were sitting in the same carriage as Chris Hinds and another young man who was wearing a sports tracksuit. The man in the tracksuit was looking at Chris Hinds before the money was taken. That evening you had a stomachache, and at about 7.15p.m. you felt sick and ran to the toilet in the next carriage.

Prepare the following information before the detective speaks to you:

- What did you do when you heard Chris Hinds shout?

1 Underline the correct alternative.

1 a place you wouldn't **choose** *to go*/*going* on holiday _____

2 something you **enjoyed** *to do*/*doing* as a child _____

3 a job you **hope** *to do*/*doing* in the future _____

4 something you **needed** *to do*/*doing* last week _____

5 housework you **hate** *to do*/*doing* _____

6 something you can't **imagine** *to wear*/*wearing* _____

7 what you **expect** *to do*/*doing* next summer _____

8 a place you **avoid** *to go*/*going* to in your town/city _____

9 a book you **didn't finish** *to read*/*reading* _____

10 someone you **need** *to email*/*emailing* soon _____

11 another language you **want** *to learn*/*learning* _____

12 a song you **love** *listen*/*listening* to _____

13 some food you **would like** *to eat*/*eating* tonight _____

14 someone famous you **would like** *to meet*/*meeting* _____

15 a present you **chose** *to buy*/*buying* recently _____

16 where you **imagine** *to live*/*living* in ten years' time _____

17 the next expensive thing you **expect** *to buy*/*buying* _____

18 a person you **want** *to talk*/*talking* to after the lesson _____

19 some advice you **decided not** *to listen*/*listening* to _____

20 a place you **hope** *to visit*/*visiting* in the future _____

2 Think of an example for 1–20.

Map A

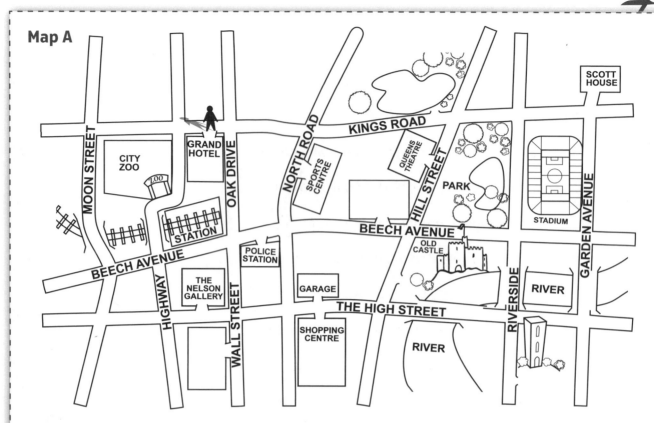

Ask how to get from:

1 The Grand Hotel to The National Museum
2 The National Museum to the Old Tower

3 The Old Tower to The Summer Palace
4 The Summer Palace to King's Park

Map B

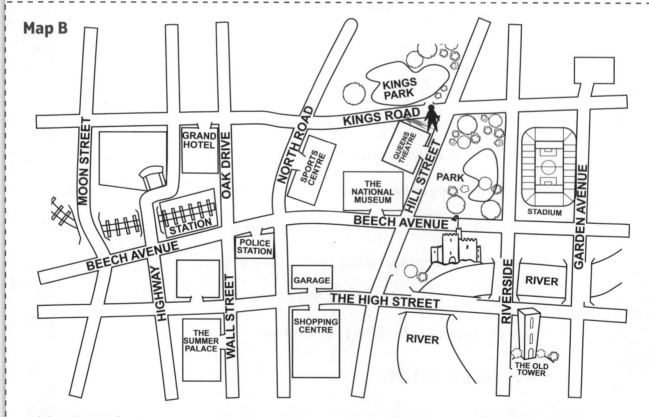

Ask how to get from:

1 The Queen's Theatre to The Old Castle
2 The Old Castle to City Zoo

3 The City Zoo to Scott House
4 Scott House to The Nelson Gallery

Worksheet A

1 **You are a town councillor, and your job is to develop sports in your area which will be good for the following categories. Choose three sports for each category.**

Good for older people:

1 _____

2 _____

3 _____

Urban sports:

1 _____

2 _____

3 _____

Expensive sports:

1 _____

2 _____

3 _____

Dangerous sports:

1 _____

2 _____

3 _____

Sports that are easy to learn:

1 _____

2 _____

3 _____

2 **Work in pairs and discuss your ideas. Decide on the best sport for each category.**

3 **Present your ideas to the class.**

Worksheet B

1 **You are a town councillor, and your job is to develop sports in your area which will be good for the following categories. Choose three sports for each category.**

Good for younger people:

1 _____

2 _____

3 _____

Rural sports:

1 _____

2 _____

3 _____

Cheap sports:

1 _____

2 _____

3 _____

Safe sports:

1 _____

2 _____

3 _____

Sports that are difficult to learn:

1 _____

2 _____

3 _____

2 **Work in pairs and discuss your ideas. Decide on the best sport for each category.**

3 **Present your ideas to the class.**

Felipe Massa
Formula 1

First played
this sport: *he was 8 years old*

Became
professional: 1998
        For: _____

Became
famous: 2003
        For: _____

Number of
competitions won: ★ ★ ★

Lionel Messi
Football

First played
this sport: *he was 5 years old*

Became
professional: 1995
        For: _____

Became
famous: 2005
        For: _____

Number of
competitions won: ★ ★ ★ ★

Tom Brady
American football

First played
this sport: *he was 3 years old*

Became
professional: 2000
        For: _____

Became
famous: 2001
        For: _____

Number of
competitions won: ★ ★ ★ ★

Tiger Woods
Golf

First played
this sport: *he was 2 years old*

Became
professional: 1996
        For: _____

Became
famous: 1999
        For: _____

Number of
competitions won: ★ ★ ★ ★ ★

Maria Sharapova
Tennis

First played
this sport: *she was 4 years old*

Became
professional: 2001
        For: _____

Became
famous: 2003
        For: _____

Number of
competitions won: ★ ★ ★ ★ ★

Usain Bolt
Running

First played
this sport: *he was 12 years old*

Became
professional: 2003
        For: _____

Became
famous: 2008
        For: _____

Number of
competitions won: ★ ★ ★ ★

Lebron James
Basketball

First played
this sport: *he was 2 years old*

Became
professional: 2003
        For: _____

Became
famous: 2004
        For: _____

Number of
competitions won: ★

Jonny Wilkinson
Rugby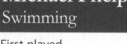

First played
this sport: *he was 4 years old*

Became
professional: 1998
        For: _____

Became
famous: 2007
        For: _____

Number of
competitions won: ★ ★ ★ ★

Michael Phelps
Swimming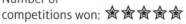

First played
this sport: *he was 7 years old*

Became
professional: 2000
        For: _____

Became
famous: 2004
        For: _____

Number of
competitions won: ★ ★ ★ ★ ★

Misty May-Treanor
Beach volleyball

First played
this sport: *she was 8 years old*

Became
professional: 1999
        For: _____

Became
famous: 2004
        For: _____

Number of
competitions won: ★ ★ ★

Beezie Madden
Horseriding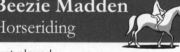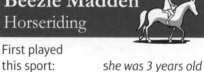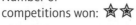

First played
this sport: *she was 3 years old*

Became
professional: 1985
        For: _____

Became
famous: 2004
        For: _____

Number of
competitions won: ★ ★

Stephanie Gilmore
Surfing

First played
this sport: *she was 10 years old*

Became
professional: 2005
        For: _____

Became
famous: 2007
        For: _____

Number of
competitions won: ★ ★ ★ ★

Student A

In the next twenty-four hours, do you think you will:	will	may/might	may/might not	won't
eat some junk food?				
walk in a park?				
tell someone you love them?				
use a computer?				
drink more than three cups of coffee?				

Student B

In the next seven days, do you think you will:	will	may/might	may/might not	won't
cry?				
buy something new?				
sleep less than five hours one night?				
forget to do something important?				
tell a lie?				

Student C

In the next twelve months, do you think you will:	will	may/might	may/might not	won't
buy a car?				
lose weight or gain weight?				
visit another country?				
move a house?				
start a new hobby?				

Student D

In the next twelve years, do you think you will:	will	may/might	may/might not	won't
start or end a relationship?				
have (more) children?				
live in another country?				
be happier than now?				
learn a foreign language?				

Patient	Doctor
	Ask the patient: • what the problem is • how long he/she has had it. • where it hurts Tell him/her what he/she should do and not to worry!

Patient	Doctor
	Ask the patient: • what the problem is • how long he/she has had it. • where it hurts Tell him/her what he/she should do and not to worry!

Patient	Doctor
	Ask the patient: • what the problem is • how long he/she has had it. • where it hurts Tell him/her what he/she should do and not to worry!

Patient	Doctor
	Ask the patient: • what the problem is • how long he/she has had it. • where it hurts Tell him/her what he/she should do and not to worry!

Patient	Doctor
	Ask the patient: • what the problem is • how long he/she has had it. • where it hurts Tell him/her what he/she should do and not to worry!

Patient	Doctor
	Ask the patient: • what the problem is • how long he/she has had it. • where it hurts Tell him/her what he/she should do and not to worry!

Patient	Doctor
	Ask the patient: • what the problem is • how long he/she has had it. • where it hurts Tell him/her what he/she should do and not to worry!

Patient	Doctor
	Ask the patient: • what the problem is • how long he/she has had it. • where it hurts Tell him/her what he/she should do and not to worry!

Who ...	Name	Extra information
1 dreams _____ working in another country?		
2 is looking _____ a new job?		
3 has given _____ something difficult?		
4 has travelled _____ their country?		
5 is waiting _____ someone to call them?		
6 is thinking _____ starting a new hobby?		
7 would like to go _____ to school or university?		
8 has moved _____ another city?		
9 is thinking _____ buying a new car?		
10 is looking _____ a new house/flat?		

Team A

1 Which company used to be called Blue Ribbon Sports?	2 What did sports car company Lamborghini use to make?	3 Which actor used to be a security guard?	4 Which American city didn't use to be in Mexico?
a) Nike	a) fridges	a) Sylvester Stallone	a) Los Angeles
b) Adidas	b) lorries	**b) Bruce Willis**	b) San Francisco
c) Puma	**c) tractors**	c) Arnold Schwarzenegger	**c) Chicago**

Team B

5 Which politician didn't use to be a lawyer?	6 Which country used to be called New Holland?	7 Which English word used to mean *teacher*?	8 Which famous product used to be called *Yum Yum*?
a) Tony Blair	**a) Australia**	a) architect	**a) Coca-Cola**
b) George W. Bush	b) New Zealand	**b) doctor**	b) Kit Kat
c) Bill Clinton	c) The USA	c) lawyer	c) Kellogg's Cornflakes

Team C

9 Which political leader used to be a spy?	10 Which football team used to be called Newton Heath?	11 Who used to work in the fast food restaurant Dunkin Donuts?	12 In which country did people use to drive on the left?
a) Nelson Mandela	a) Chelsea	**a) Madonna**	a) Australia
b) Margaret Thatcher	b) Liverpool	b) Mariah Carey	**b) The USA**
c) Vladimir Putin	**c) Manchester United**	c) Shakira	c) Brazil

Team D

13 Which job did J. K. Rowling (author of Harry Potter) use to do?	14 Which footballer used to be so poor that he played with a grapefruit, not a ball?	15 Which city used to be the capital city of Australia?	16 Which country's flag used to have three lions on it?
a) an English teacher	a) Maradona	a) Sydney	**a) England**
b) a hairdresser	**b) Pelé**	**b) Melbourne**	b) South Africa
c) a worker in McDonald's	c) David Peckham	c) Adelaide	c) Russia

Purpose – I went to university **to** study Economics.

Cause – I moved to Australia **because** I wanted a better life.

Result – I left my job **so** I had very little money.

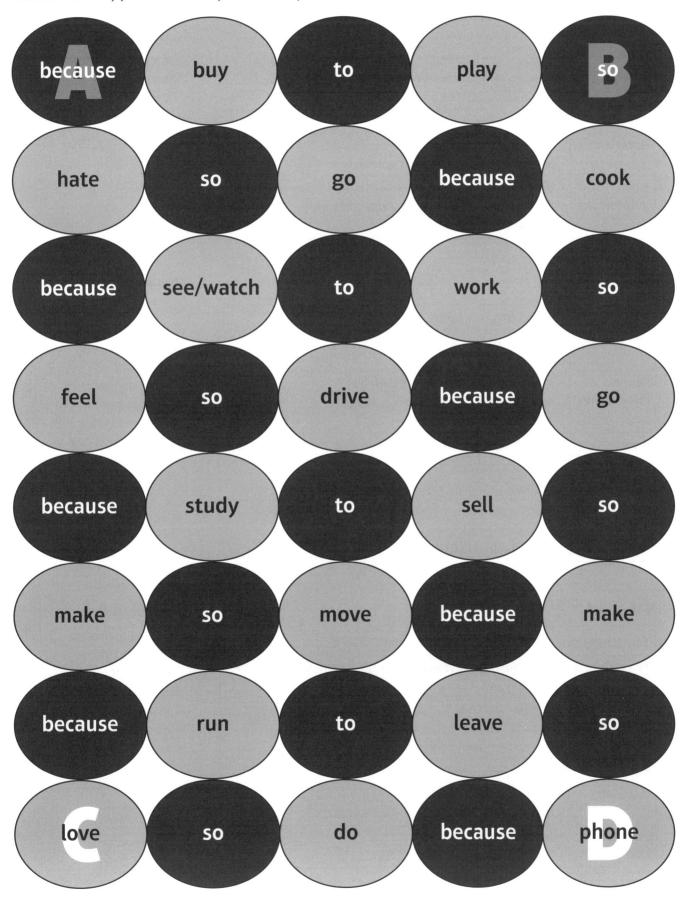

because (A)	buy	to	play	**so** (B)
hate	so	go	because	cook
because	see/watch	to	work	so
feel	so	drive	because	go
because	study	to	sell	so
make	so	move	because	make
because	run	to	leave	so
love (C)	so	do	because	phone (D)

Role card 1

Web Design Course at Eastbury Technical College

The college	• large modern college with 12,000 students • near Eastbury train station
Course information	• courses from September to May or March to November • 6.30p.m. to 9.30p.m., three evenings a week • maximum thirty-five students
Price	• $1,500
Materials	• about five books • a personal computer to do homework
Extra information	• computer rooms are open until 11p.m. Monday to Saturday • library is open until 8p.m. Monday to Saturday • need to be a creative person

Role card 2

Massage Course at Longton Adult Education Centre

The college	• small college in old house in beautiful gardens, outside the city centre
Course information	• two months long, starting every month • 6p.m. to 8.30p.m. two evenings a week • maximum twelve students
Price	• $1,500
Materials	• one book ($45) • massage oils (quite expensive)
Extra information	• practise massage on friends and family for homework • need strong hands • library is closed after 5p.m.

Role card 3

Teaching Course at Oxford International College

The college	• busy international college with 1,500 students in the city centre
Course information	• one year full time • 9a.m. to 6p.m. • maximum fifteen students
Price	• $1,200
Materials	• two books • lots of paper, pens and your own computer
Extra information	• courses are very stressful • library is open from 8a.m. to 8p.m.

Role card 4

You need to find out information about:
• the college
• the course
• times and dates
• materials you need
• when the library and facilities are open
• price

Role card 5

You need to find out information about:
• the college
• the course
• times and dates
• materials you need
• when the library and facilities are open
• price

Role card 6

You need to find out information about:
• the college
• the course
• times and dates
• materials you need
• when the library and facilities are open
• price

Team name: _____

1 How big were the largest notes ever made?
  a) about the size of printer paper
  b) about the size of a door
  c) about the size of a football pitch

2 Who were the first cheques used by?
  a) the ancient Greeks
  b) the Chinese
  c) the ancient Romans

3 How much should you leave as a tip in a US restaurant?
  a) about 50%
  b) about 5%
  c) about 15%

4 How much is the world's most expensive mobile phone worth?
  a) $500,000
  b) $1,300,000
  c) $8,000,000

5 What was unusual about some coins issued in Somalia in 2004?
  a) They were made of plastic.
  b) They were square.
  c) They were shaped liked guitars.

6 Where was the note with the biggest number made?
  a) Zimbabwe
  b) Russia
  c) Peru

7 How small was the smallest ever note?
  a) 11 mm x 19 mm
  b) 69 mm x 135 mm
  c) 32 mm x 41 mm

8 Which company invented the first credit cards?
  a) Visa
  b) Diner's Club
  c) Mastercard

9 When was the first electronic ATM used?
  a) 1939
  b) 1952
  c) 1967

10 How much did Will Smith earn for his first movie, in 1992?
  a) $50,000
  b) $500,000
  c) $5,000,000

11 Where was the first bank note used?
  a) the USA
  b) Rome
  c) China

12 Where does the US dollar sign '$' come from?
  a) a *U* over an *S*, representing the United States of America
  b) the Spanish peso
  c) Russia

Team A

The internet	Chocolate	
It's something which North American universities used first. (4 points)	It's something which Central Americans first made 3,000 years ago. (4 points)	_____ (4 points)
It's something which over half a billion people use. (3 points)	It's something which you can eat or drink. (3 points)	_____ (3 points)
It's something which you need a computer to use. (2 points)	It's something which can be brown or white. (2 points)	_____ (2 points)
It's something which you can surf. (1 point)	Nestle, Mars and Lindt are companies which make it. (1 point)	_____ (1 point)

Team B

Computer	Sandwich	
It's something which Charles Babbage invented in the 1820s. (4 points)	It's something which an English man invented in 1770. (4 points)	_____ (4 points)
It's something which is getting smaller and smaller. (3 points)	It's something which you eat. (3 points)	_____ (3 points)
It's something which is electronic. (2 points)	It's something which you eat when you want a snack. (2 points)	_____ (2 points)
Apple is one of the companies that makes it. (1 point)	It's something which you make with two slices of bread. (1 point)	_____ (1 point)

Team C

Microwave oven	Monaco	
It's something which Percy Spencer invented in 1945. (4 points)	It's a place which is on the Mediterranean coast. (4 points)	_____ (4 points)
It's something which some people think is dangerous. (3 points)	It's a place where you can find lots of casinos. (3 points)	_____ (3 points)
It's something that you can find in a kitchen. (2 points)	It's the place where lots of millionaires live. (2 points)	_____ (2 points)
It's something which you use to cook food quickly. (1 point)	It's the place where there is a famous Grand Prix. (1 point)	_____ (1 point)

Team D

CD	McDonald's	
It's something that Philips first sold in 1980. (4 points)	It's a company which started in California in 1948. (4 points)	_____ (4 points)
It's something which contains information. (3 points)	It's a company which has a Scottish name. (3 points)	_____ (3 points)
It's something which is round and silver. (2 points)	It's a company which sells food to 58 million people a day. (2 points)	_____ (2 points)
It's something which you play to listen to music. (1 point)	It's a company which sells fast food. (1 point)	_____ (1 point)

Team E

Bicycle	Jeans	
It's something which John Starley invented in 1885. (4 points)	They're something that sailors and miners first wore. (4 points)	_____ (4 points)
It's something which people use for transport and sport. (3 points)	They're something which young people often wear. (3 points)	_____ (3 points)
It's something which is very common in Holland and China. (2 points)	They're something which is usually blue. (2 points)	_____ (2 points)
It's something which you ride. (1 point)	They're something which Levi Strauss & Co. make. (1 point)	_____ (1 point)

Party Planner Card

Reason: Why are you having a party?	birthday ☐ engagement ☐ wedding ☐ anniversary ☐ graduation ☐ festival ☐ other ☐
Requirements: What do you need for the party?	food ☐ drinks ☐ food and drinks ☐ dancing ☐ DJ ☐ other ☐
Budget: How much do you want to spend?	Under $1000 ☐ $1000–1500 ☐ $1500–3000 ☐ $3000+ ☐ other ☐
Numbers: How many guests?	under 50 ☐ 50–100 ☐ 100+ ☐
Car parking: How many guests are coming by car?	none ☐ some ☐ all ☐
Accommodation: How many guests need to stay the night?	none ☐ some ☐ all ☐
Hours: What time does the party start and finish?	from: 6p.m. ☐ 7p.m. ☐ 8p.m. ☐ 9p.m. ☐ 10p.m. ☐ to: 11p.m. ☐ 12a.m. ☐ 1a.m. ☐ 2a.m. ☐ 3a.m. ☐

The Plaza Hotel

Costs	• $1000–2000 • free drinks, food $20 per person
Numbers	• up to 50 guests (Regency Room) • 50–150 guests (The Ball Room)
Extra information	• 4 bars, 3 restaurants, swimming pool • 500 parking spaces • rooms for 500 guests ($150 a night) • parties from 8p.m.–2a.m.

The Country House Hotel

Costs	• $800 • drinks not included, food $20 per person
Numbers	• 100 guests maximum
Extra information	• DJ not included • free parking • rooms for 50 guests • big old house in beautiful gardens • parties from 8p.m.–3a.m.

THE MOON RIVER BOAT

Costs	• $100 an hour or $600 all night • free drinks, food $10 per person
Numbers	• 70 guests maximum
Extra information	• 2 bars, 2 DJs • 10 parking spaces • no accommodation for guests on the boat but 25% discount at 3 star hotel which is very near • parties from 6p.m.–1a.m.

The Diamond Nightclub

Costs	• $325 • drinks not included, food $15 per person
Numbers	• 45 guests maximum
Extra information	• 1 bar, free DJ • 15 parking spaces, no accommodation • nightclub in centre of the city • parties from 7p.m.–3a.m.

Role card 1

BOB'S BOUTIQUE

Tick (✓) when you sell	Price
shirt (large, white)	$40
shoes (size 40)	$50
jeans (size 28)	$35
coat (long, green)	$95
hat (grey)	$40

Role card 3

Claire's Clothes

Tick (✓) when you sell	Price
shirt (medium, white)	$20
shoes (size 38)	$50
jeans (size 30)	$65
coat (short, black)	$85
hat (yellow)	$10

Role card 2

Fran's Fashions

Tick (✓) when you sell	Price
shirt (large, blue)	$45
shoes (size 44)	$30
jeans (size 32)	$90
coat (short, black)	$100
hat (green)	$25

Role card 4

GARY'S GEAR

Tick (✓) when you sell	Price
shirt (medium, blue)	$25
shoes (size 40)	$30
jeans (size 32)	$70
coat (long, green)	$120
hat (grey)	$15

Role card 5

Shopping list A

Tick (✓) when you buy	Budget
shoes (size 40)	$40
jeans (size 32)	$35
shirt (large, white)	$95

Role card 7

Shopping list C

Tick (✓) when you buy	Budget
coat (short, black)	$100
hat (grey)	$20
shoes (size 40)	$60

Role card 6

Shopping list B

Tick (✓) when you buy	Budget
shirt (medium)	$20
coat (long, green)	$100
hat (yellow)	$20

Role card 8

Shopping list D

Tick (✓) when you buy	Budget
hat (green)	$35
shoes (size 38)	$60
jeans (size 32)	$80

Worksheet A

1 It lives in the sea.
2 This animal can fly but it's not a bird.
3 It's a very big fish.
4 It's a big dangerous mammal.
5 It can run as fast as a horse.
6 This animal is the biggest in the world.
7 This animal is quite dangerous.
8 This animal eats lots of fish.
9 This wild animal lives in Africa.
10 It's a very small insect.
11 This animal is very slow.
12 This animal is very good at climbing trees.
13 It's the biggest animal on land.
14 This animal begins with *e*.
15 People use this animal to carry things.
16 This animal lives in all cities.

Worksheet B

1 It's an intelligent and friendly mammal.
2 It's an insect.
3 It has lots of teeth.
4 This wild animal lives in the forest or mountains.
5 It's the biggest bird.
6 It lives in the sea.
7 This reptile lives in rivers.
8 It's a bird but can't fly.
9 It has spots.
10 This animal can bite you.
11 This reptile carries its 'home' on its back.
12 It is a very intelligent wild animal.
13 It has a very good memory.
14 This animal is the symbol of some countries.
15 This animal lives in the desert.
16 Most people don't like this bird.

Worksheet C

1 It begins with *d*.
2 It has beautiful coloured wings.
3 This animal can be very dangerous.
4 It likes honey.
5 It can't fly.
6 It is not a fish.
7 It has a long body and lots of teeth.
8 It lives in Antarctica.
9 It's the fastest animal on land.
10 This animal can give you malaria.
11 It can live for a very long time.
12 This mammal is very similar to humans.
13 It has a trunk and very big ears.
14 It's the king of the birds.
15 It can live without eating or drinking for two weeks.
16 It begins with *p*.

Answer sheet

Team name: _____

1 ☐☐☐☐☐☐☐
2 ☐☐☐☐☐☐☐☐☐
3 ☐☐☐☐☐
4 ☐☐☐☐
5 ☐☐☐☐☐☐☐
6 ☐☐☐☐☐
7 ☐☐☐☐☐☐☐☐☐
8 ☐☐☐☐☐☐☐

9 ☐☐☐☐☐☐☐
10 ☐☐☐☐☐☐☐☐
11 ☐☐☐☐☐☐☐☐
12 ☐☐☐☐☐☐☐☐☐☐
13 ☐☐☐☐☐☐☐☐☐
14 ☐☐☐☐☐
15 ☐☐☐☐☐
16 ☐☐☐☐☐☐

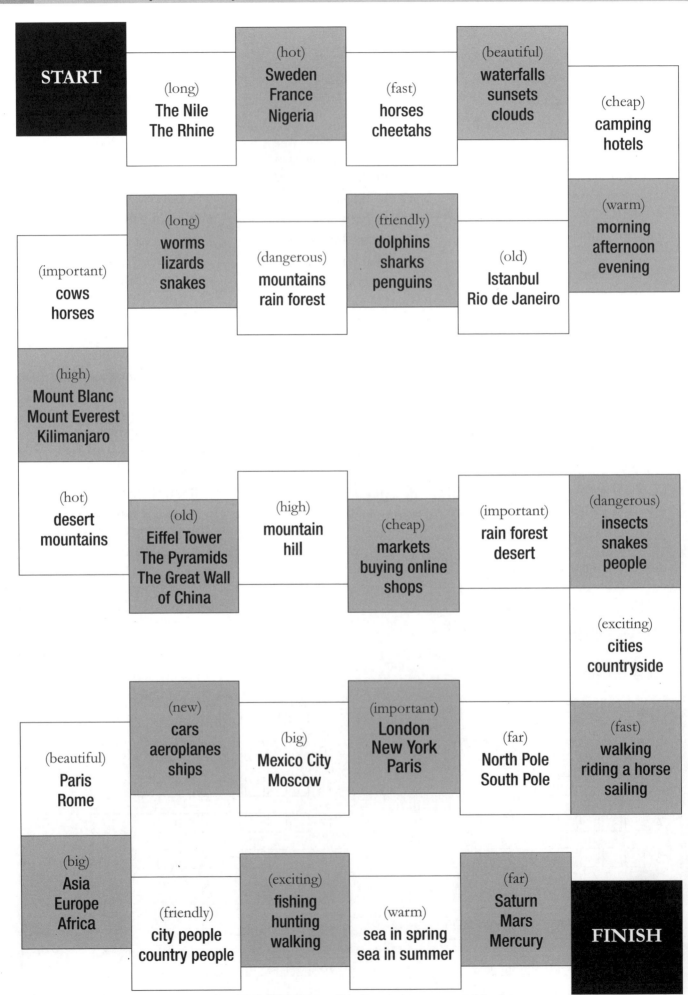

START

(long)
The Nile
The Rhine

(hot)
Sweden
France
Nigeria

(fast)
horses
cheetahs

(beautiful)
waterfalls
sunsets
clouds

(cheap)
camping
hotels

(important)
cows
horses

(long)
worms
lizards
snakes

(dangerous)
mountains
rain forest

(friendly)
dolphins
sharks
penguins

(old)
Istanbul
Rio de Janeiro

(warm)
morning
afternoon
evening

(high)
Mount Blanc
Mount Everest
Kilimanjaro

(hot)
desert
mountains

(old)
Eiffel Tower
The Pyramids
The Great Wall
of China

(high)
mountain
hill

(cheap)
markets
buying online
shops

(important)
rain forest
desert

(dangerous)
insects
snakes
people

(exciting)
cities
countryside

(beautiful)
Paris
Rome

(new)
cars
aeroplanes
ships

(big)
Mexico City
Moscow

(important)
London
New York
Paris

(far)
North Pole
South Pole

(fast)
walking
riding a horse
sailing

(big)
Asia
Europe
Africa

(friendly)
city people
country people

(exciting)
fishing
hunting
walking

(warm)
sea in spring
sea in summer

(far)
Saturn
Mars
Mercury

FINISH

The frozen continent

1	In the winter of 1911, there was the race to be the first country to reach	
2	the South Pole. Captain Scott, a famous explorer from the Great Britain,	
3	led the British team and Roald Amundsen led a Norwegian one.	
4	Scott's team took the horses, motor vehicles and a few dogs, but	
5	Amundsen was clever and took only the dogs. In November 1911,	
6	Scott's group started journey, but there were many problems;	
7	the horses died and the motor vehicles stopped working. In an end,	
8	Scott and a four men (Wilson, Bowers, Evans and Oates) continued on	
9	foot. They reached South Pole in January 1912, but they had a	
10	terrible shock when they arrived. Amundsen had arrived the five weeks	
11	earlier and they had lost a race. Scott's men were extremely tired	
12	and disappointed but they still needed to walk back 800 miles to coast.	
13	Weather got worse and worse and all the men became ill. First Evans	
14	died during night and soon after so did Oates. Three more men died	
15	in their tent, only 11 miles from their base. They were found an eight	
16	months later. Scott's diary tells a story of their final terrible days.	

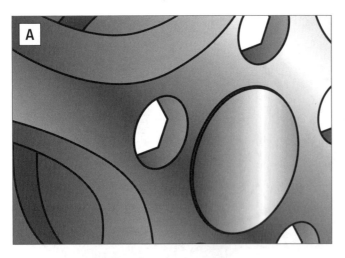

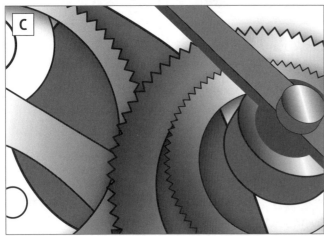

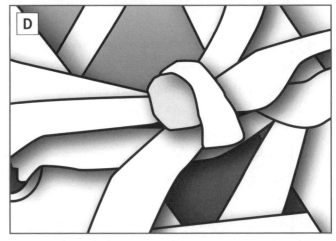

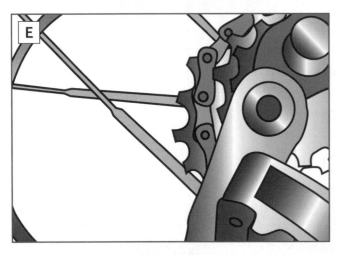

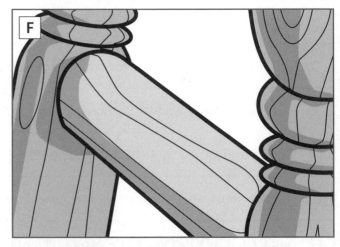

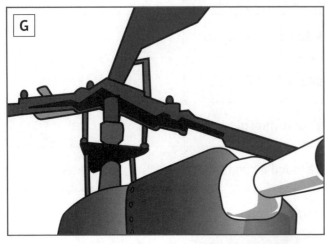

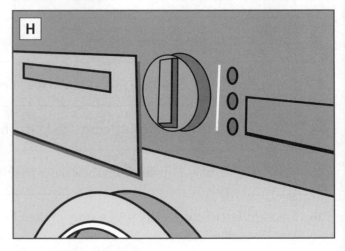

Student A

Across

1 a person who catches criminals (6, 7)
(police officer)

4 to take things which are not yours (5)
(steal)

5 the crime of stealing things from shops
(11) (shoplifting)

8 to go into a building illegally (5, 2)
(break in)

10 when the police catch criminals (6)
(arrest)

11 the crime of stealing things (5)
(theft)

13 a person who breaks the law (8)
(criminal)

Student B

Down

2 when the police look for a criminal (11)
(investigate)

3 the person who decides a punishment (5)
(judge)

4 what you do with a gun (5)
(shoot)

6 an amount of money you have to pay as a
punishment (4)
(fine)

7 the person who the criminal
affects/hurts (6)
(victim)

9 another word for *punishment* (8)
(sentence)

12 the crime of cheating people to make
money from them (5)
(fraud)

Tell your group …

• what these things are like.

• what you like or dislike about them.

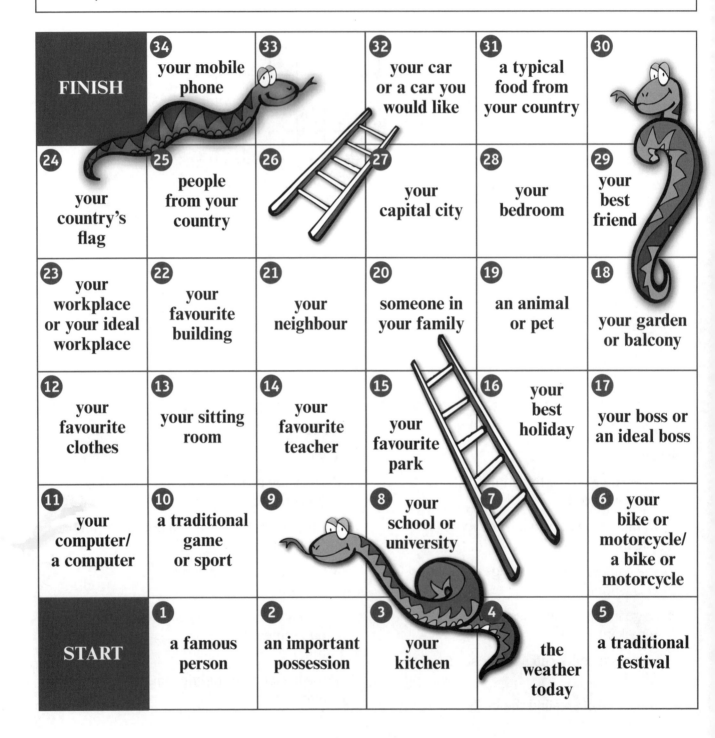

	34 your mobile phone	**33**	**32** your car or a car you would like	**31** a typical food from your country	**30**
FINISH					
24 your country's flag	**25** people from your country	**26**	**27** your capital city	**28** your bedroom	**29** your best friend
23 your workplace or your ideal workplace	**22** your favourite building	**21** your neighbour	**20** someone in your family	**19** an animal or pet	**18** your garden or balcony
12 your favourite clothes	**13** your sitting room	**14** your favourite teacher	**15** your favourite park	**16** your best holiday	**17** your boss or an ideal boss
11 your computer/ a computer	**10** a traditional game or sport	**9**	**8** your school or university	**7**	**6** your bike or motorcycle/ a bike or motorcycle
START	**1** a famous person	**2** an important possession	**3** your kitchen	**4** the weather today	**5** a traditional festival

Student A

1 Coca-Cola _____ (make) with colouring so it's not green. (true)

2 Alaska _____ (buy) from Russia for $7 million in 1867. (true)

3 The Statue of Liberty _____ (give) to the United States by Great Britain in 1886. (false)

4 In 2006, a whale _____ (see) swimming up the River Thames in London. (true)

5 The first underground system in the world _____ (build) in London in the 1860s. (true)

6 Potatoes _____ (not grow) in Europe until 1536. (true)

7 *Necessary* _____ (spell) incorrectly more than any other word in English. (false)

8 *The Da Vinci Code* _____ (write) by Paulo Coelho. (false)

Student B

1 The giant panda _____ (find) only in two countries – China and Burma. (false)

2 The British prime minister _____ (choose) by the queen or king. (false)

3 The first photo _____ (take) by the Chinese in the early 1700s. (false)

4 In Sweden, coffee _____ (drink) by children on their birthday. (false)

5 *The Mona Lisa* _____ (steal) in 1911 and lost for two years. (true)

6 *Happy Birthday* _____ (sing) more than any other English song. (true)

7 Macadamia nuts _____ (not sell) in their shells because people can't break them. (true)

8 In some parts of Wales, sheep _____ (ride) by local farmers for transport. (false)

Student C

1 *The Simpsons* cartoon _____ (show) for the first time in 1989. (true)

2 Cars _____ (drive) on the left in Sweden until 1967. (true)

3 Originally, Mickey Mouse _____ (know) as Mortimer Mouse. (true)

4 More chocolate _____ (eat) by Italians than any other nationality. (false)

5 Traditionally, skirts _____ (wear) by men in Ireland. (false)

6 Queen Elizabeth II went to hospital in 1991 after she _____ (bite) by one of her dogs. (true)

7 English school children _____ (not teach) foreign languages at school. (false)

8 The Pyramids in Egypt _____ (hide) under sand for 2,000 years. (false)

A

B

C

D

E

F

Your teacher is explaining some grammar badly.	**worried**	Your classmate is talking about a big *chicken* in her house. (She means *kitchen*!)	**worried**
It's 11.30p.m. and your fourteen-year-old child is late home.	**nervous**	Your friend has just called you and told you he's in hospital.	**nervous**
You're going to take your driving test this afternoon.	**excited**	You're going to have an important job interview today.	**excited**
You have two tickets to see your favourite pop singer.	**amazed**	Your best friend is coming home after two years away.	**amazed**
You see a boy fall from an upstairs window and then get up and walk.	**lonely**	Your friend has just won $10 million on the lottery.	**lonely**
You're staying in a hotel. It's too hot and the bed is very hard. You can't sleep.	**bored**	You're in a new country and don't know anyone.	**bored**
All your friends are on holiday and you have no-one to go out with.	**uncomfortable**	You're at home. It's raining and there is nothing to do.	**uncomfortable**
You're staying in a hotel. It's too hot and the bed is very hard. You can't sleep.	**confused**	You're wearing some new jeans, but they are too small.	**confused**

Grammar: present perfect (+ *just, yet, already*)

Worksheet A

Adam

1 not / finish / school / yet
2 already / learn / a foreign language
3 just / ride / bike / for the first time

Sam

1 just / climb / Mount Everest
2 already / climb / it / six times
3 not / be / Africa / yet

Hugh

1 already / travel / around the world
2 just / buy / a sports car
3 not / pass / driving test / yet

Johnny

1 not / find / girlfriend / yet
2 already / make / lots of money
3 just / start / playing the guitar

Colin

1 already / retire
2 just / become a grandparent
3 not / see / grandchild / yet

Worksheet B

Debbie

1 just / move / house
2 not / meet / neighbours / yet
3 already / live / ten different homes

Marcia

1 already / become / grandparent
2 just / win / lottery
3 not / fly / in aeroplane / yet

Emma

1 just / visit / hairdresser's
2 already / divorce / first husband
3 not / finish / university / yet

Angelina

1 already / make / $1million
2 just / sell / hotel
3 not / leave / home / yet

Jessica

1 already / read / lots of books
2 just / eat / ice cream
3 not / learn / swim / yet

_____ _____ _____ _____ _____

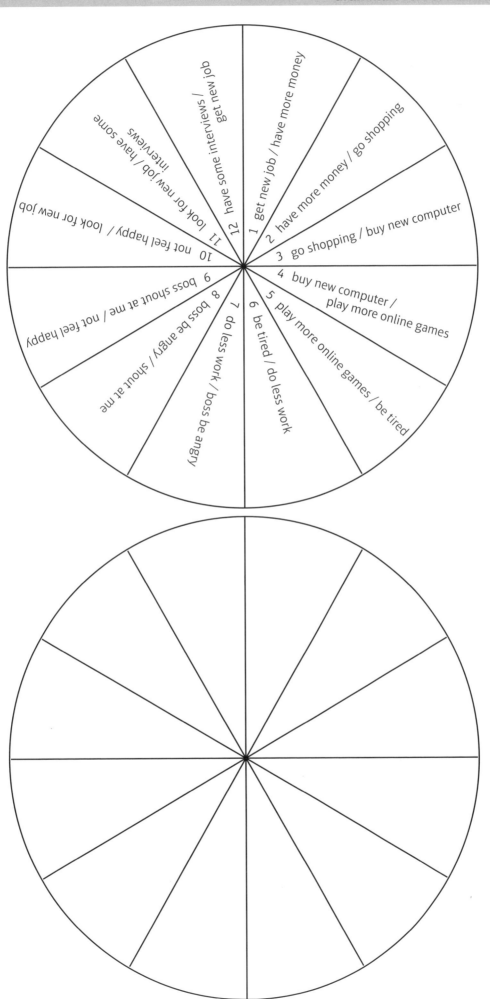

The wheel contains the following segments:

1. get new job / have more money
2. have more money / go shopping
3. go shopping / buy new computer
4. buy new computer / play more online games
5. play more online games / be tired
6. be tired / do less work
7. do less work / boss be angry
8. boss be angry / shout at me
9. boss shout at me / not feel happy
10. not feel happy / look for new job
11. look for new job / have some interviews
12. have some interviews / get new job

Functional language: giving opinions

1   Transparent toaster – watch your toast cook and decide when it's ready

2   Light shoes – you don't need batteries, just walk or run

3   Go-anywhere skateboard – use in streets, on beaches, in forests, anywhere

4   Stick-on watch – perfect for travelling light

5   Computer control headset – you think it and your computer does it

6   Solar-powered TV – you can watch TV anywhere!

a person who performs in a film or play	the company that makes films	a short part of a film	the part a person has in a film or play
a film which makes you very scared	people in films who don't have important parts	a very successful film	a film which is about the past
the person who tells the actors what to do	a film which is about the future	a film or play that makes you laugh	a film which is about real life
a film that tells the story of someone's life	the most important actor in the film	the person who organises the whole film	a very exciting film about murder or crime

Referee's answers

an actor	a studio	a scene	a role
a horror film	extras	a blockbuster	a historical drama
a director	a science fiction film	a comedy	a documentary
a biopic	a star	a producer	a thriller

Grammar: reported speech

1 **Imagine you are a film star and complete the following information.**

STAR CARD	
Personal information	
Name	
Age and birthday	
Marital status	
Home(s) and car(s)	
Three things you love	
Three things you hate	
Talents	
Career information	
Best career moment	
Worst career moment	
Present film: • type • role • actors	

2 **Now interview your film star partner and make notes.**

INTERVIEW CARD	
Personal information	
What's your name?	
How old are you? When is your birthday?	
Are you married?	
Tell me about your home(s) and car(s).	
What three things do you love?	
What three things do you hate?	
What are your talents?	
Career information	
What was the best moment in your career?	
What was the worst moment in your career?	
Tell me about what you are filming at the moment. • type • role • actors	

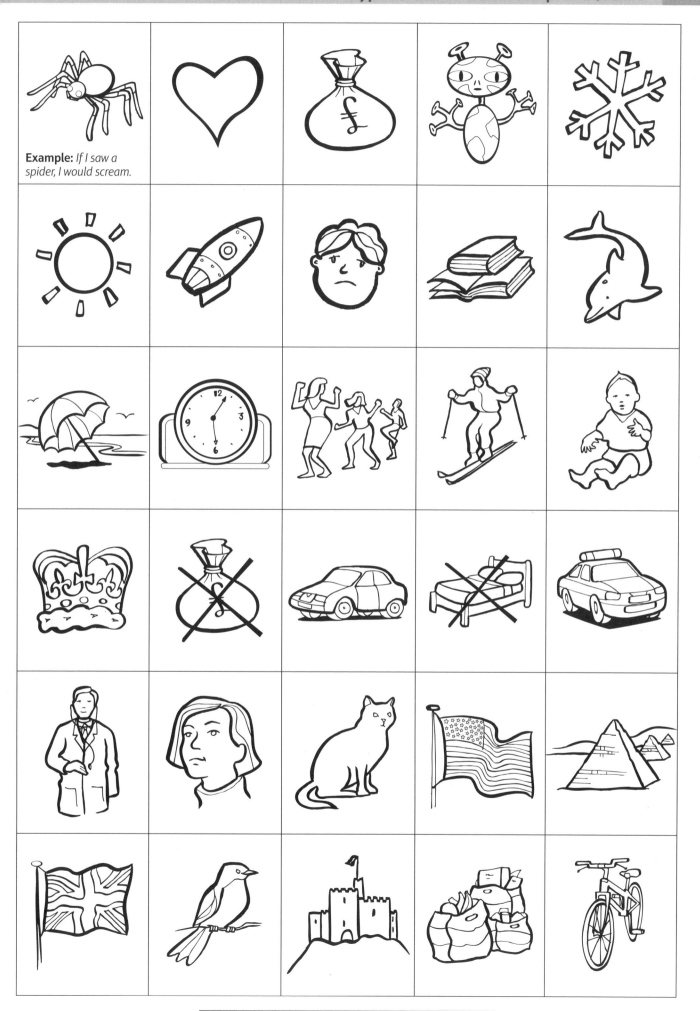

Example: *If I saw a spider, I would scream.*

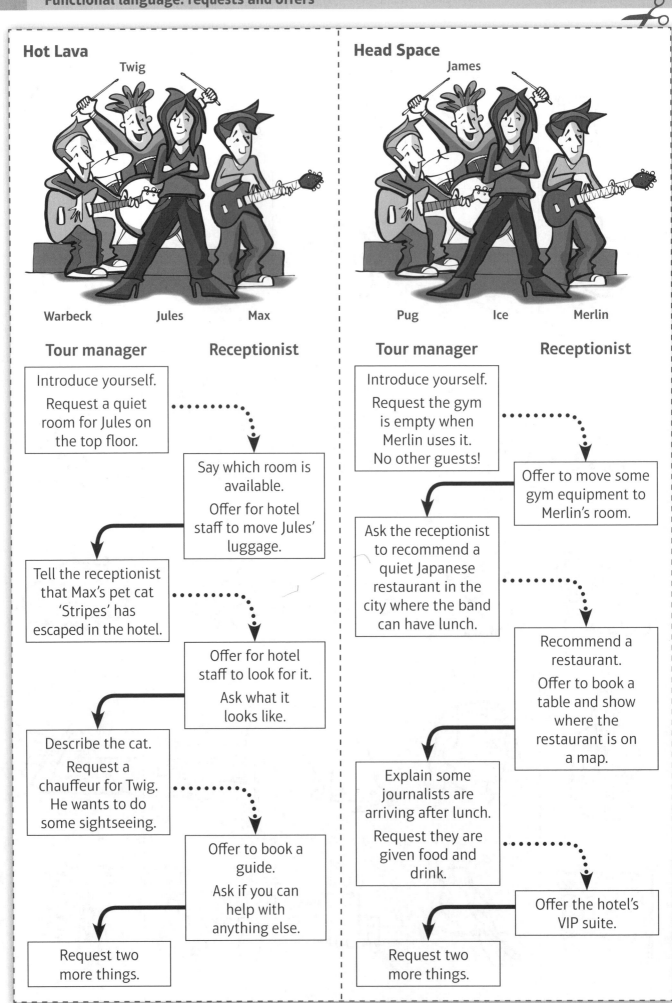

Hot Lava

Twig

Warbeck   Jules   Max

Tour manager   **Receptionist**

Introduce yourself.
Request a quiet room for Jules on the top floor.

Say which room is available.
Offer for hotel staff to move Jules' luggage.

Tell the receptionist that Max's pet cat 'Stripes' has escaped in the hotel.

Offer for hotel staff to look for it.
Ask what it looks like.

Describe the cat.
Request a chauffeur for Twig. He wants to do some sightseeing.

Offer to book a guide.
Ask if you can help with anything else.

Request two more things.

Head Space

James

Pug   Ice   Merlin

Tour manager   **Receptionist**

Introduce yourself.
Request the gym is empty when Merlin uses it. No other guests!

Offer to move some gym equipment to Merlin's room.

Ask the receptionist to recommend a quiet Japanese restaurant in the city where the band can have lunch.

Recommend a restaurant.
Offer to book a table and show where the restaurant is on a map.

Explain some journalists are arriving after lunch.
Request they are given food and drink.

Offer the hotel's VIP suite.

Request two more things.

UNIT 1

LOVE STORY

Materials: One worksheet per pair of Ss

Pre-teach *lifeguard* and elicit the job's good and bad points. Tell Ss they are going to tell a story about a lifeguard. Put them in pairs and distribute one worksheet per pair. Ss match the pictures with the words and phrases in the box.

Check answers to the matching task and then tell Ss to put the pictures in the correct order by thinking about the logical order of events in the story. Check answers.

In pairs, Ss then practise telling the story by taking it in turns to describe the pictures. Remind them to use the past simple. At the end, you can ask the class questions about the characters, e.g. *Why do you think they got divorced?*

> **Answers:**
> 1 **B** got divorced   **C** fell in love   **D** met/got on well   **E** argued
>   **F** got married   **G** got back together   **H** proposed to her/accepted
> 2 A, D, C, H, F, E, B, G

HEADS AND TAILS

Materials: One set of cards per group of Ss

Put Ss in groups of four and distribute one set of cut-up cards per group. One student deals the cards and each player places their cards face up in front of them. Explain the rules. The first student puts down a card. If the second player has the other half, they place it next to the first card. If the group agree that the two cards make a question, the second player can take the cards and put them to one side. The same student then puts down a new card. If the next student can't put down the other half of the question, they miss a turn. Ss take it in turns to complete and win questions until all the questions have been formed. The winner is the student with the most questions. Monitor to ensure that Ss form correct (and plausible) questions.

Then tell Ss to ask each other their questions – they can do this in their groups or in pairs. Encourage them to ask for extra information, especially if the questions are closed questions.

> **Answers:** (as on the worksheet)
> When did you last buy something expensive?
> When did you last go on holiday or have time off?
> What is your favourite book?
> What is your favourite sport?
> Were you feeling happy yesterday?
> Were you at home last night?
> Do you have a best friend?
> Do you spend a lot of money?
> How often do you play or watch sport?
> How often do you cook for other people?
> Where do you go out with friends?
> Where do your family live?

TALK ABOUT IT!

Materials: One worksheet and a dice per pair of Ss

Put Ss in A/B pairs and give one worksheet to each pair. Explain the rules. Student A starts and rolls the dice. The number on the dice corresponds to the numbers in the boxes. If the dice lands on 2, he/she chooses any topic numbered 2 and then talks about it for 30 seconds, using the past simple. If Student B is satisfied, the topic is crossed out and Student A wins the box. Student A can

write his/her initials in the box. It is then Student B's turn. If a student rolls the dice and there are no more topics left with that number, they lose a turn. This continues until all the topics have been crossed out. The student with the most boxes is the winner.

PARTY TIME!

Materials: One role card per student

Tell Ss that they are going to a party where they are going to meet lots of other interesting people. Review how to ask about someone's occupation and the kind of questions you need to ask about people's families, hobbies, etc. Refer Ss to the language in Lesson 1.3 for making conversation and sounding natural when you meet and say goodbye to people in social situations.

Distribute a role card to each student. Give Ss a few minutes to read their cards and check that they understand all the information. Help with vocabulary if necessary. It doesn't matter if two Ss have the same role card – they will have a lot in common when they meet!

Tell Ss that they are at the party; they should circulate to meet the other guests. The object of the activity is for Ss to make natural conversation based on the topics listed and also to do the task at the bottom of the cards. Encourage Ss to elaborate on the information on the cards so they appear as interesting as possible to the people they meet.

At the end of the activity, ask the class who they met and who was the most interesting person.

UNIT 2

WHAT DO I DO?

Materials: One set of cards per group of Ss

Review useful vocabulary from the unit related to describing jobs and write it on the board, e.g. *I work in an office/in a company/ outside/in a team/with animals/with my hands. I work under pressure. The salary is high/low. My job is boring/dangerous/exciting/creative. I wear a uniform/smart clothes/casual clothes/special clothes.*

Put Ss in groups of four and distribute one set of cut up cards per group. These are placed face down in the middle of the group.

Tell the first student to pick up a card and describe the job to the group, pretending that it is their job. They can describe various aspects of it, e.g. workplace, customers/colleagues, pay. The other Ss try to guess what the job is, and the student who guesses it correctly first wins that card. It is then the next student's turn. Ss must not show their cards to the others while they are describing them. This continues until all the jobs have been guessed. The winner is the student with the most cards.

It is also possible to do the activity without cutting up the cards. Ss choose a job but don't say or show which one it is. The procedure is the same. The first student to guess it correctly wins that job and writes their initials on the card. The student who has won the most jobs at the end of the activity is the winner.

As a follow up, invite Ss to decide the best three and worst three jobs in groups, and then to compare with the other groups. Encourage them to reach some kind of class consensus.

GRAMMAR MAZE

Materials: One worksheet per pair of Ss

Put Ss in pairs and distribute one worksheet per pair. Elicit the difference between the present continuous (used for things happening now/around now or for temporary situations) and the present simple (used for habits or permanent situations).

Explain the game and demonstrate. Tell Ss to begin at the *Start* box and to decide whether the question is in the correct tense. If they think the question is correct, they should follow the solid black arrow to the next box. If they think it is incorrect, they should follow the dotted arrow. Ss record the order of the boxes they visit by writing the letters at the bottom of the worksheet. This continues until Ss arrive at the *Finish*.

If Ss arrive at the *Finish* before visiting every box or if they revisit a box, then they have made a mistake and need to go back and consider carefully where they went wrong. Ss also need to make written corrections to the incorrect questions. Help them if they cannot see where they have gone wrong.

As a follow up, arrange Ss in larger groups to ask and answer the questions.

> **Answers: Start ✓ A ✓, D ✗** (Do you check your emails every day?),
> **F ✗** (Do you drink a lot of tea or coffee?), **C ✓**,
> **E ✗** (Do you listen to music when you work or study?), **B ✓**,
> **G ✗** (Do you like football?),
> **I ✗** (Are you reading a book at the moment?), **H ✓, K ✓**,
> **J ✗** (Do you usually sleep well?)

HOW OFTEN DO YOU …?

Materials: One copy of the board and a dice per group of Ss; a counter per student

Put Ss in groups of three or four and distribute a dice and a board (enlarged to A3 size if possible) to each group. If you don't have a dice, Ss can use a coin and move one space for heads and two spaces for tails. Ss also need a small object like a counter or coin to move around the board. Ss place these on the *Start* box.

Explain the rules. The first student rolls the dice, moves the number of places shown and makes a question from the words in the box and an appropriate question phrase from those outside the boxes, e.g. *go to the park* becomes *How often do you go to the park?* The student asking the question can ask whoever they want. The student answering can respond using any of the adverbs of frequency outside the boxes. Encourage the group to ask additional questions to find out more information, e.g. *Do you usually go alone?* Tell Ss to make their own questions if they land on a *Free question* box. While you are monitoring, pay attention to the appropriateness and accuracy of the questions, as well as more general language problems. The winner is the first student to reach the finish.

I CAN'T STAND CHEESE!

Materials: One worksheet per student

Distribute the worksheets. Ask Ss to write in the circle the name of something they like/dislike, etc. Monitor and help Ss with any vocabulary they need.

After all the worksheets have been filled in, tell Ss to mingle, with the objective of finding people with the same answers and noting their names. Ss should also find out some additional information, e.g. *A: What food do you absolutely love? B: I absolutely love pizza. What about you? B: Me too! A: How often do you eat it?*

At the end, ask whether anybody had similar likes and dislikes and also what the most interesting, amusing or unusual thing they found out was.

UNIT 3

TIME OUT TARGET PRACTICE

Materials: One copy of worksheet A and worksheet B per pair of Ss

Put Ss in A/B pairs and distribute the worksheets. Working alone, Ss write the eight words from the box into their grids. The words can be written horizontally, vertically or diagonally and can also cross each other.

When Ss have finished, explain the activity and demonstrate. Tell Ss that they have to find their partner's eight words. To do this, they give grid references to each other, e.g. Student A starts and asks for 1A. If there is nothing written in Student B's grid, they say *Miss!* and Student A should record the miss as an *X* in their grid. Student B then gives a reference, e.g. 3C, and if there is a letter written in Student A's grid, they say *Hit!* as well as the letter Student B has hit. Student B writes the letter in the correct place. This continues until one student has found all eight words.

Once Ss start 'hitting' words, the process becomes much easier and a student can guess the word from the letters if they think they know it. If they are correct, the other student replies *You've hit my (concert)!*

It is imperative to remind Ss that they must not show their worksheets to each other.

BANK HOLIDAY WEEKEND

Materials: One worksheet per student

Start by asking Ss if they have many public holidays in their country, when they are and what they celebrate. Also ask if the day of the holiday is changed so people can have a long weekend.

Pre-teach *extreme sports*, *circus*, *fair* and any other words you think Ss might not know. Give *The London Guide* listings and a diary page to each student.

Tell Ss to work on their own, choose *four* activities they would like to do and write them in the correct place in their diaries. Explain that Ss don't have to go for the whole event unless it is a performance or a football match; they can just go for a few hours. Tell Ss to leave the other slots free. Give them a few minutes to fill in their activities. Monitor and help with vocabulary if necessary.

When they have finished, Ss mingle and discuss their plans, and make further arrangements for the bank holiday weekend. They should try to fill the blank slots in their diary and to find people to do their four activities with, e.g. *A: What are you doing on Saturday afternoon? B: Nothing, I'm free. A: I'm going to the Extreme Sports Fair. Do you want to come?*

Ss should write down the new arrangements they make and the names of Ss who are coming with them for their four activities. They continue to mingle until they have a full diary, but they should only make one arrangement per person and don't have to make arrangements with everyone they meet, especially if they don't like what they are doing! When they have finished, ask Ss what they have planned to do at certain times.

IS IT ART?

Materials: One copy of worksheet A and worksheet B per pair of Ss; some photos of Banksy's work

Show Ss some photos of Banksy's work (or write *Banksy* on the board if you don't have photos). Ask Ss if they have heard of him/ if they are familiar with his work. Discuss briefly, then put Ss in A/B pairs and distribute the worksheets. Give Ss a few minutes to read the text before they start the activity. Both Ss have the same text, but different information is missing from each one. Explain that they have to ask their partner questions in order to fill in the gaps in their text, using the question words in brackets to help them. Monitor the activity, paying attention to the question forms and correcting any errors. Check answers in open class.

Suggested questions:
Student A
1 Who is Banksy?
2 What (perhaps) is his real name?
3 Where is his art?
4 Which animals are often in his pictures?
5 Who spent $2 million on his art in 2007?
Student B
1 When was Banksy born?
2 Why are there no photos of Banksy?
3 Why is his art successful?
4 Who painted over one of Banksy's famous paintings?
5 Where was his most successful exhibition?

WHO'S CALLING?

Materials: One set of role cards per pair of Ss

Put Ss in A/B pairs and distribute the A and B role cards. Give Ss a few minutes to read through the information, check what they need to do and think about the functional language they need. Get Ss to sit back to back to make it a little more like a telephone conversation. Tell them that there are two role-plays where they make the phone call and two in which they answer phone calls. Encourage them to add their own ideas where appropriate.

During the activity, monitor and listen for correct use of the functional language. You may wish to put Ss in new pairs each time, so they have a new partner for every role-play. One way to do this is to have an inner circle of Student As and an outer circle of Student Bs. For every new role-play, the outer circle rotates so every student gets a new partner.

UNIT 4

COLLOCATION FOOTBALL

Materials: One copy of worksheet A and worksheet B, one coin and one goal per pair of Ss

Write an incorrect sentence from the activity on the board and ask Ss to correct it. Tell them that they are going to try to identify whether other collocations are correct or incorrect. Put Ss in A/B pairs and distribute the worksheets and goal. Tell them not to look at their partner's worksheet.

Explain the rules and demonstrate. Student A places a coin on *Start*. Student B reads the first sentence from their worksheet to Student A, who decides if it is correct or incorrect. If it is incorrect, Student A should try to correct it. If Student A is successful, they move the coin one space towards their goal. It is then Student B's turn. If Student B is successful, he/she moves the coin back

towards their goal. Ss continue to take it in turns. If a student makes a mistake, the coin doesn't move. The object is to reach the goal squares and 'score a goal'. When a goal is scored, Ss return the coin to *Start*. Remind Ss to read slowly and clearly to each other and explain that it is only collocations that they are correcting, not grammatical mistakes.

When Ss have finished the game, they can look at each other's worksheet and discuss which statements are true for them. If time, they can change the other statements to make them true for them. Encourage them to ask additional questions.

HAVE YOU EVER …?

Materials: One worksheet per student

Put Ss in pairs and distribute the worksheets. Ask them to work together to complete the sentences using the present perfect of the verbs in brackets. Check answers with the class.

Then ask Ss to mingle and ask each other *Have you ever …?* questions using the prompts on their worksheets. They can choose any questions and in any order. Encourage them to ask further questions if they get a positive answer and record the name of the person they spoke to.

Remind Ss to use the past simple for any further questions and answers, e.g. *A: Have you ever swum with dolphins? B: Yes, I have. A: Where did you swim with them? B: In Florida, two years ago. I was on holiday with …* Remind Ss that they can use *never* for negative answers, e.g. *A: Have you ever swum with dolphins? B: No, I've never swum with dolphins./No, I haven't./No, never.*

Tell Ss to find new partners after they have both asked and answered a question. Encourage them to speak to as many different partners as possible and not spend too much time with one person or just copy each other's answers.

Answers: 1 swum 2 kept 3 done 4 driven 5 won 6 grown 7 flown 8 made 9 bought 10 lost 11 given 12 not paid 13 slept 14 caught 15 written 16 met

CLASS RULES

Materials: One worksheet per pair of Ss

Elicit/Pre-teach *contract* and clarify the idea that it is a legal document that is signed and has to be respected. Put Ss in pairs and distribute the worksheets. Ask them to look at the list of rules and decide if they are true for your class. If a rule is not true, Ss change it.

After Ss have discussed and agreed the alterations, in pairs, they add their own ideas to complete the contract using *can/can't*, *must/mustn't* and *have to/don't have to*. When the contracts are complete, pin them to the walls and ask Ss to move around the class reading them, to decide which one is the best. There could be a vote to decide this, and the winning contract could become the contract for the whole class. While Ss are reading, note any problems with the modals and deal with them in feedback.

SAVE OUR SCHOOL!

Materials: One role card per head teacher

Lead in to the topic by asking Ss about the quality of schools in their country and elicit some common problems and possible solutions. Check/Pre-teach *vandalise* and *uniform*. Divide the class into two groups, A and B. Group A are head teachers and Group B are educational advisors. Sit each group in a row facing each other – one line is the head teachers and the other is the educational advisors – and give a card to each head teacher. Explain the activity. The head teacher explains their problem to the advisor opposite, who responds by giving advice. After a few minutes, the head teachers move along one space so they can speak to a new advisor. The head teacher at the end of the row moves to the start. Head teachers should speak to all the advisors. During the activity, monitor and check Ss' use of the functional language.

When Ss have finished, ask the head teachers to describe the best advice they were given.

UNIT 5

GETTING AROUND

Materials: One copy of crossword A and crossword B per pair of Ss

Put Ss in A/B pairs and distribute the crosswords. Make sure Ss are sitting face to face so they can't see each other's answers. Tell Ss that the object of the activity is to fill in the missing words in their crossword and that they should take turns to ask their partner to describe each word, e.g. *A: What's 1 down? B: It carries lots of people. You can see it in the city, but also if you go to another city, you can take one. B: Train!* This continues until both Ss have completed their grids. You may wish to pre-teach the following useful phrases: *What's 1 down? It's something you ride/drive/fly/catch/sail. You can see it in the city/in the sky/on the water. It carries one person/four people/lots of people. It's slow/fast/expensive/cheap/quiet/dangerous.* Tell Ss not to look at each other's crossword, show their crossword to each other or use the word they are describing.

When they have finished, they can check their answers by looking at each other's crosswords.

MISSING MONEY

Materials: One set of role cards per group of Ss

Put Ss in groups of up to five Ss. If you have less than five Ss in a group, make sure at least the following roles are included: *Dick Brown, Richard Cagney, Shirley Cagney.* Check/Pre-teach *wallet, steal, be missing.* Explain the situation and set the scene. The Manchester Express was travelling from London to Manchester one evening, when one of the passengers realised his money was missing. Distribute the role cards to individuals within each group, and ask them to read the information and, working alone, prepare what they are going to say. Go round and help out with vocabulary and ideas. Give the Dick Brown role card to a stronger student, as this role involves thinking on their feet as they ask further questions.

When they are ready, Ss carry out the role-plays. The detective asks each student questions in turn. Encourage them to ask as many questions as possible, in order to find out as much information as they can. Monitor carefully, prompting Ss where necessary and taking notes on their use of language for later feedback/correction.

When they have finished, ask the detective(s) who they think stole Chris Hinds' money. Give Ss feedback on their use of language, paying particular attention to the past simple and past continuous.

Answers: Richard Cagney stole Chris Hinds' wallet. He was having problems with his business, but couldn't tell his wife. At 7.15p.m., he was reading the newspaper when he got up and told his wife he was going to the toilet. On the way he saw Chris Hinds sitting with an open bag, with the wallet showing. The train stopped and Richard Cagney pretended to 'fall' onto Chris' bag and stole his money. He then returned and sat with his wife, but looked nervous.

20 THINGS ABOUT YOU

Materials: One worksheet per student

Put Ss in pairs and distribute the worksheets. Ask them to choose the correct alternative in each prompt. Give Ss a few minutes, then check answers.

Ss then spend 5 mins writing *one* item for each prompt in the gap. Monitor and provide vocabulary for Ss if they need it.

Put Ss in groups of four. They should share their ideas and ask each other additional questions.

Answers: 1 to go 2 doing 3 to do 4 to do 5 doing 6 wearing 7 to do 8 going 9 reading 10 to email 11 to learn 12 listening 13 to eat 14 to meet 15 to buy 16 living 17 to buy 18 to talk 19 to listen 20 to visit

TIPTON TOUR

Materials: One copy of map A and map B per pair of Ss

Put Ss in pairs and distribute maps A and B. Sit Ss face-to-face so they can't see each other's maps. Tell them that they are going to visit the famous, historical town of Tipton (it's not a real place!). Ss take turns to be a tourist and tour guide, guide each other around the city and label the places on their map with the correct name of the four destinations on their itinerary, e.g. Student A starts as a tourist and Student B, the tour guide, directs them from The Grand Hotel to The National Museum by looking at their map. Remind Ss not to look at each other's worksheet or show their worksheet to their partner. When Student A arrives at each destination, he/she labels the correct box. Then it is Student B's turn.

Ss take turns until they have visited and correctly labelled all the places on their list. When they have finished, they can check their answers by comparing maps.

UNIT 6

A HEALTHY CITY

Materials: One copy of worksheet A and worksheet B per pair of Ss

Divide the class into two groups, A and B, and explain the situation. They are town councillors and as part of their job they are going to decide which sports (and facilities) should be developed for different categories in their area. Check/Pre-teach *urban* and *rural*. Distribute worksheet A to Group A and worksheet B to Group B. Give Ss time to complete their questions. Refer them to the Photo bank on p156 of the Students' Book if they need help with the names of sports.

Now put Ss in A/B pairs and explain the activity. Pairs share and discuss their lists and then need to agree on one sport which best fits each category.

When they have finished, Ss present their ideas to the class.

HOW LONG …?

Materials: One set of cards per pair of Ss

Put Ss in pairs and distribute the cards. Ask Ss to work together to complete the *For: _____* gaps on each card, using the information given, e.g. Became professional: 1998 For: 17 years (assuming now is 2015).

When they have finished, Ss put the cards in a pile face down, then divide them up between them. They must not show their cards to their partner. Elicit the questions they will need for the activity and drill them round the class: *How long has he/she played this sport? How long has he/she been professional? How long has he/she been famous? How many competitions has he/she won?* (NB: The first question/answer may sound more natural if the present perfect continuous is used: *How long has he/she been playing this sport? She has been playing tennis since she was four years old.* If Ss use this form when doing the activity, allow it, but avoid lengthy explanations as to why at this point.)

Demonstrate the activity with a stronger student. Each turn, a student picks a category on their topmost card to compare. The other student then responds using *for* or *since* and their answer. Whoever's answer is the longest/biggest wins their partner's card. If the numbers are the same, then both Ss keep their cards. The winner is the student who gets all of the cards.

PREDICTIONS

Materials: One set of cards per group of Ss

Put Ss in groups of four and distribute one card to each student. Explain that Ss have to ask each other questions using the prompts on the card and write the names of the people they interview in the appropriate column. Encourage Ss to ask additional questions and note the answers, e.g. *A: In the next seven days, do you think you'll sleep less than five hours? B: Yes, I will. B: Why? A: Because I have to work.*

Depending on the number of Ss in your class, when they have finished, you can group Ss with the same card together and ask them to compare their information. You can then ask the different groups more general questions, e.g. *Do many people think they will use a computer in the next twenty-four hours?*

WHERE DOES IT HURT?

Materials: One role card per student

Check/Pre-teach *rash* and *stomachache* and distribute the cards. Fold them so there is a patient and a doctor side. On the patient side, there is a medical problem and on the doctor side, there are prompts for the doctor to ask the patient. Ask Ss to mingle and show the doctor side of their card to another student. The other student takes the role of the doctor and asks for information about the patient's condition before telling the patient what they should do. If there is an odd number of Ss, there can be three-way conversations.

After Ss have spoken to a few doctors, they can swap cards so they have a new problem to ask advice for. Try to do this a few times during the mingle.

When Ss have finished, ask them to describe which illnesses they had, what advice they were given by the different doctors and who they think gave them the best advice.

UNIT 7

ANOTHER LIFE

Materials: One worksheet per student

Distribute the worksheets and check that Ss understand the prompts. Put Ss in pairs and ask them to complete the questions with prepositions. Allow 3–4 mins for this, then check answers.

Now demonstrate the activity by using the first question and going round the class asking: *Do you dream about working in another country?* Continue asking the question until someone answers *yes* and write their name in the correct column. Ask follow-up questions (e.g. *Why? Where?*) and write notes in the *Extra information* column. Model the other question forms with the class.

Ask Ss to mingle, find people who can answer *yes* to the questions and write their names in the correct column. They should then ask follow-up questions and note down the details in the *Extra information* column. During the activity, monitor and take notes for later feedback/correction.

When they have finished, Ss tell the class what they found out.

Answers: 1 about **2** for **3** up **4** around **5** for **6** about **7** back **8** to **9** about **10** for

DID YOU KNOW …?

Materials: One card per group of Ss

Arrange Ss into four teams of between two to four and give each team the appropriate worksheet.

Ask the first team to read out one of their questions and the three possible answers to the other three teams. The other teams listen and then discuss what they think the correct answer is and write it down. When all three teams have decided and are ready to listen, you can ask the first team to tell the others the correct answer. This is indicated in bold. Ss should not shout out their answers.

You can keep score on the board, awarding points for each correct guess. The winners are the team with the highest score.

I WENT HOME TO …

Materials: One copy of the board per group of Ss and one counter per student

Put Ss in groups of four and give each group a board (enlarged to A3 size if possible). Assign each student with a letter from A to D. Each student needs a small object, like a coin or a counter, which they can move around the board. These are placed on their letter.

Explain the rules and demonstrate. The object is for Ss to cross the board and reach the opposite corner by making sentences using infinitives of purpose, *because* or *so*. Ss make sentences using a verb in a light grey circle and *so*, *to* or *because* in an adjacent black circle, e.g. Student A starts and says *I bought a sandwich because I was hungry.* Student D might say *I needed help so I phoned my brother.* Ss can use the verbs before or after *so*, *to* or *because*. Therefore, the verbs and *so*, *to* or *because* can be in the same clause or different clauses. However, the sentence must contain the two words and clearly express purpose, cause or result. If the other Ss agree that the sentence is correct, the student moves their counter to either of the two circles which is nearest their destination. Ss may move horizontally and vertically, but not diagonally. Tell Ss not to use the circle they are on again for their next turn, but to use one which is either horizontally or vertically adjacent.

Throughout the activity, monitor closely to check that Ss are using the three forms correctly.

CAREER CHANGE

Materials: One role card per student

Start by explaining the situation. Tell Ss that they are bored with their jobs and want to change their lives completely. They go to a careers fair to find out about new careers and training courses.

Put Ss in groups of six. There are three Ss who work as representatives for colleges (Role cards 1, 2 and 3) and three Ss who need information (Role cards 4, 5 and 6). If there is an odd number of Ss, there can be two career changers or reps together. Check/Pre-teach *massage* and *stressful* and distribute the role cards. Give Ss 5 mins to read the role cards and prepare their questions/information. Then sit reps and career changers face to face. The object is for career changers to visit each college rep and ask for information. The reps should try to convince the career changers to book a course with them. College reps have to be persuasive, but truthful; career changers should ask additional questions. Every 5–6 mins or so, tell the career changers to move to the next rep.

When Ss have finished, ask the career changers to tell the class which new course they thought was the best for them and also who the best college rep was.

UNIT 8

AMAZING MONEY

Materials: One worksheet per group of Ss

Put Ss in groups of three. Give each group a copy of the quiz and ask them to think of a name for their team and write it at the top of the worksheet. Tell them to discuss the questions and circle the correct answers.

When they have finished, collect in their worksheets and give each one to a different group. Go through the answers and tell them to award one point for each correct answer. The group with the most points wins.

Answers:
1 **a)** These were issued in The Philippines and worth 100,000 pesos.
2 **c)** They were called *praescriptiones* and used in the first century BC.
3 **c)** However, this can vary, depending on how happy you are with the service.
4 **c)** The iPhone 4 Diamond Rose Edition, designed by Stuart Hughes, was made of platinum and covered in diamonds.
5 **c)** They were issued in 2004 to commemorate '50 years of Rock 'n' Roll'.
6 **a)** They were issued in 2009 and worth 100 trillion Zimbabwean dollars. They had 14 zeros on the front and back.
7 **c)** They were issued in Morocco in 1944, and worth 50 centimes.
8 **b)** Diner's Club issued 200 cards in 1951 and their customers were able to use them in 27 restaurants in New York City.
9 **c)** It was used by Barclay's Bank in Enfield Town, London. 25 years previously, an American bank had made a mechanical ATM, but later took it out of use as customers didn't like it.
10 **a)** for his role in the film *Where the Day Takes You*
11 **c)** The notes were made from deer skin, in 140BC.
12 **b)** In 1782, it was decided that they would use the Spanish currency in the USA.

FOUR GUESSES

Materials: One card per group of Ss

Tell Ss you are thinking of a common and successful item, for example, an iPod. Describe the item using relative clauses and tell Ss to guess what it is, e.g. *It's something which was first sold in 2001. It's something which is small and light.* Divide the class into five teams of two or three and distribute the cards. First, ask Ss to think of another successful, common thing like an invention, food, a famous place or even sport. They write four clues using relative clauses as in the examples. Monitor closely to make sure that the relative clauses are used correctly and that the clues are not too difficult or too easy.

When Ss are ready, tell the first team to choose one of their items and to read the first clue. The other teams listen and guess what is being described. Tell the other teams not to call out their guess, but to write it on a piece of paper. When all the teams are ready, they hold up their answers. If any team or teams guess correctly, they win the number of points in brackets for that clue. If no team or teams guess correctly, the team reading the clues read the next one and the process continues. You can keep score on the board. The winners are the team with the most points.

LET'S CELEBRATE!

Materials: One worksheet per group of Ss

Start by asking Ss about any big parties they have been to or organised themselves. Tell them that they are going to plan their own party. Put them in groups of three, distribute the party planner cards and give groups 4–5 mins to fill in the cards. Help with any vocabulary Ss may need.

When they have finished, tell Ss that there are four places they can have their party and they have to decide which is the most suitable for them. Give them the four party venues. Encourage Ss to discuss the venues using *too much/many, enough* and *very*, e.g. *The Moon River Boat is not big enough, we have 100 guests. The Plaza Hotel is too expensive.* When each group has chosen a venue, they explain to the class why they chose it and if they needed to make any changes to their plan.

CAN I HELP YOU?

Materials: One role card per student

Divide the class into two groups: shop assistants and customers. Give role cards 1, 2, 3 and 4 to the shop assistants and role cards 5, 6, 7 and 8 to the customers. Ask Ss to read their role cards. Customers have details about the items they need to buy (size, colour) and shop assistants have information about the items they are selling. The object is for Ss to mingle so that the shop assistants can sell some of the items on their cards and the customers can buy the items on theirs. Tell the customers that they have a budget and must try not to exceed it. In some cases, Ss can 'shop around' for a bargain and in others they can't because there's only one shop assistant who sells what they want. Customers must record how much they spend. Remind Ss of some of the language from Lesson 8.3, e.g. *A: Can I help you? B: I'm looking for a white shirt.*

If the customer can't find what they want, they can ask for another item or move to another shop assistant. If they do find what they want, they can tell the shop assistant they would like to buy it. When the transaction is complete, the shop assistant ticks the item to show it is sold and the customer ticks the item to show they have bought what they want. Ss must change after every transaction and continue to mingle until they have sold or bought all they can. When Ss have finished, ask how much money customers spent, if they are over or under budget and how much the shop assistants earned by selling their items.

UNIT 9

IT'S A CHEETAH!

Materials: One copy of worksheets A, B and C and one answer sheet per group of Ss; dictionaries

Put Ss in groups of three and distribute the worksheets and answer sheets. Ss decide on a team name and write it at the top. Check/Pre-teach *spots*, *mammal* and *trunk* or encourage Ss to use dictionaries.

Explain the activity. Starting with Student A, Ss take turns to read their clues to each other. When all three have been read, Ss have to agree what they think the animal is and write its name in the boxes on the answer sheet. This continues until the sheet is complete. You should remind Ss not to look at each other's worksheet.

When Ss have finished, swap answers sheets between groups for marking and go through the answers. The winners are the group with the most correct answers.

> **Answers:** **1** dolphin **2** butterfly **3** shark **4** bear **5** ostrich **6** whale **7** crocodile **8** penguin **9** cheetah **10** mosquito **11** tortoise **12** chimpanzee **13** elephant **14** eagle **15** camel **16** pigeon

COMPARE IT!

Materials: One copy of the board and a dice per group of Ss; one counter per student

Put Ss in groups of four and give each group a board (enlarged to A3 size if possible), a dice and a counter or small object each. Ask Ss to put their counters on the *Start* box and to take it in turns to move around the board. If you don't have a dice, use a coin. If it's heads, Ss move their counter forward two spaces and if it's tails, they move one. If Ss land on a grey square, they make a superlative sentence about the three items given. If they land on a white square, they make a comparative sentence about the two items given. They must use the adjective at the top of the box and can use any other language that is appropriate for the comparison, e.g. *Cheetahs are faster than horses, but horses can run for a long time; cheetahs can't. Cities are more exciting than the countryside because you can do many things like …* Some of the boxes require Ss to state facts, others opinions. Ss can challenge anything they disagree with and if a student does not know an answer to something factual, it does not matter – they can say *I think …* or *In my opinion …* The activity finishes when all Ss have reached the end.

RACE TO THE SOUTH POLE

Materials: One copy of the worksheet per pair/group of Ss

To lead in to the topic, write *explorer* on the board and discuss the kinds of places explorers go to and what kind of person they have to be. Introduce the text and ask: *Was Scott a successful explorer?* (Partially – he got to the South Pole, but lost the race and died on the way back.) Ss read the text quickly to answer the question.

Put Ss in pairs or groups of three. Tell them that each line of the text has **one** mistake relating to articles (a wrong or missing article). Ss have to identify the mistakes to win points. Ask them to look at the first line and to discuss it quickly. Invite each group in turn to identify the mistakes. Reveal the answers once all groups have responded. If they identify it correctly, they win one point and record this at the box at the end of the line. This continues for all the lines.

> **Answers:**
> **1** there was ~~the~~ *a* race to be
> **2** explorer from ~~the~~ Great Britain
> **3** Amundsen led ~~a~~ *the* Norwegian one
> **4** Scott's team took ~~the~~ horses
> **5** took only ~~the~~ dogs
> **6** Scott's group started *the* journey
> **7** In ~~an~~ *the* end
> **8** Scott and ~~a~~ four men
> **9** They reached *the* South Pole
> **10** had arrived ~~the~~ five weeks
> **11** they had lost ~~a~~ *the* race
> **12** 800 miles to *the* coast
> **13** *The* weather got worse
> **14** died during *the* night
> **15** They were found ~~an~~ eight months later
> **16** Scott's diary tells ~~a~~ *the* story

IT MIGHT BE …

Materials: One worksheet per group of Ss

Put Ss in groups of three or four and distribute one worksheet to each group. Ask the groups to speculate about what the close-up pictures are showing. Encourage Ss to use speculative language, as well as the 'Give yourself time to think' language from Lesson 9.3. They should also give reasons for their ideas whenever they can, e.g. *A: What do you think A is? B: Well, it must be a machine./It could be a car./Perhaps it's a motorbike.* Monitor and remind Ss to use the appropriate language and avoid, e.g. *It's a car! No, it's not. Yes, it is.*

When Ss have reached decisions about all the objects, do open class feedback to see if the different groups' ideas are the same. Then tell Ss the answers.

> **Answers:** **A** car **B** camera **C** clock **D** boot/shoe **E** bicycle **F** chair **G** helicopter **H** washing machine

UNIT 10

CRIME CROSSWORD

Materials: One worksheet A and B and one crossword per pair of Ss

Put Ss in A/B pairs and give one set of clues to each Student A/B, and one crossword grid to each pair. Sit Ss face to face and tell them not to show their worksheets to each other. Explain that they will work together to complete the crossword. Student A has the clues for words going across and Student B for those going down. Ss take turns to read the clues and describe the word for their partner. If the student guesses the word correctly, they can write it in the correct place in the crossword. If the student does not know the answer, he/she can try another one.

WHAT'S IT LIKE?

Materials: One copy of the board and a dice per group of Ss; one counter per student

Put Ss in groups of four and distribute the board (enlarged to A3 size if possible) and a dice to each group and a counter to each student. Quickly review the difference between *What's it like?* and *What do you like/dislike about …?* Ask Ss to take it in turns to move around the board and talk about the subject in the box they land on. After they have talked about the topic, they should also ask another student one question about the topic, e.g. *mobile phone: My mobile is silver and has a big screen. I like it because it looks very modern. Pablo, what's your mobile phone like? What do you like about it?* The other Ss can ask additional questions, e.g. *Where did you buy it?* If Ss don't own a particular object (e.g. a car), they can describe the car of someone they know instead.

If Ss land at the foot of a ladder, they go up it and if they land on the head of a snake, they go down. If you don't have any dice, Ss can use a coin and move one space for heads and two spaces for tails. The winner is the first student to reach the *Finish*.

I DON'T BELIEVE IT!

Materials: One copy of worksheet A, worksheet B and worksheet C per group of Ss

Put Ss in pairs so there are two Student As, two Student Bs and two Student Cs working together. Give Ss the appropriate worksheet. Check/Pre-teach *colouring* and *shell* and any other new vocabulary.

Ask Ss to complete the sentences with the correct passive form of the verbs in brackets – present simple or past simple. Check answers with the class.

Now regroup Ss into threes so that there is an A, B and C student in each group. With one student keeping score, Ss take it turns to read each other their facts for their partners to guess if they are true or not. They win a point for each correct guess. The winner is the student with the most points.

Answers:

A 1 is made 2 was bought 3 was given (*by France*) 4 was seen
5 was built 6 were not grown 7 is spelt (*definitely*)
8 was written (*Dan Brown*)

B 1 is found (*China only*) 2 is chosen
3 was taken (*the French, 1820*) 4 is drunk 5 was stolen
6 is sung 7 are not sold 8 are ridden

C 1 was shown 2 were driven 3 was known 4 is eaten (*Swiss*)
5 are worn (*kilts are usually only worn in Scotland*) 6 was bitten
7 are not taught (*3–5 years*) 8 were hidden (*were never buried*)

EXCUSE ME …

Materials: One copy of the worksheet per pair of Ss

Put Ss in pairs and distribute the worksheets. In their pairs, they should first identify the problem in each picture. Monitor and help them with any vocabulary they might need. Check answers with the class.

In their pairs, Ss discuss what the people complaining want from each situation, e.g. *a refund, to replace the TV*, etc. Again, help them with any vocabulary they need.

Pairs now role-play the conversations, taking turns to be the person complaining and the person dealing with the complaint. Before they begin, remind them of some of the language for complaining and sounding firm, but polite from Lesson 10.3 Encourage Ss to reach an agreement about what to do in each situation.

Answers: A insect in food **B** faulty product **C** bad haircut
D delayed flight **E** overcharged customer/incorrect bill
F sold a holiday at a hotel not finished/noisy construction work next to the hotel

UNIT 11

DOMINOES

Materials: One set of cards per group of Ss

Put Ss in groups of four and distribute the cards. Explain the activity and demonstrate. One student deals the cards and each player places them face up in front of them. The first student starts by putting down a card in the middle. Ss take it in turns to add a card to either side. If they place a card to the left, it needs to be the correct adjective. If they place a card to the right, it needs to be a situation which matches the adjective. If they don't have a match, they miss a turn. The winner is the first player to put down all their cards.

When Ss have finished, they discuss in their groups the last time they felt the different feelings. Before they begin, elicit/give them the question *When did you last feel …?*

Answers: see the worksheet (in two columns)

WHO AM I?

Materials: One copy of worksheet A and worksheet B per pair of Ss

Put Ss in A/A and B/B pairs and give the same worksheet to both Ss in each pair. Each worksheet contains information about five men or women who Ss will describe to their partner. There are also pictures of five other people who they will identify.

In the first stage, Ss make sentences with the prompts using the present perfect and *just, yet* and *already* (e.g. *Emma has just visited the hairdresser's. She hasn't finished university yet.*). These sentences will be used in a guessing game later. Monitor and prompt Ss to self-correct/correct each other.

Now put Ss in A/B pairs. Sit them face-to-face and tell them not to look at each other's worksheets. They take it in turns to read out their sentences. Their partner tries to identify who each sentence is about and writes the person's name under each picture. Explain that Ss should not reveal the answers until the end because they will make guesses by eliminating people using the information they are told.

When Ss have finished, they can look at each other's worksheets to check their answers.

CONDITIONAL WHEELS

Materials: One copy of the worksheet per pair of Ss

Put Ss in pairs and give each pair a copy of the worksheet. You can cut out the wheels, but it is not essential. Explain the activity and demonstrate. Start at number 1 in the first wheel, and elicit a conditional sentence using the prompts: *If I get a new job, I'll have more money.* Ss turn their wheels clockwise and take it in turns to make a conditional sentence, which links with the previous one. They should say their sentences to each other, but they cannot write them down. Ss do this until they reach the start again. They then repeat the whole chain, but more quickly.

When they have finished, pairs write their own conditional sentence chains in the blank wheel. These should also come full circle, but Ss don't have to use all twelve stages. Remind them to take turns, and explain that they can write prompts or full sentences. Go round monitoring and suggest ideas if Ss find it difficult to link their sentences.

When Ss have finished, they can exchange wheels with other pairs.

Answers:
1 If I get a new job, I'll have more money.
2 If I have more money, I'll go shopping.
3 If I go shopping, I'll buy a new computer.
4 If I buy a new computer, I'll play more online games.
5 If I play more online games, I'll be tired.
6 If I'm tired, I'll do less work.
7 If I do less work, my boss will be angry.
8 If my boss is angry, he'll/she'll shout at me.
9 If my boss shouts at me, I won't feel happy.
10 If I don't feel happy, I'll look for a new job.
11 If I look for a new job, I'll have some interviews.
12 If I have some interviews, I'll get a new job.

GADGETS

Materials: One copy of the worksheet per pair of Ss

Put Ss in pairs and distribute the worksheets. Ask Ss to discuss what the gadgets are for, who could use them and in what situations. Provide any vocabulary they need.

Rearrange Ss into groups of four. Tell them that they are the bosses of a company called Go Gadgets and they must choose three of the gadgets for future development. Encourage them to use the language of giving opinions and disagreeing from Lesson 11.3.

When groups have reached agreement, ask a representative from each group to tell the class why they chose their gadgets. You can write the three ideas from each group on the board. Then encourage the class as a whole to agree on the three gadgets the company should develop.

UNIT 12

NOUGHTS AND CROSSES

Materials: One copy of the worksheet per group of Ss

Put Ss in groups of three. Two Ss are players and one student is the referee. Give the players the larger grid and give the referee the answers. The object is to make a line of four squares horizontally, vertically or diagonally by choosing a definition and giving the correct word.

Explain the rules. One player starts and chooses a square. They read the definition and try to identify the word, e.g. *A film which is about real life. A documentary!* This is checked by the referee. If the

answer is correct, the student wins that square and can draw either a *O* or an *X*. If they give an incorrect answer, the referee must not tell them the correct answer. The square can still be won by the other player or the same player if they choose it again. The winner is the player with the most squares at the end of the game.

STAR INTERVIEW

Materials: One worksheet per student

Ask Ss to imagine they are a film star and create a star persona. It can be based on reality, but encourage them to be imaginative and inventive if they want. Ss work individually to complete the Star card first. Help them with vocabulary and ensure they complete their card before the next stage.

Put Ss in A/B pairs. Student A is the star and Student B is a journalist. The journalist interviews the star using the questions on the interview card and makes notes of their answers. When they have finished, they swap roles.

Now tell Ss that they are all journalists and regroup them with new partners – this can be in pairs or groups. Explain that as journalists, they are looking for the best stories to use in their newspaper. They have to tell their new partner(s) who they interviewed and report the most interesting things they found out (using reported speech), e.g. *Leon Fox told me he was filming a new action film.* Remind Ss that they should use *say* and *tell* to report the stars' answers.

When Ss have finished, you can take the role of editor of a newspaper and ask your journalists for their stories. Ss report their stories and the class decides which star(s) the newspaper will write about.

THREE IN A ROW

Materials: One worksheet per pair of Ss

Review the meaning and form of hypothetical conditionals using the example sentence on the worksheet. Write the structure on the board: *if + past simple, would + infinitive.*

Put Ss in pairs and give each pair one board (enlarged to A3 size if possible). The object of the activity is to win boxes by making conditional sentences and to make lines of three. The lines can be horizontal, vertical or diagonal.

Explain the rules and demonstrate. Point to the spider icon, read the example, then elicit another conditional sentence from a student (e.g. *If I saw a spider, I would be scared.*). Ask Ss to take it in turns to make sentences using the pictures as prompts. If their partner agrees that the sentence is meaningful and correct, they win that box and initial it. When a student has won three boxes in a row, they can draw a line through them and win one point. Ss can make lines from boxes that they have already won, and they can also stop each other from making lines by blocking. The student who has made the most lines at the end of the activity is the winner. Monitor to ensure that Ss' sentences meaningful and correct. You may wish to give Ss dictionaries or help them with vocabulary. When they have finished, elicit Ss' ideas for each picture.

ALL IN A DAY'S WORK

Materials: One copy for worksheet A and worksheet B per pair of Ss

Start by checking/pre-teaching *tour* (as a noun and verb) and *go on tour/be on tour*. Ask Ss what problems a tour manager might have. Check/Pre-teach *chauffeur, gym equipment* and *VIP suite*.

Put Ss in A/B pairs and distribute the *Hot Lava* worksheet first. Explain that Ss will do a role-play and explain the situation. Student A is the tour manager of the band Hot Lava and Student B is a receptionist. Give Ss a few minutes to read through the flowchart and think about what language they are going to use. In the case of the tour manager, they need to think of another couple of requests. Go round and help with vocabulary and ideas. You may want to revise the functional phrases from Lesson 12.3 before Ss begin the role-play. During the activity, monitor and note down problems with the target language for feedback afterwards.

When Ss have finished, tell them that they are going to do a second role-play. Distribute the *Head Space* worksheet and ask Ss to swap roles: Student B is the tour manager of Head Space and Student A is the receptionist. Follow the same procedure.

At the end of the activity, ask what other requests were made and give feedback on the use of the target language.

Pearson Education Limited
Edinburgh Gate
Harlow
Essex CM20 2JE
England
and Associated Companies throughout the world.

www.pearsonelt.com

First published 2015
ISBN: 978-1-292-12016-4
Set in Aptifer Sans 10/12 pt
Printed in Slovakia by Neografia
Illustrated by Eric Smith

Every effort has been made to trace the copyright holders and we apologise
in advance for any unintentional omissions. We would be pleased to insert the
appropriate acknowledgement in any subsequent edition of this publication.